The Organism

The Organism

A Holistic Approach to Biology
Derived from
Pathological Data in Man

Kurt Goldstein

with a foreword by
Oliver Sacks

ZONE BOOKS · NEW YORK

1995

Distributed by The MIT Press,
Cambridge, Massachusetts, and London, England

Library of Congress Cataloging-in-Publication Data

Goldstein, Kurt, 1878–1965.
    [Aufbau des Organismus. English]
The organism : a holistic approach to biology derived
from pathological data in man / Kurt Goldstein; with a
foreword by Oliver Sacks.
    p.   cm.
    Includes bibliographical references and index.
    ISBN 0-942299-96-5
    1. Neurology–Philosophy. 2. Neuropsychology–
Philosophy. 3. Holistic medicine. I. Title.
RC343.G56513   1995
612.8'2'01–dc20   94-40858
                                                            CIP

Contents

Foreword

Oliver Sacks

Kurt Goldstein (1878-1965) is one of the most important, most contradictory, and now most forgotten figures in the history of neurology and psychiatry. My own introduction to his thinking was as a medical student in the 1950s, soon after *The Organism* had been reissued as a paperback. I had a phone call from one of my closest friends, Jonathan Miller, also a medical student then – "You must read it! It is a *wonderful book!*" Indeed, it seemed to both of us to have a vigor, a vitality, a largeness of vision, that radically contrasted with the tight atmosphere of classical neurology in which we were both being educated. Goldstein had "a feeling for the organism" that seemed all too lacking in so many of our teachers and texts. He talked about "reactions" to illness, about "adaptation," "compensation," "coming to terms" – reactions that we could see in our patients all the time and that were crucial to understand if any rehabilitation was to be achieved, but ones that our textbooks completely ignored.

The history of neurology, for almost two hundred years, has consisted in part of alternations and conflicts between two points of view regarding the functions of the nervous system – points of view that neurologists sometimes speak of as "splitting" and "lumping." The splitters see the brain as a mosaic of separate functions, controlled by separate (but linked) "centers" or "modules." The lumpers, in contrast, think in terms of overall, global principles of neural organization. Paul Broca, finding, in 1861 a local basis for aphasia, that is, a center for the "motor images of words," was a splitter, and the decades from 1861 to World War I saw the confident ascription of hundreds of discrete neurological and psychological functions to equally discrete areas of the cerebral cortex. (Hughlings Jackson, a rare, philosophically minded contemporary of

Broca, was an exception.) The decades between the two world wars saw a rebuttal of this modular view, by neurologists such as Goldstein, Henry Head, and Pierre Marie; the Gestalt psychologists; and physiologists such as Karl Lashley, all of whom were intensely conscious of the plasticity of the nervous system, the organism's powers of coming to terms and adapting, and the general powers of symbolization, of conceptual thought, of perspective and consciousness, so developed in humans, which seemed to be irreducible to mere elementary or modular capacities. Since the 1950s, there has been another change in mood, the holistic viewpoints of Goldstein and others being forgotten or expelled and a new era of modularity taking its place, a school of thought that by and large, obtains to the present. Thus, for example, dozens of areas specialized for different aspects of visual processing have recently been isolated – areas crucial for the perception (properly speaking, the construction) of color, motion, depth, form – without any master area that brings all these together. There is no one area, it has become clear, where an "image" is formed – and the whole question of "splitting" and "lumping," specialization and integration, has taken on a new challenge and form.

Such a history, of course, is almost a caricature – no figure of note has ever been a pure splitter or lumper, and all have struggled, in different ways, to reconcile the two approaches. One sees this very clearly and explicitly in A.R. Luria (who in his early career was deeply influenced by Goldstein). In his autobiography, Luria speaks of "romantic" and "classical" approaches as being of equal and complementary value in neuropsychology and of his own lifelong attempt to synthesize them – a synthesis, he felt, that could only be achieved (and here only partially) by case studies of exceptional depth and detail, in which the historical, the personal, the experimental, and the clinical could all be brought together as a unity.

Goldstein himself harbored throughout his long life a similar, almost overwhelming, doubleness in himself. In a brief autobiographical note written on his eightieth birthday, he tells us that his early education and interests were all in the direction of the humanities and that, when he went to the university in Breslau and Heidelberg, he did not know whether to study natural science – or philosophy. His philosophic inclinations – he was an ardent Kantian – became subordinated for a time when he went to medical school by the rigorous classical methods he

8

imbibed there, above all from the great anatomist Ludwig Edinger and Carl Wernicke, the superb clinician who had described Wernicke's aphasia. But his philosophical leanings were later to resurface and shape many of his writings.

Under Edinger's and Wernicke's tutelage Goldstein was soon to become an astute and anatomically minded clinician too, and all his early papers (from 1903 on) show him following in their footsteps exactly. But from the start, the physician in him found the classical methods — delineating a number of isolated "deficits" — inadequate. Whatever particular deficits there might be, he felt, there was always a general reaction or change in the individual as well, sometimes farther-reaching than the deficit itself. There grew on him the sense of the patient reacting as a whole, as an organism, developing altered orientations and behaviors in response to injury or illness. This sense came to a crisis during World War I, when he was confronted with the task of treating a great number of young soldiers with brain injuries. The very complex pictures he was to see in these patients led him to formulate an ever more elaborate corpus of theoretical concepts: abstract versus concrete behavior, "catastrophic" reactions to brain injury, and so on. This work continued after the war, and the 1920s were Goldstein's most productive decade, and his happiest one too, in his deep friendship and collaboration with a remarkable Gestalt psychologist, Adhémar Gelb, and in the Institute for Research on the After-Effects of Brain Injury, which he founded and directed until Hitler came to power.

Expelled by the Nazis, Goldstein took refuge in Holland, and here, in 1934 (while awaiting his visa to the United States), he thought intensively on his rich and varied neurological experience, distilling from it the holistic system or philosophy that had gradually been gathering force within him for twenty years or more. He dictated *The Organism*, almost nonstop, over a period of five weeks — leaving himself (and his typist) in a state of prostration.

The book aroused great interest when it was published and soon after appeared in many different languages. Goldstein arrived in the United States in 1935, a world-renowned neurologist at the height of his powers, but one who had lost the institute he had founded, who had lost his collaborator, Gelb (who died in 1936), and who had lost the whole European world in which his life had been embedded for fifty years. Although he adapted in a fashion, was renowned, and remained cease-

9

lessly busy, Goldstein was never to feel fully anchored, fully at home, again. Although he lived to a great age, remarkably active to the last (he would still commute weekly, in his late seventies, between Boston and New York) and although he was to publish four more books – *Abstract and Concrete Behavior*, with his gifted psychologist colleague Martin Scheerer; *Human Nature in the Light of Psychopathology*, the William James lectures that he gave at Harvard in the winter of 1938–39; *After-Effects of Brain Injuries in War* (1942); and, in 1948, *Language and Language Disturbances* – as well as a remarkable range and number of papers and two book-length clinical studies (*Case Lanuti* in 1944 and *A Case of "Idiot Savant"* in 1945), he seemed to suffer an increasing and finally tragic isolation and unfulfillment. The subtle balance between minute empirical observation and theorizing, which had been his greatest strength, now increasingly seemed to desert him. One sees the doubleness, no longer synthesized, most clearly in his late book on aphasia, in which the first, holistic half and the second, empirical half hardly seem to have been written by the same man. But sometimes, at least, the balance was restored, and the synthesis of "romantic" and "classical," of "philosophical" and "empirical," was triumphantly achieved – most of all in his magnificent clinical studies, *Case Lanuti* and *A Case of "Idiot Savant."*

Darwin often said that one could not be a good observer without being an active theorizer, and his son later wrote of him that he seemed to be "charged with a theorizing power" that would flow into and animate all his observations. So it is with Goldstein, when (as in these case studies) he is at his best – one has the sense of observation and thought leading to one another, inseparably. "No empirical data," he writes in *The Organism*, "can ever become really intelligible unless grasped from an ideational frame of reference, and unless viewed from a conceptual plane." Much of Goldstein's theorizing has to do with what he called "concrete" and "abstract" attitudes, the regression to a mindless concreteness (as he saw it) in many forms of neurological and psychiatric disorder. What one sees in his own best work is concreteness in its healthy sense – a genius for observing a myriad of minute details combined with the power to see their sense as an organization, as a whole.

The ideal (and indeed crucial) vehicle for this was an analysis or case history of the most searching and comprehensive sort, and Goldstein's case histories, in particular, need to be made available to the present reader – some are buried in obscure academic journals, and many have never been translated from the German. They are among the most valuable and accessible of his works, and being so close to clinical reality, they show almost no dating with time. *The Organism*, indeed, presupposes in part a considerable acquaintance with Goldstein's clinical and experimental observations and is therefore couched in more general terms of methodology and philosophy.

A major theme of *The Organism* (and *the* theme of his William James lectures) is the value of pathology – its unique value in illuminating the nature of health, and of universal organismic reactions, to inner disturbances of any sort – that is, pathology as "lawful variations of the normal life process." The notion of *order* is central to Goldstein's ideas of health and disease and those of rehabilitation: "Thus, *being well* means to be capable of ordered behavior which may prevail in spite of the impossibility of certain performances which were formerly possible. But the new state of health is not the same as the old one.... Recovery is a newly achieved state of ordered functioning...*a new individual norm*." Thus, in contradistinction to a classical, "splitting" neurology, Goldstein sees symptoms not as isolated expressions of local damage in the nervous system but as "attempted solutions" the organism has arrived at, once it has been altered by disease. "Symptoms," for Goldstein, betoken whole levels of organization, adaptation to an altered inner state (and world). It is impossible, he emphasizes, to consider any illness – but above all, a neurological illness – without reference to the patient's self, and the forms of his adaptation and orientation within it. Disease, for Goldstein, involves a "shrinkage" (or, at the least, a "revision") of self and world, until an equilibrium of a radically new sort can be achieved. The function of the physician, he feels, especially if an illness is incurable and no return to the original state can be expected, is to be as sensitive as possible to all the resonances and ramifications of illness in the individual, and so help him to achieve a new organization, an equilibrium – and not force him into trying to do the old things in the old way (which can provoke, in Goldstein's vivid phrase, a "catastrophic reaction"). One must lead the sick patient through a period of chaos, gently, until he can reestablish a new organization, construct his world anew.

And to this there is a philosophical underpinning – steeped in Kantian idealism and in Husserl's phenomenology, Goldstein constantly talks of "the essence" of the individual and how it may be compromised by

11

disease. Given his clinical and philosophical hospitality to the "inward," to the actual experiences, the life-worlds, of his patients, one wonders whether he might have moved, at the time when he was writing *The Organism*, to a completely existential viewpoint, to the creation of an existential neurology comparable to the existential psychiatry being developed then by Ludwig Binswanger and others. There are certainly hints of this, here and there, in his thought; but, finally, he shrank from so radical (and, as he perhaps thought, so unscientific) a move and maintained, at least in *The Organism*, a certain abstractness, a generalizing distance, from the life-worlds he conveyed so vividly in his histories.

Or perhaps one may put this a different way. It was not so much that Goldstein shrank from an existential viewpoint; rather, he felt it necessary to propose a more general, ontological viewpoint first as a necessary *antecedent* to any personal one – this had been a constant preoccupation since his Kantian youth. Thus he gives us, in *The Organism* and elsewhere, *general* concepts of health, disease, adaptation, self, world (the prolegomena, he feels, to an as-yet-unformulated general theory). And yet Goldstein's philosophizing is never abstract but continually related to his clinical work, an attempt to give essentially clinical concepts (health, disease, etc.) the highest degree of conceptual generality. In this he might be said to have been following Nietzsche, who always felt that philosophy must start from a proper understanding of the body.

But if Goldstein in his later years was neglected or misunderstood by some of his fellow neurologists, his writings, especially *The Organism*, was central to much of the work of Georges Canguilhem and others beginning in the midforties. Canguilhem, indeed, already having achieved distinction as a philosopher, was driven to go to medical school, to root his philosophy in clinical reality; his central work, *The Normal and the Pathological*, makes constant reference to Goldstein as a pioneer in his realm. Nietzsche spoke of the need for "a philosophical physician," and Goldstein fits this description precisely. His insistence on general concepts and conceptual analysis never obscures his sense of the sufferings and strivings of his patients; the physician is never submerged or absorbed by the philosopher but retains his compassion, his voice, at all times.

Neurologists spend their lives confronting complexities – the bewildering, complex ways in which patients behave and adapt and react.

Encountering this process between the world wars, Goldstein tried to unite two traditions, the classical tradition of localizationist neurology and a noetic or holistic approach to the behavior of the organism as a whole. "The conflict of these two traditions," Luria wrote in his obituary of Goldstein, "was the basic content of his life, the attempt to construct a new neurology which had to include the truth of both was his endeavour."

Did Goldstein succeed in this? The answer must be no. But no one could have constructed a "new" neurology at this point, because the knowledge and concepts of the time did not allow it. It was similar with Lashley, his supporter and contemporary, who had first introduced *The Organism* to the English-speaking world: he too was a passionate anti-localizationist, at least passionately aware of the barrenness of the localizationism of his time, yet he was never able, any more than Goldstein, to construct a plausible global theory to put in its place. No mechanical model, no computational model of brain function, Lashley felt, would ever suffice — one needed a biological concept, a concept of dynamism, beyond any mechanical one.

Philosophically minded neurologists are rare, although neurology was in effect founded by one, the great Hughlings Jackson, whom Goldstein revered throughout his life. Hughlings Jackson was an ardent Spencerian, who tried to see an evolutionary dynamism in the development of the brain and its diseases, and spoke constantly of the "evolution" (and "dissolution") of nervous function in the individual. These too are the terms in which Goldstein thinks, coupled with the very Darwinian concepts of adaptation, fitness, selection, and so on.

But it was only in the 1960s, after Goldstein's (and Lashley's) death, that the Darwinian metaphor became more than a metaphor, that is, literalized as a new sort of population thinking, dealing not with populations of organisms, as Darwin did, but with populations of cells within each organism, *their* evolution and adaptations within the life span of the individual. A major figure in this development has been Gerald Edelman, who first confirmed the applicability of such concepts in regard to the immune system (an achievement that won him a Nobel Prize). Edelman subsequently turned to the development, adaptations, and individuation of the nervous system, envisaging an "experiential selection" as molding its development, somewhat analogous to natural selection in the formation of the species. All that Goldstein observed and brooded over – levels of organization in the nervous system, health, disease, adaptation, reconstruction – has now once again come to the fore, with the advent of new conceptual and technical tools to approach these. The global theory that Goldstein and Lashley and the Gestaltists sought may now have emerged in Edelman's theory of neural Darwinism and his concept of the brain as a sort of society, in which every part is dynamically connected, "in converse," by a process of re-entrant signaling, with every other. Edelman's concepts of higher-order consciousness, in terms of the brain's categorizations of its own categorizations, may provide a physiologically coherent way of looking at the "abstract-categorical" and at the formation of a unique viewpoint and a self.

Much that Goldstein recorded, pondered, and described for us with minute care and detail lies at the very heart of medicine and neurology and can now, perhaps, be understood – at least reapproached and reconceived – with the more powerful tools and concepts of our own time. It is fitting, therefore, to revive the observation and thoughts of this remarkable man, who saw and described so much in his own time, to see what resonances they will have for us now.

Preface to the German Edition

The intention to write this book goes back many years. It dates to that time of the world war when it became my special task as a physician to take under my medical care a great many patients with lesions of the brain. As the director of a hospital for brain-injured soldiers, my experiences compelled me to broaden the medical frame of reference to a more biological orientation. It soon became evident that only the biological approach is adequate to evaluate the changes which these suffering fellow men have undergone; moreover, the facts taught me that there was no other procedure available which could render aid, however imperfect, to these patients.

The biological orientation and method which grew out of that practice also proved fruitful in long years of other medical work and research. Many a factual and methodological result of my individual casework bears witness to the fruitfulness of this biological approach.

Not before this time of enforced leisure did I find the opportunity to survey these results systematically and to elaborate from them a theory of understanding the living organism's functioning. It would not have been possible to present my results in book form, save for the hospitality which I found in the Netherlands and for the support through the Dutsch Academic Steunfunds and the Rockefeller Foundation.

Therefore, ultimately the book owes its existence to this spirit of helpfulness, a spirit which I gratefully acknowledge. The cooperative participation which my book has thus attained becomes, to my way of thinking, a true symbol of the essence of human nature which can realize itself only where scholarly devotion to subject matter and humaneness join in united action.

Kurt Goldstein
Amsterdam, July, 1934

Author's Preface

The reappearance of a book originally published thirty years ago requires some justification for being brought out again essentially unchanged so much later. The enormous advances in the last decades in the biological sciences, to which this book belongs, may cause some doubt as to whether it would do justice to these advances, as well as whether it would be adequate to what we need today and whether it would be as accepted as before. Certainly, if I had to write this book now I would include many new observations. But in my opinion this would not change the book's essential character, which consists not so much in the communication of facts as in the clarification of the problem of method in biological research and in elucidating ways of conceptualizing the empirical material. It was this emphasis that made the book so different from other works in the field and led Karl Spencer Lashley in his foreword to say that *The Organism* is of "prime importance for all branches of natural science which are concerned with the correlation and integration of vital functions." Clarification of the methodological procedure in biology is as important today as it was thirty years ago.

The uniqueness of this book lies in the application of a new method by which I believe more justice may be done to the description and understanding of the behavior of normal and pathological living beings. The book has its origin in my practical aim to help patients suffering from severe disturbances due to defects in the brain. Having applied for many years the method of natural science and having become increasingly dissatisfied with my results, I was convinced that we needed an essentially different method for studying living beings, especially man. I realized that only a method that placed the total organism of the individual in the foreground – in our interpretation of normal functioning or disturbances due to a defect – could be fruitful.

The Organism consists mainly of a detailed description of the new method, the so-called holistic, organismic approach. Certainly, isolated data acquired by the dissecting method of natural science could not be neglected if we were to maintain a scientific basis. But we had to discover how to evaluate our observations in their significance for the total organism's functioning and thereby to understand the structure and existence of the individual person. We were confronted then with a difficult problem of epistemology. The primary aim of my book is to describe this methodological procedure in detail, by means of numerous observations.

The great number of examples from various fields in which the usefulness of the method was to be demonstrated may make the reading of the book at times difficult. But it seemed to me relevant to include such diverse observations since in this way I could exemplify the characteristic feature of the new method, namely, that by using this principle much of what we observe in living beings can be understood in the same manner. This created another advantage. Such diverse material, from the fields of anatomy, physiology, psychology, and philosophy, that is, from those disciplines concerned with the nature of man, were correlated for the reader. In this way he could observe that the method may be useful for the solution of various problems that may, superficially, seem to be divergent and that have, until now, been treated as unrelated.

I would like in this connection to mention the discussion in this book of reflexes, instincts, and conditioning; the problem of normality, health, and disease; the problem of social life, the hierarchy of life, phylogeny, and ontogeny. Furthermore, I point to many particular concepts such as specificity, antagonism, knowledge and action, life and mind, technology, education, and the comparison between natural science and the science of human beings. Finally, the problem of knowledge in general, in the similarities and dissimilarities between natural science and the science of living beings, is raised. There is a difference that frequently has led to an overestimation of natural science in our attempt to understand human beings, since the application of the methods and results of natural science may hinder the proper interpretation of life. To attempt to understand life from the point of view of the natural-science method alone is fruitless.

The holistic method cannot exclude any experiences of one kind or the other. Both belong to human beings and must be evaluated in their relevance for human existence. Therefore, the differences should be carefully considered. This is advanced by the holistic method. These and other problems have not in the least lost their importance in our time. The fruitfulness of a method reveals itself particularly in the possibility of treating new problems or raising new questions. It can be applied to material in such a way as to instigate new inquiry and achieve new unities instead of merely isolated phenomena. In this connection I would like to point to new insights into human nature gained by my changed concept of the abstract and concrete attitudes, developed after the book was first published. In human behavior I had discerned these two attitudes and assumed that they function more or less interdependently under different conditions. Concrete behavior always appears roughly concomitantly with abstract behavior and may even depend on the latter, that is to say, may be initiated by the latter. It is not so apparent that the abstract attitude also functions correctly in a concrete situation. Normal behavior demands both behavior forms combined in a unit. From such an assumption it appears surprising that at times we observe that an individual is able to exist on a concrete level alone; for example, the infant, in whom the abstract capacity has not yet developed, and in "primitive people," who seem to be primarily concrete to such a degree that it has been assumed that primitive tribes are people possessing an inferior mentality.

The infant is able to live because the people around him, particularly the mother, organize his world in such a way that he is exposed as little as possible to demands he cannot fulfill. Thus the behavior of the infant is not at all an expression of his concrete capacity alone but also of the abstract attitude of someone else. Thus normal behavior in infancy becomes comprehensible as the result of the activity of two persons. Observation of so-called primitive peoples reveals the same characteristic, as research, particularly that of Paul Radin, indicates. He showed that in all primitive communities there live two kinds of people, the "knowers," who have the capacity for the abstract attitude and employ it, and the "others," the "nonknowers," who also have the capacity to abstract but for the most part do not utilize it and thus seem to be able to live exclusively on the concrete, inferior level. The culture is so organized by the "knowers" that the others do not need to employ the abstract attitude. Thus their normal life is the result of both: the concrete and abstract behavior of different individuals. Why this is so we shall not discuss here. What is important, however, is to realize that in normal human behavior both activities are always operative, if not always in the same person. This realization is particularly important inasmuch as it renders unnecessary the assumption of a mental inferiority that on careful investigation proves to be nonexistent. And this observation warns us how easily we may be deceived in our judgment of a phenomenon when we do not apply the holistic method. (For details see my paper, "Concerning the Concept of Primitivity in Culture and History," *Culture in History: Essays in Honor of Paul Radin*, Columbia University Press, 1960.)

Another study undertaken by means of the new method revealed that human behavior cannot be understood exclusively from the concept of concrete-abstract attitude as it has been presented in this book. We thus came to the following conclusion: while in the concrete-abstract attitude ordered life can be guaranteed by the application of reasoning, to understand human life in its fullness another sphere of human behavior must be taken into consideration. When we are in this sphere, subject-object experiences remain more or less in the background and the feeling of unity comprising ourselves and the world in all respects and particularly in our relation to other human beings is dominant. This I term the "sphere of immediacy." It is not a subjective experience. It is not an irrational assumption. It is governed, like our objective world, by laws that are different from so-called logical reasoning. It is not easy to describe. It has to be experienced in definite situations.

When we try to bring ourselves into this sphere or when we are drawn to it by the attractive character which the world presents within it, the words with which we endeavor to describe our experiences may, when compared with our usual use of language, appear strange and reminiscent of the language poets use. But such words are not merely comprehensible; they also reveal a new world to which we do not generally pay attention in our practical or scientific behavior. More properly, we intentionally repress it because its influence may disturb the stability and security of the world of our culture. These experiences of immediacy originate from the same world in which we otherwise live. They even represent the deepest character of the world. For the individual is here involved in his totality, while in the subject-object world he is considered from an isolated and isolating point of view that we may prefer for some special purpose. In order to enter this sphere of immediacy we have to try to neglect somewhat the "natural science" attitude that appears unnatural in this sphere since it does not comprise total human nature. The experience of immediacy cannot be reached by the discursive procedure or by any kind of synthesis. It may be achieved only by surrendering ourselves to the world with which we come in contact without fearing to lose our relation to the ordered world.

Experience teaches us that we are able to live in both spheres, that the two spheres are not opposed to each other, that the sphere of immediacy also belongs to our nature. It shows that our existence is based not on objectively correct order alone but at the same time on comfort, well-being, beauty, and joy, on belonging together. While the appearance of "adequacy" to which I refer in my book is, indeed, important for our existence in the world, the sphere of immediacy creates a deeper existence that affords not only the possibility of living in the static condition of the abstract-concrete sphere but also of tolerating uncertainty without losing our existence. This is particularly significant for the possibility of existence in spite of failure and reveals thereby a more central layer of human nature. The sphere of immediacy becomes apparent in many circumstances of everyday life: in friendship, in love, in creative work, and in the religious attitude, and it is not even lacking as part of our experience in scientific investigation.

We are able to live in both spheres because of our capacity for the abstract attitude. This attitude renders possible our experience of subject and object separately and of shifting from one event to another, from one sphere to the other. The feeling of unity in the sphere of immediacy is the deepest foundation for the experience of well-being and for self-realization. This becomes evident, for instance, when we are deceived in our encounter with another person with whom we believed ourselves to belong together. Then we do not experience simply a feeling of error to which we pay more or less attention but we are *deeply* disappointed, even shaken. This experience is, so to speak, a shaking of our foundation, of our existence. It touches on a central human phenomenon, the experience of "being," of realizing our nature, which is possible only in a genuine unity with the other and with the world (see my paper, "The Smiling of the Infant and the Problem of Understanding the Other," *Journal of Psychology* 44 [1957]).

Before the reader embarks with a critical attitude onto the wealth of phenomena that life presents according to my method, I would like to point to a sentence in this book that is fundamental to my conviction that I am on the right path. "The attainment of biological knowledge we are seeking is essentially akin to the phenomenon that the organism becomes adequate to its demands" (see p. 307); expressed differently, "biological knowledge is a form of biological being." Biological knowledge is possible because of the similarity between human nature and human knowledge. It is an expression of human nature. This conviction grows out of participation in all the observable activities of human beings in concrete research on which my evidence is based. Here one gives an account to oneself again and again about what one is actually doing and discusses with oneself the means by which one may arrive at a comprehension of the living world, without apprehension if the factual material demands the introduction of considerations that may be termed philosophical. Only then can the term "holistic approach" stand the test of validity.

Kurt Goldstein
New York City, March 15, 1963

Introduction

If I am correct in my views, all previous attempts to understand life have followed the method of working from the lower to the higher. Under the conviction that the phyla of living beings represent a scale, at the bottom of which are organisms of relatively simple structure and function, distinguished from the "higher" ones only in that the latter show progressively greater differentiation in their development, the approach has been to explore functions in the "lower" ("simpler") animals and from there to ascend to the analysis of the "higher" (more "complex") beings. This procecure was not discarded, even by those who were rationally compelled to abandon the concept of evolution. The approach remained essentially the same whether the performances of the organism were thought to be of the reflex type or whether regulative and directive factors were introduced to explain phenomena in "higher" organisms. In the latter case, the investigator hoped to find these directive factors in their simplest form in the lower organisms. In fact, the change in biological views in recent years, the increasing movement away from the reflex concept, brought no essential change in this general attitude of biologists. Fundamentally, the determining view has remained that the lower organisms are "simpler" and can be investigated more readily. Therefore, the method of procedure from the "lower" to the "higher" has persisted.

Departure from experiences with man
The following discussion of the phenomena of life is an attempt to proceed in the diametrically opposite direction. It makes man its point of departure; from a study of human behavior it tries to obtain the foundations for an understanding of the other forms of organic life. I have

chosen the human being as my starting point not only because, being a physician, I find it more natural but primarily because, during the pursuit of my studies, I have found no concept more problematic and open to question than the concept of simplicity. Even in the analysis of human behavior, the attempt to reduce the more "complex" performances to the "simpler" ones has met with the greatest difficulties. Very often, the "simpler" performances have been found to be abstractions, and the events that the latter aim to explain turn out to be "simple" only in the presence of a specific, habitual, technical attitude of abstraction. At closer range, however, these "simple" phenomena have been found to be much more obscure. We may refer here to the traditional view of the difference between perception and sensation, or action and reflex, a relation that on closer observation has to be revised. Sensation and reflex, though supposedly the simplest constituent elements of perception and action, themselves presented a problem of increasingly greater complexity than perception and action. Such difficulties make one suspicious of attempts to differentiate between "higher" and "lower" animals, or to understand the "higher" in terms of the "lower."

The designation of an event or an organism as "simpler" ordinarily provides no indication of the meaning of the term. Usually a process is called "simple" according to the extent to which it appears to us as irreducible to more obvious and elementary ones. Thus it is assumed that the lower organisms are more easily understood in their structure and in their forms of "adjustment" to the environment: so, for example, one described the protozoa as a "simple reflex mechanism."

But are we sure that, in doing so, one does not overlook the very nature of these beings? Might they not seem so "simple" to us because, in investigating them, we simplify them artificially and see in them only that which is consistent with such a simplification? And because their nature may be so remote from ours that it makes a real understanding of them impossible, the fallacy in our procedure does not necessarily become apparent to us. We may not be aware of the degree to which our preconceptions do violence to the facts we observe and how little we are justified in picturing these creatures as simple. Such considerations are not mere theoretical speculations. The controversy over the behavior of protozoa is a good example of how helpless we are when attempting to give an incontrovertible description of the so-called simplest forms of life: To certain observers they are simple reflex mechanisms; to others their behavior becomes intelligible only under the assumption of complicated psychic processes.

The decision as to whether a certain pattern of behavior of an organism is simple or complex presupposes a knowledge of the "nature" of the creature involved. Only on this basis can we understand whether or not those traits are characteristic of this being. Only then is a comparison of the behavior of various organisms possible and a foundation laid for the discrimination between simple and complex organisms. In order to decide whether a performance of a given organism is simple or complex, it is necessary to know what demands that performance makes upon the capacity of that organism.

Thus, the problem of simplicity and complexity leads us back to the problem of unequivocal description of the very essence, the intrinsic nature of the particular organism. Consequently, man becomes the obvious starting point of our investigation, because the closer we stand in our relations to a living being, the sooner we may expect to arrive at a correct judgment regarding its essential nature. At least, it is undoubtedly easier to avoid gross mistakes in describing the behavior of man than of animals. Methodological difficulties and possible errors in procedure can be more easily noticed in the human field, since here the consequences of such faulty procedure affect the modes of life and behavior more conspicuously. By this statement I do not wish to deny or even to underrate the importance of observations and experiments on animals. Of course, the knowledge of animal behavior must be acquired by investigating the animals themselves. What I am opposing is merely the uncritical transfer of findings in one field to the other. To my mind, just as the attempt to understand man from animals would be a mistake, so also it is wrong to apply knowledge gained from a study of man directly to animals. Clearly, we have to avoid such insidious anthropomorphism. We must avoid it just as we have to avoid zoomorphism. Experiments with animals are certainly invaluable for many problems of biology and medicine, if for no other reason than that the material is so available. Their usefulness will increase to the extent that our experiences with human beings serve to guard us against methodological errors and wrong generalizations. Thus, the study of humans and that of animals have each their proper place. However, insofar as experiences in either field may be considered apt to throw light on the other, we should prefer to have the observation of human beings as the starting point and to derive from it our guiding methodological principle.

I shall confine my discussion essentially to the nervous system, since only in this realm do I feel confident that my judgment of the material will be sufficiently reliable. I believe, however, that the conclusions drawn will convince the reader that it is permissible to make some generalizations regarding processes in the other systems of the organism. Personally, I consider some such generalizations justifiable, since I do not think of a single organ as a separate system with its own functions, but only as an integrated part of the whole organism.

Biology as a science of living beings
It might be argued that biology, especially general biology, should begin with an exact definition of life and of the characteristics of living organisms before it attempts to describe and explain living organisms. As a matter of fact, this problem of definition has often been raised and attempts made to illuminate it. Hans Driesch, for instance, termed biology "the science of life," holding that the fundamental biological problem was to determine whether life should be understood as a combination of chemical and physical phenomena or as something possessing its own elementary laws. As yet, no definition has been accepted as final, and – what I regard as still more important – no attempts at a definition have contributed very much to our understanding of the living world. In any case, we are certainly obliged to admit that such an attempt presupposes a knowledge of living organisms; for a definition of life cannot be other than a concept derived from a study of their behavior. Thus, such a definition would, of necessity, be obliged to follow, rather than precede, our observations.

At what point should we begin? Perhaps we should first map out our subject matter. But is that really necessary? Does any contemporary science proceed in this manner? Not to my way of thinking! Any formalization of the subject matter of a science is useful only if it follows, not precedes the investigation. This inevitably must be the case since the subject matter itself becomes apparent only during the process of research, as it emerges from the indefinite province in which it was embedded. This is equally true for biological research. The question, "In what does living matter differ from nonliving?" presupposes that we have already separated the two. We stand in the presence of a multiformity of material that is scientifically undefined. This material is simply the world around us, in which certain phenomena immediately stand out as "living," without revealing to us the why and wherefore of this characteristic, or even challenging an inquiry concerning it. Life confronts us in the living being. These organisms, at least for the time being, provide our subject matter. With the essential nature of life, we are not at present concerned; this will gradually reveal itself, as the characteristics of living organisms become more apparent to us. Then, and then only, can we begin to ask and possibly answer the question where life begins and ends and what the difference is between living and nonliving matter.

And so it seems at least that it is the first task of biology to describe carefully all living beings as they actually are, to apprehend them in their peculiarities, to recognize, differentiate, and to "know" them, to decide whether and how they can be compared with each other, and whether and how they are related genetically. As Hermann Jacques Jordan declares, "The riddle of biology is the riddle of the systems themselves," that is, of the specific nature of the various organisms proper and not that of the changes in a system whose organization is irrelevant to the investigator.[1] To this pertinent statement I should only add that, before change can be understood, we must have reached at least a partial solution to this riddle of the systems.

But how are we to seek this solution? We have said that life confronts us in living organisms. But as soon as we attempt to grasp them scientifically, we must take them apart, and this taking apart nets us a multitude of isolated facts that offer no direct clue to that which we experience directly in the living organism. Yet we have no way of making the nature and behavior of an organism scientifically intelligible other than by its construction out of facts obtained in this way. We thus face the basic problem of all biology, possibly of all knowledge. And it is the analysis of this problem, in respect to the living world, that is here my whole concern. The question can be formulated quite simply: What do the phenomena, arising from the isolating procedure, teach us about the "essence" (the intrinsic nature) of an organism? How, from such phenomena, do we come to an understanding of the behavior of the individual organism?

Hitherto the aim of biological research has been to divide the organism, like any physical object, into parts, and then to reconstruct it. But this procedure has yielded few satisfactory results either in respect to the physical or the psychic phenomena of an organism. Dissatisfaction with these results has been one of my motives in restating the problem. It has inspired the present investigation and has dictated a critical consideration not only of the methods used until now in acquiring facts, but even of the characteristics of "facts" themselves. It appeared to me an important scientific task to decide in every case what kind of a fact an observed phenomenon represents. The basic motive, however, was not primarily a dissatisfaction with the theoretical results, but with their inadequacy in medical practice. It became more and more apparent that increased theoretical knowledge did not, by any means, lead to an improvement in the realm of practice. Despite great strides in certain fields, patients as well as physicians began to lose faith in the practical value of the scientific theory. Nor did the immense increase in the inventory of individual facts promote greater confidence in the general theoretical principles purporting to explain life processes. Again and again, new hypotheses became necessary in order to bring the facts into accord with one another. This opened the way for queries as to whether it was at all feasible to develop biology on a *strictly scientific basis* – whether transcendental and vitalistic factors were not essential to an understanding of life. Even if one vigorously rejects – as do I – all such factors, still there remains the question *whether biology as a science is at all possible.*

This book, which seeks to resolve these questions, is intended as an introduction to the practical work of the physician as well as that of the biologist. Its aim is not to offer theoretical speculations, but to present the facts themselves and discuss those explanatory concepts that these facts suggest and through which, in turn, a reliable comprehension of biological phenomena is attainable.

At this point, we cannot elaborate on the methodological process through which (despite the aforementioned difficulty) we hope to arrive at a scientific treatment of biological phenomena. The following critical discussion of the traditional procedure, and our approach to the study of a living organism, may serve to make evident the adequacy of this type of research. Subject matter and method are interrelated; the more the subject matter of our research becomes distinct, the more clearly will the method itself become manifest. Whether or not both are adequate instruments of science can be verified by only one criterion: fruitfulness in their respective fields. We must attempt to understand living organisms in the most fruitful way.

Apropos of methodology, one thing must be emphasized in advance. We will not be satisfied with any form of intuitive approach. Every natural science, indeed any science at all, must start with an analytic dissection. So, too, in biology we must first observe the "parts" of the organism. We are forced to accept this point of departure because a naive approach to the phenomena is not feasible, unless one is to be content with fictitious generalities.

Departure from pathological data

Our treatise differs from the usual one in that it proceeds from pathological rather than from normal phenomena. This approach requires some justification. The observation and analysis of pathological phenomena no doubt often yield greater insight into the processes of the organism than do those of the normal.

There is greater revelation in pathological phenomena. By this, of course, I do not mean that they immediately provide us with a real understanding of the nature of the organism. As long as one regards the pathological simply as curiosa, created by disease, we cannot hope, in studying them, to advance our knowledge of normal phenomena. On these grounds, certain investigators entirely reject the use of pathological material. Their skepticism seems justified insofar as the uncritical deduction of theoretical concepts from experiences in pathology may lead, and often has led, to improper conclusions in, and applications to, the field of normal psychology. I am thinking, for instance, of the theory of the structure of language – the so-called speech maps based on pathological phenomena. This theory was harmful in that it strengthened the associationists' claims in psychology and, in so doing, reinforced the opinion that mental life is the mere sum of isolated operations – a view that today is accepted as erroneous. But this fatal influence that pathology exercised on the ideas of normal phenomena was not occasioned by the use of pathological material as such; rather it must be attributed to an inappropriate use and insufficient analysis of that evidence and, furthermore, to an uncritical transfer of results and theoretical interpretations from one field to another.[2] Such a transfer is permissible only if one knows and takes into account the specific laws that govern the phenomena in each field of science. This aspect of the problem has often been disregarded; moreover, insufficient attention has been paid to the particular change that disease creates in a living process – a change that does not permit of any mechanical application of such pathological disclosures to the normal process. In view of this rather confused state of affairs, those who reject the use of pathological phenomena seem to be justified. They are not right, however, in the assumption that disease produces abnormal phenomena that in principle preclude an inference applicable to the normal. On the contrary, it has become increasingly evident that pathological phenomena can be recognized as an indication of lawful variations of the normal life process. And moreover, they become very useful for the understanding of normal phenomena, provided one explores and takes into account the laws that characterize these pathological conditions. Then the use of the pathological proves extremely helpful to an understanding of the normal, and a knowledge of the character of pathological condition per se acquires particular significance for biology.

Since a disease process is a modification – and indeed, a very significant modification – of a normal process, biological research cannot afford to neglect it. I hope that in this book I have succeeded in making clear how great a profit biology may draw from a study of these modified forms of normal phenomena. In recommending the use of pathological material, I wish to emphasize that the study of processes "decomposed" by disease has also led to improvements in the field of general methodology, improvements known to be of great value in the study of the normal. But, in the last analysis, is there really such a fundamental distinction between the "normal" material used in biological experiments and pathological material? The true difference between the normal and the pathological would only be evident if in our biological observations we dealt with perfectly "normal" animals; but when we experiment, or observe under experimental conditions, we actually interfere with these organisms, so that the difference between normal and pathological material diminishes considerably. So, from our point of view, experimental interference and disease mean essentially the same thing. In both cases our observations are made on substrata that have been impaired. As we shall see, the symptoms of disease and the results of experimental observations can actually be relegated to the same class. Failure to understand the similarity between the changes brought about through disease and those induced by experiment has resulted in many erroneous conclusions respecting normal process, conclusions that we hope may be corrected through the point of view introduced here.

I may be taken to task for not having cited sufficiently the views of other authors in this book, particularly since many of my findings are doubtless related or are even indebted to such sources. In answer to such criticism, I can only say that my intention has been to give a clear presentation of facts and not to supply a historical survey of how the problems involved have been treated heretofore. A thorough examination of the problems from the historical point of view would have far exceeded the scope of this volume. For the same reason, reference to the literature is made only when a particular book seems to have a significant bearing on the views expressed here. Where there is a relation between my view and others, I feel that the fact will become apparent to those who are familiar with the subject, possibly even more apparent than it is to me. While working, one cannot and should not constantly stop to consider whether a certain view or procedure owed its incentive to some worker in the field. As Goethe wrote: "The artist receives from without not merely his subject matter; he may also take unto himself foreign ideas"; and similarly, "Provided he presents the material in a refined if not perfected form, the scientist may and must make use of historical predecessors without religiously referring to the source of his material."[3] The crucial point in the evaluation of my findings will be whether my endeavor complies with these standards to some extent; in other words, whether the ideas laid down in this book are fruitful for our field of inquiry.

I should not like to present this book to the public without a grateful reference to my co-worker, Adhémar Gelb, whose untimely death I deeply deplore. Many of the thoughts voiced here are the result of more than ten years of collaboration with him, and it would be impossible to determine which of us first conceived or expressed them.

Chapter One

Method of Determining Symptoms.

Certain General Laws of Organismic Life.

Observations on Persons with

Brain Injuries

Our starting point considers phenomena exhibited when the brain cortex is damaged. This, for two reasons. First because, with some justification, we attribute a particular, dominating significance to the cortex, phenomena appearing during its injury will thereby be especially relevant for our understanding of the essential nature of man. Second, because the analysis of these phenomena enables us to demonstrate certain general laws of the disintegration of function, these laws in turn will be especially relevant for our understanding of the organism's functions.

A study of most of the former publications may convey the impression that cortical injury is usually followed by a loss of circumscribed functions, such as speech, visual perception, or motor performance. Writers on the subject actually assumed this to be so. According to this conception, they distinguished and designated various disease syndromes by such terms as aphasia in its various forms, visual agnosia, apraxia, and so on. They assumed also that circumscribed centers controlled those particular functions.

In recent years, however, improved observation has led to a change of this view. It has been found that, even in cases of circumscribed cortical damage, the disturbances are scarcely ever confined to a single field of performance. In such intricate syndromes, we deal not only with a simple combination of disparate disturbances but also with a more or less unitary, basic change that affects different fields homologously and expresses itself through different symptoms. It has also become apparent that the relation between mental performances and definite areas in the brain constitutes a far more complicated problem than the so-called localization theory has assumed.

This difference in observations should not lead us to believe that the more recent investigators are more competent than the earlier ones. The early investigations were those of experts who were highly esteemed and real masters in their field. Rather, a difference in the methodology was responsible for the emergence of other facts.

The problem of methodology has the greatest significance for psychopathology and for biological research in general. For example, in the descriptions of symptoms given by the so-called classicists on the subject of aphasia – we choose these because they demonstrate the general procedure particularly well – we find that their characteristic tendency, their reference to a hypothetical "primary symptom," renders a given symptomatology plausible. In motor-speech disturbance, for instance, an impairment of the "motor-speech images" was regarded as the "primary" symptom. Where this speech defect was found associated with a disturbance of the writing function, the latter was likewise interpreted as a consequence of the impairment of the "motor-speech images." In word deafness, an impairment of the sensory speech images was assumed to be the primary symptom. From this primary symptom, they also attempted to explain the further symptoms found in such cases, for instance, paraphasia.

The fundamental principle of this procedure is, of course, reasonable. We shall see later that we cannot obtain direct proof of a functional disturbance (see p. 108). To define the latter, we are dependent on conclusions derived from changes in performances as exhibited in the symptoms. Such procedure can be conclusive only if we ascertain, by accurate analyses of every disturbed performance, the one functional disturbance that really does account for the appearance of the various changes. This exactness can hardly be expected from pioneer work in an unknown field, in which obviously one must begin by examining the most striking features. And this is not dangerous so long as one bears in mind that the phenomena that first attract attention and are not necessarily essential, or basic, not necessarily the key to all subsequent phenomena. Such phenomena stand out only by virtue of certain circumstances; and while they may appear to be characteristic, they do not necessarily support a theoretical foundation for understanding the genesis of the whole symptomatological picture. The danger arises only when this discrimination between essential and incidental phenomena is neglected and when scientists forget that they base their theory on such a defective foundation. The incidental phenomena may have value only for preliminary orientation and may, at best, merit the position of a crude working hypothesis. The real crisis arises when, even in the face of new findings, the investigator cannot free himself from the former theory; rather, the scientist attempts to preserve it and, by constant emendations, to reconcile it with these new facts instead of replacing it by a new theory fitted to deal with both the old and new facts. This error has not been avoided in the evolution of the classical doctrine.

The Problem of Determination of Symptoms

The basic error in the procedure under consideration was the failure to recognize the complex problem involved in the method of symptoms.[1] We have become so accustomed to regard symptoms as direct expressions of the damage in a part of the nervous system that we tend to assume that, corresponding to some given damage, definite symptoms must inevitably appear. We do so because we forget that normal as well as abnormal reactions ("symptoms") are only expressions of the organism's attempt to deal with certain demands of the environment. Consideration of this makes it evident that symptoms are by no means certain to become self-apparent. Symptoms are answers, given by the modified organism, to definite demands: they are attempted solutions to problems derived on the one hand from the demands of the natural environment and on the other from the special tasks imposed on the organism in the course of the examination. We shall see below that, in the everyday life of the patient, a certain transformation of the environment goes hand in hand with each defect and tends to prevent certain disturbances from manifesting themselves. It is of primary interest that the appearance of symptoms depends on the method of examination, although the significance of this fact has been largely overlooked. By focusing attention only on certain phenomena or on a selected few, the investigator comes to isolate "symptoms." Phenomena, more striking than others, are registered first and thus give the impression of being the dominant symptom. Most likely to attract attention, of course, are the atypical reactions to a normal situation and, in particular, the complete absence of any reaction when one is expected.

In this way, complete loss of a special function tends to be the outstanding symptom and conceals the real or basic defect. On other occasions, those phenomena appear, more or less accidentally, as outstanding symptoms, which are answers elicited by specific questions presented by the examiner.

Of course, these "questions" are not fortuitous but are dictated by the investigator's fundamental ideas about the phenomena being studied. It is true that these ideas themselves may have been suggested by the data; but frequently a theory has evolved on the basis of symptoms that have gained their apparent preeminence purely by chance. This bias has often resulted in delaying the understanding of the symptoms and the advance of research. Of course, if one tried to include all symptoms in the construction of a theory, no theory could ever be elaborated. Obviously, such theorizing presumes that one has grouped the symptoms into the more and less relevant – the primary and secondary – and has tried to build only on the so-called primary symptoms. In making these distinctions, the investigator is commonly prejudiced by theoretical viewpoints that have proved useful in other fields of research and that he judges – usually without testing their qualifications – to be adequate for the material at hand.

Heretofore, psychopathological symptoms were explained in the light of concepts borrowed from reflexology and the prevailing association psychology. The theory that the structure of the nervous system is based on a number of separate mechanisms, each functioning independently, led to the supposition that circumscribed injuries would result in disorders specific to the mechanisms involved. Consequently, the investigator looked for the latter and found them, because he noticed only the disorders that best corresponded to the theory, that is, disorders that could be regarded as changes resulting from the failure of a hypothetically independent and separate function. Just as normal events had been explained as composites of *elementary* processes, so also were symptoms interpreted as changes of similar mechanisms of mental elements. When the investigator assumed that an impairment of motor-speech images was the cause of motor aphasia, or an impairment of visual images the cause of alexia, he believed that his deductions were genuinely based on the symptoms. Actually, such explanations were merely the outcome of a theoretical preconception, merely an interpretation of the phenomena in terms of a special theory, namely, association psychology.

The correctness of the basic assumption was accepted so implicitly that no attempt was made to prove that the images in question really played the part in normal speech that it was assumed they did. Nor was any attempt made to ascertain whether these images were actually defective in patients.

Once the basic concept of the importance of specific areas for certain functions was formulated and seemingly confirmed, it now determined all subsequent investigations, especially because of its applicability to practice. Thereafter, the question was confined to the decision as to whether the supposed individual centers and pathways functioned in a "normal" or "abnormal" manner. Still more serious was the fact that this concept became the criterion for determining whether or not individual phenomena belonged in the given syndrome resulting from injury to a certain area. If others besides the phenomena that had been regarded as essential symptoms were found, these were pushed aside as "complications" that disturbed the "purity" of the case and were considered the result of some injury incurred simultaneously in another area. Or an attempt was otherwise made to explain them as merely secondary effects contingent on the hypothetically primary disturbance. Yet not even the growing necessity for the most diverse modifications of the basic conception and for the most daring theoretical constructions has deterred theorists from building such auxiliary hypotheses.

Three methodological postulates

Clearly such reasoning in circles has necessarily delayed the realization that the basic concept is untenable. Yet this procedure can be regarded as characteristic of the majority of clinical, physiological, and biological research of the older school. In what respect does our procedure differ from that described? Simply put, we have endeavored to record, in an open-minded fashion, all phenomena. Pursuing this aim, there result three methodological postulates equally valid for the examination of patients or animals.

1. Consider initially all the phenomena presented by the organism (in this case it may be a patient), giving no preference, in the description, to any special one. At this stage no symptom is to be considered of greater or less importance. Only under these conditions is the description correct. It must be left for future investigation to determine how far one symptom, rather than another, is essential for understanding the underlying changes of a function.

Every unbiased and exhaustive examination of a case repeatedly

37

teaches us that alteration of a given performance, even if at first sight it appears to be very prominent, is not necessarily of primary significance for understanding the underlying functional disturbance. On the other hand, a trifle that barely attracts notice may be of the utmost importance. For example, as long as the most prominent symptom of amnesic aphasia, namely, the difficulty in finding words, was allowed to suggest the explanation of this disease, the theory that the basic disturbance consisted in a reduced evocability of speech images appeared perfectly satisfactory. But as soon as a subtle and formerly neglected alteration in the total behavior of the patient was taken into consideration, not only an entirely different conception of the underlying functional disturbance but also a new insight into the meaning of the aphasic phenomena was made possible. The difficulty in finding words, formerly regarded as the main symptom, retreated into the background. The theory of the reduced evocability of speech images became obsolete, because it could be sustained only by means of auxiliary hypotheses – hypotheses not required in our explanation – since the patients are quite capable of using the words under specific circumstances. They have not lost the use of words per se but the ability to employ words as bearers of meaning. Under circumstances in which the latter is not demanded, and the words "belong" to an action or concrete situation, the patient "has the words." The inability to find and use words voluntarily is not due to the primary defect of the speech mechanism but to a change in their total personality which bars them from the situation in which meaning is required.[2]

2. The second methodological postulate concerns the correct description of the observable phenomena themselves. It was a frequent methodological error to accept what amounted to a mere description of the effect; but an effect might be ambiguous with respect to its underlying function. Therefore, only a thorough analysis of the causes of such effects, of success or failure in a given task, for example, can provide clarification. The older psychopathological investigations usually confined themselves to the question of whether a patient actually gave, or failed to give, the correct response in a task. This "plus or minus method," however, is inadequate, no matter whether we are dealing with positive or negative results. If we regard a reaction only from the standpoint of the actual solution of a task, we may overlook the deviation from normality, because the individual completes the task by a

detour that may not be evident in the solution. Only accurate analysis, through an examination that makes it impossible for the patient to achieve a result in a roundabout way, can disclose the defect. If our capacity to observe were not so imperfect, closer attention would show that the patient has reached the goal in an abnormal manner, for, of course, under such conditions the results cannot correspond, in all details, to the normal. Once we become alert to this fact, diagnosis is often simplified by noting small and hitherto-unobserved deviations. We may use an example to illustrate this.

Patients with loss of "categorical behavior"[3] find it difficult, for instance, to consider an individual color according to a category such as redness, greenness, and so on. When we ask patients to select all red-color skeins of the Holmgren wool samples, they often place the colors "in a row": the lightest to the darkest red. On the basis of this we might assume that they have proceeded categorically, since they have apparently selected the shades according to a concept – in this case that of brightness – and placed them in a row. This assumption, however, is based on an error of observation, namely, a disregard for the slight differences that distinguish the patient's behavior from a behavior determined by the categorical attitude. It can easily be shown that they have not proceeded and cannot proceed categorically: they are not able to arrange the colors in a row as to their brightness, if asked to do so. They also fail in the task of putting together all the reds in a heap – activities that presuppose the categorical attitude.

These observations make it rather doubtful that the patient originally selected the skeins according to the category of brightness. Actually, if one more carefully examines the manipulations of the patient, one discovers that he has not really laid down a row according to brightness. What he did was to place one shade beside another, one at a time. In this way, single pairs of similar shades were formed under the guidance of the concrete sensory cohesion between the last skein and the next similar one. By this procedure of "successive pairs," he finally came to an arrangement which in toto looked like a scale of brightness but really was not. In selecting a new skein the patient was entirely and solely dependent on the skein that immediately preceded it. This accounts for the pairing of and the intervals between the skeins.[4] That his procedure was determined by this "piece-to-piece" performance could be shown by the fact that, when the examiner removed the skein the patient had last placed in position, he was unable to continue with his "series." This showed that he depended on the immediately preceding skein for the selection of the new one. We mention this example to show how vital it is, for an accurate interpretation, that description of phenomena be minute and exact. And, in order that the description be correct, how careful must be the attention given to those small matters all too easily overlooked through theoretical bias.

Equally ambiguous are the negative results of a medical examination. The wrong response is too often judged to be a simple failure, whereas actually, under careful analysis, it may throw considerable light on the mental functions of the patient. Only by this means can we discover whether there really is a defect in the ability demanded by the task or whether the patient has failed only because of special circumstances induced by the task situation (see p. 47). Furthermore, in the wrong reponse, analysis often uncovers a detour the patient has used, perhaps because the normal way was not practicable. Such facts may have an important bearing on the explanation of the capacities of the organism (see pp. 195, 197).

3. The third methodological postulate we wish to stress is that no phenomenon should be considered without reference to the organism concerned and to the situation in which it appears. We shall have to refer to this point so often that it is not worth further elaboration at this time. As infrequently as this requirement has been observed in the past, because of theoretical bias, it should nonetheless become a matter of course in the future. Many an error would have been avoided in psychopathology if this postulate, quite deliberately stated by Hughlings Jackson[5] decades ago, had not been so completely neglected. The same postulate holds to no less a degree for animal behavior observations (cf., e.g., p. 51). Later on we shall deal in detail with the fundamental difficulties following from the application of this precept, since it necessitates taking into account the organism as a whole.

We wish to refute briefly two possible objections to our methodological postulates. The first concerns the charge that, according to our postulates, one can never really determine at what point an examination can be regarded as completed. As a matter of fact, it never is. But there is still a great difference between the two forms of procedure: between the usual description and enumeration of separate disturbances, such as those of visual or linguistic performances, and our procedure, which is primarily directed toward the cognition of the whole, and, within this frame of reference, seeks to analyze as many individual performances as possible. This technique will certainly obviate the grossest errors, even though it may not lead to absolutely incontestable results. Bearing in mind this aim of completeness, it will be possible to avoid precipitate theoretical conclusions and the rigid maintenance of any hypothesis preventing us from radically revising our theories, on the strength of new experience. In the course of the examination, one comes to a point at which one feels that the analysis can be terminated without risk of gross errors in the interpretation. The examination must be carried far enough at least to ensure that (on the basis of the facts) a theory can be developed that will render understandable all observed phenomena in question and that will make it possible to predict how the organism will react, even in such tasks hitherto not investigated. Only such an analysis is to be considered adequate.

The procedure of investigating the patient, which Gelb and I have described as a case of visual agnosia, may provide an example. On the basis of our first examinations, which were not sufficiently exhaustive, we had formed a hypothesis that was not quite adequate. Further examinations drove us to the formulation of a new hypothesis that did justice to both old and new facts. The further we advanced with the examinations, the more clearly delineated did the functional disturbance in this case become. Finally, we have progressed so far toward constructing the total picture of the patient that we can predict with relatively great certainty how he will behave in any situation, even with respect to tasks that we have not yet examined. Only cases that have been investigated with such thoroughness should be used in the formation of a theory. One single extensive analysis of this sort is much more valuable than many examinations involving many patients but yielding only imperfect conclusions.

This leads to the second objection to our postulates. Our procedure necessarily enforces a limit on the number of cases investigated. To examine many cases so thoroughly would be patently impossible. It is argued that this may vitiate the conclusiveness of the statements, since we may have encountered a special instance that cannot serve as pattern for the explanation of others. This objection completely misses the point:

First, the accumulation of even a myriad of imperfectly investigated cases can in no way guide us toward recognition of the true facts. There is no alternative to carrying the examination of each case to the extent we have indicated.

Second, important though it may be to seek repeated confirmation of our findings through new case material, such confirmation adds nothing essential to our knowledge. Those patients must be subjected to investigation who offer a guarantee of unequivocal statements of fact as well as of theoretical interpretation. Under such conditions, the conclusions drawn from one case will likewise have validity for others. Since the basic laws are the same, the multiplicity encountered in various instances will be readily understood once these basic laws are recognized. True, a new observation may induce us to modify somewhat our original assumptions; but if the analysis of the first observation was sufficient, this modification can be made without conflict, whereas imperfect analysis of ever-so-many cases may be very misleading – as the literature bears witness only too clearly.

If patients with cortical injuries are examined according to these methodological principles (I am thinking primarily of patients whose "central" cortical region [see p. 56] has been injured), an extraordinarily intricate picture results, a systematic account of which has been given in a number of papers. I must forego details at this point, referring the reader to the case studies (indicated in the notes) as models for the correct methodological procedure in describing observable phenomena of a patient and arriving at an adequate symptomatology.[6]

Disintegration of Performances and the Hierarchy Within the Organism

Before outlining the features all these cases share, we must define the term "performances." We call performance of an organism any kind of behavior, activity, or operation as a whole or in part that expresses itself overtly and bears reference to the environment. Hence physiological processes, events within the nervous system, mental activities, attitudes, and affectivities are not performances so long as they do not manifest themselves in some overt action – any disclosable outward behavior. More specifically, a performance is a coming to terms of the organism with environmental stimuli by a behavioral act, be this eyelid closure under stimulation or a total movement like running toward a goal, or hearing, seeing, and so on.

The aforementioned outline may now be presented:

1. A single performance or performances in a specific field (e.g., visual, motor) will never drop out alone.[7] Invariably all performance fields are affected, although the degree to which the individual field is involved varies (see explanation below).

2. A single performance field will never drop out completely. Some individual performances are always preserved. Responses to the apparently equal demands of equal tasks do not drop out indiscriminately under all circumstances. There is a peculiar and, at first, subtle variation of reaction, even when the demand remains constant. This inconsistency is usually explained as the effect of some disturbances of "general functions," such as fatigue, or it is argued away. Actually, it indicates to us the need for further analysis.

3. The modification of performances manifested by a patient in different fields is in principle of the same nature. The different symptoms can be regarded as expressions of one and the same basic disturbance. In spite of this, we are confronted with various syndromes having to do with the question of localization. This will be discussed later (see p. 129).

4. The basic disturbance can be characterized either as a change of behavior or as an impairment of the functions of the brain matter. We have to postpone discussion of the latter (see p. 200). Here we shall merely confine ourselves to a characterization of the change in behavior. We venture to remark that whenever the patient must transcend concrete (immediate) experience in order to act – whenever he must refer to things in an imaginary way – he fails. On the other hand, whenever the result can be achieved by manipulation of concrete and tangible material, he performs successfully. Each problem that forces him beyond the sphere of immediate reality to that of the "possible," or to the sphere of representation, ensures his failure. This manifests itself in all responses such as action, perception, thinking, volition, feeling, and so on. The patient acts, perceives, thinks, has the right impulses of will, feels like others, calculates, pays attention, retains, and so on, as long as he is provided with the opportunity to handle objects concretely and directly. He fails when this is impossible. This is the reason he does not succeed at intelligence tests. This is also the reason he can grasp a little story as long as it concerns a familiar situation in which he himself has participated. But he will not understand a story – cer-

tainly no more difficult for the average person – requiring him to place himself, in imagination, in the position of someone else. He does not comprehend metaphors or puzzles. He can manipulate numbers in a practical manner but has no concept of their value. He can talk if there is some concrete subject matter present but cannot recount material unrelated to him or report it in purely conceptual terms. He is incapable of representation of direction and localities in objective space, nor can he estimate distances; but he can find his way around very well and can execute actions that are dependent on perception of distance and size.

Depending on which of these manifestations of the basic disturbance has been brought into focus, they have been named respectively: disturbance of "symbolic expression" (Henry Head), of the "representational function" (Willem von Woerkom), of "categorical behavior" (Gelb and Goldstein). With regard to the effect of the change, one may, in emphasizing the disturbance of that capacity that is a prerequisite for the performance in question, talk of impairment of the capacity to comprehend the essential features of an event.

Or we might point to the patient's inability to emancipate and withhold himself from the world, the shrinkage of his freedom, and his greater bondage to the demands of environment. The most general formula to which the change can be reduced is probably that the patient has lost the capacity to deal with that which is not real – with the possible.[8]

Inquiring now into the question of how the various performances reveal the impairment, we find that voluntary performances are particularly affected, while activities directly determined by the situation remain relatively intact. Adapting a performance so that it corresponds to the changing demands of the situation requires a voluntary attitude. Therefore, all those performances that require, for their proper execution, such a voluntary shifting must suffer, for example, all "choice reactions." The isolated performances are affected to a greater degree than the so-called total responses. This shows itself in a greater loss of isolated movements than of integrated movements, as well as in the inability to distinguish the details of a picture (the whole of which may yet be recognized) or in the inability to pronounce a single word or single letters out of context. The disintegration of a familiar function proceeds from the highly differentiated and articulated state[9] to a more amorphous total behavior.

The symptoms vary with the severity of impairment and the degree to which one area or another (see below) is affected. The basic disturbance, however, remains the same. I cannot produce proof of this assertion here, but since my concept has not remained undisputed, I should like to refer to the pertinent literature.[10] I might emphasize at the same time, however, that, for our particular purposes, the differences of opinion are unimportant. One thing is agreed on by all: cortical injury does not result in the loss of isolated performances but in systematic disintegration following the principle that certain forms of behavior will be impaired while others remain intact. Only with this in mind will it be possible to make a distinct classification of the performances that the patient can and cannot carry out, as well as to provide a meaningful description of the symptoms.

Is our characterization of the change after cortical injury satisfactory? Are we really dealing exclusively with the impairment of certain kinds of behavior? Have not "contents" also dropped out? Certainly! Yet it must be admitted that many of these losses are secondary, since it is true that certain contents appear only within certain kinds of behavior. The impairment of the behavior entails the loss of numerous contents. This is perhaps most clearly demonstrable in cases of what are known as "amnesic aphasia." Patients suffering in this way have lost the ability to call objects by their names. Seemingly, they lack the "content": names. The analysis, however, indicates that, in such cases, we are dealing with a disturbance of "categorical" behavior, an impairment of the capacity to experience and to handle "meaning," which is requisite for "naming" objects. This explains why the patients cannot find the words in those situations in which the words have to function as symbols – as representations for something. The loss of "contents" is therefore secondary.

But contents can also be embedded in other forms of behavior, namely, those which belong to acquired faculties, for example, words memorized in foreign languages. Such contents may be preserved despite a disturbance of the aforementioned behavior. To illustrate: some individuals, with a good command of language, of superior linguistic knowledge, are able to name certain objects, even when they are afflicted with "amnesic aphasia."[11] Under other conditions, these acquired performances may be lost when the substratum is damaged. Only exact analysis can show whether, in any particular case in which "contents" are lacking, we are dealing with a consequence of behavior disturbance or

of loss of these acquisitions. Only in the case of these acquired faculties can we speak of contents. The distinction is of fundamental importance for accurate diagnosis of a disturbance, as well as for any attempt
to prescribe therapeutic exercises, because only correct diagnosis of
the change can provide the correct procedure. These comments apply
equally well to the interpretation of content losses in operated animals
and to all experiments on relearning after injury and so on.

Accurate observation of many cases teaches us that disintegration
of function always results in the same pattern of distribution of the
intact and affected modes of behavior. The behavior we have characterized as categorical behavior always suffers first. We are well justified
in crediting the intact organism with a greater performance capacity
than the injured one and in admitting that the "higher" or more complex performances require a more intact substratum than the simpler
ones. Therefore, we speak of a hierarchy or descending scale of disintegration, in which the higher performances are more disturbed than
the simpler ones. Study of the phenomena in progressive and regres-
sive brain processes most clearly reveals such a hierarchy in the regular
succession of the onset of the various symptoms and their abatement
in recovery.

We might venture to say that the most complicated performances,
those first to be impaired, are probably the ones most essential and most
vital to the existence of the organism, and further, with respect to the
nature of the organism, they have the highest functional significance.
Through the deterioration of those performances, the organism loses
its most characteristic properties. We may become particularly conscious of this fact by contrasting an individual suffering from brain injuries with a normal person. Those behavioral forms that are earliest and
most markedly affected express the main characteristics of the human
species and bring to the fore its unique place in nature (cf. p. 44).

In this way, the order manifested in the disintegration may provide
us with the idea of a hierarchy of capacities and performances – a stratified structure of the organism. Of course, it is not hierarchical in the
sense that the individual forms of behavior represent performances
existing in isolation, side by side, and only linked one to the other. It
is not so simple as that. We shall later indicate how this relationship is
to be understood (see p. 363).

Characterization of Performances According to their Functional Significance or Value and their Survival Importance

Our use of the terms "higher" and "lower functional significance" or "value," requires clarification. If, from one standpoint, we characterize certain forms of behavior as intrinsically valuable because of their significance for the nature of the organism, we might, from another standpoint, characterize other performances as most important because they resist the effect of injury. Without a doubt, the survival of "automatic" performances, in contrast to that which we have characterized as "higher," more conscious, or more voluntary, is of special importance for the organism, inasmuch as they are those that ensure mere existence. In this sense, we would be justified in speaking of performances that have greater or less importance for survival. This is what is implied in the expression "the instinct of self-preservation." If this means preservation only in the sense of continued survival, we may ask the questions: Does such an "instinct" exist in the normal organism? More specifically, can it be regarded as belonging to the highest level of functioning, or is not the appearance of such a "drive," as the predominant feature in an individual, itself a symptom of abnormality – a pathological phenomenon? As we shall see, the normal organism is characterized as a "Being" in a temporal succession of definite form. For the realization of this "Being," the existence, the "mere being alive," plays, of course, a prominent but by no means *the* essential role. Under extreme circumstances, it can be compatible with the "nature" of an organism to renounce life, that is, to give up its bodily existence, in order to save its most essential characteristics – for example, a man's ethical convictions (see p. 256). Preservation of material existence becomes "essential" only after defect sets in, and possibly in certain emergencies. In the latter case, the body achieves the position of supreme importance, since all the other possibilities of self-realization are bound to it. Regarding the defective organism, the scale of performance values is likely to differ from that of the normal. In order to preclude any misunderstanding, we differentiate in the future between "functional significance" or value – by which we mean "essential to the nature of the organism" – and "survival importance," by which we mean "paramount in the preservation of its life." In the normal organism, the two usually go hand in hand inasmuch as here preservation also means preservation of the intrinsic nature so far as it is possible. In the pathologi-

47

cally changed organism, the preservation of existing potentialities, the survival importance, comes to the fore. At present we only wish to stress the importance of the principle of hierarchy indicated in the laws of disintegration, and we will subsequently return to this question with special reference to the structure of the organism (cf. p. 372).

Certain General Rules Determining Organismic Life

Normal ("ordered") behavior and "disordered" behavior.
Catastrophic reaction
A description of the mere defects does not adequately characterize the injured condition of the organism. To understand the latter completely, we must also pay close attention to the intact performances. Indeed, the question of how the organism can continue to exist in spite of such great impairments spurs us on to this task. Let us first consider another peculiarity of the injured organism, which will throw considerable light on the solution of this problem and must come to our notice if we follow our first methodological postulate. With this in mind, we find that each effective performance or each failure is an integrated feature in a definite total behavior pattern. At first, it may seem as if we were dealing with an obscure, unintelligible, unsystematic alternation between successful performances and failures. No explanation of this alternation which resorts to fluctuation of so-called higher functions or faculties, such as attention, fatigue, and so forth, reaches the core. It shifts the explanation to an allegedly underlying, but equally unintelligible, functional disturbance. We can reach an understanding of this alternation only by considering the total behavior in which the individual performance appears. Total behavior can be divided into two basic classes, objectively distinguishable; to one of these classes belong the effectual performances, to the other, the deficient performances. The first kind of behavior, we call "ordered," the second, "disordered" or "catastrophic." We shall encounter these two types repeatedly (see p. 55), but at first we must provide a more accurate phenomenological description of both. In an ordered situation, responses appear to be constant, correct, adequate to the organism to which they belong, and adequate to the species and to the individuality of the organism, as well as to the respective circumstances. The individual himself experiences them with a feeling of smooth functioning, unconstraint, well-being,

adjustment to the world, and satisfaction, that is, the course of behavior has a definite order, a total pattern in which all involved organismic factors — the mental and the somatic down to the physicochemical processes — participate in a fashion appropriate to the performance in question. And that, in fact, is the criterion of a normal condition of the organism. Hence, ordered and normal behavior are synonymous inasmuch as the behavior is normal because it is "ordered." The "catastrophic" reactions, on the other hand, are not only "inadequate" but also disordered, inconstant, inconsistent, and embedded in physical and mental shock. In these situations, the individual feels himself unfree, buffeted, and vacillating. He experiences a shock affecting not only his own person, but the surrounding world as well. He is in that condition that we usually call anxiety. After an ordered reaction, he can ordinarily proceed to another, without difficulty or fatigue. Whereas, after a catastrophic reaction, his reactivity is likely to be impeded for a longer or shorter interval. He becomes more or less unresponsive and fails even in those tasks that he could easily meet under other circumstances. The disturbing aftereffect of catastrophic reactions is long enduring. Discrimination between these two types of behavior is fundamental for the correct analysis of the performance of an organism. The solution of a task will depend on whether the task itself has arisen during the course of performances that are within the realm of the capabilities of the patient or transcend the latter.

Tendency to ordered behavior
In time the patient will — despite the persistence of the defect — return to an ordered condition. Obviously, this will be especially true of those patients whose disease came to a standstill, leaving a certain defect. The picture, during the acute state, is usually so complicated and varying as to make an unambiguous analysis impossible — which, incidentally, is analogous to the situation in animal experiments immediately after experimental destruction of certain areas. But this does not mean that the acute state can teach us nothing. On the contrary, it can yield valuable information about certain types of behavior in the organism. I am thinking particularly, in this respect, of the significance of the analysis of shock. At any rate, the picture after "recovery" is much better suited for analysis, if for no other reason than its relative consistency. Therefore, for the present, we shall confine ourselves to analyzing phe-

nomena in cases that have been "cured," although still persisting in some defects.

Examination of patients in this reordered condition convinces us that the remaining performances show a number of peculiarities that are of interest not only because of their mere occurrence but also because they throw light on the question of how the disordered organism regains a state of order. If it is correct to assume that disordered behavior results from the fact that the organism is confronted with tasks with which it cannot cope, then, in a defective organism, disordered behavior will necessarily predominate. In this state, the organism is confronted by its environment with many a task that has become insoluble on account of such a defect. But, in the face of this condition, how does the organism again achieve a state of order? Let us consider the following observations.

Lack of self-perception of defects and tendency to exclude defects
We are first struck by the observation that the disturbing stimuli apparently have no effect on the behavior. This becomes evident when we study the subjective experiences of the patients, as well as their objective behavior. Since the investigations of Gabriel Anton, this phenomenon has been known as "lacking self-perception of the defect."[12] It has been frequently observed in various disturbances: in the visual by Anton, Emil Redlich and Guilio Bonvicini, Fritz Hartmann, and others;[13] in aphasic disturbances, described by Arnold Pick and others;[14] in disturbances of the auditory sense; and in hemiplegic phenomena, alexia, and so forth.[15]

This lack of self-perception of a disturbance has been looked upon as a peculiarity resulting from a definite kind of damage to the cortex, and an attempt has been made to explain it either in terms of localization or through the assumption of faculty disturbances, such as those of attention, perception, or memory. None of these explanations has proved adequate. Redlich and Bonvicini have already pointed out that we are dealing, in such cases, with general mental disturbances that have nothing to do with abnormalities of memory, imagery, or the like; and Anton had emphasized the great similarity between the behavior of these patients and that of certain hysterics.[16] According to my observations, this resulting ineffectiveness of disturbance is also to be found in cases without any injury of the brain or mental disturbances per se, for example, where total blindness is produced exclusively by gross damage of the peripheral optic nerve. The study of such cases, and also of a great many variously localized brain injuries, has shown me that this phenomenon is certainly not confined to any specific type or place of lesion in the brain; and we cannot speak simply of psychotic reactions, even in the sense of hysteria. Rather, we are facing apparently quite normal biological reactions to a very grave defect.

Modification of preserved performances and of milieu in a defect
Disturbances, of course, can be rendered ineffective only if such demands that would provoke their coming to the fore are not made on the organism – in other words, if the patient's milieu is modified in an adequate way. This modification is partially brought about by the activity of the persons dealing with the defective organism. In experiments with animals, for instance, the experimenter tries to keep his operated animals alive and arranges the environment in such a way as to prevent any detrimental situation. Similarly, the physician plays a protective role toward the patient. But the organism itself aids in the attainment of a new milieu adequate to his altered condition. In the interest of general biology, it is of course desirable to study this process more closely. The animal seeks situations in which it is not exposed to dangers that may arise because of its disabilities. For instance, sympathectomized animals show a clear aversion to cold air and draft in the winter; they prefer to stay near a radiator.[17]

Cortical lesions. Avoidance of catastrophic situations
In human beings, this modification of milieu manifests itself in very definite changes of behavior. First of all, we find that the patients avoid, as far as possible, all situations that would occasion catastrophic reactions. Of course, this avoidance by no means implies that the patient has consciously recognized the situation and its danger. The nature of his defect usually makes this impossible for him, and actually he remains quite passive in the matter. When an objectively endangering stimulus is on its way, a catastrophic reaction sets in immediately, precluding any adequate response to the situation. The patient then appears completely aloof from the world. It is not so much that the endangering situation has been actively avoided, as that the patient has been passively protected from it. If, however, the patient has had frequent opportunities to observe that certain situations entail catastrophic reactions and

if he can learn to recognize these situations through certain "criteria" that are within his mental grasp, then he can also actively avoid the situation. We find continually that patients obstinately refuse to do certain apparently harmless things, and we can immediately understand their refusal if we keep this fact in mind.

Substitute performances. Tendency to hold to the preserved performance level
The "avoidance" of dangerous situations is brought about especially by the patient's tendency to maintain a situation with which he can cope. When we try to force him into a situation that he has identified as catastrophic, he deliberately seeks to escape through some other performance – a "substitute performance." Patients often develop great ingenuity in this respect. The content of this substitute performance may seem quite meaningless, may even be rather irrelevant, or indeed, disagreeable to the patient; but he will be less disturbed by it than if he were compelled to meet the demands of the situation with which he is actually confronted. The significance of these substitute performances rests not so much in their contents as in the fact that this mode of response lies within the capacities of the patient and that, as it takes place, nothing can happen that might lead to catastrophe. At a certain stage of disintegration, these substitute actions are the last resource, the only means by which existence can be maintained. In this sense, they are meaningful; they enable the organism to come to terms with the environment, at least in some way.

Tendency to undisturbed state
The aforementioned significance of the fact that the patient tends to perform what he is capable of makes intelligible why he is practically never idle. So long as patients are neither asleep nor at rest, they are always occupied with something. If a certain action is demanded of them, they must first be aroused – often with difficulty – from some other engrossing activities. The performances the patient can carry out and to which he always tends to cling have the character of stereotypy and exhibit little variation. This gives the impression that the patients have a pronounced disposition to maintain the most uniform and undisturbed condition. But this is not a genuine restful state of a leisurely, contemplative person. Indeed this state is susceptible to disturbance by accidental, extraneous events with which the person may not be fit

to cope. Careful observation reveals that this uniformity is "rest" only in appearance and that the patient is, in fact, never idle. By always "doing something" that he is capable of, the patient keeps himself so occupied, so engrossed, so secluded from the outside world that he remains unaffected by many events of his environment. But anything of significance to him, in the respective situation, is quite well noticed, perceived, and retained. This escape from the environment into a condition that protects him from situations that are dangerous to him has its analogy in the so-called death feint of animals. Just as this attitude in animals is not to be understood as the result of a volitional act but as a biological phenomenon occasioned primarily by shock and anxiety, so also is the behavior of the patient to be understood.

Tendency to orderliness
A characteristic means by which patients with brain injuries avoid catastrophic situations is a tendency toward orderliness. Such individuals may become veritable fanatics in this respect. The brain-injured patients whom I had under my observation for many years kept their closets in model condition. Everything had its definite place and was so arranged that the patient could find it and take it out as easily as possible. Everything, in other words, was "in order," from the patient's point of view. When we place various objects in a haphazard arrangement on a table in front of the patient we observe that if he notices them at all he will put them in order, setting side by side those things that seem to him to belong together.

Suppose a patient has just finished writing on a piece of paper. The examination is over. I take the pencil and place it carelessly on the sheet of paper that happens to lie obliquely on the table. As he gets up, the patient removes the pencil, puts the paper in line with the edge of the table, and then sets the pencil down, as parallel as possible, to the border of the paper. If, without comment, I again set the pencil obliquely on the paper, the patient, provided he has been watching, may once more place it in the same way as before. This game can be repeated several times, until he is either distracted by something else or is told explicitly that I want it this and this way. In this case, the patient resigns himself to the situation, though usually with an expression of marked discomfort.

"Disorder" is unbearable for him. What does disorder, in this sense, mean? Objective disorder is really just as nonexistant as objective order. Disorder means an arrangement that forces on one not simply a single, definite criterion such as "availability of objects" but several or many. Complete disorder, as far as this is at all possible, would not force anything on the individual, but would leave him completely free choice.

There are, of course, several possible arrangements of the same objects, depending on the attitude with which one approaches the things. For example, the appeal of an order to the active attitude will differ from its appeal to the contemplative attitude. Even in action, there is a difference in the preference of a certain order. It depends on whether a simple, habitual activity flows from the situation or whether a choice between certain ends is necessitated or the creation of new meaningful arrangements is required.

The more manifold the tasks are that a person can perform, the more his arrangements will appear disorderly to another person who is only capable of fulfilling a few tasks, be it that he can only apprehend either single objects or certain objects in a definite context. For such persons, the position of objects next to each other, or objects together in small heaps, will represent the best order, the "real" order, and everything else will stand for disorder. All patients with brain injury have a tendency toward such "primitive" order. Only by this arrangement are they able to execute, with the least expenditure of energy, performances essential to them. Only in this way can they react adequately. Other arrangements agitate and upset them, by demanding behavior that they can execute, if at all, only with great expenditure of energy and that, therefore, tend to bring about a catastrophic situation.

The principal demands that "disorder" makes on them are choice of alternatives, change of attitude, and rapid transition from one behavior to another. But this is exactly what is difficult or impossible for them to do. If they are confronted with tasks that make this demand, catastrophic reactions, catastrophic shocks, and anxiety inevitably ensue. To avoid this anxiety the patient clings tenaciously to the order that is adequate for him but that appears abnormally primitive, rigid, and compulsive to normal people. In other words, the "sense of order" in the patient is an expression of his defect, an expression of his impoverishment regarding an essentially human trait: the capacity for adequate shifting of attitude.[18]

Anxiety and avoidance of "emptiness"
The dread of catastrophic reactions must also be thought of as a reason for another phenomenon frequently observed in patients with brain lesions: the tendency to avoid "emptiness."

It is a common experience to find that patients with aphasia, if asked to write on a piece of paper lying in front of them, usually start directly at the top edge and crowd their writing as close as possible, line on line. Only with the greatest effort, if at all, can they be induced to leave a larger interlinear space or even to write in the center of a blank sheet of paper. They show analogous behavior in other performances. Attempts to interfere with this procedure disquiet them, and it becomes quite apparent how disagreeable such pressure is to them. One might be tempted to say that the patient is suffering from a phobia of empty space, but this view is derived from the world of the normal and does not do justice to that which takes place in the patient's mind. This kind of patient is not at all capable of having an idea or subjective experience of emptiness, for to do so would require an abstract attitude they do not possess. It is characteristic of the change in these patients that they can experience contents and objects only if they are confronted with something concrete, something tangible, something they can handle. In view of this condition, certainly no such object as empty space exists for them. On the other hand, there is no doubt about the anxiety, restlessness, the inner resistance they experience whenever the situation objectively demands experience of emptiness. The dread probably arises from the fact that empty space does not become an adequate stimulus and therefore leads to an inadequate catastrophic reaction. It is the dread of such reactions that makes the patients cling tenaciously to something "filled," to an object to which they can react, or with which they can establish contact through activity. In the same way as we explained the avoidance of catastrophic situations in general – that is by inference from certain situational criteria – we can explain why the patient avoids situations of empty space, even though the latter has no real existence for him. Often it only seems as if the patient were avoiding emptiness, when actually he is clinging tenaciously to its concrete contents, knowing that as soon as he gives up this point of reference he will become helpless, ineffective, disturbed, and driven to catastrophic reaction. Immediately on deprivation of such points of reference, the patient fails completely or desperately seeks devices to help him cleave to the concrete. These points of reference may easily escape the notice of a perfunctory observer, but they are extremely characteristic of the behavior of such patients. For instance, one of our patients can write only if he is first allowed to draw a line parallel to the upper margin of the paper. Whether or not he is successful in writing probably depends on whether he can keep an eye on the upper margin and hold fast to it, so to speak. Another patient can read only if an individual letter presented to him stands on a line; otherwise he fails. Or he will try to draw a line under the letter; having done that, he reads promptly.

Relative maintenance of ordered behavior by shrinkage of
milieu according to defect
These alterations of "preserved performances" imply an extraordinary limitation of the environment in which the patient naturally lives. This statement involves a fact that we will later (see p. 338) recognize as a particularly important law of behavior having general validity: a defective organism achieves ordered behavior only by a shrinkage of its environment in proportion to the defect.

These modifications in the behavior patterns of a person with a brain injury should be borne in mind in our observations of injured animals. It is to be expected that such subtle changes in animal behavior will often be overlooked, since they have escaped notice even in human behavior. Exactitude is all the more imperative since analogous modifications may impair the animal's capacities.

Tendency to optimal performance. Hemianopsia and formation
of complete visual field. The adjustmental shifts
Observation of patients with brain injury also teaches us that there is a tendency for the injured organism to maintain a performance capacity on the highest possible level compared with its former capacity. When one performance field is disturbed, the most important performances of that field survive the longest and tend to be most readily restored. A particularly instructive example of this fact is furnished by the vision of hemianoptic patients.[19] If we examine a patient with total destruction of the calcarine cortex of one hemisphere (the central termination of the optic tract), we find that he suffers from hemianopsia, that is, total blindness of corresponding halves of the visual field of both

eyes. Even though this condition appears consistently, under examination with a perimeter, the behavior of these patients in everyday life fails to indicate that they see nothing in one half — say, the right half — of the visual field. At all events, they recognize objects within an area, where stimulation, during perimetrical examination, is ineffective. Subjectively, they are aware of a somewhat impaired vision, but it is by no means true that they see only one half of the object or even that they see objects less distinctly on one side.

Precise exploration shows that the patients are not limited to half a field of vision but that their field of vision is arranged around a center like in normal patients, and that, likewise, the region of their clearest vision lies approximately at this center. As we shall demonstrate later, a visual field of such formation is requisite for the most important visual functions, especially for the perception of objects. That the organism manages to preserve this most important performance, in spite of the defect, is particularly characteristic of the way in which the organism functions in general. Therefore, we should discuss, in greater detail, such conditions.

Apparently the patient perceives stimuli originating in that part of the outer world corresponding to the blind half of his retina. That this part of the retina has not become sensitive to stimulation can be demonstrated by use of the perimeter. Therefore, we can only conclude that these stimuli have been registered with the other part, i.e., the intact half of the retina. Careful investigation actually shows this to be the case. If we present the patient with a series of figures next to each other on a blackboard and ask him to state which he sees most distinctly, he does not designate, like a normal person, that figure that would register on an area corresponding to the macula but one that lies a little further to the side. Apparently that point in the outer world seems clearest to him that is reflected not on the border of the intact retina, where the old macula now lies, but on an area within the intact retina. The latter could happen only if the eyes shifted their position from the normal. Such a displacement can actually be observed. To possess a visual field that is arranged around a center is of extraordinary importance for vision. An object is clearly seen only if it lies in the center of the visual field that surrounds this object. Normally, when we look at a series of objects in sequence, with the intention of seeing each one clearly, we move our eyes in such a way that the objects in question are always focused on the macula, in which position they always occupy the center of the visual field.

This state of affairs is attained by the displacement of the eyes. Thus, the patient regains clear vision despite the defect of his visual apparatus. That this transformation is an expression of a tendency toward maintaining optimal performance is clearly shown by the fact that it occurs only when the calcarine cortex is completely destroyed – in other words, when this side of the calcarina is really unable to convey impressions that can be used in the perception of objects.

Further illustrations of the tendency to optimal performance:
hemiamblyopia; adaptation to a defect without shift
In hemiamblyopia, where the damaged calcarina is still capable of performing this function, even though to a reduced extent – in other words, where a characteristically formed visual field still arises in the usual way – the transformation does not occur. Even though one half of the objects produce a fainter impression, this apparently does not disturb perception essentially – not to such an extent that the hemianopic displacement is demanded. As long as that is not the case, this transformation will not occur, because such transformation in itself entails disturbances of the total behavior. The eye displacement, required in hemianopsia, must limit the extent of the visually prehensile, outer world. This can involve not only mere quantitative limitations but also deficiencies of a qualitative nature: for instance, when a complete recognition of an object requires that the perception also include those aspects of the object that lie more off to the side. In addition to this limitation of the visual sphere, by the displacement of the eye, there are still some further restrictions of the total behavior of the patient. The organism bears all these impediments if a good vision is otherwise impossible; but it "avoids" them if adequate vision can still be maintained in some measure without eye shifting – as in hemiamblyopia. What is germane is not the best possible performance in one field but the best possible performance of the organism as a whole. Therefore, transformation or modification in one field will always be oriented about the functioning of the total organism. This transformation takes place according to the degree of disturbance that the adjustment necessitates within the total behavior and according to the amount of impairment in the particular field.

Accurate analysis of the behavior of a hemianopic subject, therefore, supports the view that the functioning of the organism is dominated by the principle of optimal performance. In any case, the facts are most satisfactorily explained on the basis of this theory. What we have described here is not a special peculiarity of the hemianopic but a characteristic fact that has analogies everywhere.

*Monocular diplopia. Adaptation to a defect in order
to preserve optimal performance*

Let us demonstrate this conclusion by one more of many available examples. Some patients suffer a reduction of visual efficiency in certain areas of the retina. If a good visual performance is required, it can take place only by a duplication of the object seen.[20] It could be demonstrated regularly that when the visual function is impaired effective vision is concomitant with pronounced diplopia (i.e., monocular diplopia). Objective improvement in the functioning of the visual apparatus, on the other hand, carries with it a concomitant reduction of double vision.

Numerous experimental investigations have suggested to me the following explanation: if it is essential that a good visual response be made to a stimulus affecting one area in the retina and if damage to the substrata has made this impossible, there will occur an abnormal spreading of the excitation into another area that has a better performance capacity. For instance, the excitation spreads into a field closer to the macula, which normally functions more efficiently than the peripheral zones. By this process, the object is seen better but appears to be displaced toward the macula. At the same time, a second image appears, which is correctly localized, that is, its localization corresponds to the position of the object; and inasmuch as it depends on the original excitation, it does not completely disappear. This second image is weaker than the displaced main image, in accordance with the less adequate functioning of the area that determines it. Here again, we note the tendency of the organism to attain an optimal visual performance. Since the spread of the excitation, which makes satisfactory visual performance possible, necessarily involves the appearance of a double image, the organism apparently reconciles itself to the fact of being less disturbed by diplopia than by a more deficient vision.

*Modification and preservation of performances. The rules
of adjustmental shift in defects*

We shall later have occasion to point out corresponding examples in other fields. Surveying all the facts in question, we are led to a statement of the following general rules:

1. In case of impairment of a performance field, those performances tend to survive that are most important or necessary with regard to the functioning of the whole organism.

2. As long as it is possible that the needs of the total organism, with reference to a special performance field, can be fulfilled in the usual way, the premorbid modus operandi will be maintained. If this is impossible, an adjustmental shift occurs, conforming in principle to the first rule.

3. The organism tolerates all those disturbances in other fields that must necessarily result from the adjustmental shift in any one field. Here again the principle is valid that the whole organism is less handicapped by these disturbances than it would be by the original impairment in the field that is now modified in its function.

4. Finally, we must call attention to a particularly important factor. The shift occurs suddenly. It is not a result of training, and it happens without the knowledge of the patient.

This last fact confronts us again very clearly in instances of lesion of the calcarine area. It is impossible to determine with certainty at what moment the above modification occurs in these cases. We have no definite information as to how, in the initial state of disturbance, the patient really sees things. But from all indications, the modification is to be found at the time the patient is again using his visual apparatus effectively. In any event, it is not the result of training, as the fact of its occurrence without the knowledge of the patient proves. As Wilhelm Fuchs has shown, the patient may, in a special test situation, intentionally look past one side of the object (i.e., the mentioned eye dislocation) because he experiences subjectively that he now sees better — without knowing why.[21] We must leave open the question of whether this intentional "looking past" occurs only in the experimental situation. In ordinary life, whenever he "looks at an object," the eyes assume the mentioned displacement without the patient being at all aware of the fact.

If we conclude from these data the general rule that the organism tends toward an optimal performance, we may be met with the following objection: Is not the eye displacement (i.e., the adjustmental shift) of the hemianopic patient a pathological phenomenon from which we have no right to conclude that a normal organism is governed by the same tendency? To this we offer the answer that the behavior of the hemianopic is in principle not different from that of a normal person. To appreciate this fact clearly, we must observe more carefully the change produced by the adjustmental shift. A more detailed discussion of this matter is justified because these statements have an important bearing on the problem of localization.

After the adjustment, only those stimuli are available for the visual field that are registered on one half of the retina. It is usually accepted that, in normal conditions in which the formation of the visual field is determined by the functioning of the whole retina, each part of the retina serves a specific operation with respect to visual acuity, color, and space perception. Such conditions do not apply to our case. A region of the retina, which in relation to the center of clearest vision (the anatomical macula) is located relatively peripherally, now assumes the role of that center. A new region of best vision, a new fovea, a so-called pseudo-fova, has developed. But with this alteration, the function of every point on the retina must likewise have undergone transformation. Centrally located areas are now hypofunctioning, or, to express it otherwise, they now function as peripheral zones normally do. Fuchs's accurate investigation of visual acuity in such cases has shown that it decreases from the new center toward both sides – the decrease involving even the anatomical macula. It has been shown that, in visual acuity, the new point of clearest vision, the pseudo-fovea, may surpass the anatomical fovea by $\frac{1}{6}$, $\frac{1}{4}$, or even $\frac{1}{2}$. Concomitantly, with this displacement of the point of clearest vision toward the functionally intact part of the retina (i.e., the retinal area corresponding to the unimpaired area in the calcarina), the functioning of all the other retinal points is modified not only in visual acuity with respect to black and white but also to colors and spatial values. Ordinarily, the patient sees those objects, which are projected on the pseudo-fovea, as lying straight ahead, just as normal people see "straight ahead" the objects projected on the anatomical fovea. In a corresponding degree, all other spatial values, determined by their position relative to the new center, must also have changed. In short, the functional value of every point of the retina has undergone a change involving, necessarily, every point of the calcarine area. The change, however, does not produce a new formation that is fixed once for all. The investigations of Fuchs have shown that the position of the center of acuity, the pseudo-fovea, varies (and with it, the properties of each part of the retina) according to the particular visual object that confronts the patient. Comparing these findings with those in normal people, we discover that even in the latter case there is no constant relation between a particular part of the retina and a particular function, but that the contribution of any part of the retina to the total performance changes according to the task with which the organism is confronted, and according to the kind of adjustment that a specific situation requires. This holds, for example, for visual acuity in any one part of the retina. The acuity in each point varies with the functional significance of the contribution that that point makes toward an adequate perception of the object. According to Gelb's findings, visual acuity of any point of the retina is determined by its participation in the configurational process, corresponding to a definite object.[22] It depends on the pattern of excitation of the entire retina and on the general attitude of the organism toward the object. Analogous conditions prevail for other performances of the retina. According to observations made by Erich R. Jaensch, also in normal individuals, the "straight ahead" experience is not invariably associated with stimulation of the macula, even though it usually occurs under these conditions.[23] When attention is concentrated on an object registered on the periphery, there may be some uncertainty as to whether the peripheral object is not regarded directly, that is, whether the observer does not see it straight ahead. Unquestionably, localization of an object as "straight ahead" is usually determined through excitation of the macula, but even normally it is not necessarily bound to that excitation. Fuchs has emphasized that this relation is evidently not even essential. The essential condition for experiencing something as straight ahead is that it appear in the center of the visual field. As experiments by Jaensch show, the visual field even in normal people varies in accordance with the attitude of the individual toward the object. If, for any reason, an object that is registered on the periphery assumes greater importance for us, this peripheral point becomes the center of the visual field and gains certain properties that under other conditions would belong to objects focused on the fovea: such, for instance, as the experiences of being "straight ahead," "directly regarded," "distinct," and so on. Observations on patients with operated strabism show, among other things, that spatial values do not depend absolutely on the excitation of definite retinal points.[24] Such investigations also show that the shift of spatial values after the operation does not occur as a result of training, but suddenly.

Thus, the change in function of individual points in the calcarine region, which at first seems so striking in the hemianopic, fits completely within the frame of normal occurrences. The coming-to-terms with visual stimuli by the hemianopic is not fundamentally different from that of normal individuals. If, in hemianopsia, one calcarine area is still capable of responding to external stimuli in such a way that a complete visual field is formed, then we are merely dealing with a specially striking instance of normal function.

Energy and performance
Finally, there is the question of the dependency of performance on the available energy. Before presenting the facts, let us introduce the problem with a few brief remarks about the source of this energy. It must be remembered that external stimuli not only initiate the process in the nervous system but also represent sources of energy. This is true not only of the stimulus that evokes the most prominent reaction but for the host of manifold stimuli that continuously impinge on the organism. Besides the external stimuli, those that affect the nervous system from within play a considerable part. I should like to point out especially that the connection between the nervous system and the rest of the body is not to be ignored. We must not overlook the fact that the whole organism presents one unit, in which the nervous system, if considered by itself, is only an artificially isolated part. Inasmuch as the nervous system in vivo is an integral part of the organism, its sources of energy must be the same as those that sustain the activity of the whole organism. In carrying out this function, individual organs (e.g., the ductless glands) have a specific significance. To appreciate the range of the nervous system's functions, we must take into account its special relation to the general sources of energy, such as the nutritional factor, the oxygen content of the blood, and so forth. Only in this way can we hope to understand the characteristics of the symptomatology in a given case. The symptom analysis suggests a few conclusions:

The available energy supply is constant, within certain limits. If one particular performance requires especially great energy expenditure, some other performance suffers in the process.

Relevant to this, I should like to point out certain facts to which I called attention years ago while I was trying to obtain an understanding of hallucinatory phenomena.[25] At that time I remarked on the antagonistic character of the energy distribution between sensory and thought performances, which manifests itself in the reduced vividness of our sensory experiences and in our inattentiveness to them during the thought process. A similar antagonism exists between motor and sensory phenomena, between verbal and nonverbal performances, and so on. In these and similar cases, we can assume that one performance is weakened because the available energy is being used to maintain activity in that mechanism on which the other performance depends. This becomes particularly evident in pathological conditions. It can readily be assumed that a brain lesion will impede the functioning. Expressed in terms of energy, this means that special energies will become necessary to maintain a function. This assumption is founded on the observed fact that patients fail in those performances, which they otherwise can accomplish, when performances involving an injured area are simultaneously required of them. If we ask an aphasic patient to read aloud, he may not be able to understand what he reads, because of the impediment of the speech activity. The energy is exhausted in coping with this impediment. But if he reads silently, he may be able to read with full understanding. This dependence of performance on the available energy may manifest itself in a phenomenon that is, at first, rather surprising: frequently, patients who suffer complete destruction of a field essential to a certain performance may on the whole be less afflicted than those who suffer only partial destruction. A patient with hemiamblyopia (a less intensive injury of one calcarine area) is, to a certain extent, actually more distrubed in his vision than a patient with a total destruction of this area. In terms of energy this is easily explainable: the organism tends to function in the accustomed manner as long as an at least moderately effective performance can be achieved in this way. This is true in minor calcarine lesion, where the afflicted area remains in use. Under these conditions, the energy distribution is the same as before. Because of this damage to the area, poor vision results. If, on the other hand, one of the calcarine areas is completely destroyed, the total amount of energy at the disposal of both calcarinae flows into the one that is intact. The flow into the destroyed region is, so to speak, blocked. The high energy charge of the intact side effects a shift of the entire brain activity, so that a more efficient result is actually obtained, at least as far as vision is concerned.

Otto Pötzl offers a particularly instructive example of the difference in shift of energy – the difference depending on whether a field is still functioning to some extent.[26] The patient in question was suffering from complete word deafness, subsequent to disappearance of initial disturbances. After a certain time he began to comprehend some words to the extent of being able to repeat them. Concomitant with improvement of the word deafness his "inner speech" appeared to undergo a deterioration that manifested itself in paraphasia during spontaneous speech and reading, in his failure to understand what he had read, and in a grave inability to find words. When later, because of a new lesion, the word deafness again became total, this inner speech improved. Thus, we see demonstrated a clear antagonism between two speech performances. As long as the word deafness was complete, the total energy could be placed at the disposal of the apparatus of inner speech, as was evidenced in the good performances in this respect. But as soon as the return of function in the region of "word deafness" demanded a particularly strong energy supply, the substratum of inner speech, now supplied with a smaller quantity of energy, decreased in function, as the accompanying disturbance of inner speech indicated. Pötzl talks of a total capacity of the activating energies that are "distributed among the two spheres of the outer and the inner world. The energies which turn outward, becoming effective in speech comprehension, predominate over those involved in inner speech. Therefore, if the region of word deafness is restored to a certain extent, as soon as stimuli from the environment can become effective at all, any additional helpful impetus from these activating energies is turned more into this channel, thereby being withdrawn from inner speech, which on this account is impaired." If now, the possibility of the environmental influence on language is again eliminated, inner speech can be restored, because the activating energies are all turned toward it. This aspect of differential energy distribution must be taken into full consideration in every symptom analysis.

The quantity of available energy depends essentially on the total condition, not only of the brain, of the state of nutrition of the brain, and so on, but also of the entire body. Thus, it becomes intelligible why the patient's performance will vary in accordance with his well-being, degree of fatigue, and so on.

Reference of symptoms and performances to the whole of the organism.
Is the organism a whole, and if so, how can we recognize it as such?
Analysis of the phenomena resulting from cortical lesion has revealed to us a number of general laws governing the life of the organism. Again and again, the principle of the close relationship of the individual phenomenon to the "whole" of the organism forces itself on us. Subsequent considerations will show us that this relation holds equally well for those performances or symptoms due to injuries to other organs of the body. We should like to stress the fact that the relationship is not at all confined to the phenomena resulting from the function of the cerebral cortex.

But what do we really mean by this word "whole" that we are careful to place in quotation marks? As long as we confine ourselves to a statement of general rules regarding the part-whole relation, we can leave the question of the essential nature of the whole untouched. But if we wish to understand an individual performance this is no longer permissible. If we say that the organism tends to modify itself, in spite of the defect, in such a way that those performances most important for it are made possible, we are positing certain essential characteristics of the organism, without offering any explanation for the way in which this knowledge has been obtained. Thus, for example, we say that a particular form of vision, or some similar activity, characterizes the organism concerned. This procedure is appropriate, because only in this way can we attain knowledge of the general rules of holistic and organismic processes. Yet this remains insufficient. The procedure is always exposed to a certain skepticism regarding these rules. Above all, it is inadequate for an understanding of an individual response, primarily because it is doubtful whether the characteristics we have assumed are in fact "genuine" properties of the organism concerned. In fact, each single performance that we observe introduces anew the question of whether we are dealing with a phenomenon that is really equivalent to an essential characteristic of the organism.

In order to answer this question we must truly know the organism. There can be no doubt that this knowledge is attainable only through

the scientific or *analytic*, *"anatomizing"* method, that only the empirical data obtained thereby can be considered.[27] To be sure, this analysis
may take any one of several forms. It may bring into focus the morphological and physiological organization, or the physical and chemical
composition, or the so-called somatic and mental phenomena, and so
on. Of course, we cannot simply survey this manifold material and see
what sort of a picture of the organism will emerge therefrom. We have
to deal first with the more fundamental question of whether, and to
what extent, the material yielded by analysis is at all suitable to provide a picture of the organism. We are concerned with the question of
what light this material throws on the performances of the organism;
whether or not it impels us to regard the organism as a whole, and if
so, how we arrive at a conception of the "whole," as represented in this
organism. For this purpose it is immaterial which sort of facts we take
as our point of departure. We will connect our discussion with that
material embodied in the theory of the so-called reflexes. And this will
be done because such data seem best fitted to deal with the methodological approach leading to an understanding of the organism.

The Organism Viewed in the Light of Results Obtained Through Atomistic Method. The Theory of Reflex Structure of the Organism

According to the view underlying the reflex theory, the organism represents a bundle of isolable mechanisms that are constant in structure and that respond, in a constant way, to events in the environment (stimuli). These responses are usually understood as depending on the existence of a more or less differentiated nervous apparatus. This is the view held not only of the nervous system but also of all phenomena. For example, even chemical processes are considered as related to the activity of very definite mechanisms. From this point of view the influences to which the organism is exposed represent the sum of the stimuli to which it reacts in a regular manner. The aim of research, according to this conception, is to dissect the behavior of the organism in order to discover those "part processes" that can be considered as governed by mechanistic laws and as unambiguous, elementary reactions to definite stimuli. To work out these laws exactly, one exposes the organism to single stimuli, using various means to control conditions so that the reaction, which corresponds to that particular stimulus, may occur in almost complete isolation. Ideally this principle can only be realized by segregating from the whole that part of the organism under investigation. Therefore, for those who adopt this view, "analytical" experimentation has become the ideal foundation of knowledge. When such a procedure cannot be used, the attempt is made to arrange conditions so that one stimulated part of the organism is relatively isolated – for example, one sector of the nervous system in relative isolation from the rest. To this isolating technique, we owe our knowledge of reflexes, of the difference between sensory and motor activity, and of the so-called agonistic and antagonistic processes. To it we owe furthermore much information about the vegetative system, such as the specific role played by the vagus and sympathetic system, the specific effects of the duct-less glands and other humors of the body, and so on.

The Observable Phenomena Do Not Correspond to the Definition of Reflexes

Individually disparate mechanisms as alleged constituents of behavior
Since the premise is made that the organism consists of separate mech-anisms, it matters little for this doctrine whether these parts function in isolation or not. Concerted functioning, involving reciprocal facili-tation or inhibition of the effects of a single apparatus, merely produces an effect that is more complicated and less easily analyzed with regard to the significance of the contribution made by a single mechanism to the total performance. Notwithstanding this, it is assumed that the responses of the special apparatus under examination by the analytic method are identical with the reaction of this same apparatus, even when such reactions are occurring within the activity of the whole organism. The life of the organism is considered to be composed of these disparate mechanisms.

By virtue of its methodological clarity, this approach would cer-tainly be considered ideal, if it really made possible an understanding of the behavior of the organism. Before we discuss the question of whether it does, let us scrutinize the facts more closely, especially those on which the theory of reflex organization of the nervous system is based. This theory represents the most typical example of the analytic procedure outlined above. Do the facts support the reflex concept?

The facts: No constancy
In the strict sense, is there any such phenomenon as reflex? Although this may seem a strange question, it requires very serious consideration. It is by no means as easy to establish the existence of constant responses to specific stimuli, as the reflex concept assumes. Unprejudiced obser-vation of reflexive responses to stimuli should convince us that usually a large number of diverse reactions to the same stimulus occur. The "patellar reflex," for example, has proved to be by no means invariably constant in the same individual. It varies, depending, among other things, on the position of the limb, on the behavior of the rest of the organism, and on whether or not attention is paid to it. Changes in the

mode of attention will also change the reflex in a particular manner, as Paul Hoffmann and F. Kretschmer have shown.[1] A certain kind of attention diminishes the response, another kind exaggerates it. Furthermore, the response appears intensified in lesions of the pyramidal tract. To explain all these variations, it was necessary to go beyond the processes in the so-called reflex arc and to assume that the course of a reflex is influenced by other factors. Hence one thinks that the reflex is normally inhibited by impulses that pass along the pyramidal tract, and when these inhibitions cease — in lesions of the pyramidal tract — the reflex becomes abnormally strong. This shows that, even under normal conditions, the reflex cannot be properly understood in terms of the isolated mechanism alone.

Analogous facts are found in all animal and human reflex investigations. The unusually voluminous literature on animal reflex investigations reveals a multitude of variations of normal reflex action, which may be briefly illustrated here.

Variation of reflexes according to receptive fields and kinds of stimuli
In the first place, it would be oversimplifying matters to assume that eliciting of the reflex depends on stimulation of one definite and constant place. Therefore, reference is usually made to a receptive "field." But the excitability of this field is not the same throughout all its parts. Moreover, the excitability is not identical at all times, under all circumstances, or to all stimulations.

According to Charles Scott Sherrington, the limits of the field of the scratch reflex in dogs, for example, can vary on different days.[2] Furthermore, even though the stimulus remains the same, different reactions may occur. Some of these variations may be due to the fact that the place of stimulation has not always been exactly the same; for example, if the outer side of the plantar of the "spinal" monkey is tickled, we obtain a stronger reaction in the peronei, whereas if the inner side is tickled, there occurs a more pronounced reaction in the Tibialis anticus.[3] This can also be observed, occasionally, in human beings with spastic disturbances. However, there are some facts that cannot be explained in this manner. E. Sanders has described a group of cases that can only be understood by assuming that the sensory field contains various receptors that are related to the various reflexes.[4] This shows that, apparently, not only the place but also the kind of stimulus determines which reflex will appear. From many examples, especially those cited by Sherrington, we know that, often, even apparently slight modifications of the stimulus determine whether or not a reflex will take place; for example, a decerebrated cat will promptly swallow water placed in the pharynx but it will not swallow it if a small amount of alcohol is added. This small modification of the stimulus produces an entirely different response, in the form of "wiping movements of the tongue."[5] The ear reflex can be elicited through fine mechanical stimuli but not through dull pressure. The "extensor thrust," according to Sherrington, is elicited only by mild pressure against the sole, or removal of such pressure, but not by other stimulation.[6]

Variations according to harmless and harmful stimuli
These variations might possibly be considered merely the expression of different reflex responses to different kinds of stimulation. Aside from these variations, such a statement fails to explain cases where a special selection among the stimuli, leading to the response, takes place.

For example, the flexor reflex in the dog can be elicited through pricking, heat, pinching, and chemical stimulation, but not through touch and simple pressure. This means a differentiation between a more "neutral" and a more "unpleasant" character of a stimulus. Therefore, one can classify stimuli into "harmful" and "harmless" and assume that the effect will vary according to the harmfulness or harmlessness. Sherrington was the first to state this important fact. As a means of explanation, he has assumed special "nociceptors," an explanation, however, that is not very satisfactory. In any event, a hypothesis is thereby introduced that cannot be reconciled with the view that the reflex is a simple connection between a specific stimulus and a definite reaction. It demands a preestablished value scale, especially in view of the further fact that the nociform reflexes prevail on simultaneous provocation of other reflexes. The problem becomes still more complicated when we note that, under certain conditions, this scale can be reversed. In human beings, even in the face of pain and injury, no avoidance reflex will appear if the subject needs to obtain information regarding the nature of the stimulus.

Variation according to stimulus intensity
Whether or not a reflex occurs, seems, therefore, to depend partly on

the "value" of the stimulus – on its functional significance for the whole organism. As Silvestro Baglioni has pointed out, there is a similar situation in the case in which two reflexes are simultaneously stimulated but only one is realized.[7] The attempt to explain this phenomenon as the mere effect of the greater intensity of one stimulus is not at all successful.

Balthasar Luchsinger has shown that, simply by touching the skin, one can inhibit the intensive rhythmical bodily movements that are found in the "spinal" snake.[8] The explanation certainly does not lie in the strength of the stimulus. But if we seek the explanation in the comparative strength of the two reflexes, we are only saying that one reflex predominates in its effect, and the question still remains, Why? Thus, Victor von Weizsäcker says: "In no sense is it possible to establish a generally valid rule for predicting which stimulus or which reflex will prevail."[9] I would like to add that such a pronouncement is true only when phenomena that arise from parts in isolation are considered.

Particular difficulties arise when the reversal of a response to one and the same stimulus appears. These phenomena probably first became known through the observations made by Jakob von Uexküll and Hubert F. Jordan in vertebrates.[10] If, according to the procedure of Uexküll, one arm of the ophiuroid starfish is isolated, so that there remains only its connection with the central nervous ring, we obtain a bending movement of the arm toward the stimulated side. This occurs, provided the arm is resting horizontally so that both sides are in a state of equal tension. But if we suspend the arm at the raw or cut end so that it hangs down, and thereby one side is stretched more than the other, then we usually obtain a bending toward the side that is stretched, irrespective of which side is stimulated. We thus have a reversed effect. The fact that apparently slight variations in the stimulus intensity can lead to a reversed reaction is confirmed by many experiments. Sherrington and S.C.M. Sowton have shown that an ipsilateral extensor reflex appears in place of the flexor reflex if one applies weak galvanic or slowly increasing stimuli.[11] J.S. Beritoff was able to produce reversal through slight changes in stimulus intensity.[12]

Variation according to postural factors. The so-called reflex reversal
Likewise, change in position of the limb in which the reflex occurs may lead to reversal of movements. In the usual experiment with a flexed

leg, one obtains an extension of the crossed leg when the sole of the other foot is stimulated. If the crossed leg is passively extended, one obtains a flexion. On the basis of such findings, Rudolf Magnus spoke of a position factor.[13] According to his investigations, tactile and other stimuli (e.g., changes of the position of other limbs) also produce reversal of a reflex. We know from Sherrington, furthermore, that poisons may reverse the reflex effect, for example, strychnine. Fatigue produces similar results: a reflex effect may revert to its opposite through frequent repetition.[14] The existence of one reflex influences the course of others in various ways, not infrequently by inducing its opposite. A weak flexion reflex is inhibited by the contralateral reflex. But if it is strong, the contralateral will facilitate it.

Reflexes and total condition
It is, furthermore, remarkable that reflexes can turn out very differently, depending on whether we are dealing with "decerebrated" or "spinal" animals, and finally that the outcome depends on the total condition, on the "general mood," on the "mental set" of the animal. The latter is particularly well known in regard to the reflex investigations in human beings. The Babinski phenomenon in human beings is one of the best instances of "reflex reversal." When the sole is stimulated in such cases, we do not observe the "normal" plantar flexion of the toes but a dorsal flexion, in particular, one of the large toe. To be sure, we find this phenomenon only under pathological conditions – but they are certainly not more pathological than the dissection of the spinal cord in an animal. Today, we also know from John F. Fulton and Allen D. Keller that injuries in animals (primates) lead to the same reflex reversal when the sole is stimulated. But alluding to a pathological causation is in no way an explanation. Actually, entirely different factors have been suggested in explanation – for example, the loss of inhibition – and we shall have to discuss whether this is justified.

The equivocal relation between stimulus and response, which we have referred to, is especially pronounced in the field of the vegetative nervous system. Only in very special circumstances, under the most complete isolation of one part, do we obtain constant responses to one specific stimulus. Such a multitude of examples are available in this connection that it is almost impossible to survey them.[15] Let us mention only a few instances.

We know that the separation of autonomically innervated organs from the central nervous system, that is, from the respective ganglia, leads to a change, particularly to an increased response to the same stimulus. When the dilator pupillae is separated from the cervical ganglion, it responds to adrenaline with stronger dilatation than normal, as we know from Rudolf Lewandowski. Anderson showed that removal of the ganglion ciliare causes changes in the form and reaction of the pupil on the operated side. When the vagus has been cut through, an increased responsiveness of the heart to acetylcholine results, according to Ogir. There are many more examples. A change in the effect of the stimulus, however, results not only when the relation to the central organ is modified but also when the relation to any of the other processes in the organism is changed. Thus, the reaction is determined by the condition of the reacting organ. John N. Langley's work has shown that, when the cardia is open, stimulation of the vagus causes contraction; when closed, relaxation. Furthermore, according to Langley and Anderson, the pregnant uterus reacts to hypophysine in a manner opposite that of the nonpregnant. Stimulation of the sympathicus increases the tonus of the stomach when the muscle is relaxed and reduces it when it is contracted. The stimulation of the heart, of the bladder, and so on, with adrenaline, shows similar phenomena.

Variation according to humoral conditions. Vagus and sympathicus
These variations of the stimulus effect are found to depend not only on the morphological condition of the reacting organ but also on the humoral condition. Today, we may assume that the effect of the stimulation of the sympathicus or vagus on the reacting organ comes about by way of humoral processes that take place on the periphery during the excitation. This may be regarded as a chemical transmission substance, possibly a vagus or sympathicus substance, or as metabolic products of the physiological activity of the organs themselves, for example, the heart.

Friedrich Kraus and Samuel G. Zondek interpret the influence of the sympathicus, or vagus, as due to the transmission of calium or calcium to the cell wall membrane. Thus, we can understand that humoral conditions cause changes of the response similar to morphological ones. Even a previous exposure to the same drug has analogous results. Stimulation with adrenaline influences the end organ, so that further stimulation with adrenaline may reverse the first action of the drug. After preparatory treatment of one organ, for example, the heart of a frog, with acetylcholine (which is equivalent to the parasympathetic "transmission substance"), adrenaline acts like the parasympathetic substance, as shown by Pick and Kolm. The parasympathetic end organ now responds to the sympathetic substance, adrenaline. It seems that the stimulation of an end organ also makes it sensitive to nonspecific drugs, even to those that would otherwise have had the opposite effect. Pick and Kolm term this a displacement of the stimulus effect toward the locus of higher excitability. Yet it is not a simple displacement but rather a reversal of the stimulus effect. At best, one could talk of a qualitative displacement.

Drugs and hormones
In the same way, we may understand the facts in those cases of "aorta insufficiency," in which calcium, which normally slows down the pulse, now accelerates it. The explanation, according to Kraus, is that this pathology involves increased excitability of the sympathicus.

Pilocarpine is an even better example than adrenaline of the variability of effects of the same drug under different circumstances. While pilocarpine is usually a vagus stimulant, it can also act as a stimulant for the sympathicus, as Erich Schilf, in particular, has pointed out. Ergotoxin, which usually increases blood pressure, produces a reduction of blood pressure, if treatment with sufficient quantities of the same drug has preceded; in this case, stimulation of the sympathicus also reduces blood pressure. Following previous treatment with nicotine, stimulation of the vagus produces acceleration of the heartbeat.

The stimulation appears still more complicated, almost confused, if we take into account all the other humoral factors that influence the excitability of one or another division of the automatic system: innumerable experiments illustrate this point. It is quite impossible to deal with them here; we can only refer to the main factors that bear on the question. According to Franz van Brücke, besides the "local hormones," which seem to be effective only near their place of origin at the nerve, we must consider the multitude of "distant hormones," of which adrenaline is a particularly good example. Furthermore, we must consider the products of internal secretion of various glands and the humors of many, possibly all organs. Hypophysine, like thyroxin, is said to sensitize the organism for the effect of adrenaline. On the other hand, the effect of adrenaline can be inhibited through extracts from the liver, lungs, kidneys, thymus, and so on. Albumins produced in the body, and derivatives of albumin, as, for instance, the lipoids, are of the greatest importance for excitability. According to Dresel and Sternheimer, the latter plays a fundamental role in the functioning of the automatic end organs. The mixture cholesterol-lecithin, in the cell wall membrane, seems to be of great importance. We know what significance cholesteremia has for "essential hypertension." It has been further shown that the sensitizing action of adrenaline in cholesteremia depends on a reaction that occurs only in a neutral or an acid medium.

This leads us, finally, to recognize the important influence that the ionic state has on the functioning of the autonomic and sympathetic systems. But the ionic state itself only represents one aspect among many that determine the reaction. According to Kraus and Zondek, the proper functioning depends on the establishment of a definite equilibrium between the electrolyte and colloidal particles. Also, the cell wall potential, which influences the colloidal state of the cells, which in turn is so important for their activity, is, according to these investigators, dependent on a great number of factors: the cell membrane, the salt-electrolyte, the hormones, poisons, and the vegetative nervous system.

*General interaction. Reflex and retroaction of periphery on
nervous center, and vice versa*
Finally, the facts compel us to acknowledge that all the numerous factors that have been isolated are really influencing each other. The more many sided the investigations are, the more they show the manifold interrelation of a multitude of factors influencing the life process. Of all these factors I wish to emphasize only the influence of the peripheral processes on the function of the central nervous system. By stressing this influence, we close the circle of our discussion.

We started by a consideration of the dependency of the peripheral processes on the function of central apparatus, and now we have to recognize the converse influence. We know that this influence occurs partly through afferent nerve action, for example, the regulation of breathing, and partly it takes a physical form, as in the regulation of temperature, or it may be of a chemical nature and play an important role in circulation, respiration, and metabolic processes.

We must further insist on the relation between vegetative and spino-cerebral processes, especially, the psychic processes. As Brücke has particularly emphasized, probably all tissues of our body, not only the so-called viscera, are under the influence of the vegetative system. We know this to be true with regard to muscle tonus, muscle metabolism, and also with regard to the sense receptors. When the vegetative system is influenced by drugs, changes are found in the chronaxie of the peripheral sense organs according to Otfrid Foerster, H. Altenburger, and Michael Kroll. Friedrich Achelis found that similar conditions were revealed in changes of the water metabolism and regulation of body temperature. The spino-cerebral system is probably influenced by processes in the vegetative system, just as they, in turn, influence the latter. After transsection of the vagus, or the cervical sympathicus, changes have been noticed in the cortical fields, according to Louis Lapicque. Conversely, in cases of cortical lesions – as the experiences with brain lesions during World War I very clearly showed – changes in blood pressure, pulse rate, trophic activity, blood picture, innervation of the pupils, and so on can be observed.

Finally, recent research has disclosed an extraordinary number of facts that demonstrate a far-reaching interaction between vegetative and mental processes. It must be stressed that such a relation holds not only for emotional processes but also for sensory perception. Even the preparedness for mental performances in general shows more and more its dependency on the automatic nervous system. In this connection we should mention the investigations of Walter Hess regarding the influence of the vegetative nervous system on waking and sleeping.

Critique of Reflex Concept

The so-called inhibition, shunting, and so on
I have made this survey of the various factors that, along with the external individual stimulus, determine the reaction, because practically nowhere outside this carefully investigated field is it so evident how impossible it is to attempt the isolation of a single factor and to consider it the sole determinant for the effect of a stimulus. On the basis of this material, it really seems beyond discussion that practically nowhere can a simple stimulus response relation, corresponding to the strict reflex concept, be directly observed. Such a claim could be

defended only if one construes the reflex as an abstraction from very involved facts.

If one regards the responses to a given stimulus without bias, one can distinguish between two essentially different types of reaction:

1. So-called constant reactions.

2. Reactions differing in strength, which may change qualitatively, even to the extent of the appearance of the opposite reaction. If we investigate in what ways the situations differ, wherein the constant and the variable reactions occur, we find the constant reactions require (a) strict isolation of the stimulated and the reacting part from the rest of the organism, and (b) provision for a sufficient interval between the various individual reactions, that is, an isolation regarding time (cf. our discussion on adequate time, p. 98). Variable responses occur, if such an isolation does not take place, that is, if we observe the reactions in the more "natural situation" of the organism. The customary method attempts to reduce variable to constant reactions, seeing in the latter the basic ones and regarding the former as modifications. This tendency is understandable as a natural desire to deal with constant factors. The supposedly greater simplicity of constant reactions lends itself as a starting point for a theory, in that the variable responses can then be understood as complexes derived from the more simple and constant ones. However, there is no question but that the so-called variable processes are, in reality, no less constant, if one takes into consideration all their causal conditions. Concerning the question of simplicity and complexity and whether the complex can be deduced from the simple, we shall see, in our later discussion, that the converse view is proabably nearer the truth. But for the time being, we want to leave this point aside.

Let us consider how the variety of reactions is explained on the basis of the reflex concept. The "modifications" are usually reduced to various factors, such as inhibition, facilitation, neural switching or shunting of different kinds, influence through peripheral factors, such as the state of tension of the muscles, position, enforcement or diminution through other reflexes, "central" factors, and, in particular, among these, psychic factors. Again and again, new experimental revelations have led to additional theoretical assumptions that usually were not mutually compatible and thus necessitated further hypotheses. Against this view it must be said:

1. There is no justification for calling one the normal reflex and the others variations of it. If one does think this way, he does so only under the theoretical preconception that claims that a phenomenon is normal when found in the artificial isolation of an analytic experiment.

2. Whence come the inhibition, the shunting, switching, and so on? What directs them? This theory does not raise or answer these questions, and it completely overlooks the fact that such procedure always leads to the assumption of new factors, to wit, new inhibitory mechanisms, about which nothing can be said, except that they do inhibit, that they do shift, and so on (i.e., ad hoc hypotheses).

3. The advocates of this theory further overlook the fact that this viewpoint is entirely negative (cf. p. 146) and leads to an endless regress, a regress that is usually not obvious because the isolated phenomenon alone is held in mind.

4. An unbiased observation of the facts shows that the assumption of inhibitory and other factors cannot be maintained, if for no other reason than that actually one cannot determine which of two events is the inhibited and which the inhibiting one. In reality there is always a mutual interdependency. This is a statement of fundamental importance, which, up to now, has not been taken sufficiently into consideration in the discussion of reflexes.[16]

The reversibility of all reactions; exemplification by the phenomena of tonus
Not only does an effect depend on the stimulus and on the condition of the receptor apparatus, but "reception" itself is also determined by the condition of the effector apparatus. We have already mentioned a number of facts pertaining to this point. The effect of the degree of muscular tension on the distribution of the excitation can also be described as follows: the efficacy of the outside stimulus is, in part, determined by the effector itself; in other words, the effect is really caused by the effector, or rather it does not depend on the stimulus alone. This fact is of paramount significance. Therefore, I should like to give further illustrations.

Through Magnus, we have learned about the so-called "neck reflexes," which involve a fixed relation between certain postures of the head and certain postures of the arms and legs.[17] This relation is often very marked in certain patients. If one turns the head of such a patient toward the left, one obtains, as in animal experiments, an increase of the extensor tonus in the left (i.e., in the homologous or "chin") arm and an increase in the flexor tonus in the right, or opposite arm. This becomes apparent through an extension and abduction of the left arm and a flexion and adduction of the right arm, and similarly, although less pronounced, in the corresponding leg. I was able to show in many observations, which have been confirmed by others, that one can prove an influence of the posture of the extremities on the head posture as well as an influence of the head posture on the extremities.[18] There exists a complete reciprocity of the influences.

To digress for a moment, let it be said that if these facts have not as yet received general recognition, this is partly due to the fact that, strange as it may seem, other investigators have failed to follow the experimental directions contained in the publications of myself and others, which are indispensable for eliciting the phenomena, and consequently have not obtained the same results. This must be stressed, because it shows how a theoretical bias can block the proper elaboration of facts. Because these investigators were so convinced of the reflex nature of the "Magnus reflexes" and consequently of the nonreciprocal character of the relation, they thought that my findings represented something totally different that had nothing in common with the neck reflexes and that consequently did not need to be taken into account for their evaluations. Therefore they did not even try to observe the necessary precautions in the experiments. Even if they had wanted to, however, they could not have done so, because the meaning of the experimental directions were obscured by their theoretical bias. These directions were based on a more subtle analysis of the phenomena themselves and could only be understood in this way. Disregard of my procedure prevented the fuller understanding of the phenomena themselves and made impossible an adequate appreciation of my criticism regarding the reflex nature of the neck reflexes. Actually we are confronted with a defective empirical method here, as well as in the interpretation of the neck reflexes. A more accurate empiricism shows very clearly the reciprocity of the events and also discloses why, under certain circumstances, phenomena equivalent to "neck reflexes" appear and why they were first discovered. Observability of muscular changes depends, to a certain degree, on their intensity. The change depends on the relation of the mass of the "inducing" muscle to the mass of the "induced" muscle in which the abnormal tension, or movement, occurs. In this respect, the relation between the strength and volume of the neck muscles and that of the muscles of the upper extremity was particularly favorable to produce and exhibit an influence on the muscles of the extremity by the neck muscles. But it was unfavorable for manifesting the reciprocal influence. The neck muscles are more massive, the head is less mobile than the upper extremities. Therefore, especially in animals where one must confine oneself to the grosser phenomena, the first phenomenon (the "neck reflex") was more readily observed than the reversed phenomenon, especially if the idea of the possibility of the latter had not been entertained. Thus, it was understandable that the "neck reflexes" were the first phenomena of this kind to claim Magnus's attention, and it could seem quite conclusive, to the animal experimenter, that he was dealing with a true "neck reflex." In man, however, conditions are much more favorable for the observation of the opposite behavior, if for no other reason than that the differentiation of the limbs is much finer. Thus, it was possible not only to discover many new facts through experiments with humans but also to carry the analysis of the phenomena much further. Of course, it was necessary at first to become somewhat emancipated from the descriptions of the animal behavior in these experiments and from the theories that were drawn from them and to approach the material itself without bias. Unfortunately, students have seldom followed this rule. As usual, the suggestiveness of animal experiments was so great that investigators were satisfied to seek the same phenomena in men. It was even thought that observed deviations from the results of the animal experiments should be rejected. Consequently, it was claimed that the "induced tonus phenomena," which I discovered, had nothing to do with the reflexes of Magnus, in spite of the fact that I was able to prove that both were based on the same laws and that the Magnus reflexes can be explained as a special case of the "tonus phenomena," under definite conditions. Practically nowhere has it become so evident as here, how completely the reflex concept can prevent the progress of knowledge.

To resume our main discussion, I wish to summarize a few main results of the investigations that bear on our general discussion of the reflex theory.

1. The effect depends not only on the "stimulus" that is the result of change in the stimulating organ: the "stimulator" (the neck muscles).

It also depends on the condition of the stimulated organ: the "receptor" (the arm muscle).

2. The relation between stimulating and stimulated organ is, ipso facto, reversible. In order to produce an effect the only prerequisite is an adequate gradient between the two organs, in respect to strength and volume.

3. The "strength" of a limb, at any one time, depends not only on the respective posture and structure, but also on the condition of the rest of the organism, inasmuch as it codetermines the condition of the stimulated as well as the stimulating organ. Therefore, where the effect appears, it depends not only on the stimulus but on the total conditions prevailing in the organism at that time. We shall subsequently return to the significance of this last statement. At this point, we are primarily interested in proving the reciprocal relation of so-called reflex phenomena. The problem of reciprocal relations confronts us especially in the field of the vegetative nervous system. Vegetative life is regarded as regulated by the antagonistic effects of the vagus and the sympathicus. Each of these nerves is said to be excitable through specific stimuli and lead, in reflex fashion, to specific performances that are antagonistic to each other. It is said, moreover, that the vegetative activity of the organism results from these antagonistic processes. The problem of this antagonism will occupy us again later. Here we want to point out only those facts that prove that it is absurd to speak of two different reflexes – actuated by the vagus and the sympathicus, respectively, each reflex taking a course of its own. In this instance, we see quite clearly the complete reciprocity of effects that renders impossible the application of such concepts as inhibition, shunting, and so on. If one open-mindedly surveys available material one does not find a single event that can be conceived as the univocal effect of one definite stimulus.[19] All such explanations, as those in terms of inhibition, for example, obscure the fact that, by introducing theoretical conceptions that have no factual support, the assumption of reflexes is really untenable. We shall see, later on, that such concepts are not necessary for univocal description.

The so-called reciprocity and self-regulatory cycle of processes
The realization that it is factually impossible to reduce the processes in the organism to univocal relations between a single stimulus and a

single response has prompted certain authors, with a broader outlook, to regard the vegetative processes as belonging to one great system. Christian Kroetz calls it "a system in which a continual circle of self-regulative vegetative processes takes place."[20] Consistent thinking must, of necessity, always reach such a view, if one starts from the facts in "isolating experiments" and tries to understand the life of the organism on that basis. However, the assumption of circular self-regulative processes is not satisfactory if one really wants to understand the events in the organism. How can a definite performance ever result from it? At best, such a dynamism would continuously transform disorder in the organism, resulting from events in the environment, into order. Actually, authors who adhere strictly to the reflex theory see the organism as merely a system of regulations that compensate the changes that arise by restoring the organism's equilibrium. According to this view, everything seems to be made for the preservation of the equilibrium state of the organism. But if the life of the organism consisted merely of an interplay of elementary factors that kept each other in check, how could any movement, any dynamics, enter into the situation to give direction to behavior? And direction is what we actually find as the outstanding characteristic in the performances of an organism.

Whence Comes the Direction in the Activity of the Organism?

From without?
Whence does this direction come? With this question, we stand before the fundamental problem of life processes. Indeed, direction is the essential characteristic of every vital phenomenon. Two answers, different in principle, seem possible. (1) The direction is effected through a specific environment in which the organism lives. (2) It is effected through a certain determination and force issuing from the organism itself.

The first view seems to be the more justified one, especially on the basis of accurate investigations that have shown that the individual organism is always fitted into a very specific environment, and that its existence, in spite of all variability, hinges ultimately on an environment that is adequate for it. Uexküll's research is basic to this point and is so generally valid that it no longer meets with much opposition.[21] In cases of brain injuries, our experience has everywhere shown the equivalent results.

Criticism of the purely environmental theory. World and environment (milieu)
On the other hand, the fact that the organism finds itself in an ordered
state only in certain environments, and can only live in such an environment, does not mean at all that the environment creates this order.
This would only be possible, in general, if the life of every individual
organism were actually fitted firmly into a segregated ("insulated") part
of the world – into its own environment – and if the rest of the world
were nonexistent for it. In this event the problem of the organism would
be referred to that of the environment regarded as a definitely fixed part
of its world. But actually the situation is not like this. Each organism
lives in a world that by no means contains only such stimuli as are adequate for it. It lives not merely in its "own environment" (milieu) but in
a world in which all possible sorts of stimuli are present and act on it.
The organism must cope with this "quasi-negative" environment. Actually, some sort of continuous selection among the events in the world
takes place, namely, from that point of view wherein events are, or are
not, pertinent to the organism. The environment of an organism is by no
means something definite and static but is continuously forming com-
mensurably with the development of the organism and its activity. One
could say that the environment emerges from the world through the being
or actualization of the organism. Stated in a less prejudiced manner,
an organism can exist only if it succeeds in finding in the world an adequate environment – in shaping an environment (for which, of course,
the world must offer the opportunity). An environment always presupposes a given organism. How could it then be determined by the environment? How could it achieve order only by the environment? Of course,
as soon as it has an environment, it has order. Order is only achievable
if there is the possibility of obtaining an adequate environment. But
the possibility alone is of no avail. Environment first arises from the
world only when there is an ordered organism. Therefore, the order
must be determined from somewhere else. From where? From within
the organism? We are ultimately referred back to the organism itself.

The fact that the milieu is determined by the particular characteristics of the organism becomes especially clear in the diseased. For
this altered organism, to whom the formerly normal environment has
now become strange and disturbing, the basic prerequisite of existence
is capability to shape once again an adequate environment. We have
already indicated how this occurs and shall refer to it again later.

Sherrington's concept of integration
Our evaluation of the concept of the environment, of course, renders dubious at the very outset all attempts to explain the order in the organism in terms of an effect from the outer world. Sherrington's work is based on such an attempt. It is imperative to consider his work most carefully, not only because he deserves the highest esteem as a scholar but also because no one else has defined and employed the reflex concept as clearly as he has. Nowhere else can we find such an indisputable starting point for our critical analysis that, above all, must avoid any ambiguity of concepts. We shall see later on that there are certain authors who, while defending the holistic theory, would like at the same time to retain the reflex concept in some way. This procedure endangers the clarification of the entire problem. Sherrington starts with the simplest reflex, where one stimulus causes a reaction by way of one receptor and effector, while the rest of the organism remains completely unaffected. He chooses this reflex for methodological reasons, appreciating very well that he is dealing with an abstraction. The actual reality is, for him, the sum total of the reflexes, since each single one is codetermined by the other reflexes. This sum represents the instrument of order that governs the activity of the organism. The activity of the organism is guaranteed through the synergy of the reflexes that appears as a sum of numerous parts, which, however, regarded in isolation, do not exist at all, because they are merely abstractions. Order is established by the fact that this complicated reflex apparatus becomes active, and is kept active, through the total stimulation of the environment. For such a summative concept of the whole, it is a scientifically correct approach to start from the reflexes and to study their changes under varying conditions. The laws of reciprocal inhibition, facilitation, shunting, and so on, are genuine scientific principles by which order is brought to this sum. On the basis of the original assumption, this approach is logical. That the scientists who proceed in this manner fail to notice that order is not comprehensible on this basis is understandable by virtue of the fact that they never deal, in their concrete work, with the organism as a whole. They are content with painstakingly minute and marvelously accurate detail work. They can be content with the results of this approach because their interest is, and so remains, essentially in animals. But we, who are especially concerned with human beings, are impelled to comprehend the performances of the whole

organism; thereby, the impossibility of conceiving the behavior of the organism as constituted by reflexes is evident.

Is the direction issuing from the organism itself?
The theory of coordination centers
There are, however, other types of quasi-holistic approach. The relation between the parts and the whole is considered either as given in the organism itself – for example, the various biological organismic theories – or it is considered adventitious, as, for instance, in the form of an entelechy. We shall refer subsequently to these views. Here we must discuss the theory of coordination centers and other attempts to explain order.

The theory of coordination centers usually postulates higher centers of the nervous system, which regulate other processes. In this connection one speaks of "higher performances"; and with this concept a genuine part-whole relation within the organism is not necessarily or usually intended. The idea of coordination centers must be rejected in the light of our explanations regarding the lack of utility of the concept of inhibition. Albrecht Bethe has made a thorough critical discussion of it and has refuted it.[22] Through the analysis of a great number of phenomena, especially in the invertebrates, he arrives at the conclusion that "each small part of the nervous system is at the same time a primary reflex center and, with regard to the neighboring parts, a center of co-ordination.... The co-ordination is located everywhere and nowhere."[23] He rejects the assumption of coordination centers for movement by pointing out the following very interesting facts: in worms and myriapoda and other animals of segmental structure, movements occur essentially unmodified, even when the connections between the segments are interrupted. Each part of the transected animal shows the same characteristic mode of locomotion as the whole animal.

The "resonance" theory of Weiss
Bethe proceeds then to discuss the various theories advanced today for an understanding of nervous processes and refutes them all. Since we agree essentially with his criticism, we need only to repeat these theories briefly. J. Moritz Schiff, on the basis of his experiments with transection of the spinal cord, recognized that function is not determined by a definite anatomical connection.[24] He assumed that any

existing nervous tract may transmit various excitations. Therefore, "ordered" performance could only be explained if certain areas of the central nervous system were brought in tune with each other in the manner of resonators. In more recent years, Paul Weiss has attempted to build up a corresponding theory on the basis of his brilliant transplantation experiments.[25] He found that an implanted additional extremity executes exactly the same movements as the adjoining normal extremity that is in its proper location. He concludes from this that the performance is the result of tuning between parts of the central nervous system and peripheral effectors. As a result of this tuning, it is assumed that each specific wave of excitation brings only the specific muscle group into action. Thus, it is altogether immaterial with which nerve the transplanted muscle is connected, for it will always become excited when its characteristic form of excitation is emitted from the central organ. Bethe was correct in pointing out that this hypothesis, attractive as it may be, does not explain the adjustment that becomes necessary if the old performances are to take place in spite of interchange of muscles or nerves. In order to explain this we would have to presume a modification of the tune of the resonator, and by so doing we would be no nearer to an understanding than if we assumed any other form of shunting. Bethe is furthermore correct in his objection that this hypothesis really presupposes the existence of preformed and specific centers, from which the specific wave of excitation issues. It is exactly against such an assumption that the critique is directed, on the basis of recent experiments. The resonance hypothesis cannot explain where the direction of the processes originates. It can only explain at best why, when one part is excited, other parts are also brought into play. But this does not carry us any further in overcoming the fundamental difficulties. The theory of resonance introduces a constancy that does not correspond to the manifoldedness of the phenomena.[26] It leaves completely unexplained the relation of each single performance to the whole organism. Uexküll, in particular, long ago recognized the difficulties that lie in the assumption of firmly established centers and has tried to overcome it through certain hypotheses regarding the distribution of the excitations.[27] According to him, three factors must be considered as regulators in this connection. First, the state of extension of the muscle. There is no doubt that a series of phenomena can well be explained by the postulate that the excitation flows along the more tensed muscle. On

the other hand, it can also be readily shown, that this is not always necessarily the case. In an attempt to understand these deviations Uexküll
introduces a second factor: the operation of additional laws. One of
these laws is the different effects of strong and weak reflexes. He found
that, in the sea urchin, certain muscles contract under weak stimulation but relax under strong stimulation. We have mentioned similar phenomena before (p. 71). Uexküll explains these phenomena by a shunting
mechanism that is brought into activity by the force of the stimulus.
Bethe, however, refutes this view, claiming that we find such shunting
brought about by various stimuli in a great variety of responses. These
responses always indicate a dispositional change ("*Umstimmung*") that
cannot be explained simply by differences in strength of the stimulus.
The reason for the shunting still remains completely unexplained. On
the basis of our previous expositions, we agree fully with Bethe.

The theorem of Uexküll

Finally, Uexküll emphasizes as a third law the effect of the so-called
tonus valley (*Tonustal*). There is no doubt about the facts. Because of
his astute and unbiased observation, Uexküll was probably the first to
find that the same stimulus can become effective in quite different ways
and in different localities and that it depends on the prevailing condition of the various regions concerned, where the excitation will, so to
speak, "be caught." If the excitation at one place is prevented from
spreading, possibly through the destruction of a part of the nervous system or through the artificial impediment of a movement, it spreads to
another part, as if there were a valley into which it flows like a stream.

There are a great number of examples of this process in the invertebrates, where up to now it has been particularly well demonstrated.
But we know of it also from numerous instances with patients. One
example may suffice as an illustration. If a patient with a cerebellar
lesion is made to raise the arm of the diseased side in the forward direction, we find that the arm will deviate at the shoulder joint toward the
outside. If one prevents this deviation by holding the arm at the shoulder joint, then the deviation takes place in the elbow joint. If one also
prevents this, the deviation makes its appearance in the wrist joint; and
finally if this is impeded, in the finger joint. Thus, through the proper
experimental control, one can determine at will in which part the deviation is to occur.[28]

Our theoretical standpoint is in agreement with Uexküll's, inasmuch as he has abandoned the customary concept of excitation in the nervous system being an oscillatory process and instead introduces a model of a displaceable fluid. But such a concept still leaves unexplained how this fluid attains a definite formation, especially how it is dammed up in one place of the "tonus valley." The idea becomes no clearer if we include the law of the tensed muscles and the phenomenon of the weak and strong reflexes. All these laws, like the reflex laws themselves, hold only for definite experimental conditions, where, through the situation created by the experimenter, the distribution of the excitation is determined in various ways. They teach us nothing regarding the actual life process. It would again be necessary to assume new specific centers, centers of coordination, higher integrating agencies that regulate the tonus. Uexküll's "*Representanten*," which are supposed to determine the shunting, are of this nature. But again, this has not carried us any further.

Bethe's principle of gliding coupling

According to Bethe, the coordination is determined partly by events that take place outside the animal and partly by those that take place inside. Each situation brings about the appropriate coordination. As a prototype for this Bethe mentions the principle of the "gliding coupling" or "gliding regulation." He demonstrates this principle by the following example, which explains the coordinated operation of the parts of the hand, as depending on the varying environmental conditions:

In an artificial hand, the pull on a wire, Z, is not directly effective on the four levers $W_1 \ldots W_4$ that are to be moved but is transmitted through the mediation of one long lever and two short levers. If the resistance that has to be overcome in order to move the levers $W_1 \ldots W_4$ is equal for all four levers, then they all move over the same angle if Z is pulled. If, however, one of the levers meets outside resistance, it is brought to a standstill, while the others move on until they are prevented from further movement, either simultaneously or consecutively. At this equilibrium point, a stronger pull can first become effective through equally increased pressure, on the part of all four levers, against the outside resistance. If the four levers, corresponding to the anatomic structure of the hand, are again subdivided into three parts, so that they correspond to the fingers, the hand thereby gains greater adaptability and sensitivity. If one adds a simple automatic commutator one creates a considerable capacity of the hand for bending in the shape of very different objects. Sometimes all four levers will move, sometimes only two, while the others remain extended, depending on the shape of the object to be grasped. To set the hand going, there is only one equal and constant innervating impulse needed on the part of the individual whose arm muscles are connected with the artificial hand. The variety, in effect, is produced only through the conditions of outer resistance.

Possibly the principle of "gliding coupling" is an adequate explanation for the changing muscular interplay in the artificial hand, in its varying environment, but it is hardly sufficient to explain the events in the living organism. After all, one could only explain in this way the variation of the muscle play, corresponding to the variety in the environment, if one assumes an equally constant pull, one single constant impulse, as is actually the case in the use of the artificial hand. But does this correspond to the events, when various objects are grasped by the natural hand? Hardly. It does not even agree with the facts, if one maintains that, in grasping an object with the hand, only the general impulse of closing is sent into all hand muscles, and that this movement is continued until each finger meets with resistance. Rather, as Bethe has argued, "the retroaction on the central organ through the receptors causes the respective muscles to put on the brake or lock, but the impulse still remains active in the other muscles, until they too are locked."[29]

At best, however, such a sequence of events is found only when completely unfamiliar objects are involved, and then only if the intention is to grasp, but not to use, the object (cf. below). In such cases, one sees clearly how hesitantly and imperfectly the grasping takes place.

Whenever objects are familiar (even where familiarity is established not through visual but possibly only through touch perception), then even the first movement is not one of equal closure for all parts of the hand but is graded in the various muscles, corresponding to the peculiarity of the object. Therefore, this gradation does not take place in accordance with the peripheral influences but is "centrally" innervated. We have the "feel" of a familiar object even before we grasp it.

But there is still another factor that speaks against the suggestion that order is brought into the movements through the "gliding coupling." The grasping of an object is practically never an end in itself; it is usually only the first link in a movement of manipulation. The innervation of the separate muscles by no means takes place on the principle of grasping but on the principle of progressive use, which in turn is directed by central points of view, by the "intention." Under abnormal conditions, we find a simple grasping, corresponding to the "holding" of the artificial hand, in the so-called forced grasping. In this case, the behavior could possibly be explained on the principle of the "gliding coupling." But here, we are dealing with an activity divorced from the center and one that is, in effect, peripherally determined. The result is not a purposeful reaching for an object but a meaningless clutching, so contrary to good sense that the stronger the pain, to wit, the peripheral stimulus, the tighter the object will be held. If we are to consider this as the constant basic process, conditioned through couplings, then we need a further central regulation for the normal, meaningful grasping of an object. In other words, we still have not progressed any further. It would be a great injustice to Bethe if one insinuated that he thought only outside influences acted as regulators. On the contrary, only a few lines above, he calls attention to the fact that coordination depends on the conditions within and without the animal.[30] He is trying to avoid the assumption of fixed centers of coordination. This is why he places so much emphasis on his principle that does not require such an assumption, at least not for the holding of an object. In other words, he wants the principle of the "gliding coupling" to be regarded only as an analogy. But it does not seem to us to be a very suitable analogy for the understanding of the performances of the organism, because it does not contain an account of the part that the organism itself plays. Perhaps Bethe thinks one could correct this error by adding another principle. The following sentence, in another place, seems to indicate he holds such an opinion: "It is hardly probable that one single, basic principle will be found by which all nervous phenomena can be explained."[31] Whether such a principle will be found at all is certainly a problem. But it seems to me that the living processes will become intelligible through one, and only one, basic principle. The danger in assuming additional principles lies in the fact that one too easily overlooks the faults of the original principle. This, for example, is the case in the theory of inhibitions, in the reflex hypothesis. The assumption of several principles, furthermore, always requires a regulation – in other words, an additional, higher authority. Either the second principle is only an elaboration of the first, in which case the first becomes really unnecessary, or it is in contradiction to the first, and then the relation between the two must be explained. This again leads us to the centers of regulation, which we have refuted. We shall have to deal with this problem in our discussion of antagonistic innervation. It is our conviction that organismic life, according to all indications, is governed by only one principle, which manifests itself in certain situations in various forms but always remains basically the same. These forms do not represent the manifestations of new principles. The principle of the tensed muscle is, for example, only a special case of the principle of the "tonus valley." This, in turn, is only a special case of our principle of equalization (cf. p. 97), which in turn can be reduced to the principle of "adequate coming to terms" (cf. p. 104). The careful analysis of the special instances that have led to the assumptions of various principles shows again and again that they are, in reality, cases in which the basic principle manifests itself, under the special circumstances, in one form or the other. These instances are then erroneously explained as the effect of new principles. This almost invariably implies the end of further analysis and hinders the progress of knowledge. The principle of the gliding couplings seems to us well suited to construct artificial hands that are able to hold various objects in a correct way, but it does not help our understanding of real performances. Only the centrally directed movements of the arm are apt for purposeful manipulations.

The elements posited by the reflex theorem cannot offer an understanding of the organism

Our expositions thus far have aimed at showing that the ordered activity of the organism cannot be understood on the basis of such elements as the reflex investigations furnish and that we cannot obtain a picture of the structure of the organism on that basis.

We had to discard as unsuitable the explanations of all the experiments in question, which were carried out to adduce evidence that the performances of the organism are based on the interplay of individually separate phenomena. Before we discuss additional facts, which in our opinion will lead us to a more appropriate explanation, we wish to outline a preliminary sketch of our view of the functioning of the organism, which is essentially based on facts that we have already discussed or know from other sources.

93

CHAPTER THREE

Theoretical Reflections on the Function of the Nervous System as Foundation for a Theory of the Organism

The Nervous System a Network.
The Course of Excitation in Such a System

The following theoretical reflection on the function of the nervous system is based on the analysis of numerous normal and pathological phenomena.[1] Although primarily intended as a systematic explanation of the events in the nervous system, our conception seems suited for generalization, in order to arrive at a theory of the functioning of the whole organism. It is based on the view that the nervous system, not only of invertebrates, but also of vertebrates, including human beings, is a network in which ganglia are inserted at various places and that is related to the external world by means of the sense organs and the movable parts of the body. This network, in which the excitations take place, represents an apparatus that always functions as a whole. To these excitations are related the performances of the organism, but the particular form of this relation cannot as yet be clearly described. From analyses of the performances the following laws governing the course of excitation may be deduced.

1. The system is never at rest, but in a continual state of excitation. The nervous system has often been considered as an organ at rest, in which excitation arises only as a response to stimuli. This was due to the fact that only those phenomena that became particularly pronounced on stimulation were considered as expressions of the processes in the nervous system. The fact that the nervous system is continuously under the influence of stimuli and is continually excited was overlooked. It was not recognized that events that follow a definite stimulus are only an expression of a change of excitation in the nervous system, that they represent only a special pattern of the excitation pro-

cess. This assumption of a system at rest was especially favored by the fact that only the external stimuli were considered. Too little attention was given to the fact that the organism is continuously exposed, even in the apparent absence of outward stimuli, to the influence of internal stimuli — influences that may be of highest importance for its activity, for example, the effect of stimuli issuing from the blood, the importance of which was particularly pointed out by Thomas Graham Brown.[2] Our view has received support by the investigation of the action currents of the brain, for it has been shown that even while the organism is not exposed to any external stimuli regular excitation processes occur in the brain. Stimulation appears in the curves rather as a disturbance of the regularity of the currents.

If, in the following description of functional events, we employ terms borrowed from physics like "course of excitation," "distribution of excitation," "state of equilibrium," "disequilibrium," and so on, we do not wish to imply any statement regarding the nature of these processes. We merely wish to characterize the respective kind of dynamics involved, and thus we feel justified in applying the same terminology whether we are dealing with physical processes or performances.

2. Since we are concerned with a system that always functions as a whole, a given stimulus must produce changes in the whole organism. Actually, however, effects by no means appear everywhere but usually only in one more or less extended area. The reason for this is as follows: in a system as extensive as the nervous system the changes in response to a stimulus do not take place everywhere simultaneously and to an equal degree. They appear earlier and with greater intensity near the point at which the stimulus is applied than in regions further from the point of the stimulus application. I shall call this the "local near effect."

Distribution of excitation through the spatial and functional "near effect"
We know from experimental evidence in lower animals that the intensity of the excitation in a nervous system, which is a network, decreases with the distance from the point of stimulus application — that the excitation process in a nervous network suffers a "decrement" (a "metabolic gradient"; cf. Charles Manning Child[3]). The existence of interposed ganglion cells is especially responsible for distribution of the excitation. This, too, we know from experiments with lower animals.

The destruction of ganglion cells results, experimentally, in principally three sequelae:

1. In a preparation deprived of its ganglia – for example an aplysia, from which the central nervous system has been removed – stimulation results in more intense excitation.

2. The preparation does not react in the normal, localized area alone, but over a wide region, with a more homogeneous energy distribution.

3. The stimulus effect is of greater duration.

These changes in the reactions, following the elimination of ganglion cells, can be understood if the ganglion is considered as a structural enlargement of the system of functional elements. This assumption is supported by the fact that the structure of the ganglion cells consists of fibrils and that these fibrils are connected with those in the general network. In this context we shall speak of an enlargement of the system. Because the ganglion enlarges the system it is, in the first place, well suited to effect a channeled distribution of new energy through the enlarged network.

This wider distribution of the given amount of energy results in reduced strength of excitation per given area. The strength of the excitation is less than if the system were free of ganglia. Consequently, in a preparation containing ganglia, the strength of the stimulus effect is weaker. On the other hand, because the ganglion is interposed between one part of the system and the remainder, it prevents the otherwise rapid distribution of the excitation over more distant parts of the system. In other words, it causes a relative limitation of the extension of the changes, with a markedly strong excitation in the "nearer part" – and thus a more localized effect. In a preparation lacking ganglia the radiation of the effect is greater. The effect is less localized. Finally, the ganglion causes a decrease of the excitation at the point that was first stimulated, because at this point an equalization takes place between the higher excitation level and the lower excitation level in the rest of the system. The result is the gradual decrease of the reaction at this point – the equalization of the excitation. Thus, on the one hand, the ganglion slows the flow of excitation from one part of the system to the whole system, causes, so to speak, a piling up in one part of the system.[4] On the other hand, the ganglion reduces the increase of the excitation in this part of the system by enlarging it, ultimately causing a slow equalization of the differences in excitation. The first effect induces the appearance of the decrement, the second reduces the effective value of the decrement, while the third favors the equalization of the effect at various levels in the different parts of the system and thus reestablishes a state of equilibrium, the "average state of excitation."

The significance of adequate anatomical structures
The decrement effect, the "near effect," is, however, not only determined by the proximity of a part of the nervous system to the point at which the stimulus was applied, but also in the more or less greater appropriateness of the stimulus for the various parts of the nervous system. The latter show varying degrees of adequacy to the different types of stimuli, on account of the organization of the respective organism and on account of the individual differences in receptiveness toward various constellations of stimuli (familiar as well as unfamiliar ones). The eye is more receptive to light rays than is the rest of the body, the ear is more receptive to sound waves, and so on. In a part that is especially adapted to receive a certain type of stimulus, this stimulus will produce a greater change than in less adapted parts. In a part well adapted to receive a stimulus, easily recorded effects occur. In other words, "effective" changes are produced; the same stimulus will not elicit a response in a less well adapted part or in an inadequate part. There it remains "subliminal." We shall designate this type of effect the "functional near effect," in contrast to the "local near effect." Those parts that are better adapted to receive a given stimulus, are functionally homogeneous, and therefore exhibit the "near effect" must not necessarily be in local proximity but can be spread over distant parts of the nervous system. An adequate stimulus that impinges on any point can thus become effective at very different, widely separated regions, whereas other parts of greater local proximity but of different adequacy remain relatively untouched. In large regions of the system, which are functionally related, the change will not everywhere be equally strong and simultaneous but will occur sooner and more strongly in that part which is nearer the point of stimulation. In the case just mentioned, the reverse may in time become true; that is to say, in the nearer part, the equalization may have already begun, whereas in the more distant parts, the effect may have just started. Hence one stimulus can affect performances having temporal sequence. We can differentiate between near effects of varying degrees. The degree is determined, on the one

hand, by the more or less greater local proximity to the onset of the stimulus and on the other hand by the greater or lesser adequacy of the stimulus for the part of the system involved. Parts that functionally belong together have a specific structure acquired through specific "practice." This structure favors the effect of specific stimuli appropriate to it. Normal performance, that is, the normal reaction to a specific stimulus, is linked to the normal structure. This is where the significance of the anatomic structures becomes evident for the distribution of the excitation in the system.

We cannot here attempt to explain the origin of these structures. This question is related, on the one side, to the problem of the so-called origin of species, and of the origin of various forms of living oragnisms in general, and, on the other side, to the problem of the specific pattern that the organism acquires during experience. Likewise, we can only state that the structure of any organism is such that it makes possible performances that are the fulfillments of the requirements of its environment. The structure is best understood as the result of a process of adaptation of the organism to the environment. The normal structure corresponds to the normal performances of the organism, which remain generally quite constant, the regular and prompt course of which, in turn, is guaranteed through the structure itself.

The processes in the "distant part." Figure-ground formation
The pattern of the excitation that occurs in the system as the result of a stimulus cannot be sufficiently characterized by noting merely the state of excitation in the "near part." The rest of the system, the "distant part," as we shall call it, is also in a very definite state of excitation.

Each movement of one part of the body is accompanied by a definite change in the posture of the rest of the body. When, in response to a stimulus, one definite part of our field of perception becomes prominent, the entire perceptual field changes simultaneously in support of the perception proper. We can conclude from these and similar facts, which could be multiplied ad libitum, that simultaneously with each near change, a corresponding change in the remaining system takes place. This change in the distant part is, in a certain sense, antagonistic to the first and is necessary not only for the maintenance of the balance in the entire system but also for the accurate execution of the required performances (i.e., the result of the processes in the "near part"; for example, were it not for this balancing process, we might fall when lifting one arm sideward). A reaction at one point of the organism is the more accurate the more it is in configurational contrast to the rest of the organism – the more it stands in the "foreground" as compared with the "background" (which is represented by the rest of the organism). In other words, a reaction at one point of the organism is more accurate the more precise the relation is between the near process ("the foreground process") and the process in the rest of the system ("the background process"). Whenever we analyze the structure of acts or performances we meet this same configuration. I am therefore inclined to regard this configuration of excitation, the foreground-background relation, as the basic form of the functioning of the nervous system.

The foreground process comprises at times narrow areas, at other times wide areas of the organism, depending on whether a greater or smaller part of the structures of the organism is required to deal with the actual task.

Experience shows, particularly in patients, that the execution of individual performances, the formation of individual figure-ground processes, is evidently of varying difficulty for the organism. The analysis of performances, or of the degrees of disturbance in a lesion, discloses that the figure-ground formation is the more difficult (i.e., makes the greater demands on the nervous tissue) the more precisely a definitely circumscribed, unitary formation has to stand out from the ground, and the more isolable elements it contains in a characteristic organization. The difficulty varies according to its familiarity, thus depending on the tuning of the substratum gained through experience. In certain adjustments, namely, in those that have been experienced frequently, the formation of the figure occurs more promptly and is firmer. Those adjustments that have been acquired in childhood seem to be particularly stable. All the factors mentioned determine the "functional significance," the "valence" of each single performance. It depends on this valence whether, in a case of impairment of function, one performance can be executed better than another performance of "higher" or "lower" valence. We conclude all this from exact observation as to which performances remain intact and which performances become disturbed when the function is reduced through damage of the substratum. In the latter cases we always see that when the performance capacity of a substratum is impaired the execution of separate actions suffers first and foremost, while the more "general reactions" that correspond to a less clear figure-ground formation are still possible. We see further that a differentiation within the performance especially suffers; that the performance loses in precision and discreteness of shape of the contributing "single elements." We can understand this if we realize that a well-functioning substratum is certainly required to maintain a high tension in a narrowly circumscribed area and that tension is necessary for the execution of the aforementioned performances. Any slackening of function leads, therefore, to a leveling, to wit, to a greater uniformity of processes in the concerned regions of the system, or possibly in the entire system. Later on we shall examine these laws of "dedifferentiation" of the figure-ground processes.

The distribution of excitation depends on the condition
of the organism as a whole
There is a continuous alternation as to which "part" of the organism stands in the foreground – and which in the background. The foreground is determined by the task the organism has to fulfill at any given moment, namely, by the situation in which the organism happens to find itself and by the demands with which it has to cope.

The tasks are determined by the "nature" of the organism, its "essence," which is brought into actualization through the environmental changes that act on it. The expressions of this actualization are the performances of the organism. Through them the organism can deal with the respective environmental demands and actualize itself. The possibility of asserting itself in the world, while preserving its character, hinges on a specific kind of "coming to terms" of the organism with the environment. This has to take place in such a fashion that each change of the organism, caused by environmental stimuli, is equalized after a definite time, so that the organism regains that "average" state that corresponds to its nature, which is "adequate" to it. Only when this is the case is it possible that the same environmental events can produce the same changes, that is, can lead to the same effects and to the same experiences. Only under this condition can the organism maintain its constancy and identity. If this equalization toward the average of adequate state did not occur, then the same environmental events would produce diverse changes in the organism. Thereby, the environment would lose its constancy for the organism and would alter continually. An ordered course of performances would be impossible. The organism would be in a continual state of disquiet, would be endangered in its existence, and actually would be continuously "another" organism. This, however, is actually not the case. On the contrary, we can observe that the performances of the organism show a relatively great constancy, with fluctuations around a constant mean. If this relative constancy did not exist it would not even be possible to recognize an organism as such; we could not even talk of a specific organism.

The distribution of excitation depends on the condition
of organism at the onset of a reaction
This kind of coming to terms of the organism with the environment we call the basic biologic law. It is supported, for instance, by the following facts: We find in experimental investigations that the same external change, "the same stimulus," may act quite differently. The effect depends, first of all, on the condition of the system at the moment of exposure to the stimulus, which we call the starting situation; and it usually appears as a definite process in that sector of the organism in which the near effect takes place. We know this law from psychology, where it has found expression in the Weber-Fechner law, which describes the dependence of the differential limen on the relation of the stimulus increase to the basic stimulus. Whether this law holds in its specific formulation – and many objections have been raised against its general validity – there is no doubt as to the significance of the starting situation for the stimulus effect. A similar law holds apparently for all life processes.[5] I have indicated the significance of the starting situation for the explanation of many phenomena in the motor system. It becomes especially pronounced in the vegetative system, for example, in the following phenomena: the effect of a small amount of adrenaline, which reduces blood pressure, becomes – according to Walter Bradford Cannon and William G. Lyman – the more apparent the higher the tonus of the vascular muscles. According to Hess, a vessel that is narrower has a greater inclination toward dilatation than one that is wider. Inez Wilder has studied these and similar facts, and summed them up in the form of a "law of initial values" (i.e., the value of the initial state), which attempts to bring into regular relation the quantitative dependency of the stimulus effect on the initial situation.[6] This law is, how-

ever, not sufficiently comprehensive because it takes into consideration only the quantitative relation. But we are actually dealing here not merely with a quantitatively different effect of the same stimulus.

The Equalization Belongs to the Excitation Course

We have seen that under certain conditions the stimulus effect can be reversed. This reversal can be understood if we keep in mind that the stimulus effect is represented not only in the change of excitation but also in the equalization of that change. The curve of the effect has an ascending and a descending slope, the latter corresponding to the return of the excitation to the adequate mean. The organism tends never to remain, beyond a certain time, in a state of tension that lies above or below the "mean." In our opinion, the reason for this is that in either event the same stimuli would lead to different reactions. Thus, each stimulus acting on an organism always initiates a return of the state of excitation to the mean, before a noticeable – an "effective-effect" – appears. Therefore, the same stimuli are less effective when the condition of excitation of the organism is below the mean than when it is at the mean. In a condition of abnormally high excitation the same stimuli have the opposite effect, namely, of reducing the excitation toward the mean.

We know of a number of facts from the field of the vegetative system that actually show this. If the stimulus meets the organism in a condition of abnormally low excitation, its effect may be relatively low as compared with the amount of change from the normal excitation level taken as the starting situation. In this case the effect above the mean can be relatively small – smaller than the effect of the same stimulus in a starting situation of greater excitation. If we measure the effect of a stimulus on the change of the excitation with respect to the starting situation, we find that an equally strong stimulus shows a lesser effect, in the case of a high excitation level of the starting situation. The effect never goes beyond a certain level. If the same stimulus becomes effective in a starting situation in which the excitation is very nearly at its possible apex, the effect is actually less. If the state of excitation in the starting situation is actually at its apex, the same stimulus may have no effect at all or a reversed effect. In this last case, the stimulus actually leads to a reduction of excitation.

Kroetz has expressed this law in general form by stating that the individual effect of the autonomic nerve stimulation usually proceeds in such a way that the existing extension of the smooth muscle fibers tends to approximate a mean position.[7] Adrenaline, for example, increases the tonus in the stomach when the muscle is relaxed but reduces it when the muscle is contracted. We may assume that this law has general validity for all stimulus effect. What the "mean" in each individual case signifies, however, will have to be discussed later.

Equalization toward an "adequate" average level in
an "adequate" time: A basic biological law
These facts indicate that in the stimulus effect relation we are not dealing with a performance that is strictly caused by the stimulus alone but that the simultaneously occurring processes prevent too great a deviation from the "mean," that is, the resulting performance is part of a total process that regulates the course of excitation so that it never deviates in an inadequate way from the mean. Since this process assumes essential importance for the maintenance of normal life, we may be well justified in calling it a biologically basic process.

Both the excitation and the equalization process require time. In any performance, for its total course as well as for its part events, a definite configuration of its temporal sequence is characteristic. Any change in the temporal course of excitation changes the excitation as well as the equalization; we shall see later on under what conditions such a change occurs. The temporal relation between impinging of the stimulus and reaction of the organism is normally so regulated that new stimuli, in order to set up new performances, become effective only after the equalization has taken place in accordance with the situation. The result is that approximately the same effect always corresponds to the same stimulus. If, however, equalization has not yet taken place, that is, if the new stimulus follows the preceding one too rapidly, we obtain an effect of the new stimulus, which differs from the effect normally obtained by the same stimulus. This is the case in the experimental facts that we have cited. Thus, a different effect is the result of an "inadequate" stimulation. We shall see subsequently that we find this also in cases where inadequate reactions of the organism are obtained on account of changes of the functioning of the substratum due to disease.

Under both conditions, the normal course of equalization is disturbed. From this we conclude – for the evaluation of the results in experimental investigations – that we must be very cautious in regarding them as normal phenomena. In any event, the laws that we have outlined must be very carefully considered in appraising the results of experimental investigations. The "basic biologic law" determines the process of a stimulated substratum. This law corresponds to the manner of functioning throughout the organism. Whenever the organism is exposed to stimulation it responds in this way. Therefore, in this respect, I speak of a "basic function." Any injury means a disturbance of this basic function, which leads to a change of the performances according to very definite laws (cf. p. 115). To prevent misunderstandings, we want to stress that this basic function in itself is not identical with the functioning of the organism as a whole, even though, in any part of the organism, it is not independent of the whole. The manner in which any substratum reacts (according to the basic function) would be the same, even if the organism consisted of isolated parts.[8]

The equalization process and the milieu of the organism.
The catastrophic reaction
The above-mentioned maintenance of a relative constancy, distinctive to each organism, is only possible when there is a definite configuration of the stimuli, that is, of the milieu. Actually, only such events that make the above-discussed equalization possible belong to the milieu of the organism, exist for it as a stimulus, and lead to the experience of definite contents.

For each organism, not everything that occurs in the outer world belongs to its milieu. The only events that normally prove themselves as stimuli are those with which the organism can come to terms in a manner such that its existence (i.e., the actualization of the performances that constitute its nature) is not essentially disturbed. In other words, this adjustment must permit an equalization that is peculiar to the individual nature of the organism. Events in the outer world that do not permit this do not become effective in the normal organism, except when they are of abnormal intensity. In this case they do not lead to actual performances but to the phenomenon of shock of the whole organism, which endangers its continuity as a system and that I have therefore called catastrophic reaction.

We must make a clear distinction between the surrounding world, in which the organism is located, and the milieu that represents only a part of the world – that part that is adequate to it, that is, that allows for the described relationship between the organism and its environment. Each organism has its milieu, as Jakob von Uexküll has emphasized.[9] Its existence and its "normal" performances are dependent on the condition that a state of adaptation can come about between its structure and the environmental events, allowing the formation of an "adequate" milieu. This is normally the case for a living organism.

An organism responds, at first, to any stimulus acting on it, by a "turning-to movement" toward the stimulus source. This is followed by further reactions that lead either to the acceptance or rejection of the stimulus object. Some reactions seem to consist merely of rejection; actually the organism must always first come somehow into "contact" with the stimulus object before it can turn away from the object – before it can repel it. Reactions of acceptance and rejection are essentially the same kind of behavior, only their direction is different – they are simply different kinds of apprehending the stimulus object. Whether acceptance or rejection or possibly partial elimination ultimately takes place depends on the degree to which the stimulus object is adequate to the entire organization of the organism in question. Everything is eliminated that endangers the permanent continuity of the system, that is, that renders impossible the return to the adequate mean.

Distribution of excitation corresponding to the "all-or-none law"
Any change in the organism has the tendency to continue for a while in the same direction (tendency of perseverance) and to reach a definite state. This tendency is relatively independent of the strength of the stimulus. The processes do not run in a continuous flow but go from one "preferred" condition to another. All stimuli are used more or less according to the "all-or-none law." Some scholars have doubted the validity of this law. One must not interpret it as being completely definitive, that in spite of varying intensity of the stimulus the effect must be, under all conditions, the same. That concept would be erroneous, if for no other reason than because the stimulus value is always determined by the situation in which the whole organism is found at a given time. Thus, we cannot talk generally of "strong" or "weak" stimuli or, accordingly, of the same effect of various stimuli. Rather, the all-or-none law postulates that, relatively independent of the intensity of the stim-

ulus, those reactions occur that correspond to the best utilization of the part of the organism at the time, to wit, "preferred" utilization. In so doing, various reactions can take place depending on whether an organ is exposed to the stimulus, in connection with the whole, or in "isolation." Hence we may find quite different effects as the expression of preferred utilization that, although corresponding to the meaning of the all-or-none law, may create the impression of deviations from it, as long as one regards a single situation and its resulting effect as the "normal." From these considerations it follows that the validity or nonvalidity of any biological law can never be proved through simple comparison of actual, single phenomena but only through careful analysis of their relation within the respective total situation. It seems to me that such an analysis, properly understood, will demonstrate the validity of the all-or-none law. Such an analysis demands, of course, that one include our concept of the essential nature of the organism. This all-or-none law, from our point of interest, is equivalent to the law of pregnanz (cf. p. 293), a term introduced by Max Wertheimer in connection with Gestalt psychology. The end to which each process normally tends is determined by its significance for the essential tasks of the whole organism. Although it is always modified by the changes of the situation, it remains essentially constant.

If we assume that every reaction is determined by the nature or "essence" of the organism, if we regard equalization as an equalization toward a mean, adequate to the nature of the organism in a given situation, then the question arises: What do we mean by the term "nature"? It is the same question that we have encountered previously: How do we arrive at the knowledge of this "nature"? The procedure of natural science, as such, cannot yield other than isolated facts in the physical and psychological realm; as much as we may refine our methods of observation, we will never actually get beyond statements of such a piecemeal kind. We do not at all propose to abandon this principle of natural science. But how shall it enable us to arrive at an understanding of the "whole"? This is not possible through the simple summation of these piecemeal results, these "parts." It is certainly not possible to reconstruct the behavior in the organism directly from the parts. What I have explained so far about the parts is certainly not suited for such a construction. We remember how equivocal, even contradictory, reactions to the same stimulus can be, and how, up to this point, we have been lacking any guiding principle to bring order into this chaos. But before advancing our own theory we must carry our analysis further. First, we have to inquire more thoroughly why the "part phenomena," which we have considered so far, are unsuited to serve as a basis from which a concept of the whole of the essence of the organism could be derived. To answer this question we must scrutinize the methodological procedure that has brought these "parts" to the fore. From such a reflexion on methodology we may gain material that might be appropriate for settling our problem, or we may learn how to obtain material more useful for the understanding of the organism. The discussion below of the method by which the reflex phenomena have been studied and arrived at may help us here. It may, at the same time, assure us of a better understanding of the nature of reflexes.

Discussion of the Physico-Chemical and So-Called Physiological Facts

First, some preliminary remarks regarding two possible objections to our view of the functioning of the organism or of the nervous system. At the outset, our conception requires a justification, inasmuch as it does not consider the customary hypothesis that the performances are the expression of certain physico-chemical processes. Certainly, in a complete theory of the organism, we must also take these processes into account. However, according to our view, they play no greater part than the other phenomena but are only coordinated with them. At the present stage of the theory, they are actually without specific significance. True, we talk of excitation, of configuration of excitation, and we attempt to develop pertinent laws for normal and abnormal conditions. But we do not presuppose anything regarding the nature of physical or chemical processes. This is not done without a purpose and requires justification.

What is usually understood by physico-chemical or physiological investigation and theory is by no means unequivocal. The approach that is attempted by present-day physiology, and that is regarded as the ideal, is to examine the organism by physical and chemical methods and to form a concept of the functioning of the organism on the basis of results thereby obtained. Such investigations are usually called physiological, and thus one contrasts research of physico-chemical processes within the living organism with investigations of physico-chemical processes outside the organism. A theory, formed on the basis of physico-chemical investigation, probably enjoys such great esteem because it is based on the extreme exactness of results obtained by this method and also because one believes that this method can convey a particularly direct insight into the events in the living substance. Of course, there are authors to whom it is a foregone conclusion that life processes can ultimately be resolved into physico-chemical processes and to whom the failure of this explanation of the biological process is only due to the incompleteness of our present state of research. Therefore, these authors maintain, the physico-chemical investigations provide the only incontestable material no matter how incomplete it may be at present. Also, those who do not believe that life can be comprehended by physico-chemical methods regard the physico-chemical facts solely as the necessary fundament from which an understanding of the functioning of the organism must ultimately arise, even if additional factors have to be included. This entire view seems problematic to us, to say the least, because it could be questioned whether anything at all that will clarify the performances of the organism can be discovered by this method. Could not the application of physico-chemical methods possibly mean, in principle, such a destruction of the organism (cf. p. 104), and could not the onset of the experiment alter the activity of the organism in such a way that we always obtain a modification of its normal functions that deviate irreparably from the normal processes? In that way will we ever be able to understand the normal functions, whatever correction we may introduce? Can this method teach us more than something concerning certain prerequisites for the course of normal activity, the knowledge of which may be of great importance for certain practical questions (as, e.g., for the purpose of influencing the processes)? Can it really teach us something about the functioning of the organism? Is it not altogether a mistake to talk about physiological facts where it would be more correct to say that we are dealing with physics and chemistry applied to a living object, but not with a physical and chemical research of life processes? But aside from these arguments, because of the holistic concept of the function of the organism here presented, we must reject the assumption that in this way processes in the organism can be grasped directly.

Even those authors who are not very hopeful regarding the direct physico-chemical approach to the nervous system still claim that, for functional analyses, they regard the physiological method as the only firm foundation by which to obtain laws governing the processes in the organism. In this sense, Constantin von Monakow has spoken of physiological phenomena in contrast to psychological ones.[10] To attain a conception of localization in the cerebrum, he fights strongly against starting from psychological data and repeatedly emphasizes that only "physiological" considerations can lead to the goal. He certainly did not have in mind physico-chemical research on the nervous substance but analysis of bodily phenomena. The procedure of many physiologists, for instance, Ivan Pavlov and others, is quite similar. J. Stein, in particular, with his presentation of the pathology of perception, has in principle refused all attempts to derive a conception of physiological processes from psychological events.[11] In his opinion such procedure, which deals only with physiological processes, imagined as parallel, is not physiology (see p. 112). Although the results of phenomena analysis might yield material for the exploration of separate physiological realms, they will never lead directly to a physiological theory, according to Stein. The physiology of excitation, or another branch of physics, would have to decide whether the modification of a sensation under constant stimulation can be explained by a characteristic change of excitability or of the course of excitation and so on. According to the special value Stein ascribes to the method of chronaxie, physiology means to him results obtained by an electrical method. We mention in particular Stein's view because it seems to us to be paradigmatic for a conception of the term "physiological" that is different from what we have first characterized. This kind of physiology is believed capable of coming closer to an understanding of the processes in the organism through the physical — especially the electrical method — than would be possible through a simple analysis of behavior, be it somatic or psychic. But even the authors who advance this point of view are overlooking the fact that in these findings, for example, in chronaxiemetric findings, we are by no means dealing with direct manifestations of the activity of nervous substance or the course of excitation but only with expressions of the nervous system or of the organism under specific conditions, namely, under the definite demands as are exerted by stimulation through the electric current. They overlook the fact that the laws of the course of excitation in the organism, which they have thus derived, represent only inferences from experimentation. These "physiological facts" do not furnish a direct representation of the functioning of the nervous system. They do no more than any performance analysis, for example, the experimental analysis of a course of movement, or of a certain behavior act, or of any psychological performances. True, Stein in another place refuses to base the concept of sense perception on such a procedure as the chronaxie method: "It cannot be the objective of depicting the excitation process and comparing the stimulus event with the phenomenon of sensation, to refer simply to the action currents (as important as it may be to make visualizable by the action current, certain processes underlying sensory excitations); but in no way can the content of the sensory experience be understood thereby." According to Stein, this would represent nothing but a return to Gustav Fechner in the hope of finding a parallelism. At this point we completely agree with Stein and merely consider it inconsistent that he rejects this view for the understanding of sensory experiences, while at the same time attributing such fundamental significance to the results of chronaxie. Granted the fact that they are particularly valuable, because they are suited to take the so important time factor into account, yet in principle they in no way differ from other electro-physical experiments on the organism.

I cannot see why, on the basis of chronaxie investigations, we should arrive, in principle, at a better understanding of the course of excitation in the nervous system than through the analysis of other performances. After all, we are also dealing, in these experiments, with performance experiments. On the basis of Stein's objection, the usefulness of such experiments for the determination of the course of excitation in the nervous system would have to be rejected, just like others. Such investigations would lose their value for those who hope to be able to determine directly the course of excitation during the activity of the nervous system. But it is indeed a question whether such a determination is at all possible or whether the only possible way is not the analysis of the performances. In that case, of course, men like Stein would have to renounce any attempt to gain a concept of the activity of the nervous system, that is, to study "physiology," if one understands under physiology the sum of phenomena obtained by certain methods, for example, the physical or chemical method. Life processes can be conceived properly only when this understanding is derived from the investigation of performances. We have already seen how much we can learn, by such investigations, about the function of the organism. Later on we shall show how far it will take us on the road to a proper understanding of the nature of the organism.

The investigations by Stein demonstrate that the electro-physiological methods do not actually achieve any more than the "phenomenal analysis" (if we take this expression in the wide sense in which it means the description of kinds of behavior). The chronaxie investigations, so to speak, confirm the findings that the investigations of perception have yielded. Even regarding the functional significance of time in the course of excitations, one can draw such conclusions equally well from these investigations as from chronaxie investigations. One of the most valuable facts determined by Stein, namely, the lability of threshold under pathological conditions, was, after all, discovered prior to the application of the chronaxie method. Laws that Stein has formulated on the basis of his findings have been found similar to those obtained through the psychological analysis of the performances, that is, by a method totally different from Stein's. He points out that the assumed importance of the time factor may arise from my investigations, as a postulate, and that it achieves a physiological foundation only through the facts explored with the chronaxie method, which he has published. I cannot at all concede this, but rather believe that neither he nor I have checked directly, by physiological methods, the functional significance of the time factor. Stein writes: "If the chronaxie is increased, then tachistoscopically presented stimuli lead to sensations only if the exposure-times are long enough to correspond to the degree of increasing chronaxie."[12] But one can say just as well: "If one finds a disturbance of tachistoscopic vision and discovers that the possibility of visual performances is dependent on an increased exposure time, one can conclude that the chronaxie values are increased."

We see that both methods of investigation yield the same results, namely, disturbed performances; and the analysis of these "performances" by either method permits us to predict how tests with the other method will turn out in a certain respect. Neither one is any better than the other, except that the chronaxie-metrical investigation is more precise in administration and offers the possibility to represent results more clearly. Hence, both methods can only corroborate each other by their results, but neither one can of itself bring us nearer to the real processes than the other. I quite agree with Stein that it is not possible to arrive through psychological findings at a theoretical understanding, in the sense of physics and chemistry. But one can very well arrive, in this way, at a theoretical understanding, in the sense of "physiology," if one considers such findings, as the chronaxie investigations show, as "physiological." Everybody will probably agree with Stein that such findings should be considered physiological ones. We shall refer again later on to this question of the relation between psychology and physiology (cf. pp. 261f.).

The compatibility of our theory with the anatomical facts
Every theory of the functioning of the organism must be such that it can be brought into accord with the known anatomical facts. However, the question arises: What really are these facts? Things are not as simple as they seem on the basis of the usual presentations. Today it is no longer necessary to prove that the neuron theory, which provides such a good anatomical basis for the functional course of the reflexes, is not an established fact, if we regard the fibrils as the conducting constituents of the nervous system. Even by assuming the fibrillar structure of the nervous system, the relation of the parts to one another is by no means stated in unequivocal terms. I recall that the argument is not yet settled whether the endings (telodendrones) of the neurons are only in contact with each other (at the synapse) or whether a direct continuity exists. Likewise here it depends on the method of investigation, how the "facts," the anatomical structure of the nervous system, present themselves to us. Also on this point, we depend on the evaluation of symptoms that in turn depend on the way the questions are raised – on the method used. How do we know to what extent the structures which have been explored are not artifacts? Even the existence of the fibrils, as they are described in histological preparations, has been doubted in the living organism (Leopold Auerbach); and writers such as Max Verworn, Mihäly Lenhossek, and Goldschmidt are inclined to regard the fibrils only as supporting tissue. We can doubt altogether that the anatomic structures described in histology are at all essential for the functioning of the nervous system. One could ask whether the functioning elements of the nervous system are really the so-called neurons. One may be justified in stating that this generally adopted view is probably not correct in its exclusiveness. Aside from the problem of the methodological dependency in examining these structures, there remain other questions: What is the functional significance of the gan-

glia and of the various other structures, and what significance may have to be attributed to the fluid parts of the nervous system that so far could not be represented as structures? Conrad Rieger warns against an over-rating of the "solidum," as compared with the "liquidum," in our quest for processes in the brain that are equivalent to the functional phenom-ena.[13] As long as all these questions cannot be practically answered, all theories of the functioning of the nervous system, based on the so-called anatomical facts, are of very problematic character — a fact we must always bear in mind. Actually, anatomy cannot supply a completely firm basis for the theory of nervous function. However, it is to be under-stood that a theory of the functioning of the nervous system should attempt to do justice to the anatomical facts, as we know them at pres-ent. The theory that we present here, is compatible throughout with the prevailing anatomic evidence.

If our theory is correct, if it provides a true picture of life in the nervous system, it will help to determine which of the structures, represented by the various methods, are the actual ones, that is, which are best suited to reveal a material foundation for the course of the func-tion. From this point of view, the conception represented by the fibril theory seems to us to be the most adequate for the time being. How-ever, we must keep in mind that this theory does not necessarily state that the excitation takes its course in or by way of the fibrils. Possibly the fibrils have only the function of facilitating the connection of the various parts of the nervous system so that they may act as functionally unifying apparatuses.[14]

CHAPTER FOUR

Modification of Function Due to

Impairment of the Organism

If we wish to understand the nature of part processes, the best approach is the study of phenomena found in diseased persons. Here we are dealing with performances that take place in isolated parts, because all damage severs parts from the organism, or to put it more precisely, divides the organism into parts. A circumscribed injury to the neural substratum modifies the excitation process in two ways: (1) by directly affecting the functioning of the substratum concerned and (2) by isolating the excitation spread in one part from the excitation in the rest of the nervous system.

The "Dedifferentiation" of Functioning in the Impaired Substrate
Since the excitation process in the organism represents an organized whole, these two types of effects will not be independent of each other, and we can separate them from each other only by proceeding somewhat artificially. But even though the principle of functional disturbance is always the same, one can observe different phenomena, for the injury sometimes predominantly affects the substratum itself; at other times it chiefly affects the substratum's relation to the rest of the organism. This expresses itself in different changes in performance, inasmuch as some modifications of performance are caused more by the damage of the substratum itself, while others occur in the isolation of the connection between the substratum and the whole of the nervous system.

Impediment and retardation of the excitation process. Defective equalization. Abnormal stimulus bond. "Dedifferentiation" toward greater homogeneity
We may assume that the injury of the substratum, which always means a loss of ganglion cells, affects those events that we have learned exist

through the interposition of the ganglia. This will lead to encumbrance and retardation of the course of excitation, to a dedifferentiation in structural organization, and finally to a defective equalization. It rarely happens that an injury is so severe as to suspend the functioning of one field completely. We seldom deal with a total destruction of the substratum but rather with cases in which functional disturbances appear that manifest themselves in modifications of the performances. A short survey now follows of the symptoms as they appear in lesions of various parts of the nervous system, with an attempt to explain their respective functional disturbances.

When a substratum, which is directly stimulable by the outer world, is injured, when, for example, a sensory area is injured, we find a raised threshold (e.g., of visual acuity); this means that responsiveness is reduced, requiring stronger stimulation, and at the same time is retarded. In this condition, increased intensity and duration of stimulation may still lead to normal or even to abnormally strong and lasting sensations due to retarded equalization (as in the case of "blinding"). The dedifferentiation shows itself in the reduced differential threshold, lowering of visual acuity, vagueness or diffusion of contours, and defective localization of stimuli. The dedifferentiation also shows itself in defective power to differentiate between qualities (e.g., a reduction of color perception in the sense of red-green blindness or even a lowering to such an extent that only black-and-white sensation is retained). We find corresponding phenomena in the motor field and in the field of reflexes, in the latter not infrequently in the form of diminution.

In this case, functional disturbance usually affects performances of circumscribed areas of the body. To what extent this disturbance of performance actually impedes the behavior of the damaged organism can only be understood if we consider it in the light of the whole organism (cf. our discussion of disturbances in calcarine lesion, p. 57).

In the peripheral areas, severance from the rest of the organism does not play such an essential role compared with direct injury of the substrata. In centrally located injuries, however, isolation from the rest of . the organism is very important.

The effect of isolation
In many symptoms we are dealing principally with the effect of isolation. Isolation creates essentially the same changes that we have

mentioned above. In addition to dedifferentiation, we find changes of performance due to modification of the reactions. These modifications take the form of abnormal stimulus bonds, "forced responsiveness" – abnormally strong effect of the stimuli, abnormal dependency on the quality of the stimulus, and extension of the stimulus effect with respect to space and time, and so on. Finally, we find a particularly strange and apparently contradictory phenomenon, which becomes intelligible if we appreciate the effect of isolation properly: the phenomenon of alternation between opposite reactions. Under certain circumstances, we have an abnormal perseveration and under other circumstances a great lability, that is, the reaction alternates between opposite extremes.

Dedifferentiation Exemplified by Phenomena of Lesions in Various Parts of the Nervous System

Symptoms of isolation in the spinal cord

When the spinal cord is cut at any level, we find, as the direct effect of damage to the substratum, the loss of certain performances that are "localized" at the level of the damage, such as reflexes, sensitivity, and so on. We find as the result of isolation a reduction of the threshold of excitability of the proprioceptive reflexes. The patellar reflex may be elicited from zones that are normally not reflexogenous or by otherwise subliminal stimuli. We find furthermore an increased reaction, abnormal duration of the movement, and permanent spasms (in the muscles, in consequence of defective equalization). In the Babinski phenomenon, we have at the same time a particularly good example of the effect of the dedifferentiation in a specific field, namely, the motor field.[1] For this reason, we want to discuss this fact more carefully.

Explanation of the Babinski phenomenon as the effect of dedifferentiation of motor performance. The nature of flexion and extension performances

Usually this phenomenon is regarded as the result of a disinhibition of the dorsal flexion that is supposed to represent in human beings an inhibited reflex response to the stimulation of the sole and a meaningful reflex in animals. We reject this interpretation first of all because of the meaningless concept of inhibition. Further, the phylogenetic interpretation has been rendered very improbable in the light of recent facts.

Investigations on the plantar response in animals, especially in monkeys and apes, conducted by Fulton and Allen D. Keller, have shown that the Babinski phenomenon is not the characteristic reaction in monkeys to plantar stimulation and that it does not occur in them under normal or pathological conditions.[2] These facts speak directly against the phylogenetic explanation of the phenomenon. Moreover, it seems possible to arrive at an intelligible explanation of the phenomenon without the hypothesis of disinhibition. Therefore, an analysis of the Babinski sign may be useful and at the same time give us an opportunity to comment on the problem of reflex reversal in general.

The difference between the normal plantar response and that occurring in lesions of the pyramidal tract consists, apart from the "fanning" of the toes, in the fact that the normally occurring plantar flexion of the big toe is changed to an extension, that is, dorsal flexion. We explain this "reversal" of reaction by a change in the relation of the distribution in excitability between flexor and extensor. The stimulus, always spreading diffusely, becomes effective and leads to reactions where the threshold of excitability is lowest. Normally, the greatest excitability is to be found in the flexor muscles. Investigations of chronaxie leave no doubt that in lesions of the pyramidal tract we are actually dealing with such a reversal of the ratio of excitability between flexors and extensors. While normally the chronaxie of the flexor is lower than that of the extensor, the opposite is now the case.[3] Thus, both the normal plantar reflex and the Babinski are explicable on the same principle, namely, by the relation between the excitability of the muscles and their response to stimulation. How does a lesion of the pyramidal tract produce this change of the normal ratio of excitability?

To answer this question we must briefly discuss the cause of the normal excitability ratio. The reversal will then prove to be the expression of the dedifferentiation of the motor performances of the organism, in consequence of the impairment of cortical function.

Sensitiveness of a muscle group facilitates the reaction of the group to stimulation. This is significant for fulfillment of the task the organism is set for in a given situation, because it guarantees the exact activity of these muscles. The normally greater sensitivity of the flexor muscles is thus an expression of their greater significance for carrying out the most important activities of the human being, the voluntary actions (see p. 365). From this it becomes understandable that, for both, for voluntary actions as well as for innervation of flexor muscles, the brain cortex is of paramount significance.[4]

The reversal of the excitability ratio between flexors and extensors corresponds to the diminution of voluntary actions in damage of the cortical motor system and the coming to the fore of automotive reactions that are performed in particular by extensor movements related to activity of the subcortical motor system.

In damage of the cortical motor system the organism is no longer able to adjust itself to previously normal stimuli; they now represent a danger. Therefore the organism reacts to them with protective automatic defense or flight reactions. Which of them becomes dominant depends on the particular locus of lesion of the motor system.[5]

In pyramidal tract lesions, flight reactions to stimulation of the sole show in withdrawal of the whole leg. In human beings the withdrawal may represent itself only in a rudimentary form, namely, in an isolated dorsal movement of the big toe, while in animals a withdrawal of the whole leg, even the whole body, occurs. In other words, animals react with a greater part of the body; human beings, only with an isolated movement. This difference becomes understandable if one compares it with the difference of the structure of the motility in general between animals and human beings. The more an organism is conditioned to react with highly specialized movements, the more also its flight reactions will consist of more isolated movements of the leg or only of the big toe in stimulation of the sole, instead of a general withdrawal. The flight reactions occur as isolated movements chiefly in the highest organisms in which isolated movements physiologically play an important role in general.[6]

Hence we come to the result: the Babinski phenomenon is to be understood as an expression of the change of the excitability ratio because of a dedifferentiation of the motor system that brings flight reactions and, with them, sensitivity of extensor muscles abnormally to the fore. It becomes evident that we cannot consider the phenomenon a reversal of the normal plantar response to stimulation of the sole, which is an essentially different reaction, namely, a rudiment of a voluntary grasping.

The normal plantar reflex and the Babinski phenomenon thus represent different forms of the organism's coming to terms with a stimulus (in this case plantar stimulation) under different conditions of the whole organism.

In viewing the Babinski phenomenon as a flight reaction, we are in accordance with a number of authors who have studied it. We deviate from them only in seeing in the occurrence of the flight reaction not the effect of a disinhibition of a primitive mechanism, as some of them do, but a kind of reaction that prevails in a damaged organism, corresponding to the greater danger in which the organism lives and against which it protects itself by this kind of reaction. By damage we mean the isolation of the stimulated part from the cortical influence, which entails impairment of the proper utilization of the stimulus.

From our discussion we may draw the following general conclusion. To each performance belongs a specific distribution of excitability in the nervous system. To performances in a certain state of dedifferentiation a definite change of distribution of the excitability corresponds. If a stimulus becomes effective, it is responded to by a reaction commensurate with the excitability predominant in that state of dedifferentiation. Thus we see, under normal conditions, a dominance of flexor performances in cortical stimulation, a higher chronaxie in the flexor muscles than in the extensors, and, finally, a flexor movement in stimulation of the sole. We find in a lesion of the pyramidal tract, to wit, a dedifferentiation of the motor system of a definite kind, concomitantly with the predominance of flight reactions, a distribution of excitability that shows itself in the lowered chronaxie of the dorsal flexors as well as in the appearance of the dorsal flexion (extension) in plantar stimulation – the Babinski phenomenon. Thus, neither one of the responses to plantar stimulation, be it the normal or the pathological, represents a reflex or a disinhibited reflex; both represent the different ways in which the organism, under different conditions, utilizes the stimulus: The so-called reversal of reflexes is not really a reversal of a fixed reaction, but in both phenomena, the "reflex" and the "reversal," we are dealing with different performances that have nothing to do with each other.

The difference expresses itself in two different movements in reaction to the same stimulus, movements opposite in kind, because by the change of conditions (in the case of Babinski through a definite pathology in the motor system) the ratio of excitability in antagonistic regions has become reversed for reasons we have already explained.

Further analysis would show that, as the Babinski phenomenon is an expression of a definite dominance of flight reaction and of a corresponding distribution of excitability, defense reactions are explainable on the same principle, another kind of dedifferentiation that goes along with another distribution of excitability.

Other phenomena in plantar stimulation due to isolation by disease
If our assumption is correct, namely, that the cause of the Babinski phenomenon is a reversal of the conditions of excitability, we would expect to obtain the dorsal flexion of the big toe when conditions are changed by factors other than lesions of the pyramidal tract.[7] On the other hand, even in lesions of the pyramidal tract the Babinski phenomenon must disappear if, owing to yet other conditions, the relation of the excitability between flexor and extensor is changed in favor of the flexor.[8] Both assumptions can be proved by facts.[9] We know that dorsal flexion occurs in plantar stimulation if the plantar flexion is damaged alone or damaged to a greater degree than the dorsal flexion in cases of peripheral paralysis, paralysis of the sciatic nerve, or in lesions of the anterior horn having specific localization. In these cases, the reaction to the plantar stimulus can be almost exactly like the "genuine" Babinski sign.[10] We know, furthermore, that in lesions of the pyramidal tract, dorsal flexion disappears or changes into plantar flexion, if we modify the relation of excitability in the flexor extensor field of the big toe by changing the posture of the leg (flexion in hip and knee), of the body (ventral position), or of the head (Walsh). These facts of so-called reflex change, which have been considered merely as curiosities, can be properly understood if one regards them from the point of view here represented.

Abnormal excitation spread under isolation
Let us now consider additional phenomena evidencing the effect of the isolation of parts of the spinal cord. Abnormal spatial diffusion of the stimulus is seen not only in an increase of the area that becomes receptive (as we have mentioned already) but also in the wider spreading of the effect in the motor field. There is no longer a functional relationship between a definite stimulus and a definite muscle area. In other words, the motor figure formation, necessary for a definite performance that corresponds to a certain stimulus, has suffered. Many parts that were formerly background now become figure. The distinction between figure and ground becomes less articulate, consequently the plantar stimulus may be followed, sometimes by a dorsal flexion of the toes,

sometimes by withdrawal of the entire leg. Animal experiments have shown quite different results when the stimulus was applied to one or to both legs. Until now, however, no uniform explanation of these differences has been reached. According to our view, this is quite understandable. When one leg is stimulated, it depends on the "strength of the stimulus"[11] whether flexion or extension occurs. When the stimulus is weak we obtain extension of the stimulated leg; when strong, a flexion – while we may find, simultaneously, an opposite movement in the other leg. Whether the same reaction takes place in both legs or whether an alternating reaction occurs, also depends on the stimulus strength. When the stimulus is weak, extension results in both legs; when it is stronger, flexion results, but only ipsilaterally. We find the same phenomenon when the nervous system is injured through asphyxia.[12] In these cases, uniform movements are preferred to alternating ones. Finally we must mention that alternating reactions appear more readily in the decapitated than in the decerebrated preparation: in the latter, we usually find tonic reactions (Sherrington). How can all these phenomena be understood under one principle?

Let us consider certain facts that they all have in common and try to understand them.

1. The weaker the excitation, either because of weakness of the stimulus or because of injury of the substratum, the more do homogeneous and ipsilateral reactions preponderate. We obtain the homogeneous reaction because the alternating reaction corresponds to a more complicated figure, and because the reactions become more homogeneous through dedifferentiation (cf. p. 134). We obtain the one-sided ipsilateral reaction, because this reaction, on the nearer side (i.e. ipsilateral), is a simpler one, on account of the stronger near-effect.

2. Weaker stimuli lead to an extensor reaction, and stronger stimuli lead to a flexor reaction, because the extension is simpler. It is more automatic. In cases of decerebration and cerebellar disturbances, the extensor reactions predominate, for the spinal cord acts as a sort of extensor pulley (cf. p. 119). We can say that, as one last remaining adjustment in a stage of severe dedifferentiation, only the equalization of the stimulus is still possible, but no further utilization of it. In this case that means extension, "turning to the stimulus." In this same way, all varying reactions can be understood without having to assume disinhibition, reciprocal innervation, and so on.

The alternating reactions. Rigidity and lability in the figure-ground
process as expression of isolation of an apparatus
Not infrequently one finds in cases of cross-section lesions that the plantar stimulus is responded to by alternating movements of both legs,
which resemble "walking movements." We regard them as indications of
the lowered stability of the figure formation and the resulting increased
lability of the processes. This phenomenon seems to be particularly well
suited to illustrate the nature of lability.

One might be tempted to explain these alternating movements by
positing that the isolation of the spinal cord causes a stagnation of excitation and with it an excitation of performance fields in the spinal cord,
which normally would not respond to the plantar stimulus, that is, of
that part of the mechanism of "walking movements" that is located in
the cord. Such a theory, by the way, would not necessarily require the
premise that walking corresponds to a spinal pattern or that "walking
centers" are located in the spine. Later, in discussing localization, we
shall see how unjustified, in general, is the assumption of such centers.
But this entire explanation is not necessary and actually does not suit
the data. Closer observation shows that the alternating movements
resemble walking movements only very superficially. If the preconceived
opinion that these were walking movements had not actually retarded
an adequate investigation, the difference between these two phenomena would have stood out immediately. Leaving this attempt at explanation aside, we may ask, What causes these alternating movements?
We can understand them best if we consider them in connection with
other reactions. In some cases, the plantar stimulus is followed by a
flexor reaction that may even become fixed in a spasm of variable tension and duration. In other cases, an extensor reaction takes place. In
still other cases, stimulation of one plantar causes the flexion of the
stimulated leg and the extension of the other leg. In all these reactions,
we are dealing with various abnormal near effects that, because of isolation, manifest themselves in various symptoms, depending on the differences in the locus of isolation relations.

We have already shown that a certain ground process accompanies
each figure process. In performances of the normal organism, the total
organism forms the background against which the figure process, taking place in a circumscribed area, stands out. But the entire organism
does not form the background in a homogeneous way. In the execu-

tion of a movement the "ground process," in the rest of the motorium, is probably more closely related to the figure process than the processes in the rest of the organism at large. But the whole system always participates to some extent. In the same way, the equalization process involves the whole organism, but here too, those parts of the system nearer to the actual figure-ground process are more intimately concerned. In this sense, the ground process in the relatively circumscribed parts (in our example, the motorium) is set off, so to speak, as secondary figure against the rest of the organism as ground.

But the stimulus reaction changes, if it takes place in relatively isolated parts of the system. As a matter of fact, we then observe either an abnormal perseveration and rigidity of the figure, as in the case of spasm, or an abnormal alternation between opposing phenomena. The following examples show that this alternation of phenomena is really related to the course of the excitation process, in a part that is relatively isolated from the whole. We can expose our visual apparatus to relatively isolated stimuli as in the so-called afterimage experiments, where we allow a color to act intensively on our eye. In that case, we obtain, on the one hand, an abnormal aftereffect, but, on the other hand, a repeated change of opposite color sensations. Or take a similar phenomenon in the motor field, as in the so-called Kohnstamm experiment. If, with the arm hanging loosely, one presses the hand against the wall so that the deltoid muscle is strongly innervated, and then gives the arm free space for movement, one experiences the arm rising by itself. This phenomenon is particularly striking if the subject pays as little attention to the arm as possible, thereby isolating it. If one succeeds in this isolation, one experiences an alternating movement, the arm rising and falling several times. Similar observations can be made following experimental stimulation of the labyrinth: nystagmus or "arm tonus reactions," induced by stimulation in the labyrinth.[13] Other phenomena of a similar nature are the so-called induced tonus phenomena,[14] the nystagmus-like oscillation of seen objects, which one can normally produce through a cold stimulus on one side of the neck, and other phenomena.[15] All these are cases in which the excitation takes its course in relative "isolation." The subjective experiences support the assumption of the isolation of each of these processes from the whole. We feel that these events take place almost against our will. While they occur in our body, we have really nothing to do with them. The isolation becomes particularly clear if we succeed in bringing one of the phenomena in closer relation to ourselves. Then the character of lability disappears, or at least decreases strongly. The event gains definiteness and stability. If, for example, we ask a patient with nystagmus to fixate on an object, then the nystagmus is reduced.

The phenomenon that interests us here becomes particularly clear if we look at ambiguous figures, for example, in the well-known drawing of Edgar Rubin.[16] Depending on our attitude, one or other part of the total configuration becomes the foreground, and accordingly two entirely different figures can alternately arise. We may see either two dark faces on a light background or a light vase on a dark background. When we take a passive attitude toward the drawing and regard it purely as such, then a fluctuation between the figures becomes very pronounced (cf. p. 124). But the fluctuation decreases, and one figure becomes more constant, the more the entire organism participates in the activity of focusing on one or the other part of the drawing. This is also the case if we regard the figure not merely as a picture but try to perceive the faces or the vase as real objects. Not everybody succeeds in doing this, but if one does, the alternating fluctuation disappears almost completely. Perception of one part of the drawing as a real object can be facilitated by adding some lines which enhance the character of concreteness and vividness, as Mary R. Harrower has shown.[17] When this is done the phenomenon of lability is decreased, and no specific attitude is needed to yield a stable perception. Apparently, under normal conditions, any figure formation determined by a stimulus has the whole of the organism as its background. Excitation and equalization, as well as the utilization of other stimuli required by the task in their functional significance for the particular figure – all this takes place in a manner adequate to the total organism. If the figure formation loses its stability, though a defective articulation of the figure-ground relation in the whole, then the outer stimuli become abnormally effective, in an inadequate, "random" fashion. If they are very strong, an abnormal fixation of one figure results. If such a stable figure cannot be formed, either a disturbance or disorder sets in; or the "ground" processes will press forward, become figure, and consequently performances will occur that correspond to the ground process. This second alternative may take place when the effective stimuli are more adequate to the ground process and therefore influence it directly so that the ground process undergoes a stimulus increase in an abnormal way. Thus we may find a permanent and abnormal perseverance of the ground, or an alternation between figure and ground, which we shall encounter in many other phenomena.

This figure-ground relationship explains the appearance of lability as such but not the appearance of directly antagonistic performances; for example, in vision, why is the after image red and green, or black and white, and so on, and in the motor field, why does an "antagonistic" movement appear in the place of the "agonistic"? These phenomena can be understood in this way: in those performances that involve the entire organism, the contents of figure and ground differ widely. This means that the change does not involve a directly opposite phenomenon. However, the more the figure-ground process is restricted to smaller areas, the more do the local effects become similar, representing opposite stages of one and the same process. For this reason, we obtain the above-mentioned aftereffects in the visual field, of green after red, of black after white, and the antagonistic reactions in the motor field, and so on. Now, if lability occurs in a circumscribed section of that sort, it must manifest itself in the alternation of opposite reactions. We find this situation particularly in the pathological or experimental isolation of certain parts. Therefore, alternating flexor and extensor movements occur if the spine is transected. Let us assume that at first the stimulus produces a flexion of the ipsilateral leg, because the situation favors this (cf. p. 122). To this movement there also belongs, under certain circumstances, an extensor movement of the other leg as a functional near effect. This figure, however, is unstable. A reversal takes place; the ground that is formed in the ipsilateral leg, through the extensor, and in the opposite leg through the flexor, now becomes figure. Thus it is possible that the tension of the antagonist (which has become abnormal on account of the isolation) to some extent plays the role of the stimulus in bringing forward ground-process phenomena as figures. This abnormal tension permits the antagonistic figure to gain the upper hand for a while, until reversal again sets in. Thus, one, single, outer stimulus may produce alternating movements. Their continuation comes about through the abnormal processes that take place in the antagonist field simultaneously and that have the same effect as a new stimulus, until finally the relative equilibrium is regained.

Alternating processes and rhythmic performances
Our explanation seems to resemble that which Wilhelm Trendelenburg
has advanced for the crawling movement. Yet it is only a superficial similarity, since we regard the alternating movement not as a normal but as
an abnormal event. To us, the performance that corresponds to the normal, forward, stepwise movement is not only determined by the periphery, as the alternating movement is, but by the whole. Therefore, it
shows much less "exactness," because it depends on the total situation;
the walking movement changes and becomes irregular, as compared
with the machinelike promptness of the pathological "reflex" movement. Even a superficial inspection shows the careful observer that the
"alternating" abnormal movements have an entirely different character
from the normal rhythmic performances. Therefore, we may, at least
for the present, restrict our explanation to the pathological "alternating processes," differentiating them sharply from the "rhythmic performances" of the normal processes. In doing so, we agree with Graham
Brown who regards rhythm as a central phenomenon, not of the reflex
type.[18] We shall return to this subsequently, especially to the question
of whether these alternating processes might possibly have significance
for the rhythmic performances, and what this significance may be. Here
we are only interested in the fact that, under certain circumstances during application of one stimulus, alternating phenomena can be understood as the expression of a figure-ground process that has become
defective through isolation.

Symptoms of isolation in the cerebellum
Let us now consider several symptoms that appear, following the elimination of the function of the cerebellum.[19] In cases of disease of the
cerebellar cortex in men, characteristic symptoms have been found in
the form of the so-called deviation, the "past pointing," the tendency
to fall, and similar phenomena. Careful analysis leads one to reject the
assumption that this is the result of the loss of certain centers of coordination and equilibrium in the cerebellum. We are led, rather, to the
assumption that these are instances of abnormal stimulus reaction in
subcerebellar mechanisms, because of the loss of the cerebellar participation in the reaction. This becomes particularly evident if we take
into account the fact that the phenomena do not present an irregular
disturbance of equilibrium but a systematic change of certain perfor-

mances. These changes become intelligible if one regards them as the reactions of special apparatuses functioning in isolation from the cerebellum. The resulting performances show the specific characteristics due to isolation, namely, abnormal stimulus bond, abnormal aftereffect, and so on. As described elsewhere, cerebellar coinnervation of the subcerebellar motor mechanisms particularly favors the flexor and adduction movements. Through these flexor movements, the stimuli which act on the limbs from without and that otherwise would elicit abduction extension movements are checked (the "turning-to reaction"). These stimuli are not only kept in check, so that they cannot become effective independently of the total constellation, but are integrated with the latter. In this way it is possible for us to stand erect, keep one arm lifted forward, and so forth, without continuously and consciously counteracting the change of posture caused by the varying external stimuli. When this cerebellar coinnervation is impaired, the isolated subcerebellar mechanisms are exposed, to an increased degree, to the effect of peripheral stimuli. This manifests itself in one-sided lesions, through abnormal abduction and extension tendency in the limbs of this side, and so leads to a deviation of the stretched-out arm, to the tendency to pass pointing, and to similar phenomena.

The cerebellar symptoms, therefore, are the expression of a dedifferentiation of the motor performances of the organism, which manifests itself in a decay of the flexion and adduction and an increase of the extension and abduction performances. This form of dedifferentiation is intelligible only if one grasps the functional relation of these various performances to the whole organism.

There is scarcely another field of disease in which these effects of isolation can be so clearly seen as in diseases of the cerebellum. They are seen in the following symptoms: abnormal stimulus bond as indicated by the abnormal effect of all kinds of stimulation during movement of the body, abnormal effect of perception, attention, and bodily posture; the abnormal spreading of the stimulus effect (e.g., spreading through the entire body following stimulation on single parts of the body); the abnormal duration, in the lack of equalization (abnormal aftereffect of postures, movements, perceptions, in abnormal duration of assumed postures, and so on); the appearance of alternating reactions (induced tonus phenomena and sensory events); the dedifferentiation of the figure (the just-mentioned phenomenon); and the abnormal appearance of homologous phenomena in the form of abnormal, associated movements. (With reference to all these points, the summary mentioned on p. 127 may be consulted.)

Symptoms of isolation in the cerebral cortex
All the phenomena of direct injury to the substratum and of isolation appear equally clearly in cortical lesions, in the form of changes of the mental processes. From the extraordinarily large amount of available material, which can be found particularly in the publications quoted on pages 395ff., we want to mention only a few examples. Let us begin with the retarded effect of a stimulus, the well-known symptom of cortical diseases. Here, one speaks of retarded responsiveness, of a difficulty in assuming a psycho-physical set. We observe it in perception as well as in motility, thinking, and so on. It requires considerable time before a perception is consolidated. However, once a stimulus has produced an effect − has registered, so to speak − then the effect can become abnormally strong, indicating the stagnation of excitation in the circumscribed area, because of the isolation. At the same time, an increase of duration and a diffused distribution may occur over a larger area, the latter finding expression in a lack of precision in the figure formation. The abnormal radiation, in combination with imperfect differentiation, may be the reason a cutaneous stimulus is followed by an abnormally diffused sensation, which at the same time is incorrectly localized by the patient. It seems that the more circumscribed this sensation becomes, the less correct is the localization − as though the energy were not sufficient to enable the proper total figure formation to occur with the two necessary aspects: setting into relief and referring to a definite place. Sometimes, when one finger is touched, this sensation is localized at the correct place but on any of the fingers. This is not the result of a good figure formation in the finger that the patient indicates but of defective figure formation in general. Therefore, the patient is not sure whence the stimulus originated within the homogeneous area, which in this case is formed by all the fingers. Apparently, he experiences only that the stimulated point lies within this field. In the motor field, we know of defective differentiation (in the form of the so-called synkinesis); for example, stretching the index finger can only be achieved with simultaneous stretching of all the other fingers.

Defective figure-ground formation can manifest itself in various ways: in the leveling of the differences between figure and ground; in an impaired preciseness of the figure; in the appearance of performances that correspond to so-called "general" reactions; in a preponderant effect of the environmental stimuli on the figure formation; in the lack of stability and of closed configuration of the internal processes; in the formation of simpler figures that show impoverishment in content; in the instability of the figure, and therefore in a tendency to inversion of figure and ground; and finally in the uncertainty as to which is figure and which is ground. The latter will occur if individual stimuli become so abnormally intense that they drag along with them those processes ordinarily belonging to the ground.

The relative uncertainty or incompleteness of the functional evaluation of the stimulus shows itself, indirectly, in the fact that perceptions and imagery, which may be defective, can attain greater stability through prompting. A patient may suffer from fragmentary visual imagery so that only isolated pieces stand out, although with abnormal clearness. By the aid of a drawing, however, the figure may gradually be formed. Furthermore, an introduction of outer stimuli may improve the formation of images, or a certain motor process can be brought back into memory through the execution of a pertinent movement.[20] In the visual field, dedifferentiation shows itself in a simplification of the organized units, in the loss of characteristic peculiarities, and in the appearance of simpler patterns, as when a patient sees two parallel lines instead of a triangle. Many so-called illusions are based on such processes. Actually, the patient does not misapprehend but sees something else that he recognizes correctly, inasmuch as it is familiar to him; to us, this may appear as a complete misapprehension. Only by taking this factor into account do many such delusions of patients become intelligible. Not infrequently these changes of phenomena are erroneously attributed to fluctuations in attention or in similar "higher" functions. However, it is nothing but the change in the functional evaluation of stimuli, which we have met repeatedly, as the result of isolation. Examples of this, in cases of lesions in sensory fields, are the appearance of "threshold lability" in Stein's work and, in vision, a corresponding phenomenon in the form of the so-called annula scotoma of Goldstein and Gelb. One frequently makes the observation that definite performances can still be accomplished in definite situations, namely, where the whole organism participates more fully, but cannot be carried out if required under greater isolation, that is, less participation of the organism. This factor is of particular importance for the appreciation of behavior in animal experiments, because here it is more difficult to evaluate correctly the specific situation from which the animal's behavior arises. In human beings such an analysis is frequently very enlightening; a patient, for instance, may not be able to recall the numbers, but when he counts money, he can accompany this action with the appropriate "number words."

The impairment of figure formation may concern very different fields and attain different degrees. It may manifest itself in an inability to execute an isolated movement, in an inability to evoke images volitionally, in the impairment of the aforementioned categorical behavior, and in innumerable other phenomena.

Because of the isolation, certain figure formations may be of abnormal firmness and rigidity. This explains the strange observation that patients, in certain tasks, create the impression of performing abnormally well: patients, who are otherwise severely disturbed, may react in a simple reaction experiment with unusual promptness and regularity once they have "warmed up" to the task. We also find similar phenomena in animal experiments.[21] For example, the scratch reflex is executed more correctly and better by the spinal animal than by the normal. This unusual promptness is abnormal and is caused through isolation, which precludes interference by other stimuli that would otherwise influence the process and therefore make it more plastic and fluid. The impaired organism can be less susceptible to interfering stimuli that are alien to the given task. This abnormal bond to an action once set in motion could also be explained through the curtailment of energy. When the total energy is reduced, then the energy consumption in one part impairs and prevents the function of another part to a larger extent than is normally the case.

Abnormal distractibility and abnormal stimulus bond as expression of defective figure-ground events
Frequently we find abnormal alternations and abnormal bonds ("forced responsiveness") side by side. Analysis often reveals, with great clarity, the relation of both phenomena to the same defect, namely, to the impairment of figure-ground formation. As long as a "correct" performance has not been accomplished, the patient seems to be affected by

any stimulus, to be highly distractible, and to have difficulty in concentrating. By a correct performance we mean one in which the task is objectively fulfilled and the patient has the feeling of correctness. If we express this in terms of the physiology of excitation it means that the tension that the task creates has become equalized, that is, a stable figure has been formed. As soon as a good performance has been accomplished new stimuli no longer seem to be effective; the patient is inattentive with regard to them. If he is confronted with a new task, which he cannot perform, he keeps on repeating the old performance, he perseverates, as it is called. Our view explains why perseveration occurs so frequently after a good performance and why the patient cannot carry out subsequent tasks. It shows why the same patient can exhibit abnormal "fixation," and at the same time abnormal "distractibility." If no solution can be found that leads to the goal, that is, if no good (closed) figure takes place, then the organism remains restless. Any new stimulus can find access, because a disequilibrium of excitation still exists. Any new stimulus can usurp the excitation until a stable figure has been achieved.

CHAPTER FIVE

The Nature of Partitive Processes

What is a Reflex?

The reflex as expression of experimentally produced injury

Now that we have seen that reactions attain certain peculiarities when they occur in separate, more or less isolated parts of the organism, let us return to the findings of the experimental research we have already discussed. In the light of the experience gained from a study of pathological phenomena, we wish to examine particularly the reflex phenomena. Our main question is: What is a reflex? We shall start again with the example of the Babinski phenomenon. We have attempted to show above that in cases of lesion of the pyramidal tract the cortex is prevented from contributing to the functional utilization of the stimulus, that is, from influencing the reaction to the plantar stimulus. This makes the dorsal flexors outweigh the plantar flexors – the stimulus being more effective in the former, because under the prevailing circumstances their excitability is greater. We obtain a relatively isolated movement of the toes for two reasons: first because of the experimental arrangement and the demand imposed on the organism by the external stimulation and second because of the pathological condition. The latter prevents certain parts from participating in the reaction to the stimulus and thus pushes the normally relevant performances into the background. In this situation, the reaction of dorsal flexion remains the only functional utilization of the plantar stimulation. Dorsal flexion is the contraction of the muscles that are in the closest local relationship to the stimulus and hence respond most readily to it. Thus, we may state that the following factors determine the outcome of a reaction:

    1. The external milieu, that is, the environmental constellation

which constitutes the demands on the organism's reactivity, and the specific task it is confronted with (in our example, the experimental arrangement and the plantar stimulation)

2. The internal milieu, the condition of the organism (in our example, the pathological condition, resulting in altered distribution of excitability in the muscle groups concerned)

3. The potential reactivity present in that particular field through which the stimulus spread radiates by virtue of the internal and external milieu. Besides these three factors, a fourth must be considered, which is not so apparent in the case of the Babinski phenomenon.

4. The special quality of the stimulus and its particular effectiveness in the given situation, which is particularly marked in the variable effects of the so-called nociform stimuli referred to earlier, as well as in the different effect of weak or strong stimuli.

All this shows that in the reflex, so-called, we are dealing with a special type of coming to terms of organism and environment – a performance of the whole organism in a peculiar configuration, thanks to pathological or experimental causes. This explains immediately why such diversifying factors are determinative for the course of the reflex and why the total condition of the organism is decisive. As a rule, whenever one refers to an event that is confined to a separate part of the organism, one can do so only by disregarding the behavior of the rest of the organism; and then one is forced to make auxiliary hypotheses to explain all the variations of the part reactions. The facts, however, call for another interpretation: the reflex, just like any other reaction of the organism, must be understood as a response of the whole organism. The allegedly "isolated" phenomenon, which one alludes to by the term reflex, is in fact a "figure" in a reaction pattern of the whole organism. The "reflex" is the figure, while the activity of the rest of the organism is the background. This is clearly confirmed by the fact that any change in the remaining organism at once modifies the reflex, the figure.

The individual reflexes as sequelae of different forms of isolation
If, with this in mind, we survey the facts yielded by our study of the reflex, we come to a general conclusion implicitly grounded in our foregoing discussion. The reflexes and the reflex laws are an expression of the organism's reactions, when certain parts are isolated. The isolation is effected either by the artificial (experimental) elimination of the rest

of the organism that is not supposed to enter into the reaction or by the pathological segregation of single sections, through disease. There is a similarity between the experimental and the pathological phenomena, inasmuch as both have their origin in isolation.

The peculiarities of the reflexes find an explanation, if we regard them as the result of the "formal" change of the course of excitation in the isolated part. Abstractly, one may distinguish between formal changes and those of content, because of isolation. As formal changes, we can list the following:

1. The relatively circumscribed effect of a stimulus may be observed, if one artificially prevents the participation of the remaining organism, or if one disregards the events that do occur in it.

2. The relative constancy depends on the fact that further stimuli, beyond the one that releases the reflex, are prevented from becoming effective at the same time.

3. The exaggeration of the reflexes under pathological conditions, or in certain experimental situations, becomes intelligible if we regard it as the outcome of an abnormal stimulus effect in an isolated part (artificial subwhole) of the system. The same explanation accounts for the prolonged reaction that results from imperfect equalization; and it accounts as well for the greater spread of the reaction on the same side of the body, or for its appearance on the opposite side.

As changes of content we can indicate the following:

1. The modification of the content of the reaction is due to the fact that isolation causes other apparatuses to enter into the reaction. For example, peripheral influences or certain attitudes can become abnormally effective. These other apparatuses, entering into the reaction to a certain stimulus, may change its normal content completely.

2. Dedifferentiation causes a leveling of the reactions, that is, a greater homogeneity of the events in the whole organism, which homogeneity goes along with the spread of excitation over larger fields of the organism.

3. Because of defective figure formation, the individual events are less distinctly separated from one another and so induce each other more easily. This is normally prevented by the fact that the functional values of the individual events differ and that, depending on this difference in value, there will be participation of the rest of the organism to a greater or less degree in a given performance.

135

4. By virtue of the greater homogeneity of the processes it is possible, further, that stimuli that in themselves are not adequate for a reaction may exaggerate it. Conversely, a stimulus may hinder the progress of a reflex in action by releasing another reflex that becomes dominant.

So-called reflex reversal is actually not a reflex reversal. The reverse reaction has nothing to do with the former one. It is conditioned by a change of the inner situation, to wit, by isolation of other parts of the organism that makes the stimulus effective in those parts. Consequently, a change results in the functional value of the stimulus, calling for another performance (cf. flight reaction instead of normal reaction in the Babinski phenomenon).

The reaction to stimulation is always determined by the functional significance of the stimulus in that part of the organism within reach of the stimulus. In the intact organism this reaction is determined by the whole; in the injured organism, by the part that is relatively isolated.

In my opinion every phenomenon of known reflex activity can be explained from this point of view, provided sufficient data for examination are available.

The Meaning of the Reflexes

Proprioceptive reflexes as the expression of equalization —
the most primitive type of reaction
As we have seen, reflexes are not abstractions. In saying this, we are at variance with Sherrington, who, in accordance with his basic views on the functioning of the nervous system, regards them as such. The reflexes are certainly processes of a special kind, but since they take place within the organism, we are justified in asking what meaning they have, if any, for the organism.

Up to the present, only a few reflexes could be meaningfully related, in an integrated manner, to the activity of the organism. And the explanation of even these required very farfetched assumptions. For example, in order to explain the Babinski reflex, one had to assume a phenomenon that was meaningful for animals but that became inhibited in human beings.

We want to understand any reflex, or any of its modifications, as representing occurrences in the organism that are pertinent to a given situation. Furthermore, we want to determine whether or not we are dealing with a performance essential to the nature of the organism, whether it is "adequate."

Among the reactions of the organism, the constant ones, which are usually termed reflexes, merely represent a special class and do not differ from other reactions in principle. They are brought about by the fact that the situation causes such a dedifferentiation of the relevant substratum that only the most primitive reaction of living substance is possible, namely, the equalization process. In this state, the organism is capable of coming to terms with the stimulus only by the "turning-to" reactions. All simple reflexes can be explained in terms of this turning-to reaction.

Normally, this turning-to reaction is only the first stage of a more meaningful one. But even when it can only take place in isolation it is not meaningless, because it fulfills an important task for the organism. It brings about equalization and thereby, so to speak, removes or renders harmless stimuli that are disturbing the organism. From this point of view, we can understand the different reactions in starfish (ophiuroida) under the following experimental conditions: (1) the amputated arm of the ophiuroida turns toward the side on which the stimulus is applied; (2) when the position of the arm is changed, and thereby the muscles of the contralateral side are extended, the same stimulus is now effective on this side. This demonstrates that equalization takes place in both cases but expresses itself in different ways. The extension of the muscles on the contralateral side works as another stimulus, causing a release of a corresponding equalization tendency on this side and so making the first stimulus more effective here than on the side where it impinges. Thus, the stimulus reaching both sides produces an effect more readily in the extended (the contralateral) side, where equalization is more urgently needed. Moreover, this effect has to be regarded as even more significant because once a greater change in the contralateral side has been produced, our method of investigation may not even reveal the effect on the homologous side. But it has not been determined to what extent an effect on the stimulated side may be latent and thus possibly reduce the contralateral effect. In connection with this question it is noteworthy that the effect is by no means constant, since the arm sometimes swings toward the side of the stimulus as well. This apparently indicates that the local near effect (and with that, the equalization) may outweigh the effect on the opposite, more distant side. Apparently a competition takes place at times (cf. p. 224). Our explanation is supported by the fact that extension is usually followed by contraction, that is, equalization takes place.

According to what we have said, the patellar reflex, like all "proprioceptive reflexes," can be regarded as an equalization phenomenon. If one taps the patellar tendon of the quadriceps the muscle contracts because of the equalization of the tension, caused by the tapping. The stimulus probably reaches the flexors also and produces a contraction there (as in the work of Gollar and Joseph Paul Hettwer), but since the tension there is much less, so also is the effect.

Most reflex phenomena become intelligible if one understands them as an expression of this primitive type of meaningful response to a stimulus. In all pathological reflexes, and in all experimentally produced reactions that result from isolation, a mere "rendering the stimulus harmless" is all that is achieved. This is true even when the reactions involve large areas and appear to be very complex. Such behavior does not contribute much to the whole organism, and cannot, since it only represents an isolated functioning.

What is the role of the so-called reflex in a real performance? It might seem reasonable to suppose that, in abnormal tension of a muscle during a performance, reflexive contraction might furnish relief. But is one justified in assuming that, in normal, voluntary innervation, such a strong extension takes place that the differentiation of the central impulse is inadequate and that subsequent peripheral control is therefore required? This is hardly likely, in view of the fact that innervation undoubtedly occurs in accordance with the requirements of the milieu. Why should one expect the peripheral to have a finer differential threshold than the central process? If that supposed control were of this retroactive character, how would a differentially, really well articulated and smooth movement be possible? The idea of such retroactive control of a process, which has already been set going, is frequently adopted to explain quite diverse phenomena, but it seems to us to introduce an entirely unbiological principle. This idea implies, furthermore, the unproven and improbable presupposition of a primal separation between peripheral and central process. The central innervation of a voluntary movement involves a state of excitation in the muscles, as well as in other peripheral parts with a configuration, such that there is no need for correction by means of special peripheral processes. If for any reason a special tension, which does not belong to the performance, exists in the periphery, the central innervation changes in accordance with this inadequate condition of the whole system. Hence, the innervation centers around a certain mean.

Proprioceptive reflexes as expression of reactions in border situations

It is probable that those phenomena that correspond to the proprioceptive reflexes appear only when the muscle is relatively detached, in function, from the center. This may be the case in isolation through induced extension (as in reflex experiments) and possibly in certain danger situations. This leads us to a question of general importance for the understanding of reflex phenomena. The muscle can become relatively isolated from the center if, because of certain special environmental events, a tension in the whole system or in a part of it, occurs either above or below the average mean. This can happen either because the organism is not "prepared" for such an event or because it is not quite capable of coping with the changed situation. A muscle, for example, may be stretched by burdening it with a heavy object, and the organism may not be capable of reacting with a voluntary counterinnervation sufficient to keep the external pressure in balance. Or, the muscle may be burdened so rapidly that it cannot adjust itself to the changed condition. In these cases an abnormal extension of an isolated muscle can occur, and the proprioceptive reflex would then set in. An example, which Bethe suggests, is pertinent: in running down a mountain, the heel of the advanced leg first strikes the ground, then the extended muscles of the anterior side of the lower part of the thigh and the quadriceps become contracted. Should one explain this contraction as the effect of proprioceptive reflexes? Plausible though the explanation may seem, it cannot be correct. Actually, the contrary phenomenon can also be observed. For example, in another situation that Bethe describes, "if the toe of the foot gets caught behind a root or a stone, the muscles, just referred to, become suddenly extended. However, now they do not contract, but relax their antagonists, and the muscles, of the posterior part, contract strongly, in order to free the caught foot and prevent a fall." This is a very neat example; but here we are not dealing with a reflex. Here the essential features of reflex action – a definite stimulus and a definite reaction – are not to be found. Rather, this is a response that can be understood only as determined by the whole organism.

Hence one should not consider the contraction of the muscles of the advanced leg, in the first example, as the result of a reflex. Rather, both phenomena should be considered as reactions, which result from holistic utilization of stimuli, which vary when the stimuli appear in different total situations or, to put it differently, when they have a different meaning for the organism. Though Bethe presents this example to demonstrate the worthlessness of the usual reflex concept, he does not entirely relinquish its basic assumption. Questioning the stringent character of constancy of the reflexes, he tends to modify the concept by admitting a certain plasticity, an adaptability of that reaction to the given circumstances. But this leaves open the question of how this adaptation is determined. Bethe would like to relate this question to the principle of "gliding couplings" (cf. p. 90). In doing so, however, he refers almost exclusively to the sphere of external stimuli. Though we have no certain proof that in such danger situations we are really dealing with a sort of reflex reaction, we should here consider, seriously, the possible existence of it. If this be true, then the reflex would be a phenomenon that appears in a "border situation," that is, when a catastrophe is imminent. The necessary conditions for such border situations are (1) when a reflex is elicited in an experiment, which of course artificially eliminates possible counterinnervation, and with that prevents the subject from taking into account the "milieu," and (2) in normal life, if emergencies arise that we cannot foresee – then reflex reactions may appear.

Adaptation of this sort to certain milieu conditions that cannot be foreseen might take place through contraction as well as through tonic extension of the muscles. Thus, one could speak, as Viktor von Weizsäcker does, of the adaptive and compensatory effects.[1] But one must not interpret these terms as referring to phenomena of normal movement or posture. The milieu in which a movement normally occurs belongs initially to the nonconscious "plan" of the movement. Weizsäcker is quite right in saying that "the environment and the pattern of the environment is an image which, for all animals and man also, is the product of a passive-active, sensori-motor process of perception and knowledge." By analyzing a number of movements of my patients I was able to prove that the execution of movement is determined by the "milieu" that goes with the intended action.[2]

The meaning of the proprioceptive reflexes

Thus, in normal performances, compensations and adaptations that may be determined by the milieu will play a part only insofar as certain stimulus variations – which of course occur continually, even in a familiar milieu – can be utilized. This does not mean that such behavior must necessarily occur voluntarily, but it cannot occur in isolation from the holistic process of innervation and therefore does not require the action of special reflexes. Only in completely abnormal situations are such adaptation and compensation processes initiated in isolation. Characteristically enough, Weizsäcker, in an attempt to illustrate the operation of such special reflexes, has to take recourse to the example of a man walking over a newly plowed field in the dark. This is certainly a rather unusual situation, somewhat related to the conditions in reflex examinations, inasmuch as a relatively isolated activity of the cutaneous sense organs in the feet and legs is called into play. Perhaps, in such a situation, certain reflexes do become effective. But we also have evidence here only of so-called proprioceptive reflexes. To be sure, we include among the proprioceptive reflexes, insofar as the equalization process for individual performances is concerned, several phenomena that, according to the definition of Hoffmann, would have to be classified among the exteroceptive reflexes (cf. p. 142).[3] According to his definition, the criterion for the proprioceptive reflex is the close anatomical association of receptor and effector. But some of the reflexes, in which receptor and effector are anatomically separated, are certainly intimately akin to the proprioceptive reflexes, as, for instance, pupillary reaction to light. This response is related to the nature of proprioceptive reflexes, in the sense that abnormal wear and tear of the eye mechanism is avoided by the cutting down an abnormally strong light that would otherwise cause excessive visual excitation. It would perhaps be more correct to distinguish between proprioceptive and exteroceptive reflexes, not on the basis of their anatomical differences but rather on the basis of whether they are subservient to a self-regulative process within the organism or facilitate a direct adjustment to the environment. Although the various proprioceptive reflexes would not show the same excitation threshold, they would certainly have in common their major characteristics, presenting therein a clear contrast to the exteroceptive reflexes. The former are relatively simple in comparison to the latter, which involve more coordinations and are more variable in respect to the intensity of the stimulus, for example. All these features become intelligible when we realize that the exteroceptive reflexes are concerned with the more complicated stimulus configuration of events in the external environment.

Exteroceptive reflexes are performances, not reflexes
If we accept this differentiation between exteroceptive and proprioceptive reflexes, the question arises as to what bearing exteroceptive reflexes can have on normal performance. Weizsäcker, taking into consideration the fact that the latter can be released centrally, through cortical stimulation, as well as peripherally, is inclined to ascribe only a regulative function to them. But he is quite right in adding that this view raises a new question instead of providing an answer. I venture to predict that some day the term reflex will cease to be used in the description of all these so-called reflexes, as for example the scratch "reflex." These are real performances that also may possibly be aroused without the cerebrum. They are real reactions of the whole organism. In common with all other performances they undergo the regulating effect of the periphery. They are reactions of the whole – intelligible only in terms of the whole, and not in terms of the isolated stimulus, nor of the simple compensatory behavior represented in the proprioceptive reflexes. Through them the organism does something that is important for it as a whole, which aids its coming to terms with the environment. The exteroceptive reflexes are not embedded in performances, they are performances themselves.

At best, therefore, reflexes have little to offer toward the understanding of a normal performance. They may have significance in "border situations"; but the latter can certainly not form the starting point or basis for an understanding of normal performances. The phenomena connected with them are of a totally different nature, even to outward appearance. They lack the well-integrated character our other performances display. They are different, single performances occurring in sequence. The example of walking in the newly plowed field illustrates this. The conditions do not allow us to stroll naturally. On the contrary, our walking is rather imperfect and halting. Conversely, if we walk over familiar territory, not only is our walking better but it is entirely different. All this should go to prove that normal behavior is not composed of reflex processes.

*Reflex and equalization process as the simplest reaction
of living substance to stimuli*
With our view of reflexes in mind, we may ask, therefore, whether the
assumption of special reflexes is necessary at all, even in border situations. The process simply represents the general tendency to equalization toward the mean of excitation – its particular expression, on any
occasion, corresponding to the structure of the particular system that
is in disequilibrium. What we call the reflex is then only the tendency
of a relatively isolated part of the system to return to the preferred situation. The isolation may be caused by a sudden, intense stimulus. The
reflex thus represents nothing but the simplest possible reaction of the
living substance, namely, an equalization that is reached by turning
toward the stimulus. Obviously, the phenomena in border situations
cannot be offered as the explanation of normal functioning, since they
are the simplest catastrophic reactions and represent protection against
destruction. Neither is the organism's activity focused on any special
object, nor do these reactions convey any object content to the organism, as is the case in a performance. True, on the basis of normal functioning, the reflex can be explained as a modification of that functioning,
conditioned by circumstances – as the most primitive, meaningful
response supplying protection against destruction; but normal function
can never be explained on the basis of reflexes.

The "higher" organism exhibits more reflex phenomena than the lower
If the organism were so perfect that it could perform unhindered at
all times, we would never have an opportunity to observe reflexlike
phenomena. Since the optimal performance requires a complete integration, a perfect "centering" and adaptation of the organism to its environment, this can obviously be achieved only on rare occasions. Thus,
in normal life, reflexlike events have to occur quite frequently, but the
more an actual "centering" is achieved, the more do we find real performances, and the less frequently do "reflexes" appear. It is necessary
to carry this idea to its ultimate conclusion – which certainly is at variance with the traditional one:

The highest organisms, owing to the complexity of their organization and environment as well as to the difficulty of the required
adjustment, possess on the one hand a higher degree of centering; on
the other hand this centered organization, owing to its subtlety, is

more susceptible to environmental disturbances and border situations. Therefore, they manifest reflex behavior much more frequently than the lower organisms, which are very adequately embedded in their limited environment.

To be sure, this view is diametrically opposed to the usual one, which would regard the lower organisms as reflex machines and would even reduce the processes in a higher organism to the same mechanical basis. Another reason why reflexlike phenomena appear in the higher organism lies in the fact that these organisms are capable of producing artificial isolations in themselves. This may possibly apply only to humans. Human beings are able, by assuming a special attitude, to surrender single parts of their organism to the environment for isolated reaction. Usually, this is the condition under which we examine a patient's "reflexes." If, in examining a man's pupillary reflex, we obtain a relatively constant contraction of the iris, this is possible only because the individual, so to speak, surrenders his eye to us and completely foregoes the usual act of seeing, that is, the visual prehension of some environmental feature. Of course, it is true that in real vision the diameter of the pupil changes according to the amount of light on the seen object. But it certainly is not true that the same light intensity will produce the same contraction when it affects the organ in isolation (as in the reflex examination) and when it acts on the eye of the person who deliberately regards an object. Although it is not easy to prove this experimentally, one only needs to contrast the pupillary reaction of a man looking interestedly at a brightly illuminated object with the reaction of an eye that has been exposed "in isolation" to the same light intensity. The difference in pupillary reaction is immediately manifest. The nature of the contraction will depend on whether a bright light is striking the eye suddenly, under everyday conditions, or whether we are examining the pupillary response to light. This, by the way, is a problem that requires further investigation. As far as my clinical experiences on this point go, they corroborate my theoretical conceptions.

The question of reflexes within the continuation of a performance
Still another problem arises in considering the organism's performance in its various phases in relation to the reflexes. One might argue that only the onset of a performance is determined holistically and that its continuation is guaranteed by reflexes. Perhaps the process continues

automatically under the influence of outer stimuli. This is true to some extent, but even here, the sequence is not left to separate mechanisms, for each phase is still determined by the whole. In such cases, what unfolds itself is in its course fundamentally a holistic performance throughout. Into its pattern previous training is integrated, and its course is maintained through outer stimulation belonging to the situation in which the performance occurs.

Methodological Conclusions

The diagnostic significance of the reflex

By denying that reflexes can be adequately considered from an atomistic standpoint we have questioned their existence, as posited by the traditional view. But by this we have not meant to minimize the importance of investigation of "reflexes" for furnishing information of great practical value. Their marked significance and their changes through disease remain of unquestioned value for purposes of diagnosis, especially local diagnosis in nervous disease. But this is a very different problem from our present theoretical one. The practical problem concerns the possible utilization for diagnostic purposes of empirically discovered correlations of certain diseases and certain locations of disease. We do not deny that such correlations exist. But we believe that our view makes possible a greater certainty and a greater univocality of these correlations than does the customary view. Our wish is to point out that the clear recognition of the relation to the whole of the organism, in the different phenomena of the "Babinski," for example, not only renders the "deviations" intelligible but also makes it possible to inquire more intelligently about the connection between the symptoms and the location of the injury. Our view then, rather than hinder the diagnosis, allows for a refinement, if for no other reason than that it leads to more differentiated investigations. Finally, I would emphasize that what we have said about the usefulness of studying "reflexes" for diagnostic purposes applies equally to the observation of all other "part processes."

Significance of reflex investigations for the understanding of performances

Even if we have contended that the analysis of reflexes has contributed little to the understanding of the real performance of the organism, that is, of its "nature," yet we know that their study yields various hints for a theory of the performances.

First, the analysis has given us some information about the functional significance of the various forms of performances. We have learned that the greater uniformity of figure and ground indicates a simpler and more primitive form of stimulus reaction and that a stimulus reaction in which an individual process stands out from a more homogeneous ground represents the more differentiated form of performance.

We have learned further that the instability of a performance, its alternation between opposing phases, is the expression of an imperfect centering of the whole organism. From this arose the suggestion that a fundamental importance has to be attributed to shock as an inadequate form of coming to terms of organism and environment (cf. pp. 48, 105).

We also gained some information regarding certain performances essential to the organism. The analysis of the Babinski phenomenon and the reflex phenomena in cerebellar patients has called attention to the uniqueness of the flexor performances as compared with the extensor performances. We shall see later that we are dealing here with significant manifestation of two fundamentally different modes of behavior.

Only theories working with "positive" factors are acceptable

Finally, our analysis has demonstrated emphatically a methodological point of view that is likely to become a guiding principle for understanding all reactions to stimuli. We have found it futile to try to understand one pathological phenomenon by attributing it to the loss of another function, an explanation generally implied in theories of disinhibition and so on. We have established the fact that the only fruitful and scientifically unobjectionable explanation is one that confines itself to those factors that can actually be found in the situation. We may regard this methodological principle as a general postulate. Where an explanation on this basis is not possible, it is preferable to attempt no explanation at all; for to make assumptions ad hoc, which do not rest on facts, merely obscures the problem.

This methodological postulate implies that there is nothing "negative" in nature. It implies further that any negative determination can, at best, be of provisional value for knowledge. Knowledge based on facts is always of a positive character (cf. p. 320).

The Conditioned Reflex

Criteria and characteristics
The so-called conditioned reflexes require a special discussion. In common with the unconditioned reflexes, there is a constant relation established between stimulus and response. Here the connection is especially precise in respect to both stimulus and effect. Aside from this feature, the two phenomena differ in essential factor, which we must examine more closely to understand how conditioned reflexes are brought about and to determine what light, if any, they throw on the understanding of the performances. The following are the principal characteristics of the phenomena:

1. Conditioned reflexes are functions of the cortex of the cerebrum. For their formation and their course, the cortex is requisite. When the cortex of the cerebrum is removed, they vanish.

2. They can be formed only in connection with an unconditioned reflex. That conditioned reflexes have a lesser efficacy than the latter appears from the fact that they will not occur if an unconditioned reflex is brought into operation immediately before the conditioned one (A.N. Krestovnikov).

3. They are unstable and not permanent. They can easily be disturbed and destroyed by other processes. They last only a certain time beyond the period of their establishment. If they are to be preserved, the association with the unconditioned reflex has to be renewed from time to time. They can be disturbed, or "inhibited," through a second stimulus.

4. Any stimulus repeatedly applied without the associated, unconditioned stimulus produces a state of sleepiness ("inner inhibition," so called by Pavlov).

5. Their formation follows the principle that the reaction, at first, is bound to a somewhat undefined perception, for instance of sound or light, to wit, to a more diffuse field of stimulation. Only gradually is a connection established with a more specialized stimulus, such as the sound of a particular wave length, the sight of a particular visual form, and so on. The impairment of the conditioned reflexes, which takes place when the cortex is damaged, proceeds on the same principle, but in reverse order. At first, all conditioned reflexes are affected, and a chaotic state ensues similar to that which exists during their initial formation. During the period of rebuilding the conditioned reflex,

147

the response occurs first to any visual stimulus rather than to the definite pattern to which the response was formerly conditioned.

Surveying these facts, one may conclude that conditioned reflexes share the characteristics of processes that occur in isolation, since on the one hand, they show an extraordinary precision and rigidity, and on the other hand, lability. Not being firmly rooted in the whole organism, they are easily destroyed. Since they are "inferior" to performances that are closer to the organism, such as the unconditioned reflexes, they are "inhibited" by them. Further, they can easily be disturbed by other processes, such as the simultaneous intrusion of an indifferent stimulus. In short, they are easily lost, for since they are only loosely related to the organism this relation must constantly be renewed through repeated association with the unconditioned "reflexes" – which are nearer to real life. Any injury to the organism easily impairs them. How alien to the organism these conditioned reflexes are is evidenced by the fact that they produce somnolent states when they are repeatedly administered. We are inclined to interpret this as a typical catastrophic reaction – in other words, a reaction that, like sleep, has the effect of excluding stimuli at large.

In general, we might characterize them as drill results (see the explanation of this term on p. 379). They are acquired through the influence of performances that are really meaningful to the organism but are difficult to execute in and of themselves. In forming and maintaining them, the total psychological situation plays an important role. It is known that they are easily disturbed by a psychic shock.

What is their meaning for the normal organism? Do these "drill results" enter into performances? Are the latter intelligible in the light of the former? Their position, in principle, is that of achievements that are produced through routine drill. This we shall discuss later (pp. 379f.). The ingenious experiments of Pavlov and his pupils are of greatest interest for the problem of training and drill. But it is impossible to derive from them any general conclusions on the question of whether the natural environment would ever present an occasion or set of conditions suitable for the formation of such reflexes.

Significance of conditioned reflexes in man
There is probably an essential difference between animals and man in this respect. The formation of conditioned reflexes in man plays a not

unimportant part in education and self-education. It requires a certain attitude, an adaptation to unaccustomed, unnatural situations that probably only man is capable of achieving. The conditioned reflexes represent the highest achievement in such adaptation. In the infant, where this attitude is not yet developed, the reactions are achieved through external pressure exerted by the educator. Thus, the toilet habits of the child can be built up as conditioned reflexes. But they will never remain such reflexes proper. The infant has acquired these reactions without insight into their significance. Later, their control is accomplished by insight and by integrating that action into its activities. The habit is then determined by volitional and purposive behavior. The urinary control, for example, is no longer in any way a conditioned reflex but a voluntary act. If, for instance, this status is not achieved, because of retardation in the child's general development, especially the mental, then the proper toilet habit will never be perfectly attained. This proves that drill effects can only be utilized when they can be later embedded in "natural" performances and when the effect of training or drill can become subservient to, and instrumental for, the performances. The fact that human beings possess insight into the necessity of forming bonds allows the building up of associate connections, though these may be quite alien to the nature of the individual; it allows these connections to "run off" rather independently and relatively undisturbed by intervening influences. Only very severe shock effects can destroy such connections. Even a connection of this sort, however, is never the passive result of outside influences but originates in concomitant activity of the person himself or his fellow human beings. This is the reason conditioned reflexes in animals differ so markedly from those in human beings. They can originate only through man's interference with the animal's life and can be maintained only through persistent human influence; otherwise they disappear. This is because the above-described reference of the connections to the individual's insight, the relation to the whole, can never take place in animals. In human beings alone is the necessary "attitude" possible. In animals, consequently, they are more easily lost, requiring for their preservation constant renewal by reference to the unconditioned situation that, in turn, only the experimenter is capable of creating.

All this goes to show that conditioned reflexes may teach us something about the origin of particularly unnatural reactions and thus, indirectly, something about the essential nature of the organism under consideration. If it could be proved that conditioned reflexes develop in some animals, without human influence, we might accept this as evidence of a particularly "high" species similar to man. But conditioned reflexes do not offer an adequate basis for understanding performances of the organism in general. From the viewpoint of figure-ground formation, they are not simple but complicated patterns. Indeed, one might even say they are the most intricate. In this connection, we may remind the reader that conditioned reflexes, in their formation and disintegration, seem in principle to resemble performances connected with cortical function.

The Phenomena in Cortical Stimulation

In connection with our discussion of conditioned reflexes, it is of particular interest to consider the phenomena observed in cortical stimulation. These also are isolated excitations, inasmuch as the stimuli employed are certainly not "adequate." The facts indicate, in many details, close conformity between the typical reactions in reflex experiments and those resulting from cortical stimulation — notwithstanding the fact that some differences exist.

Within a certain range of stimulus intensities, reaction is limited to a certain field; when the intensity is increased beyond this, the reaction spreads into other fields. Repeated, weak, ineffectual stimuli can produce an effect through summation.[4] The same increase of reaction may be effected by stimulating another place, possibly even the periphery.[5] We have already found something analogous to this to be characteristic of reflexes, and here again we have evidence of the reciprocal interrelation of effects. Through repetition of the stimuli, the reaction reaches its maximum, after which it may subside.[6] The reaction related to one cortical point can be changed in a homologous way, by stimulating other points. Thus, an effect opposite to the usual one can occur if, while one point is being stimulated, another is simultaneously excited.[7] And identical stimulation can produce different results, according to the milieu in which it takes place. According to Graham Brown, this varied effect need not be ascribed to a difference in spatial spread of the excitation current during the stimulation. The repeated stimulation of one point may result, not only in abatement, but even in a reversal of the effect, for example, flexion of the elbow instead of extension.

To account for this, one is forced to assume either that no specialized function exists for a stimulated point or that the aftereffect does not directly result from the stimulation but through processes in the stimulated (activated) muscle when the stimulus effect abates. We would then be dealing with a secondary induction, similar to that occurring in alternating movements. The explanation of this might be that the point is not specific, inasmuch as its stimulation can yield opposite performances that only differ according to their excitation threshold. This view receives support from the fact that reversal occurs more readily in the primary extension reaction than in the primary flexion reaction. We might expect from this a higher threshold for the extension reaction and find, in confirmation, that we can obtain flexion even when stimulation of a flexor point has been immediately preceded by stimulation of extensor points, whereas the opposite is less commonly the case (as in the work of Graham Brown).

This result would suggest a difference in the thresholds of the different performances rather than an effect dependent on any particular point of excitation. The effects produced by identical stimuli depend on conditions at the point of their application, at other parts of the cortex, or at peripheral parts. The effects, therefore, may differ so widely that even such competent students as Sherrington and Graham Brown find it difficult to determine unequivocally the function of any particular point. In summing up the similarity of the stimulus effects in reflexes and in cortical stimulation, we can say:

1. Constant results are only obtained when the stimulus is in complete isolation locally and temporally.

2. Numerous variations are possible – even reversal of effect – under identical stimuli.

3. There exists a hierarchy of performances, according to a scale of their functional value. When the performance capacity is reduced, as well as when the stimuli become weaker, certain performances are favored – which corresponds to what we found in the case of reflexes (cf. p. 121).

4. It must be noted that the stimuli effects do not necessarily disturb the volitional performances, a fact that would indicate that the holistic (e.g., the volitional) performance has a higher functional value than the isolated performance (as represented in the effects of cortical stimulation; cf. p. 150).

All these phenomena can be explained as the outcome of a more or less extensive isolation of the stimulus effect. Certainly, in real performances, such variations are not possible. Therefore, real performances must owe their origin to a different form of excitation that determines their constancy. The varying value of the stimulus effect points again to the determining role of the holistic factor. Examples of this sort could be multiplied ad libitum. We may conclude: from pathological material that has come under my own observation and from that which is described in the literature, I would say that there is no pathological phenomenon that cannot be explained as the effect of direct injury or as the effect of isolation of a substratum. It is particularly significant that, in regard to the "formal change," there is no difference between those phenomena that we usually ascribe to peripheral, central, spinal, cerebellar, or cortical abnormalities. We wish to stress particularly, in this connection, that the function of the cerebral cortex is to be considered in no respect different from that of the other nervous substrata. The differences, evident in performances, depend on the degree of differentiation and the extent of that part of the system that is under excitation. It is this difference in extent and differentiation that renders the organism capable of dealing with contents of varying scope and articulation.

The So-Called Instincts

In our attempt to comprehend the organism we have already found reason to contest the view that reflexes are elements and that the performances are their composites. What now about the instincts thought to explain so much in the life of animal and man? We can afford to discuss here only a few fundamental questions. It would be quite impossible to treat the vast literature or all aspects of this complicated problem.

Characteristics and criteria. Variability and end effect

Instinct actions are markedly set off from reflexes, as well as from the learned performances. The instinct action is characterized by the fact that an organism carries out some complicated movements that appear very purposeful, either for its own life or for the life of its offspring. This is done without previous experience, independently of training, and often without any possibility of knowing in advance something of the success that is to be achieved. To be sure, an attempt has been made to reduce instincts to chain reflexes, but this view already has been refuted on several occasions. I might refer in this connection to H.J. Jordan, Kurt Koffka, Gordon W. Allport, and others.[8] Koffka is right in insisting that instincts constitute behavior that tends to a definite, necessary end situation and that in this respect they resemble rather the phenomena of "willed responses." This is not the place to elaborate on pertinent and relevant differences between willed responses and instinct. This much, however, may be said: the instinct actions are always strictly related to a definite effect, and the condition under which the same effect is reached can vary greatly. Corresponding to this change of the condition, the performance itself has to change, and this change continues to take place until the effect is reached. All this cannot be based on a fixed apparatus, and it speaks just as well against the theory of a mechanical summation of single reflexes in "a chain." Moreover, such an assumption would have to posit all the possible variations as potentially and anticipatorily included in the very release of the instinct mechanism. So we would still be left with the same problem we faced in reflex variation. As in the case of reflexes, we must view the instinct action holistically, in terms of its reference to the whole organism and to the variables of the situation — understandable only from the respective nature of the organism.

In many of their characteristics, instincts apparently are more closely related to the whole than to reflexes. For instance, it is often pointed out that locomotion is so adjusted to the stimulus that it seems to be purposeful, that is, it seems to take into account the entire field of the organism. Even alterations of the stimulus, though appearing irrelevant to the observer, may lead to modifications of reactions and, moreover, may reverse them. Such phenomena are only intelligible as an expression of the principle of "suitability for the whole." They depend, furthermore, not merely on the effectiveness of the stimulus but on a particular total condition of the organism, for instance, the need for food. We must note, finally, that although the organism performs a purposive response, the purpose cannot enter as a determining factor into the present execution because its fulfillment will occur only in the future.

Reference to the whole as such would not allow for a discrimination between instincts and reflexes, because we have seen that this principle also applies to the reflexes. But they are distinguishable from the reflexes, on the basis of another characteristic. Instincts are released through "natural," external, or internal stimuli. They are processes that belong essentially to the life of the organism. They are not artificial reactions, elicited to serve the investigator's purposes, nor are they reactions occasioned by virtue of an inadequate milieu in "border situations" – both being the case in most reflexes. Koffka and Jordan call the instincts "processes in the nature of Gestalten." Jordan cleverly analyzed a number of known instinct processes from the holistic point of view, while Koffka attempted to bring them into line with Köhler's physical Gestalten. According to our view, an understanding of the instincts can be attained only through a holistic analysis of their respective nature, in the respective whole to which they belong. The problem is made more difficult, in that factors essential to an entire species play a particularly important part. In spite of an enormous amount of work bearing on this subject, we still lack, above all, a description of this behavior sufficiently accurate and unbiased to allow us to uncover the "constants" (cf. pp. 282f.) that might furnish us with the groundwork of knowledge about its nature.[9] Let us analyze a relatively simple response, which will at the same time serve to demonstrate that some phenomena, regarded as instincts, involve entirely different processes, to say the least. It is particularly important to verify this, because if there is any hope of ever clarifying the much disputed instinct concept or of understanding the nature of its underlying processes, we must examine it carefully.

Instinct, equalization process, and turning-to reaction
In the reflexes, we have distinguished between those phenomena that have as their end only the equalization of abnormal tension – the so-called proprioceptive reflexes – and those that we have described as "performances." In my opinion, a similar differentiation is called for between two types of behavioral activity, usually classified as instinctive. For example, the behavior of the newborn infant who turns toward a stimulus from the very first day, is sometimes called "instinctive." This, however, is nothing but the tendency toward equalization – not necessarily a special instinct, but an instance of the common reaction of living substance in general. The observation that only "corresponding" individual movements occur, for example, eye movements through stimulation by light, mouth movements by touching of the face, and so on,

is not quite correct phenomenally. If we leave the child unencumbered and undressed and observe everything it does, we find that its turning-to movements are much more comprehensive than in the above description. The entire organism, so to speak, strives or orients itself toward the stimulus. As far as some differentiation appears, it occurs because in contiguous parts that already represent a functional unit, stronger effects arise through the influence of their proximity. For example, they are related by their sensitivity and motility as eye and surrounding muscles, sensitivity of the cheeks and mouth, sensitivity of the hand and muscles of the hand, and so on. That "partitive" reactions appear so pronounced in the newborn infant is furthermore explainable by the relative isolation of certain parts, through defective centering.[10] The turning-to reaction is in the foreground at this phase of the development, because other reactions are not yet possible at that stage of maturation. It is not necessary to assume a special instinct to understand this phenomenon. The impression of a reflex or instinct action is suggested by the fact that the reaction seems to occur only in those muscles that are functionally conneced with the stimulated sense organ. But this is not an entirely correct observation. If the infant has the possibility of moving his entire body, we have seen that its reactions are more or less performed with the whole body.

Koffka is quite justified in saying that "the so-called instincts of turning-to and turning away, imply nothing more than that certain stimuli, having disturbed its equilibrium, the newborn infant attempts to restore it through positive or negative movements. But this must not lead us to assume the existence of special, preformed connections."[11] I would prefer, therefore, not to use the word "instinct" for describing these processes, because essentially they are not a special capacity possessed by some creatures or species, but, as stated before, a general type of reaction common to all living substance. In saying this, we do not overlook the fact that, even in the beginning, the reaction is colored by the "nature" of the respective organism.

If one considers sucking, for instance, one sees that the reaction is not fixed. It is not adapted solely to the nipple of the mother's breast, for the child is able to suck from another nipple, a rubber nipple, or a finger.[12] The movement each time is different – corresponding to the difference of the object – but it is carried out with the same promptness. On the other hand, the action differs as to the quality of the milk, the fatigue or freshness of the baby, and especially to the state of hunger or satiation. We have to deal with a complicated action, which reveals a dependence on the condition of the whole organism and which is to be understood only from the effect to be attained.

Another example: The newly hatched chick is determined, in its first activities, by exactly the same tendency as the newborn infant. Its pecking is nothing but a turning-to reaction. But very soon this is altered by "experience" to a purposive pecking. At first, the newborn chick pecks at all available objects of a certain size and within a certain distance – because such objects belong to the environment for which, by nature, it has an affinity. Conwy Lloyd Morgan has shown that the chick, at that time, also pecks at certain caterpillars that it will, however, "spit out." When Morgan presented such a caterpillar to the chick a second time – a day later – the chick did not peck at it. It had learned to suppress its "instinct" of pecking.[13] It is interesting that a single experience was sufficient to change the "instinctive" action. That shows how poorly fixed these "instinct" actions are, and how much they depend on the momentary condition of the whole organism.

"Instinct action" and experience

We have here a perfect analogy to the behavior of the human infant, except that the latter requires a longer interval to develop the ability to act purposively. But there is no justification for talking about instincts and their modification through experience, when, in reality, we are dealing with two entirely different processes: on the one hand, with a mere equalization process, the effect of incomplete maturation, and on the other hand with the disappearance of that turning-to reaction and its substitution by a real performance, related purposefully to the nature of the organism. In the beginning of the development, we observe responses, in which we are actually dealing with the equalization phenomenon, as an expression of the immaturity of the organism. Later, that response becomes a purposeful performance corresponding to the nature of this individual organism. The initial pecking of the chick is considered to be an instinctive reaction, because it seems to be so very purposeful. However, the chick first turns toward many things not fit for it, in the same way as does the human baby. In the chick, these unpurposeful reactions are not to be so easily observed. For the change in pecking takes place with maturation, which occurs very quickly in the chick. This maturation is characterized, in the differentiating between fit and unfit objects, by the use of experience. The chick undoubtedly reacts by "turning to" a stimulus, as often as the newborn infant. But these forms of behavior are easier to observe in the human infant. We do not notice these other turning-to reactions, because we do not think of them as related to a "purpose," even though, in their nature, they represent the same phenomenon. The change in the way of pecking is concomitant with maturation, and the new type of pecking represents an entirely different performance. Of course, this maturation unfolds under the influence of outer stimuli, since it represents the adaptation of the organism to the environment — an adaptation between the forming organism and the "forming" world, or "milieu." At first, the chick pecks at everything, reacts to any disturbing stimulus, through the tendency toward equalization. But once it has pecked at something distasteful to it, the reaction becomes modified, so that an inadequate object, such as a caterpillar, will no longer be a stimulus. The organism is "closed" against the caterpillar, or as someone else might say, it has become "inhibited." At this point, we can only repeat the question we have already raised so often: Who has proof that inhibition is the case, and what has caused it? The chick, maturing very rapidly, gains a new attitude, making it peck at only certain kernels that, because of their good effect, have come to be regarded as "peckable." Two characteristics observed by Morgan are noteworthy: the rapidity of the learning, sometimes after a single experience, and the reproducing of the learned response after an interval. These facts give evidence that this is not the acquisition of a performance through repeated experiences but that the organism came into a situation in which its capacity, corresponding to its state of maturation, could cope successfully with the situation. And this is the prerequisite, as well as the nature of learning.

We must content ourselves with these remarks to illustrate that "instincts" offer the same fundamental difficulties as "reflexes." In our opinion, the same methodological errors are usually made here and can ultimately be traced to the usual, faulty point of departure: that "parts" — in this case, the so-called instinctive reactions — are to be thought of as the constant components of behavior, without due regard to their "belongingness" to the nature of the whole organism.

"Instinct actions" inseparable from the whole

Thus we can say, the so-called instinctive actions, too, are not executed separately from the whole of the oragnism but take place in connection with all other activities. Indeed, the urge to "deliver" them is very great. But we are not forced to follow that urge, we can postpone its realization, if we think that something else is of greater importance to us at that moment. Some observations of Lashley speak in favor of the connection between the "instinct" and the total individual. Lashley could show that in rats the mother instinct and other instincts depend on the function of the cortex.[14] From operations on the brain cortex, he could adduce evidence of the decisive role of the cortex in sexual behavior, even in lower animals.

Transitoriness of "instinct" in relation to the whole

William James has pointed to another phenomenon, important for an understanding of the instinct actions. He stressed that the "instincts" appear at a certain life period, and disappear later, because in that new life situation they are of no further use. This shows that they are related to some special phases in the life of the individual – that they correspond to a certain stage of development, as an expression of maturation. One could conclude from these facts that the instinct actions have nothing to do with experience. In some respects, this is true. But this does not place these actions in a different category from other capacities of the organism with regard to the important role of experience. Certainly, the instinct actions, like all other capacities, are inborn, in a potential form, and become mature at a specific time. The concrete behavior, the abstract behavior – these and other capacities are not learned. They belong to the nature of the organism, but they are utilized only by the organism in the course of its encounter with the outer world and its coming to terms with external stimuli. Thus, they develop with the attempt of the organism to adjust itself to the environment in a certain way. The development of these capabilities is dependent on the possibility of a specifically formed environment suited to the use of such capacities. The same is the case with the so-called instincts. They are special, inborn, more or less functional potentialities, which become actualized only when the situation in the outer world makes that possible; and, if that is not the case, they may vanish.

It is not difficult to notice in human beings that the instinct actions are connected with the whole personality. For instance, actions corresponding to the mother instinct are often first observed only after the child is born. Only then has the woman entered the situation in which she really acquires the attitude and position of a mother. If women frequently appear interested in the motherly behavior before that time, the reason for this phenomenon is found in the capacity for imagination and anticipation, which is so characteristic of the human being. It depends on the differences of the whole personality, whether the so-called mother behavior first occurs after the child has been born or before. Not infrequently, a child must even reach a certain age before actual mother behavior comes to the fore.

The whole theory of instincts is to be understood only from its origin, namely, from observations in animals and in children. Regarding the inference from animal observations, it seems to me that Allport has pointed out, quite correctly, that the question of instinct in animals should not confuse the issue of the instinct problem in human beings.[15] There are such great differences between both that it is impossible to understand both in the same way. It should be added that, since the condition in animals is so much more difficult for us to understand than the behavior of human beings, we have every reason to confine ourselves especially to the observations of the latter in order to avoid running into errors and misleading conclusions. Furthermore, we have to scrutinize the behavior of children, since it has been regarded as evidence of the instinct theory. Certainly, children seem to be driven very strongly by some "instincts": thirst and hunger seem to call for definite actions. However, in reality, children too are not always forced to follow a certain drive. A child can "forget" hunger, when he is playing, for example. In that way, the more the child matures, the less a single "instinct activity" determines his behavior. More and more factors acquire importance for the actions of the individual, and whether one factor is effective or not, and how it becomes effective, can be understood only from the relation between these factors and the whole of the organism. True, the life of the child seems particularly to be governed by instinct actions. But that is to be explained by the fact that children are not yet such centered beings as adults are, and therefore a part of their organism can become isolated to a relatively large extent, so that it can determine their behavior and give the appearance of a special "instinct." The more centered the organism has become, the less it manifests this type of behavior, the less it appears to be governed by single, so-called instincts, and the more it is guided by the attitude of the whole organism with reference to the entire, given situation. Here, too, I agree with Allport that the instincts in adults are nothing more than "a constellation of emotions, habit, and foresight, better called sentiments or interests."[16] While it is true that they are based on some tendencies of the organism in question, these tendencies that belong to its nature become effective in various ways, according to the special constellation, which is determined by the organism and the situation as a whole. And it is this relation we have to grasp, when we wish to explain this behavior.

Summarizing, we are justified in concluding that the so-called instinct actions are reactions of the whole organism. They are distinguished from other performances only by the fact that inborn and nonconscious factors play a much greater role than in the other performances, as, for example, in the voluntary actions, the highest form of performances. Whether an organism presents "instinct performances" alone or both the instinct and voluntary performances depends on the difference in the organization of organisms. The assumption of capacities, which operate without knowledge or awareness of the origin of the respective performances on the part of the organism, is not in contrast with a theory that considers each performance as being an action of the total organism and that sees in the different performances only the sequelae of different attitudes on the part of the organism as a whole.

The learned, voluntary performances represent only a special type of behavior. Another type is the performances that take their course on the basis of nonconscious activities (pp. 240f.). These performances emerge as reactions of the organism during certain states of development, of maturation. To this group also belong sitting, walking, speaking, grasping, and so on. In the voluntary actions, the "drive" works through the medium of intention, of thinking, decision, and motivation on the part of the individual. In the instinct action, the performances are set going directly by the "drive" (see p. 163). Both types of performances are dependent, however, on the activity of the organism as a whole – both are expressions of the nature of the individual organism. Ultimately there is no reason to consider the so-called instinctive reaction as belonging to a type of behavior different in principle from the higher form of self-actualization of the organism.

The So-Called Drives
We have to deal here with a problem more difficult than any other. The pertinent discussion in the literature is in a state of confusion, which renders it difficult to obtain any orientation on this basis. Therefore, let us look at some phenomena in pathology and see what we can learn from observations on patients, concerning the essential problem in question, namely: Toward what are the drives driving?

Drives as release of tension – a pathological phenomenon
Observations in patients present us with a phenomenon important for the theory of drives. The sick person has the tendency to avoid catastrophic reactions, because these are even more dangerous for him than for normals. He is not able to bear them, and he is hindered by them to a much higher degree than normal individuals in the execution of performances. He therefore tries to avoid them. Many peculiarities of patients are understandable only from this condition. Catastrophic situations are especially favored by abnormal tensions in any field. In pathology, abnormal tensions occur relatively often in single fields, because reactions tend to take place in isolated parts and because the process of equalization is disturbed. Therefore, the sick organism tends especially to remove abnormal tensions and seems to be governed by the drive to do so. For example, the sick, suffering from a tension in the sex sphere, seem to be forced, above all, to release this tension. From such observation arose the idea that it is the real goal of all drives to alleviate and to discharge the tension and to bring the organism into a state of nontension, to wit, it is the goal of the drive to release itself.

We have spoken about the difference of the equalization process in normal and abnormal life. In the state of isolation, as in sick people, the discharge of tension is in the foreground, and the tendency to remove any arising tension prevails. In sound life, however, the result of the normal equalization process is the formation of a certain level of tension, namely, that which makes possible further ordered activity.

The tendency to discharge any tension whatsoever is an expression of a defective organism, of disease. It is the only means of the sick organism to actualize itself, even if in an imperfect way. Such a state is possible only with the support of other organisms. It will be remembered what we have said about the fact that the life of a sick organism, its entire existence, depends on other organisms. This shows clearly that life, under such conditions, is not normal life, and that mere discharge or release of tensions cannot be a characteristic of normal life.

The "drive for self-preservation" — a pathological phenomenon
The basic tendency of the sick organism is to utilize the preserved capacities in the best possible way, considered in relation to the normal nature of the organism concerned. The behavior of patients is to be understood only from such a viewpoint. We may recall here especially the different behavior of patients with hemianopsia and with hemiamblyopia; both are understandable from the just-mentioned viewpoint. Our comparison of the behavior of the patients with that of normal individuals left us no doubt that normal organismic life is also governed by this rule. We can say that an organism is governed by the tendency to actualize, as much as possible, its individual capacities, its "nature," in the world. This nature is what we call the psychosomatic constitution, and, as far as considered during a certain phase, it is the individual pattern, the "character" that the respective constitution has attained in the course of experience. This tendency to actualize its nature, to actualize "itself," is the basic drive, the only drive by which the life of the organism is determined. This tendency undergoes in the sick human being a characteristic change. The patient's scope of life is reduced in two ways. First, he is driven to utilize his preserved capacities in the best possible way. Second, he is driven to maintain a certain state of living and not to be disturbed in this condition. Therefore sick life is — as we explained — very bare of productivity, development, and progress, and bare of the characteristic particularities of normal organismic and especially human life. Frequently, the law of maintaining the existent state — the self-preservation — is considered as the basic law of life. I believe such a concept could arise only because one had assumed, as a starting point, the experiences in abnormal conditions or experimental situations. The tendency to maintain the existent state is characteristic for sick people and is a sign of anomalous life, of decay of life. The tendency of normal life is toward activity and progress. For the sick, the only form of self-actualization that remains is the maintenance of the existent state. That, however, is not the tendency of the normal. It might be that sometimes the normal organism also tends primarily to avoid catastrophes and to maintain a certain state that makes that possible; but this takes place under inadequate conditions and is

not at all the usual behavior. Under adequate conditions the normal organism seeks further activity.

Only one drive: self-actualization
Normal behavior corresponds to a continual change of tension of such a kind that over and again that state of tension is reached that enables and impels the organism to actualize itself in further activities, according to its nature.

Thus, experiences with patients teach us that we have to assume only one drive, the drive of self-actualization, and that the goal of the drive is not a discharge of tension. Under various conditions, various actions come into the foreground; and while they thereby seem to be directed toward different goals, they give the impression of independently existing drives. In reality, however, these various actions occur in accordance with the various capacities belonging to the nature of the organism and occur in accordance with those instrumental processes that are then necessary prerequisites of the self-actualization of the organism.

The concept of different, separate drives is based especially on two groups of observations, namely, observations on young children and on animals under experimental conditions. That is, observations are made under circumstances that represent a decentering of the functioning of the organism. They are derived from a condition we have characterized as favoring an abnormal "coming into relief" of activities corresponding to the functioning of isolated parts of the organism (see p. 116).

Discharge of special tension — a phenomenon of defective centering
Let us first consider the observations in children. Indeed, we very often have the impression that the actions of infants, in the beginning of life, are directed toward the goal of discharging a tension. Tension and removal of tension can be observed in the whole behavioral aspect of the child, in pertinent situations. In a situation of hunger or thirst the child appears governed by the desire to release those tensions corresponding to the phenomenal goals — for instance, sucking. In another example, the child appears satisfied only if he can grasp the object by which he is stirred up. But we should never forget that such descriptions of the child's behavior can be wrong. Our descriptions of the behavior of children always lack certainty. More accurately stated, we

do not know anything definite about the child's reactions, about what is really the stimulus for the child, about the desires or needs by which it is driven, and by what reactions they are released. Let us look at some facts. For instance, there is the first turning-to movement of the head, which, as we believe, can be explained as simple equalization. Here we might assume as the essential factor of the process the release of a tension produced by the stimulus. It may be that, in such reactions, the infant also experiences some tension and the release of it. The situation changes, however, when the infant becomes more mature. Then the character of the head turning is totally different.

It is difficult to say how many of the reactions of the infant are reactions of "single tension release." I like to regard the first grasping reactions of the baby as such an equalization phenomenon – as long as the grasping is restricted to objects placed in the hand of the baby and the baby tends to hold the object without doing something else with it. The Moro response is a phenomenon of that kind.[17] If the interpretation of these reactions is correct, namely, that we have to deal with release phenomena, then we may speak here of a drive for release of a tension produced by a stimulus. However, to speak of a drive for release would state nothing concerning the character of drives, in general. In the mentioned examples, we are faced with phenomena under inadequate conditions, that is, during the stage of immaturity of an organism. We have no right to conclude from such observations anything about the nature of drives in adult life. One could say that the infant itself does not tend to grasp, but his hand separately grasps if it is stimulated without the organism as a whole being concerned in that activity. In the case, however, where the infant tends to grasp the object, if it is not placed in his hand, and then tries to use it in a way that corresponds to his capacities, we have to do not only with a discharge of a tension but also with the organism's tendency to come to terms with the object – not only with a reaction of a part of the organism but with a performance of the whole organism. What impulse in the infant might be satisfied by this action is difficult to say, but we are certainly not faced merely with a discharge of a tension. The same might be the case in sucking. Here especially, we seem to be justified in speaking of a release of a tension in one field. But are we sure that the sucking, with its effect – the intake of food – relieves only a desire for food? Perhaps it would be possible to describe the situation in the following way: the desire is only a partial aspect of a feeling of deficiency of the whole organism, which makes its activities, that is, its self-actualization, impossible; and the sucking and the intake of food are the means of bringing the whole organism into a condition in which it is able to perform again, corresponding to its nature. Then we should not speak of a special drive but of a special condition of the entire organism. Such a description would be supported by facts. The observations of the infant lead us to assume that sucking is dependent on the condition of the whole organism, as we mentioned before in the discussion about the instinct actions. It changes, corresponding to the changes of the condition of the whole organism. We could describe the whole phenomenon as a tension of the organism in general, which disturbs its functioning and finds its special expression in the desire for food, and as an action of the entire organism, which, by the sucking act, brings the organism again into the state of being able to perform normally, as a whole. Then we would have to consider, as the goal of the drive, the tendency to come into a condition in which the organism can perform normally, that is, corresponding to its nature. The sucking movements would be suited to return the organism to this condition, because they are means for removing a certain disturbance. In that case, we would have to deal not with a special drive and the release of it but with a tendency to remove a condition that makes any adequate performance impossible. We would have to deal not with a discharge of any tension but with the tendency to self-actualization, which renders necessary, under certain conditions, some characteristic actions. We would have to deal with an action that is only one phase in the activities of the organism, which correspond to the process of actualization of its nature.

I cannot prove that the situation in children is of the type I have tried to characterize. However, I think that our explanation has at least the same degree of probability as the usual theory of drives, yet I am inclined to assume that my interpretation rests more on facts. Be that as it may, our example illustrates that we have to be very careful in any derivation of a theory of drives from the behavior of children. It is so difficult to obtain a real insight into the condition in children that ultimate certainty here is not to be realized. Therefore, we should be cautioned against drawing on observations in children in considering the behavior of adults with regard to possible existence of drives.

This criticism must also make us cautious if we try to build up a theory of drives from the experimental facts. As we have stressed so often, we have to deal here with a condition of uttermost isolation, and all facts found in this state are liable to the fallacies we have discussed.

The impression of drives arises because the organism is governed at one time by one tendency, at another time by another; because one or the other tendency in the given condition becomes more important for self-actualization. This is especially the case when the organism is living under inadequate conditions. If a human being is forced to live in a state of hunger for a long time, or if there are conditions in his body that produce a strong hunger feeling, so that he is urged to relieve this feeling, it disturbs the self-actualization of his whole personality. Then he appears as if under a hunger drive. The same may be the case with sex.

A normal organism, however, is able to repress the hunger feeling or the sex urge if it has something very important to do, the neglect of which would bring the whole organism into danger. The behavior of a normal individual is to be understood only if considered from the viewpoint that those performances most important for the organism are always fulfilled. That presupposes a normal centering of the organism and a normal, adequate environment. Because these conditions are not always fulfilled, even in normal life, the organism might often appear to be governed transitorily by a special tendency. In this case we have to deal not with a normal situation but with an emergency situation, one that gives the impression of a special, isolated drive. This is particularly to be found if the organism is not allowed to actualize one or the other potentialities for an abnormally long time, as, for example, if the reception of food is hindered a long time. Then the harmonious attitude of the organism to the outer world might be thrown out of gear and the individual is thereby driven to fulfill that potentiality because only in this way can the existence of the organism be guaranteed. We are confronted here with a behavior corresponding to that which we have discussed where only those activities prevail that are important for mere existence in situations of danger. But these are not the activities by which normal behavior can be understood.

From our discussion, I think we are in no way forced to assume the existence of special drives. I believe that the facts taken as foundations for the assumption of different drives are more or less abstractions from the natural behavior of the organism. They are special reactions in special situations and represent the various forms in which the organism, as a whole, expresses itself.

The traditional view assumes various drives that are foregrounded under certain conditions. We assume only one drive, the drive for self-actualization of the organism; but we are compelled to concede that, under certain conditions, the tendency to actualize one potentiality is so strong that the organism is governed by it. Superficially, therefore, our theory may not appear so much in conflict with others. However, I think there is an essential difference. From our standpoint, we can understand the latter phenomenon as an abnormal deviation from the normal behavior under definite conditions; but the theory of separate drives can never comprehend normal behavior — without positing another agency that makes the decision in the struggle between the single drives, which means any theory of drives has to introduce another, "higher" agency. Here we again meet the same situation as in the discussion of reflexes and instincts and must again reject this auxiliary hypothesis as unsuitable to solve the problem. "The tendency of the organism to actualize itself" always confronts us with the same question. We do not need the drives!

Potentialities ("capacities") and self-actualization. Tendency to perfection
We reject the theory of drives from yet another point of view. If one of these potentialities, or one we can abstract from the whole of the organism, is taken as a distinct faculty we fall into the errors of faculty psychology.[18] This isolation changes the capacity, exaggerating it in the same way as every behavioral aspect is changed when isolated from the rest of the organism. And starting from the phenomena to be observed in such situations of isolation, we can never understand the behavior. False concepts arise, such as the determining importance of single drives, sex or power, and so on. A judgment about such phenomena as sex and power, and so on, is to be made only if one considers them outside of their appearance in isolation and looks at their appearance in the natural life of the organism, where they present themselves as embedded in the activities of the organism as a whole. With this approach to the problem, the way (most often obstructed by some preconceived idea of isolated drives) is free for new investigations. That should be the essential outcome of our critique.

What are usually called drives are tendencies corresponding to the capacities, the nature of the organism, and the environment in which the organism is living at a given time. It is better that we speak of "needs." The organism has definite potentialities, and because it has them it has the need to actualize or realize them. The fulfillment of these needs represents the self-actualization of the organism. Driven by such needs, we are experiencing ourselves as active personalities not, however, passively impelled by drives experienced as conflicting with the personality.

A special form of this self-actualization is the need to complete incomplete actions. This tendency for completion explains so many of the activities of the child. In the innumerable repetitions of children, we are not dealing with the manifestation of a senseless drive for repetition, but with the tendency to completion and perfection. The driving force is given in the experience of imperfection — be it thirst, hunger, or experience of being unable to fulfill any performance that seems to be within our capacities — the goal is the fulfillment of the task. The nearer we are to perfection, the stronger is the need to perform. This is valid for children as well as for adults.

The urge to perfection brings about a building up of more or less perfect instruments in any respective field. These in themselves become a further impulse for use of the instrumental mechanisms, because that makes possible perfection in other fields. As long as the child's walking is imperfect, he tends to walk and walk, often with no other goal than walking. After he has perfected the walking, he uses this instrument to reach a special point that attracts his attention, namely, to complete another performance, for example.

Drives, capacities, and habits
It was believed that it is possible to reduce the drive to those instrumental mechanisms. The mechanisms themselves were supposed to be originated from conditioned responses, built up as means of adjustment of the organism during development. The drive then is considered nothing more than a neural process or habit corresponding to this neural process that releases these mechanisms. There is no doubt that habits incite the activities. But the problem is how these habits originated and whether for their acquisition a special activity and tendency — a "drive" — is not the necessary cause. The question is brought back to the problem of the origin of habits or mechanisms. There are two pos-

sibilities to be considered: the mechanisms develop with maturation of inborn neural patterns without any active interference on the part of the organism, or they are built by the activity of the organism in connection with experience. Nobody will doubt that the development of mechanisms is based on inborn dispositions corresponding to the nature of the organism, on inborn capacities that develop with maturation. But the question is whether these capacities develop without any activity of the organism. I think experience teaches us that this is not the case. The development of the mechanism takes place during the organism's procedure of coming to terms with the outer world, because of the tendency, the drive for self-actualization. Walking and speaking do not develop without impulse on the part of the child. If this impulse is lacking, development even of these definitely inborn capacities is retarded or missing. Thus the development of the mechanisms presupposes the drive for self-actualization, notwithstanding the "functional autonomy" (Allport) the mechanisms achieve later.

From these mechanisms, from these habits, arises a strong impulse for actions. These mechanisms then become instrumental for the performances of the organism and make the self-actualization of the organism easier; therefore there is a strong urge to use them. Insofar do we agree with Robert S. Woodworth, who has placed emphasis on the fact: "The means to the end becomes an object of interest on its own account."[19] But normally this "functional autonomy," as Allport called it, is meaningfully integrated in the whole of personality; that is, the "means to an end," the "mechanism," and the "habits" achieve an independency only insofar as they are not in conflict with the "needs" of the whole organism and the life situations. Whenever they attain an actual autonomy, then we are dealing with a quite different phenomenon – namely, with unnatural isolation. Many of the customs, habits, and symbols in civilization and culture have, in the course of history, attained a certain emancipation from the original contextual intention and can govern the behavior without the individual being aware of the original purpose. Notwithstanding the unjustified tyranny they may exercise and the obstacles they may offer to free development, it should be said that they are still embedded within the purposive setting of the situations and social framework in which they play a part.

If this emancipation, however, reaches a degree whereby the mechanisms become practically detached from the personality, then we encounter pathological conditions, with a sequelae of a defective centering of the organism.

The So-Called Chemical Parts

Is starting from the "parts," discovered by chemical analysis, justifiable? True, marvelous observations have been made that seem to be in favor of such an approach, for example, the discovery of the effect of the smallest quantities of certain hormones on the development of such apparently fundamental characteristics of the organism as its sex characteristics. These facts are certainly worthy of serious consideration in regard to our theory. Perhaps even more startling has been the fact that some chemical substances are extremely important for the so-called introduction of growth of tissue of certain structure. Hans Spemann has transplanted small parts of the dorsal tissue of the gastrula of an amphibian larva, cells that would later normally develop into the nervous tissue of the spinal cord of the brain, to that part of another larva that would normally develop into something quite different, for example, the peritoneum.[20] He has found that the transplanted part develops into a nervous system at the new locus. Recently, Johannes Holtfreter has shown that to achieve such a result it is not even necessary to transplant the living "organizers" but that even "mortified" tissues, which have lost their histological structure and can only be evaluated on the basis of their chemical constituents, can be transplanted successfully.

But do all these amazing facts indicate anything more than that the substance, which has been determined in an isolating investigation, is significant for the existence of, and the formation of, a very definite property of the organism? They tell nothing about the property itself or about the life process as a whole. A chemical description will never adequately explain a biological process. It can never do more than disclose factors – essential ones, we concede – necessary to the course of the performances and can only show how they appear under isolated conditions. To understand the phenomena, and by means of these to understand the organism, requires above all behavior analysis. What we call "chemism" will certainly play a part in this analysis, more important than we sufficiently realize today. But I believe that what we have learned from analyzing reflexes applies equally to all knowledge gained through similar methods. And what we have learned is that the phenomena observed, in isolating investigations, have special properties, from which it would be impossible to draw any valid inferences about the real nature of the organism.

After I had completed the above summary of the conclusions of our investigations, I read the very noteworthy discussion by H.J. Jordan on the value of causal analysis in understanding processes in the organism, and I am glad to report a confirmation of my views, which is all the more gratifying to me inasmuch as I myself do not feel qualified to speak competently on the subject of physico-chemical processes.[21] Jordan asserts that the physico-chemical explanation is "valid only for short ranges."[22] The statement that the laws of diffusion account for oxygen penetration through the alveoli of the lungs to the haemoglobin is valid only if we assume a system of harmoniously grouped factors that, we might say, cooperate in effecting the process. In other words, the process exists only in a limited field, and only when that is embedded in a definite way in a larger relation – exactly as we have found to be true of reflexes. According to Jordan, the problem of biology is the determination of this relation. The aim, "explanation of life through causal analysis," must be abandoned once and for all.[23] In order to explain life, synthesis is necessary. It cannot be denied that the problem of synthesis, involving the relationship of the parts to each other and to the whole, becomes a scientific task of the first order.[24] But Jordan does not indicate how to arrive from the parts to this synthesis. He confines himself to a negative statement. He argues that the chemico-physical facts do not permit such a simple synthesis and that the solution of the problem is not to be expected in our age.[25] This negative statement is very important to us, although our endeavor is to reach a more positive determination of the approach from parts to whole.

CHAPTER SIX

On the Conception of the Organism

as a Whole

The Phenomena in Individual Parts of the Organism and the Events in the Rest of the Organism

Our studies have shown why the results of reflex investigations do not offer the fundamentals for building up a concept of the organism. However, the reflex investigations, as well as the observations of the behavior of patients with brain lesions, have repeatedly taught us one thing: the relationship of each individual performance to the whole organism. We shall now follow up this idea and consider further facts that will make this relationship even clearer.

Any change in one locality is accompanied by a change in other localities
We have seen that the reaction to a given stimulus can vary, and also that no process ever completes itself in a circumscribed reaction. We have seen, moreover, that wider areas, indeed the whole organism, always participate in any reaction. Thus, it follows that, with any change in one locality in the organism, simultaneous changes occur in other localities.

Even such an apparently simple reaction as the response of the eye to light is by no means limited to the contraction of the iris. For here we observe a variety of phenomena occurring throughout the body. Although they are perhaps of as much importance for the organism as the contraction of the iris, we usually overlook them because the examination of the pupillary reflex is the purpose of the stimulation. The effect of light on the organism is manifold, shows itself emphatically, and can be traced in changes in motoric and sensory fields.[1] We know, furthermore, that movements in one part of the body manifest themselves in changes of the motoric processes in various other parts of the body. This becomes particularly clear in the so-called induced tonus processes we have already mentioned; for example, in a case of cerebellar injury, if one flexes passively the hand of the diseased side, one may observe a corresponding flexion of the foot but also the reverse movement. Similar observations can be made on normal persons, only they are not so easily elicited.[2] This phenomenon, which has been described by Walther Riese and me, and the validity of which has often been doubted, has been confirmed through the chronaxie investigations of Kroll.[3] He found in normal individuals a change in the chronaxie value of the flexor and extensor muscles of the arm, corresponding to differences in the head positions and conforming with the relations between head and arm muscles as they come out in the so-called neck reflexes.

Investigations with a string galvanometer have also shown that a movement in one part is accompanied by electrical changes in analogous muscles of other parts of the body. Thus, an action current in the foot flexors was found when the fingers were flexed.

The more carefully we investigate, and the more we get out of the habit of observing only those phenomena that, for definite theoretical or practical reasons, seem most important to us, the more we find that, whenever a change is induced in one region, we can actually observe simultaneous changes in whatever part of the organism we may test. We encounter here the same state of affairs we have met above in the discussion of the symptoms in a circumscribed cortical lesion. This furnishes additional confirmation of the general validity of our second methodological postulate (cf. p. 35).

Homologous and heterologous changes in different fields
Inasmuch as we are dealing merely with homologous effects on various parts, one might assume that the strength of the stimulus breaks through the boundaries set by the reflexes and causes coexcitation of fields that otherwise would not enter into the reaction (in line with the theory of irradiation). This assumption, which cannot be disproved by mere academic discussion, cannot, however, be valid for those cases in which the effect on various parts of the organism is a different one; for one would be obliged to presuppose that the excitation may radiate to so-called heterogeneous fields. Now, as a rule, effects do take place in heterogeneous fields. We find that the differences in the effect of identical stimulation are due to the extent of the excitation in the

parts of the organism, and this effect is in proportion to the limits imposed on the excitation by the experimental setting or by a circumscribed defect through disease. A given stimulus produces heterogeneous effects when it spreads over more or less extensive parts of the organism. How far the excitation will spread depends on the experimental conditions or on the lesion in certain areas.

Stimulating the sole of the foot by a pinprick produces withdrawal of the leg. At the same time, however, pain is felt, and various corresponding phenomena appear in the whole of the body: the muscles, the vaso-motors, the pupils, and so on. If, however, the sensory tract to the cortex is interrupted through a lesion of the spinal cord, we may obtain only a reflex phenomenon without any of the other reactions – thus the reaction seems to be much simpler. On the other hand, however, the effect in the leg can be prevented by conscious effort, and the concomitant reactions become more intense. The dependence of the distance of spread of the stimulus effect on the condition of the whole organism (which can be codetermined by still other simultaneous activities) shows itself most clearly in cases of so-called reflex variation, in which entirely different systems are suddenly activated by the same stimulus.

When the "flexor reflex" is elicited, a simultaneous relaxing of the extensor "normally" takes place. A stimulation of the nerve of the knee flexor at the same time increases the flexor reflex. This seems natural, because the new stimulus acts in the same direction as the stimulus that elicits the flexor reflex. However, when we elicit the flexor reflex and stimulate, at the same time, the nerve of the knee extensor, we obtain the same effect, although the second stimulation should have resulted in a contraction of the knee extensor, because of the proprioceptive reflex. In other words, this contraction does not take place when the flexor reflex is elicited simultaneously. Why? Apparently there are additional factors that have caused the preference for, or the predominance of, the flexor reflex and the omission of the extensor reflex.

A distinction has been made between so-called associated and antagonistic reflexes, that is, reflexes that support or inhibit one another, the reason being really unaccounted for. Theorists have tried to introduce a number of factors that provide the cause for the predominance of an individual reflex in a given situation. But no explanation has, as yet, proved satisfactory. The effect certainly does not depend on the intensity of the stimulus that elicits the reflex, for the intensity of the stimulus would only affect the amplitude of the reflex reading. When two reflexes are stimulated, we can conclude only retrospectively, from the predominance of one, that it was the stronger. The strength of the reflex is not determined by the stimulus alone, and it need not be the same under varying conditions. To draw any conclusion as to strength of a reflex from the predominance of one reflex over another would be merely circular reasoning. The homolateral reflex (e.g., the homo-lateral flexion reflex) seems to prevail over the contralateral reflex (e.g., the contralateral extension reflex). Why? One has attempted to explain this by the time factor of the reflex onset: the stronger effect of the reflex that appears later is ascribed to some fatigue of the one already under way. For this explanation, the fact was especially suggestive that the effect of the second reflex is the stronger, the later it is applied and the longer the first one has been in effect (thus having been more fatigued). But this factor cannot always be the determining one. It is true that the flexion reflex is the more influenced the later the contra-laterally produced extension reflex sets in. If, however, one elicits the contralateral extension reflex first, and then the flexion reflex, the for-mer is, on the contrary, the more readily disturbed the sooner the flexion reflex sets in. This would not be possible if fatigue were the determining factor.

The Relation of Every Individual Reaction to the Organism as a Whole

In all these examples, which could be multiplied ad libitum, the reac-tions exceed the limits set by the theory of reflexes. Moreover, their course is really determined by the condition of the rest of the organ-ism. This shows that the reflex phenomenon is not only modified by the state of the rest of the organism, as has been generally accepted, but that the reaction, from the very start, depends on the condition of a field far beyond the reflex arc. The "reflex variations" are not varia-tions caused by the influence of other fields on the constant field of a reflex arc. They are events taking place in fields having a different extension. At first, it remains obscure how these wider fields become involved and why, at one time in one way, at another time in another way. All attempts to explain the phenomena by assuming the existence of certain further part processes apply only to definite, individual phenomena. However, other facts that contradict these assumptions appear again and again.

The stimulus effect is determined by the "functional significance" of the stimulus for the organism. The so-called nociform reflexes

There are further experiences that show that the effect pattern depends primarily on the functional significance of the stimulus for the whole organism. We have already remarked on the important fact that the nociform stimuli, indeed any stimuli relevant to the whole organism, outweigh other stimuli. However, as we have seen, there are exceptions to this law, for example, when the recognition of the stimulus object is more significant than the warding off of harm.

There are situations in which an individual endures pain, for example, for the sake of "higher" interest. The defense of the organism against injury is then not the most significant or the most essential task of the moment. This proves that stimuli are dominant not because they are nociform, not because there may be special noci-receptive organs (Sherrington), but because this injurious effect under certain circumstances becomes more important for the organism than all other stimuli to, or actions of, the organism. Again we see how important a factor the functional significance of the stimulus is.

This factor can be well demonstrated when an individual succeeds in interrupting strong bonds between definite stimuli and definite reactions. This is particularly marked if these connections are unusually strong, as in pathological cases. The patient Pf., described in detail elsewhere by me, presented the following peculiarity: if he turned his head toward one side, say, the right, the left arm described a forced movement in the opposite direction, that is, toward the left.[4] In this position, it remained tonic as long as the head remained fixed in this posture. Now, if the patient were asked to point with his left arm to somebody who stood on his right, he was unable to do so as long as the head remained turned to the right. One observed pointing-movement attempts in the left arm, while the head moved slightly toward the left. But actually the left arm reached the right side only after the head was completely turned toward the left. Conversely, where the head had not been brought into a special position beforehand, the patient was able, on demand, to point to somebody at the right with the left arm in a normal way. The same was the case if the patient pointed to somebody spontaneously. In both cases, we find (as in normal persons), together with the movement of the left arm toward the right, a head or eye movement in the same direction. Undoubtedly, we are not dealing here with a deliberate overcoming of "subcortical bonds." The patient is by no means capable of overcoming the forced bond by direct, deliberate counteraction. Furthermore, the altered reaction occurs much too promptly and spontaneously for this explanation to hold. The factor that determines his inability to execute a movement in the one situation and his ability to do so in the other is that, in the one situation, an action of an isolated part of the organism is required (i.e., to execute a single movement), while in the other the action occurs as governed by the whole organism (i.e., by the intention to perform an act adequate to the situation). In the first case, the pathological bond existing in the area that has to come into action is brought to the fore because the excitation takes place under artificially isolated conditions. In the second case the excitation in the same fields is apparently so different that the otherwise abnormally active bond between head and arm cannot become effective and may not even be present, even though the action brings the head into the same position as in the first case. It is always decisive whether or not the innervation takes place under the influence of the intention to point in compliance with the meaning of the total situation. The stimulus utilization (in this case, the stimulus given by the head posture) indeed depends on the whole. Probably also in the case in which two reflexes are elicited, the predominance of one can be accounted for by its greater functional significance for the organism as a whole in a given situation. At all events, other explanations are inadequate for certain cases.

The various phenomena in different fields form a unitary whole
All these facts indicate the existence of the relation of any reaction to the whole of the organism. Still another factor points in the same direction. Changes that can be noted in various regions of the organism are never independent of one another; rather they stand in a very definite relation to one another. They constitute a functional unit. It is impossible to inhibit artificially any one change without influencing the phenomena in other regions.

Impediment in one part of a reaction disturbs its total course
Adolf Freusberg found that the rhythmical, pendulous movements of the spinal dog can be prevented by holding one leg fast.[5] We have frequently observed that very complicated forms of tremor of one hand, or abnormal, pseudospontaneous arm movements can be stopped by holding fast one part of the limb in motion. If, in the course of a typical pseudospontaneous movement that concerns the entire half of the body, one prevents a member, for example, the small finger, from moving, then the entire movement stops: arm and leg become relaxed and hang down. For the course of such apparently relatively isolated, abnormal movements (like a tremor of one hand) to exist, a definite configuration of the rest of the body is necessary. This is shown clearly by the fact that certain positions or passive movements of the nonaffected parts of the body interrupt or modify the tremor. This is particularly pronounced in striatal or cerebellar phenomena.[6]

Meaningful modifications in cases of impediment: the righting reflex in the starfish; the wiping reflex in the frog; scratching in man
Another phenomenon illustrates the relation to the whole in still another way if, through an event in the rest of the body, an activity is not merely interrupted but modified in a meaningful way, so that the purpose of that activity can be fulfilled: if one brings a starfish into an abnormal position, then naturally its most important activity of the moment is the return to the normal position. As the experiments by William Preyer, Georges J. Romanes, and especially Herbert S. Jennings have shown, one can vary the abnormal position considerably and still find that the starfish returns promptly to the normal position.[7] Thirty variations of this return, depending on the starting position, have been observed, each being entirely different and immediately adequate, and impress one, as Friedrich Alverdes points out, "as having from the outset, reference to the whole, and as being carried through holistically."[8] The execution of these movements is certainly not the result of trial and error. If one elicits, in a frog, the wiping-away reflex by applying acid to a certain part of the body and amputates the leg by which the wiping movement normally is executed, the frog will immediately use another leg to do the wiping, as shown by Eduard Pflüger. E. Gergens has found the same to be true for the scratch reflex.[9] If one holds the leg, which is "adequate" to a definite location of the stimulus, the animal uses another

leg in the appropriate way. During the clasping position, stimulation of the nose of the clasping male toad, which otherwise elicits a reflex movement of the forelegs, now leads to a corresponding reflex in the hindlegs. This alteration of the locus of reaction apparently occurs in order to prevent a disturbance of the clasping. This explanation seems the most appropriate for understanding why, under these circumstances, the stimulation of the nose elicits a corresponding movement in the hindlegs.[10] Likewise the dog, if placed on one side, thus preventing the use of the extremities of that side, will always scratch with one of the upper legs, no matter where the stimulus is applied. This may lead to a procedure quite contrary to the usual one.[11] Similar phenomena are known to exist in men. Depending on the site of the itch in the body, we scratch ourselves with different limbs, but always so that the scratching takes place in the simplest manner with the least expenditure of energy and by the shortest route. This is also the case when the action of certain members is impeded. Then, without our awareness, another member executes the scratching movements with equal promptness, and also by the shortest way, in spite of the fact that the conditions are entirely new as compared with the normal.[12] I was able to observe similar phenomena in patients with brain lesions whose consciousness was dimmed. They grasped for an irritating stimulus and shoved it aside, in quite the same way as normal people: that is to say, with the appropriate appendage, which, if impeded, was promptly replaced in action by another appendage.

Only one performance is possible at the same time.
Exemplification by reflex phenomena
The fact that the whole organism is involved in each performance manifests itself furthermore in the phenomenon that basically only one performance is always possible at a given moment. It is difficult to decide whether there are exceptions to this rule in certain invertebrates and whether it be true that, in some echinoidea (sea urchins), the "pedicels, stingers and prehensile suckers operate seemingly independently of one another, and this, not only when they are located in distant, but also in neighboring parts of the body." Bethe himself is not quite sure of this, since otherwise he would not say "seemingly."[13] We cannot attempt here to decide whether or not we are dealing with a holistic performance corresponding to the respective situation. To do so, it

would be necessary to know the nature of the organism of the sea urchin much better. We mention this example to point out how careful one must be if one wants to determine whether, in a not very well known organism, we are dealing with one performance or with different, simultaneous performances side by side (when the events in question appear to us as different). One unfamiliar with the structure of human walking, one who did not know that arm, leg, and head movement belong together, would say that in the process of walking different things occur simultaneously, whereas actually it is a unitary performance.

Exemplification by the medusa; by mental processes in man
In the medusa, even according to Bethe, the conditions are unequivocally in favor of the law of "exclusiveness of each process in the nervous system," as he calls the phenomenon we have in mind. If the subumbrella of a medusa is touched anywhere, the manubrium turns in this direction. If, however, another point is stimulated simultaneously, the manubrium immediately changes its direction. Bethe has shown in a great number of examples that definite reactions in one part of an organism (cephalopod) cannot be executed at the same time as definite reactions in other parts. Bethe writes that this exclusiveness becomes particularly apparent in the behavior of the medusa toward the small, fast-moving crustaceans that live as parasites on its subumbrella. Sometimes the animal tries to remove them by a movement of the manubrium, sometimes by violent swimming movements. If swimming movements appear, the manubrium hangs down relaxed; if the defense with the manubrium takes place, then the swimming movements cease. Alverdes says of the nymphs of the ephemerida that they are not capable of following two different activities simultaneously, as, for example, walking or cleaning of the mouth apparatus while beating with the fanlike tail in the direction of an approaching object.

In our discussion of the fact that one reflex is inhibited by another or that a pseudospontaneous process is disturbed by other processes not belonging to the former, we have met corresponding phenomena also in human beings. We are familiar with this exclusiveness, particularly in psychic processes where it is usually described and studied under the name of the "limit of consciousness." Apparently we are here dealing with a very general principle that can be described by saying that at one time only one performance can take place in the organism.

*Every reaction is a "Gestalt reaction" of the whole in the form
of a figure-ground configuration*
These phenomena could still be interpreted in the sense that, while
one process takes its course in one part, the rest of the organism cannot become active in a way alien to this course. The facts, however,
point to an even closer relation of the individual action to the rest of
the organism. They show that the condition of the rest of the organism
is not an indifferent factor for the course in the part but that changes
in the rest of the organism influence the latter in a definite way. Consequently, we must regard the process in the rest of the organism as
belonging to that in the part; moreover, both constitute a unit. Once
one has become accustomed to taking into account the behavior of the
rest of the organism, which seemingly does not belong to the performance under observation, then one recognizes clearly that the process
in the rest of the organism is, by nature, part of the individual, apparently isolated performance. This holds true in the course of such simple
performances as reflexes — as well as in voluntary acts and perceptions.
We really must always speak of a reaction Gestalt that comprises the
entire organism. As we have discussed, one can differentiate in this
Gestalt, although only in a certain abstract sense, between two components — the "figure" and the "ground" (cf. p. 99).

When do processes appear in a part of the organism?
This view might seem exaggerated. Are there really no processes in the
organism that take place in the periphery exclusively? And are there
really no reactions during which the organism is at least not essentially
affected in its entirety? Certainly these may exist, but they are the
exceptions. We may find them in animals in that kind of artificially
isolated reaction as the conditioned reflex and those actions built up
by special "drill" and coercion, for example. However, even in these
instances, the rest of the organism is really not uninvolved. One mis-
judges the actual facts in these phenomena because one easily overlooks
the fact that the course of the process has been restricted to a compar-
atively peripheral sector by artificial interferences imposed by the
experimenter, by the artificial shunting off of the rest of the organism.
It would be more correct to say that the rest of the organism, because
of the minute experimental arrangement, remains in a definite and
constant state, thus representing a uniform background on which the

performances stand out. Such conditions arise also in the "border situations of life." We find, furthermore, relatively isolated performances in patients, in whom disease produces such isolation of parts. Finally, we know such performances occur in very intricate mental settings, for example, in certain psychological experiments.

The Relative Independence of the Performances from the Functioning of a Specific Locality to Which "Normally" They Are Related — The Holistic Relation of Performances. Exemplifications

The holistic relation of performances is furthermore expressed in their relative independence of specific regions to which they are normally related. This relative independence can be widely demonstrated in the most diverse performances. It is particularly impressive in the adaptation phenomena of cases with irreparable defects in specific regions. We have already discussed the instructive case of the unilateral calcarine destruction. We shall here relate a few further examples of defects in the periphery and in other parts of the nervous system, including those in the cortex.

Transplantation of nerves and muscles

We know that, if one transplants a part of the proximal portion of a peripheral nerve into the distal portion of another cut nerve and if neurotization of the distal portion is achieved, the previously paralyzed muscle can recover its voluntary activity. The process usually takes place in the way that Foerster has described in the case of transplantation of a part of the central portion of the accessorius to the peripheral portion of the facial nerve.[14] At first the facial muscles cannot be moved, either in an attempt to innervate them intentionally or through innervation of the accessorius. In a second stage, when the central accessorius fibrils are grown into the facial muscles and the electric stimulability has again become approximately normal, a contraction of the facial muscles occurs simultaneously with each voluntary elevation of the shoulder, this elevation being mediated by those branches of the accessorius that have not been transplanted. However, the facial muscles still cannot be innervated alone. But this condition changes, according to Foerster. The patient very soon succeeds in again innervating the facial muscles, directly and voluntarily. At first, the shoulder moves at the same time, but later the movements of the facial muscles and the shoulder are again separated. This development is most likely not a mere training effect. Of course, the patient tries until he achieves a proper innervation; but once the innervation is successful, it always takes place promptly thereafter. It is not possible to determine unequivocally how the proper innervation is achieved and what part the factor of practice plays in these partial nerve transplantations, because we cannot decide definitely at which moment anatomical conditions make the movement of the muscles possible. In total transplantation of a nerve, as Bethe has done by crossing the sciatic nerves of the dog, the conditions are more clear.[15] There we find that the correct innervation takes place without any preceding incorrect movements. This is also true in the transplantation of muscles, a condition particularly instructive because the new connection is established directly by the operation. In this case, we observe that the proper movement occurs immediately after removal of the bandage. For example, in transplantation of the flexor tendon – in the case of a peripheral paralysis of the radial nerve – "incorrect movement does not occur" at all. In such cases, in which the correct innervation appears immediately in the first movement executed, the assumption of any form of relearning is clearly impossible.

The usual interpretation of the results of these transplantations rests on the atomistic premise that the relation of each area in the cortex to its corresponding motor nucleus is independent. The isolated excitation of an area, and also the innervation of the corresponding muscles, supposedly is brought about by the fact that those "cortical excitation patterns," which underlie the "idea" of a movement (here the facial movement), are assumed to be separately localized and to have a distinct connection with the area (here the facial area). Through transplantation, this cortical excitation pattern, corresponding to the facial movement idea, acquires a connection with the cortical area for raising a shoulder. When this cortical excitation pattern is in excitation, the shoulder-raising area at first responds as a whole. Therefore, when the attempt is made to make facial movements, all the muscles are innervated that have a part in the raising of the shoulder. But the movements of the shoulder finally cease during the volitional innervation of the face. This is due to the fact that, within the cortical area for shoulder raising, a dissociation of the elements that are assigned to the individual shoulder-raising muscles has occurred. Thus, the cortical elements that correspond to the raising of the shoulder are innervated independently of the other elements, separated from the cortical excitation processes that correspond to the intention to move the face. Foerster says: "It is possible that now a tract is put into service which runs from the cortical facial focus to the accessorius nucleus, and which formerly was not used simultaneously with the volitional facial innervations."[16]

One must raise the question: How should the cortical "center of facial movements" now gain a relation to the shoulder focus, if this relation were not always existent? Or why should a connection between facial focus and accessorius nucleus, which existed right along, start to function now, whereas it had not functioned previously? And why should this connection have existed, if it were not necessary for functioning? This last assumption on the part of such an eminent scholar as Foerster illustrates exceptionally well what difficulties this view encounters, what paradoxical ad hoc assumptions it is forced to make. Actually, both assumptions appear completely unintelligible. One cannot be surprised if, on the basis of such conceptions, Foerster has to confess that "in the desire to explain the restitution processes, we can never succeed beyond a certain point" and that he himself was not able to explain the processes without resorting to a principle of "purposefulness." This principle could at best give the reason for the new formation, the impulse for it. It tells us nothing, however, as to how this formation itself is brought about.

The adjustmental shift requires no training of innervation
and no preformed histological connections
If we wish to obtain an understanding of how the new innervation is brought about we must concentrate on the fact that correct innervation is not the result of practicing but that the very first performance is already correct. This fact precludes the hypothesis of newly formed tracts or the training of tracts not formerly used. If the basic concept of normal innervation necessitates such an assumption in order to explain the results of transplantation, then very serious doubts as to the correctness of that concept must arise. In our opinion, the results of transplantation clearly show that this concept is untenable. Careful investigation reveals that it does not even fit normal conditions. Whenever we intend a certain movement we do not innervate individual

muscles or muscle groups, but a change in the present state of innervation of all the body muscles takes place. Thus, a pattern of innervation
results, in which one definite single contraction, namely, the intended
one, stands in the foreground. For the appropriate contraction of one
muscle group, that is, for that contraction by which a definite effect
results, a certain state of innervation of the remaining body muscles is
requisite. To be sure, we do not notice this state of innervation, because
it seems to be insignificant for the intention of that movement. But it
is not at all insignificant, it rather enables the organism to execute the
movement correctly.

One can observe, especially in cases of peripheral paralysis, that,
when a certain movement is intended, the excitation decidedly does
not propagate only into the nerve and muscle field in question. We see,
as in a case of peripheral facial paralysis, that, through continued effort
to innervate the paralyzed face, the excitation flows into other muscles
and results in false movements, especially of those muscles related to
those in which the effect does not occur. We can always observe that,
when innervation is rendered difficult, more or less extended so-called
associated movements occur. This, however, is only possible if there are
connections between the various fields, which are usually regarded as
isolated. The explanation of such facts offers no difficulty for our view
of the net structure of the nervous system, but it remains completely
unintelligible for the theory of isolated mechanisms. A definite configuration of excitations in the entire organism, especially in the nervous system, corresponds to any single movement, as well as to any
performance of the organism. The movement of a definite muscle group
is only the particularly outstanding part of the whole event. If the possibility for its realization is disturbed peripherally, as in the case of
paralysis, then that movement drops out, the excitation in the rest
of the organism is malformed, and thus the various associated movements occur.

How the excitation pattern comes about, when a specific movement
is intended, we cannot as yet determine with any degree of certainty.
Here we are facing the problem of how to explain volitional performance in general. In this regard, we can say at this time only the following: The intention of a volitional performance, like a volitional facial
movement, means a very definite attitude of the organism toward certain demands of the environment. This attitude finds its expression in

a special configuration of the organism and becomes apparent as the innervation of a definite muscle group. Thus, the explanation of innervation becomes part of the general problem of the adjustment of the organism to the environment, in fact, of the origin of a specific form of coming to terms with the world. The idea we are advancing here is in line with the general biological principles we have developed above. These principles enable us to explain innervation after transplantation on the same basis as normal innervation. To us, innervation of a particular muscle group does not correspond to the activity of an isolated apparatus. But under certain circumstances, the excitation takes its course through these apparatuses, because they offer the easier way to effectuate the innervation. From this view, it is not surprising that the innervation is effected equally correctly in that case in which the normal connection between the central nervous system and the peripheral part is disturbed and another connection is established. In other words, it is not surprising that correct innervation occurs as long as any connection whatsoever exists.

For our view, it is immaterial by which apparatus the new connection between the muscle and the organism is brought about. As long as a connection exists at all, the innervation succeeds because the total excitation pattern, which corresponds to the intended movement, can effectuate itself. This is because the total excitation pattern is not confined to a definite anatomical structure but represents a definite excitation Gestalt that can utilize, for its course, any available structure. This is the same phenomenon as the scratching reflex that promptly sets in (with the aid of other muscles) when the "adequate" muscles are impeded. The performance is based not on the activity of certain mechanisms but on certain potentialities of the organism that realize themselves by utilization of all sorts of substitute means when the "normal" means are out of order.

Phenomena similar to those just described become especially apparent in transplantations in the vegetative nervous system, as in transplantation experiments of vagus and sympathicus. Langley has connected the central end of the vagus to the peripheral end of the sympathicus and obtained a sympathicus effect when the central part of the vagus was stimulated.[17] Correspondingly, after connecting the central end of the sympathicus with the peripheral end of the vagus, he obtained a vagus effect when the sympathicus was stimulated. In Brücke's well-known experiment, the heartbeat is retarded when the depressor is stimulated – even if both vagi are transected – as long as the sympathicus remains intact.[18] The retardation takes place by way of the "vagus center," the excitation of which now becomes effective by way of the sympathicus. If one explains this phenomenon through reduction of a sympathicus tonus or through the excitation of inhibiting fibrils in the sympathicus, one simply makes auxiliary hypotheses ad hoc, which are completely unnecessary. According to our view, this phenomenon finds a simple explanation. The "mechanism" stimulated in this situation is composed of depressor, vagus center, and sympathicus. The performance in question, corresponding to the change that a stimulation of the depressor produces, is retardation of the pulse. It is mediated by the so-called vagus center that, when stimulated, reacts with pulse retardation. The channel used for this mediation is any available connection of the central nervous system with the heart, in this instance the sympathicus. It is immaterial by what channel the retardation of the heart is effected; as long as a nerve relation exists between the central organ and the heart, the retardation occurs. This shows that the sympathicus in itself neither accelerates nor retards the heartbeat. It is, like the vagus, the mediator of a performance that results from the total situation, or from the excitation of a mechanism that is in connection with the heart.

The sequelae of amputation
As a second group of examples, which prove the same point, we want to refer to the phenomena in amputation of one or more extremities in animals. If one amputates any extremities, as in arthropoda, the animals immediately walk with the remaining extremities in the most efficient manner, although under the new conditions, extremity and muscle combinations quite different from "normal" ones are used. Relevant experiments were first made by Wolfgang von Buddenbrock and were then carried out very systematically, especially by Bethe and his pupils in various animals.[19] In these investigations, the laws that govern the development of the new gait have been clearly elaborated.

The most important aspect of these significant experiments is, for us, that the shift to the new gait takes place correctly in the first attempt of the animal. This means that a complete change of the distribution of excitation in a large part of the organism takes place as soon as the demand of a performance requires it. This becomes particularly impressive when the new locomotion is of an entirely novel kind, never used before, as the experiment by Martin H. Fischer especially shows. All the legs of a guinea pig were amputated. Soon after awakening from the anesthesia, the animal began to roll around its longitudinal axis. Rolling was now the only possible means of locomotion.

The adjustmental shift in hemiplegia. Writing with the left hand without training: a further proof of holistic relation
We know of corresponding phenomena also in man. If one hand cannot be used, as in hemiplegia, or if one hand is lost through amputation, we find very often that the intact hand takes over the performances of the other with extraordinary promptness, and not infrequently after only a short period of transition. This is particularly pronounced when the right hand, the so-called predominant hand, is rendered inactive and performances are demanded, for the execution of which the use of the right hand is merely a "matter of course," as in writing. Persons whose right arm is paralyzed or amputated learn very quickly to write with the left. It is not really correct to say "they learn"; they do not need to learn because in principle they know it already at the first trial. What they really learn is how to overcome obstacles.

At first, they must overcome a psychological resistance against writing with the left hand, because they believe that they cannot write with the left hand. They must become accustomed to the necessity of holding the pen somewhat differently and to a somewhat different position of the paper as compared to right-hand writing. Furthermore, they must get accustomed to the fact that the written part is covered by the writing arm, if they write in the usual fashion from left to right, and that therefore they cannot immediately control with their eyes the process of writing. But once they have overcome these resistances, they soon write with the left hand as they once wrote with the right, although objectively not as correctly, and subjectively with somewhat greater effort. But it is not a question of having to learn to write the letters with the left hand in the way we all had to learn to write with the right. In principle, this capacity of writing with the left hand becomes particularly clear if the patient does mirror writing with the left hand, as is the case in some right-hand hemiplegies. The patient certainly does not learn this. He is surprised himself that he produces mirror writing when he uses his left hand in an unreflective or naive way. We do not want to discuss here the question of why mirror writing occurs. The essential point for us is that the patient is able to write promptly without any special training – be it with the left hand or with practically any movable member. Other performances are also soon promptly executed by the left hand.

Any normal person is immediately capable of writing with any part of the body that can be used at all for writing movements. But we are also able to write in quite unusual positions of the hand, for instance, if we turn the palm of the hand up or rotate the hand even beyond that position.[20] This is certainly not a case of training, nor does it indicate the existence of definite nerve connections. There is scarcely a more instructive and simpler experiment to demonstrate that a performance is not bound to specific anatomical connections and to prove that it is not the course of excitation within a specific apparatus that is essential for the performance but rather the functional pattern of the excitation. It shows further, that it is not a specific and constant way of execution that is basic but that a certain end has to be reached, no matter in what way, and that this way is always detrmined by the condition of the whole.

The shift is facilitated when a performance becomes entirely impaired
The following observation of Trendelenburg is also very illuminating.[21] After operation on the cortex of a baboon, by which the white matter below the arm and leg area of the left cerebral cortex was destroyed, only the left hand was used for the grasping of fruit by the animal. Seven weeks after the first operation, the left arm was amputated. Now the animal tried immediately to reach with the right hand for food brought into its cage. The following day, it was already capable of a more differentiated use of thumb and index finger toward each other, so that after a short period the right hand was used almost like a normal one. Now, a deep incision in the arm region of the left cerebral cortex was made. This again destroyed the capacity of reaching for food with the right hand. This reaching movement, however, could again be brought on if the food was not carried into the cage, but was placed outside, so that the animal could reach the food only by use of the arm. Although the reaching movements no longer turned out so well, still the arm was continuously used for grasping when the situation required it.

Similar to the way we have presented it in case of calcarine lesion, the general rule is that the adjustmental shift takes place when execution of the performance in the customary manner has become totally impossible. As long as an injured member is still capable of some performance, though imperfectly and impeded, the use of the other members for certain unaccustomed performances develops more slowly than in the case of complete incapacitation. Thus, after amputation, persons learn to write much faster with the left hand than persons with hemiplegia. The general functional impairment usually present in cases of hemiplegia, to a greater or lesser degree, certainly does not account for this difference.

We find the same difference also between incomplete and complete paralysis of the hand due to noncortical nervous disturbance. The adjustmental shift is facilitated if the customary execution of a performance has become impossible. The difference, as well as the promptness of the shift in general, becomes particularly clear in reactions of great vital importance, which are certainly rooted in the whole organism. While patients cannot possibly be made to carry out on demand volitional movements with the "inadequate" hand, this usually occurs very promptly in such vitally important reactions. For example, patients with a paralyzed hand usually remove promptly an irritating stimulus on their body with the intact hand, no matter where the stimulus occurs, even if this be a place where normally the other (now diseased) hand would be used to remove an irritation. But characteristically enough, this is the case only when the motor capacity of the "adequate" hand is absolutely insufficient for the performance. One often then sees that at first, such movements appear in the not completely paralyzed hand, which could bring the arm to the irritated place if the motions could be executed to a sufficient extent. But after a few futile attempts the movements in the damaged arm cease, and the other arm promptly takes its place and removes the irritation as much as possible. This is not due to deliberate and voluntary behavior of the patient but is tied up with a much deeper, more vital process. This is indicated by the fact that the process – at first the futile use of the damaged arm, then the prompt execution of the performance with the undamaged one – always takes place in the same manner. It is confirmed by the fact that the same behavior can be observed even when a patient is unconscious.[22] Patients with disturbed consciousness grasp the irritating stimulus object particularly promptly with the adequate member. If the adequate member is partially paralyzed, one first sees attempts to reach the stimulated place with this member. Only if the attempt does not succeed is another member used, the next adequate in line. Obviously it is essential for the organism to free itself from the irritating stimulus object. Normally, this is not always done with the arm; a person with undisturbed consciousness has a number of defense means at his disposal. He can defend himself against the stimulus by a glance, or a speech, or by withdrawing the entire body. If he realizes that the danger is after all not so great, he may even tolerate the irritation for certain reasons, as is the case in examination of a patient with sensory disturbance. All this is impossible if an individual's consciousness is disturbed. Only one behavior is available for such a person, and it occurs compulsively. It is the behavior that is suited for removing the danger by the fastest and safest means: by reaching with the hand. It is particularly interesting to see how an organism with disturbed consciousness protects itself when this adequate behavior is prevented by the adequate member being held back by force. At first the arm moves violently – apparently to free itself. At the same time there is an onset of all kinds of general reactions, like twitching of the face, and of that part of the body that is near the stimulus, and possibly a general unrest. If it is impossible to free the adequate arm, these general reactions cease, and the other arm, which is now the most adequate member, promptly reaches for the locus of the stimulus.

Bethe has found that the dung beetle, after removal of the middle leg, easily achieves a shift to an ordered gait. Rupprecht Matthaei amputated the lower part of the middle leg.[23] As a result, the animal moved practically without change, on a rough surface such as a blotter; the stumps were used like regular limbs, and the "remaining legs" accordingly showed the normal ambling gait. If, however, the animal were placed on a smooth surface, the stumps were no longer moved and the other legs now shifted, in the sense of a trot. In other words, an inability to reach the ground with the mutilated limbs had the same effect on the animal as if the limbs were missing, as if they had been totally destroyed; and in that case the shift occurred. But if the use of the stumps still proved effective for the gait, as on a rough surface, the normal mode of locomotion was maintained even if the walking itself were not totally normal. Kuehl observed similar phenomena in the crustaceans. Bethe and E. Woitas were able to determine that *Dyticus* maginalis, a beetle that normally swims only with the rear pair of legs, uses the stumps of these legs for swimming as long as that succeeds.[24] Only when this is no longer possible does it shift to the middle legs for swimming. Matthaei suggests the explanation that the shift occurs only when the receptor correlate of the movement of the partially amputated leg drops out. I do not believe that a proprioceptive report represents the essential factor. I am much more of the opinion that the shift occurs if the performance in question can no longer be accomplished in the ordered fashion. In support of this view, I may point out that the use of the stump does not give the identical sensory report as did the use of the entire leg. If, through the use of the stump, an essentially ordered performance is achieved, there is no real occasion for a shift. But as soon as this ordered performance drops out, then the shift sets in. Our explanation also makes intelligible another experiment, which Bethe has described. It is not necessary to amputate a leg of a dog in order to produce a shift; rather it is sufficient to tie a shoelike apparatus under a foot, by which a strong pain is produced with each step. In that case as well, the shift takes place. Obviously the strong pain makes the usual, normal gait impossible. Ordered behavior is therefore only reestablished after the pain has been eliminated by using the remaining limbs exclusively. For the same reason, fastening the leg to the body has a different effect than amputation, for it does not cause a shift. The fastening does not produce a simple impediment of the movement but a continuous irritation of the animal. Thus the animal is continuously urged to free itself from the fastening. The impossibility to do so leads to continued general unrest, to catastrophic reactions that prevent a new order, that is, the shift to a different use of the extremities for walking. Yet, according to Matthaei's view, it should lead to a shift. Apparently the adjustmental shift occurs always with regard to the whole organism. The essential factor is not the nonoccurrence of a sensation but the impossibility of producing the effect. Of course, sensations, or better, the total changes in the organism that appear during the effect and that continuously influence the action during performance, play a part. But they do this only after the shift has taken place. When one leg is missing, the stimuli sensations from this leg, which would be associated with the normal gait, are also missing. Beside the lack of the proper effect, this state may, at most, produce disorder in the act of locomotion itself, with the result of a catastrophic reaction. And so the lack contributes indirectly to the shift.

If the movement of the fastened limb is impaired, through transection of the sensory and motor roots, then the fastening does not hold up, or prevent the shift, as Bethe has shown. This is plausible, because then there is no reason for unrest and for attempts of the animal to free the limb. The small movements that occasionally occur in the free end of the fastened leg, according to Bethe, are not essentially disturbing. It is noteworthy that Bethe emphasizes that these movements do not correspond to movements that would be normal for the four-leg gait. Rather they fit into the changed rhythm of the three walking legs; thus they do not actually disturb but may even support the three-leg gait. They are not movements at all comparable to those in the attempt of liberation; neither are they random movements. Apparently, they "belong" to the three-foot gait. Thus, it becomes intelligible that the shift cannot take place when these small movements of the stump are prevented through a very strong fastening, as, for instance, putting the leg into a plaster cast (as done by Bethe), apparently because this causes a serious state of general unrest that hinders the shifting.

Just as in dogs, in crustaceans, and in starfish, so also in human beings with disturbed consciousness, the fastening of the member, which is adequate for the removal of a given stimulus, hinders the appropriate shift. As long as the adequate arm is held, so that the patient can still execute certain movements with it, movements occur in the arm. If no ordered removal is achievable, we find, besides the attempts to free the arm, general reactions that are rather the expression of the general shock and that appear not very appropriate for riddance of the stimulus. But if one holds the arm tighter, so that any movement is practically precluded, then the movements to free the arm soon stop and "ordered removal," with another extremity, takes place. This behavior, in a person with disturbed consciousness, shows clearly that, although these reactions can be modified by consciousness, they are not caused by it. We are dealing, rather, with phenomena that are deeply grounded biologically and that become intelligible only if we regard them holistically.

Dependence of substitute phenomena in cortical impairment on the whole
If a certain part is so completely destroyed that an adjustmental shift in that field is no longer possible, the relation of the reactions to the whole becomes especially clear in the characteristic substitute phenom-

ena that form in other fields. To what extent such substitute formations in animals play a part cannot be stated definitely. Sufficient specialized investigations, in this respect, are not available. But it seems beyond doubt that, for example, in animals, the total loss of vision can be compensated to a certain extent through a specific utilization of the intact senses and the motorium. At least animals with such disturbances do not simply perish. In any event, observations are available to indicate that animals, even in their natural life situations, have survived with such defects.

But the observations in patients are more revealing as to the rules of substitute phenomena. Some patients, because of a motor speech disturbance, have lost the ability promptly to solve tasks of the multiplication table, because in performing this task in their premorbid state they have predominantly drawn on motor speech series. They knew the performances, so to speak, motorically by heart. We see then that such patients create substitute means by utilizing performances of visualization whenever they are compelled to calculate; and thereby the individual's premorbid skill plays a considerable role. One of my patients proceeded as follows: He made a chart (matrix) of ten-by-ten squares, wrote in the first row and in the first column the figures from one to ten, and then wrote, in each one of the squares, the figure resulting from the multiplication of each figure of the first column with each figure of the first row. Thus he obtained a complete multiplication table from one to ten. When he had to solve a problem he drew on his visual image of this table, looked for the place that corresponded to the result of the multiplication, and "read off" the results. Naturally, to form such a substitute, a particularly well developed visual imagery is necessary.

Generally stated, individual premorbid skills are necessary for the formation of substitutes. Therefore the type of the respective substitute formation is not arbitrary. Hence the physician cannot develop substitutes arbitrarily, on somewhat purely theoretical grounds. Rather, in order to obtain a good substitute, it is necessary to know the individuality of the patient very well. It is interesting, from a general biological standpoint, that the utilization of a special ability may take place, on the part of the patient, completely "instinctively." The patient usually cannot render an account to himself as having had any special ability in that field. This became particularly clear in the substitute formation of the "mind-blind" patient, on whom Gelb and I have reported. The visual performances of this patient were disturbed to such a degree that he was unable to recognize even the simplest visual objects. Nor did he have the correct visual experience of "straight" and "curved." Therefore, he was also unable to identify letters or figures from purely visual impressions. To him, everything was a chaos in which he could recognize only light and dark spots. But he very soon learned to read without anybody instructing him. As we have reported in detail, he read by tracing stepwise along the light-dark margins, by making the macula, so to speak, glide over them. The experienced movement constituted, to him, a letter in the same sense as, for us, the seen letter. It is no question that he had achieved this kind of reading all by himself, really knowing neither how he developed it nor what he was actually doing. Not before we disclosed the nature of his procedure and had explained this to the patient did he become aware of the fact that he read differently than normal individuals do and than he himself formerly did. It is very doubtful whether he ever understood completely in what the difference consisted. But he learned one thing: namely, to use his new way of proceeding with great virtuosity. Since he saw only spots in front of him, the shape of which he was not able to comprehend, the tracing with his eyes was guided only by the borders between light and dark. Of course, he was not at all certain whether he started his tracing at the appropriate, right point and whether he continued in the right direction to gain the motor image characteristic for the individual letter. It was at first entirely a matter of chance whether he obtained a good result. Later, he learned to develop the tracing systematically on the basis of certain criteria and so arrived at a specific method of determining where to begin and how to continue the movement. That made it possible to "read" with greater speed and accuracy. The patient behaved similarly in "recognizing" other seen objects. He attained such perfection that his "detour" behavior was hardly noticeable and that he was eventually able to follow a vocation in which accurate measuring was very important: he had to cut women's leather bags of a certain form and size.

On the basis of these minute observations, we find that the general laws of forming substitutes are the same as in adjustments. Here as well, the cause is the complete incapacitation of a certain performance of particular importance for the individual. And here also, the impulse arises from the experience of a catastrophic reaction that sets in if such a performance is completely impossible. The substitution is formed without consciousness. Of course, the patient first tries and makes many errors till he finally reaches the right result, that is, one that gives ordered behavior. He maintains the procedure that he experienced on those occasions but without understanding how it leads to the good result. He remains without insight, in this respect, even when he improves the result volitionally by developing certain aids, which he has experienced as leading him more quickly to the goal; so for example, when he starts to read at the left, or when, after having traced a part of the object, he checks whether these experiences and his visual sensations coincide with one or another familiar kinesthetic image and so forth. Thus far, training can improve the performance but does not change, in principle, the procedure in the substitute formation. The adequacy of the substitute formation depends on the potentialities of the respective person and on the demands made on him. Thus it is pronouncedly related to the whole. The influence of the demand manifests itself in the fact that if the demands are too little, the adjustmental shift is imperfect, worse than it should be according to the kind of injury of that field, the impairment of which makes the adjustment necessary. Such demands, which are too small, can be caused by extraneous factors or, further, by defects of the organism itself. If the overcoming of difficulties is too much facilitated from without, the level of the performance drops too far, just as greater demands increase the performance level. We can observe this whenever we have occasion to study the behavior of different patients with almost the same defects in different life situations. The patients (as well as observers) are surprised to see what performances they can accomplish if one makes greater demands on them. Of course, the demands must be adequate to, and not beyond the capacity of, the patient. Patients with apparently serious defects are capable of extraordinary performances if certain life situations compel them, as Walthard has shown particularly well. But a too-severe shrinkage of the milieu, too great a reduction of demands, can be caused through further impairments.

Thus the shift or substitute formation may take place only insufficiently, or not at all, if it becomes useless on account of further defects that preclude the use of the preserved functions to such an extent that, by their use, the impaired organism could not achieve essential performances. One observes quite often that patients sustain certain disturbances without developing adaptations, either because in their case impairments in other fields forced them into inactivity or because such demands, suitable to cause the shift, do not even reach the patient, on account of the other defects. The adaptation varies, depending on whether a patient lives continuously in the protecting milieu of a clinic or whether he lives outside, where certain demands of everyday life compel him to utilize his capacities as widely as possible.

This difference became particularly impressive in two cases of mind blindness, which I had occasion to observe.[25] The analysis brought out clearly the various factors that favor or obstruct adaptation. The one patient showed impairment of visual perception to a high degree. But in spite of this lasting impairment, he developed such a far-reaching adjustment that in general this defect was not noticed at all. He was able to follow his vocation and to father a family. Closer examination revealed that this was not attained by adjustmental shift but by substitution (cf. p. 194). The patient had developed an unusual mastery in motor performances that enabled him, in spite of his impairment of visual perception, to meet all demands of his milieu. The other patient, whose vision was less disturbed, so that he was able to recognize quite a few things purely visually, also had developed certain motor substitute performances, but to a much lesser extent. They were so imperfect that he practically could not move in the dark and was able to execute movements only when looking at the moved member. The second patient, on the whole, seemed much more helpless than the first, also with regard to the motor field. Various factors account for this difference. Possibly the good substitute formation of the first patient was supported to a certain degree by his particularly good motor-kinesthetic endowment, which the second patient did not possess. We must consider, as a second factor in the development of the substitute, that the purely visual performance capacity of the first patient was extremely poor, that he would have been very helpless if he had relied on his visual experience alone, and would have continuously undergone catastrophic reactions. The second patient, on the other hand, was able to accomplish, by vision alone, performances that were essential for him. But probably still more significant than these factors was the fact that the whole situation compelled the first patient to develop much more the substitute means and made the performance, thus attained, appear to him as particularly valuable. This was not the case with the other patient. The first patient had no essential disturbances besides his visual impairment; his walking movements were not impaired, he was able to employ his hands skillfully, and he could communicate very well by language. He lived in a situation that made great demands on him. He had children for whom he had to care, and this he tried to do well, in accordance with his character. He followed a vocation, and the money he earned was important for his entire standard of living. In addition to this, he was an intelligent person of sound character. The seriousness of his visual disturbance very soon forced him to develop a substitute, if he were not to be continually exposed to catastrophic reactions. He soon realized that a definitely planned procedure of utilizing motor processes was necessary. Since he had married during his hospitalization, his life circumstances compelled him to leave the hospital. His vocation – in which he was, by the way, very successful – as well as his entire above-described life situation, constantly induced him to employ his preserved capacities to better advantage and to improve the substitute.

With the second patient, the situation was entirely different. Besides his visual disturbance, he suffered from a severe paralysis of the right arm and leg; he had a serious motor aphasia that in itself hindered him in the most primitive functions. He, too, was quite intelligent, perhaps even more so than the other, and possessed also a certain ingenuity and a great desire to make the most out of his life. But the scope of his milieu always remained extremely small. There was no question of learning or of following a vocation. On account of his general helplessness, he never even left the hospital and was continuously in need of care by nurses. To raise a family, for example, would have been utterly impossible for him. His remaining vision, although defective, was almost sufficient for the minor performances demanded by his narrowed milieu. Since this milieu did not require a better performance than he was able to accomplish by his preserved vision, only very poor substitute formations were developed.

We have treated these last two examples in somewhat greater detail because they were especially suited for a thorough analysis and because the results obtained point very clearly to the holistic relation of all biological phenomena. It will never become possible to achieve an insight into the problem of adaptation in animals to such a degree as obtained in humans, since we are never able to search thoroughly enough into their conditions of life. Yet, only then will it be possible to understand biological reality.

Localization and Specificity

The significance of anatomical structure in the brain cortex
The relative independence of performances, from the activity of a specific mechanism, must raise doubt as to whether one is justified in "localizing" specific performances in a circumscribed apparatus. This question, of course, leads to the still deeper problem of specificity in general. Are there substrata of specific functions? Are there "specific" tissues, nerves, sense areas in the brain, and so on? If the answer regarding the specificity of circumscribed apparatus is negative, the troublesome problem of specificity of functioning in general is not alleviated. In that case, the new question arises whether and how the phenomena, to which the term specificity alludes, are intelligible from an organismic viewpoint.

This specificity appears to be clearest and most self-evident in the difference between the various organs as to their structure and function. Who would wish to doubt the specific difference of liver, stomach, heart, brain and its substructures, and so on? Yet, we shall see later that this doubt is not altogether as absurd as it at first seems. Let us here take up the problem of localization of isolated functions in the cerebral cortex. The available material regarding the question of separated localization of individual performances has led to very heated controversies and seems particularly well suited to clarify the subject.

It is beyond doubt that the cerebral cortex contains tissue of highly diversified structure. Furthermore, these differences of structure hold a special significance for the relevant functions. The stratified structure, the differential complexity of that structure in veretebrates, the differential structure at the various places of the cerebral cortex, the indubitable relation of certain characteristically stratified fields, like the sensory and motor fields, to certain areas and certain fields of the sensory, or motor periphery — all these and many other facts point emphatically to differences in function. But how much beyond this is really ascertained? We cannot answer this broad question. Here we can only scrutinize the validity of various methods used to justify the claim of a differential functional significance of separate areas in the brain cortex. Thereby we are attempting to develop an approach to the localization problem, which is in line with the facts.

That the various areas of the cortex are heterogeneous becomes evident in ever-so-many investigations. The least certain and most indefinite results are those offered from the study of the morphology of the brain surface, of the differential development of the gyri in animals, in various human races and in individuals of different capabilities, especially in individuals with outstanding achievements. Such investigations have not even yielded important material for the purely anatomical comparison of animal brains and for the comparison between the brains of men and animals.

The microscopic studies have been, at any rate, more instructive. If we survey this field of research, we can assume, with a fair degree of certainty, that there are areas designed to receive excitation from the environment and others to mediate the motor performances.[26] Here also we find a one-to-one correspondence between certain sectors of the periphery and certain areas in the cortex; that is, an anatomical localization is possible. But it remains unsettled how these cortical areas, which I called the periphery of the cortex, do function. Only performance analysis can provide information on this point. Besides this periphery of the cortex, we have large sectors that, judging by their structure as well as by their relatively loose connection with the projection system, undoubtedly have a significance of their own relatively independent of the peripheral cortex. They represent, so to speak, domains of a higher order. I called them the central sector, which comprises the parietal, the Insula Reili, and particularly the frontal lobe, which is especially well developed in the higher mammals and particularly in man. Besides this differentiation as to central and peripheral sectors, we find one within the stratified structure, inasmuch as the individual strata apparently have a different functional significance. That is already expressed in the differences of fiber relations of the various strata to other parts of the brain. Some are in direct relation to the spinal cord, others to the pons, and still others to the cerebellum, whereas the fifth stratum seems to be of special importance for sensory performances. Opinions on this subject are far from unified. But one fact seems to be certain, namely, that within a specific area, one can also differentiate between a peripheral sector and one that is more related to other cortical parts themselves — a central sector.

What is the meaning of differentiation?
What can we deduce from the anatomical differences? Not much more than that the various species of vertebrates show certain conformities and certain differences in the structure of their brain, that the variations in structure are distributed around a basic type that is valid for all vertebrates. As far as the differences are concerned, we learn only that there are such, between the "higher" and the "lower" mammals and between the higher mammals and men, and that we find certain stratifications only in a human brain and never in an animal brain. This holds especially for certain fields in the frontal, the parietal, the temporal lobe, as well as in the Insulae Reili, all of which undoubtedly have a particular functional significance.

I shall pass over views that have been developed regarding the relations between the structure of the cortex and certain psychological performances, as the relations of specific strata to images and of others to perceptions. Most objections that we shall have to raise against the localization theory in general concern these views as well and render their significance very problematic, if for no other than methodological reasons. In fact, they seem by no means to be a contribution to our knowledge.

What the histologist has actually contributed to our knowledge, by his differentiations, is the possibility of topographical delimination of areas, their identification, and their divisibility into peripheral and central sectors. This delimitation and identification have true relevance if one wishes to compare injuries in different places inflicted on animals or destruction of different places through disease in human beings. Regarding function, the histological differentiation gives us hardly any essential information.

Only by comparing a definite performance with a definite brain locus, as attempted by brain physiology and brain pathology, could we learn anything in this respect. The relevant discussion leaned, on the one hand, on the observations of aphasic symptoms in circumscribed brain lesions and, on the other hand, on the results of experiments, where circumscribed parts of the cortex were stimulated. These experiments, first performed by Fritsch and Eduard Hitzig, and later repeated by many others on animals and human beings, have shown by the stimulus effect a strict relation between circumscribed cortical areas and circumscribed muscular and sensory fields. However, they have taught us very little regarding the functioning of the cortex. For this, the electrical current is too inadequate as a stimulus. And, more important, if a certain phenomenon arises through isolated stimulation, this does not provide any information regarding the organization of a performance and its relation to any definite area of the brain. The objections raised above against the reflex theory hold true here as well. In this connection, it is interesting to note that stimulation of the same cortical points by no means always yields the same results. In other words, the same stimulus may, under different circumstances, lead to different performances, a fact that we found so typical of the reflexes. At this point, we are essentially interested in the fact that these experiments again prove that stimulation of identical circumscribed foci is not always followed by the same effect and that here also any stimulus effect can be evaluated correctly only by considering the condition of the whole organism. The effect is only to be understood if one regards the process at the stimulated point, as "figure process" in a larger "ground process." As far as we find constant stimulus-effect relations, we are dealing with a special case of figure-ground process corresponding to special conditions.

Localization of mental phenomena

The theory of localization of mental phenomena is historically connected with the names of Franz Josef Gall, Bouchard, Dax (father and son), and especially Paul Broca and Carl Wernicke. Innumerable papers have been written concerning the minute construction of brain maps that were supposed to demonstrate the relation of certain performances to circumscribed brain areas. For a while, it seemed the ideal of a complete brain map was coming closer and closer to realization. (Head calls this the era of the "diagram makers.")

So strong was the suggestion that emanated from these brain maps, with regard to topographical diagnosis, so eminent were they in medical practice, that most investigators had not the slightest doubt that the research was on the right track. Until about one or two decades ago, the tenor of the entire literature was, in general, one of extreme assurance. Of course, more and more cases became known in which the symptomatology could no longer be fitted into these schematic constructions and in which the anatomical facts by no means corresponded to the theoretical premises. However, these difficulties were overcome by special, usually ad hoc explanations, which were presented and received with a surprising lack of critical attitude. One receives a very accurate impression of these attempts in glancing over the numerous diagrams in the survey François Moutier has given in his book on Broca's aphasia.[27] Today, one cannot read this survey without deploring the enormous but mostly futile scholarship that these attempts represent.

During the last decades, a more thorough examination of the anatomical, clinical, and psychological facts has finally severely shaken the so-called classical approach. To be sure, even today one finds authors who defend the principle of the localization theory in the old sense, thinking that all discrepancies can be overcome by a more thorough procedure along the same lines. However, the voices raised against the basic principle of the theory become increasingly more numerous, and the arguments continue to prove themselves of increasing weight. Thus, we find in wide circles today at least great skepticism toward the customary localization theory. But we cannot content ourselves with this skepticism and with a rejection of any attempt to form a concept of the differential significance of the various parts of the brain for different psychological functions. We cannot simply regard the mental activity as the expression of a functioning of the total cortex. The differences of symptoms, when the lesions are localized in different places, are much too convincing. We believe that the best way to obtain a correct stand toward the entire localization problem is by examining the objections that can be raised against the usual localization theory. These objections can run in three directions. The first concerns the anatomical foundations and is based on a critical evaluation of the anatomical facts that we owe especially to the untiring efforts of von Monakow.[28]

Superficial observation shows a difference in symptoms, whereas apparently the location of the lesion is roughly the same. These are, furthermore, cases that are negative in two ways: characteristic symptoms may be absent while there is a definitely localized lesion, while symptoms may appear without the presence of a correspondingly localized lesion. All this shows that it is impossible to regard the presence of symptoms as simply depending on the locus of the injury. From a purely anatomical standpoint, the locus is usually regarded too schematically, without considering sufficiently the nature of the injury. One overlooks the difference of the histopathological change in various diseases, or at various times of the illness, probably because one usually cannot observe the anatomical state simultaneously with the syndrome.[29] Generally, the anatomical state of the brain can be compared with a syndrome only as it was found before death. On account of the premortem and postmortem changes of the structure, this is, however, often only of very problematic value for our determinations. It is obvious that such determinations are not very reliable.

Furthermore, one is too readily inclined to evaluate anatomical differences only quantitatively, which is certainly incorrect. The different ways in which the various strata are involved are usually very difficult to evaluate properly and must certainly lead to qualitatively different symptoms.

The inaccuracy of the judgment regarding the anatomical facts is increased because we really do not know the relation between a specific state of an anatomical condition and a specific performance. We are far from being able to decide whether the preserved tissue is still functioning sufficiently to allow for a certain performance. We have no definite criteria for this decision. We do not even know the functional significance of the cortex in general and its various strata in particular for various performances. We do not know which performances are connected with the fine association fibrils and the subcortical tissue. We do not know to what extent each of these areas must be intact to maintain normal functioning. We are facing here a methodological difficulty that, as far as I can see, can scarcely be overcome at all. We shall probably never get beyond conjectures; yet only a definite knowledge, in this direction, can offer a basis for a solution of the problem of localization. Many errors and many controversies are caused simply by this uncertainty, which in a given case is so conducive to opinionated judgments.

Frequently, one has also overlooked the great importance of the condition of the rest of the brain and even of the whole organism for the development of syndromes in cases with local lesion. This was realized, particularly by von Monakow, who demanded a fundamental revision of the customary view on this point.[30] He emphasized the basic difference between initial and residual symptoms, which can be explained only if one considers the condition of the rest of the organism. Usually, the initial phenomena were explained by the initially larger expansion of the pathological process, which causes the injury of additional centers, although these are not directly damaged by the gross focus. It is further said that these phenomena disappear after the injury confines itself to a smaller region, because of a retrogression of the pathological anatomical process. But this explanation is not satisfactory, because, as von Monakow justly emphasized, the difference between initial and residual phenomena is by no means only quantitative but is also qualitative. Some symptoms almost invariably disappear to a large extent, in cases of exclusively local injury, whereas others do not disappear at all, or only very incompletely in cases in which the local injury goes only a little deeper. As von Monakow shows, these permanent symptoms are of a different, more primitive kind than the initial symptoms.[31] They represent losses of movement, of sensory functions, and so on, whereas the initial disturbances are of a more complicated nature. They are the "mnemic" defects proper, the apractic disturbances, mind blindness, disturbance of inner speech, and so on. These differences are caused, according to von Monakow, by a difference in relations of the various performances to the brain matter. The more primitive functions can be lost permanently because they are really related to a specific locus and correspond, in their localization, to parts of the periphery, inasmuch as these loci are the most essential point of entrance for nervous excitations from the periphery into the brain. However, the assumption of such a relation of certain loci to mental performances proper is out of the question. The fact that mental performances, in cases of circumscribed lesions, are in principle subject to regeneration proves that they are not limited to the function of certain places of the brain but that much more extended parts of the nervous system correspond to them, which are only temporarily incapacitated by a focal lesion, by the so-called functional diaschisis. By this term von Monakow understood "the dynamic distance effect" radiating from the locus of the cortical lesion. This distance effect produces a suspension of function in such places where fibers, emerging from the area of the focus, terminate in the gray substance, although the latter was not primarily injured. Thus, the responsiveness of the elements, within a definite physiologically well defined area of excitation, is reduced or abolished. This effect of the diaschisis, by its very nature, can be restored in varying ways. The more complex and less used the functional connections are, the longer they remain disturbed through diaschisis. Above all, the effect depends on the nature of the disease, on the vascular supply, and on the condition of the entire brain. It is evident that, in such a relation of the performance to the nervous system, the condition of those fields that are not directly damaged will have the greatest influence on the symptomatology. Thus, a proper evaluation of the connection of a syndrome with a circumscribed lesion cannot be referred simply to the locus of the lesion. One therefore has to conclude that a decision on any question of localization is extremely difficult, especially if one considers how little we know, up to now, regarding the brain neuron connections corresponding to an individual performance. We must further consider how little we know as to which performance is more difficult, which one is easier, and what part the individual's capability plays for any performance. Of course, it would be very important to comprehend configuration of the neural structure, in which the excitation during a certain performance takes place, and to know the functional significance of each particular locus in this configuration. But this determination encounters extreme difficulties, since our knowledge in this field is still very imperfect. Here, the study of anatomy alone takes us but little further. Those who discuss these matters merely from the anatomical viewpoint usually neglect another factor: the destruction of one part of the brain never leaves unchanged the activity of the rest of the organism, especially the rest of the brain. On the contrary, there usually occurs a change of the distribution of excitation. If we do not consider this fact, the syndrome, in case of a local injury, remains altogether unintelligible.

In summarizing our discussion of the possibility of a correct anatomical evaluation, as a basis for localization, one thing seems certain: it renders rather unsatisfactory service to determine simply the location of a lesion. Whether a certain symptom will appear on account of a local injury, especially whether it will become a permanent symptom, certainly depends on many other factors: on the nature of the disease process, on the condition of the rest of the brain, on the state of the circulation, and on the psycho-physical constitution of the patient. It also depends on the "difficulty" of that performance, the disturbance of which represents the symptom, and, finally, on the reaction of the entire organism to the defect.

Criticism of the localization theory on a symptomatological basis
The criticism of the localization theory, on the basis of symptomatological considerations, has become even more serious than the anatomical criticism. We have previously shown that the usual procedure in disclosing symptoms did not comply with the most necessary method-

ological postulates. We saw, furthermore, that if subjected to greater scrutiny than is usually the case, the classic assumption of specific, separate losses of individual performances cannot be maintained. We found, rather, that a systematic reduction (dedifferentiation) results, a dedifferentiation that can be evaluated properly only in relation to the whole organism. Depending on the part of the brain that is injured, this reduction affects one circumscribed performance field more than others. When the so-called peripheral areas are injured the reduction is relatively more isolated in one motor or sensory field. When the central areas are injured the reduction always affects all fields. But in the first case also, we do not find "dropping out" of isolated performances but rather a systematic dedifferentiation of the functioning of that entire field. Only in subcortical lesions is a loss in a circumscribed sector possible. For this is almost the same as if a peripheral sector itself had been affected, to wit, it interrupts the relation between the organism and a certain part of the outer world.

We cannot discuss in detail the changes in circumscribed lesions of the brain cortex. They can be classified and understood very clearly from the general point of view of the disintegration of nervous functions (cf. pp. 42, 115).

Can an analysis that is methodologically incontestable prompt us to form a concept of the localization as to mental performances, that is, as to a specific significance of definite areas? In this connection, we must refer to an argument having general bearing: von Monakow in particular has emphasized that we are by no means justified to infer directly, from a relation between a localized defect and a functional disturbance, a relation between the area corresponding to that defect, and a performance. If this difference between the "localization of the disturbance" and "the localization of the performance" is not strictly observed (as is frequently the case, especially in animal experiments), then the consequences are fatal and lead to unnecessary disputes.

On the basis of thorough investigations, which are reported elsewhere, regarding the entire localization problem, I have come to a conclusion, which I will cite here briefly and which demonstrates what direction, in my opinion, our science will have to take in the future.

Localization of a performance no longer means to us an excitation in a certain place, but a dynamic process that occurs in the entire nervous system, even in the whole organism, and that has a definite configuration for each performance. This excitation configuration has, in a certain locality, a special formation ("elevation") corresponding to the figure process. This elevation finds its expression in the figure of the performance. A specific location is characterized by the influence a particular structure of that area exerts on the total process, that is, by the contribution that the excitation of that area, by virtue of its structure, makes to the total process.

The so-called specificity of the senses
With the above conclusion, the posited specificity of certain circumscribed areas in the cortex, conceived as related to single mental performances, seems untenable in principle. Nevertheless, the question remains whether we should not have to assume specific substances or processes for such definite qualities as color, tone, and so on, complying with the so-called theory of the specific energy of the senses.

Of course, to say anything with regard to this question, the facts ought to be more clarified than they actually are. The problem of the specific sense energies in itself is today very much open to discussion. We have met new "senses," as, for instance, the sense of equilibrium and vibration. It seems that the cutaneous sense is being divided more and more into diverse senses, and we must first of all be clear about the following: all these single senses owe their delimitation to a certain procedure, to the isolating segregation of single experiences from the total pattern of phenomena that occur when the organism reacts to a so-called sensory stimulus. In this way, we could perhaps find a great many more distinct senses. But here too, the question arises: Are these separate senses not perhaps the product of this procedure? Do such specific experiences really exist, or do they not, perhaps, owe their existence to this special attitude of introspection? It is a just description to say that, even while assuming this attitude, the phenomenon exhausts itself in that particular experience. And do we, in everyday life, behave in any such fashion? Fundamentally, we are faced here with the same question as in the case of the reflexes, namely: Do not the specific sense modalities possibly owe their discreteness to the isolating procedure? And what is the meaning of the facts, thus determined, for the life of the organism? The decision on this question is certainly not without interest for the question of localization and specificity. The data of observation pointed to very intricate processes and very complicated figure formations as basic to various performances in general. In the same way, the experience of an isolated color or tone would be indicative of a very intricate brain process. This complicated brain process in itself, however, could certainly not be thought of as a foundation for the understanding of the phenomena of sensation as such. What we call sensation, in a special sense modality, is but a very complicated special instance of a total reaction pattern of the organism during its coming to terms with those events of the environment that demand sensory experience.

Even the bare content of perceptual experience is by no means exhausted in sheer sensory content, as color, for example. Other experiences are probably still more important in normal life, for example, all that we generally call "mood" or "atmosphere," into which we are brought by a certain sensory stimulus. Artists especially, for example Goethe and Kandinsky, have not only recognized this effect of sensory stimuli, but have considered it to be the essence of perception.[32] Our language contains manifold traces of such experiences, as, for instance, when we talk of the softness, the gaiety, the vigor of a color, of its coldness, of its piercing character, and similar attributes. Such experiences are particularly pronounced when the "objectifying" attitude is not as much in the foreground as is customary, either because of the situation or some lack, as in disease.[33] As an instance of this we find, in patients, that these types of emotionally saturated experiences become particularly marked. Patients may present descriptions of their experiences occasioned by color, which show an extraordinary agreement with those of Goethe and Kandinsky.[34] This points to a close and constant relation between these special experiences and the total reaction of the organism to sensory stimuli. We may conjecture that animals have experiences similar to these, whereas very serious doubts exist whether they have objectified color experiences.

Yet even the inclusion of these phenomena by no means exhausts the entire range of sensory events. Numerous investigations have shown that, simultaneous with the perceptual phenomenon, a great variety of additional somatic events takes place. The so-called tonus processes, especially those that occur during optical and tactile sensations, are the best-known examples. We are justified in assuming that a certain muscle tension corresponds to every sense impression. Of course, this tension will differ according to the total situation, since it also depends on other processes. Thus, we were able to state that usually quite the opposite effects go with green and with red color stimulation.[35] If one asks a patient, preferably a cerebellar patient (who exhibits these phenomena, often exceptionally clearly), to raise his arms forward so that they are in a somewhat unstable position, and if one exposes him to various colors (e.g., large sheets of colored paper), we notice that green and blue stimulation lead to a change of the position of the arms in the opposite direction as that induced by yellow or red stimulation. In the first case, the arms move together (if before they were in a definite position); in the second case they move apart. We shall have to discuss later on what this difference, adduction in one case and abduction in the other, means for the organism. We know, further, that color stimuli do affect a diversity of other performances and events in the body; for example, that color influences the volitional movements. Under red and green lights, movements are carried out with a different speed, without subjectively experiencing the change in speed. Likewise, the estimates of traversed distances vary as to length; seen and felt distances, time intervals, and weights are judged differently under the influence of different colors.

It has been shown that, under the latter condition, the organism behaves differently, even morphologically. We have been able to demonstrate, in a very interesting case, that the refraction of the lens can vary to an objectively noticeable degree depending on whether the eye is exposed to green or red light. With green lights the refraction in this patient was normal; with red lights it was changed, as in a myopia, by several diopters.

It is probably not a false statement to say that a specific color stimulation is accompanied by a specific response pattern of the entire organism. The contention is made for all sense organs that to every sense stimulation there is a corresponding specific response pattern of the entire organism.

We may go even further and say: this pattern formation is not limited to stimulus objects that evoke specific sensory experiences; it also occurs under stimulation that does not involve sensory objects. This can be due to infrared or ultraviolet light where the effects of stimuli are not mediated by an organ appropriate to the stimuli. We should mention here that a differential effect of colors is by no means limited to stimulation of the eye, but that it also holds for light stimulation of the skin in general, although to a much lesser degree. (It is hardly necessary to emphasize that during these experiments all optical influences were excluded and the subject was prevented from seeing the light.)

These last observations are important because they show that the sensory organs are not the only inlets for the influence of specific stimuli, though they, of course, play a preferred role as entrance gates for those stimuli, and perhaps indirectly also for the achievement of specific optimum performances, as, for instance, objectifying experiences. These findings enable us to eliminate the possible source of error for a proper appreciation of the generalized effects of stimuli, the source of which lies or could lie in an inference from conscious sensory experience.

We can even determine more precisely the response pattern of the organism to color, inasmuch as it differs for the individual color quality. We have already mentioned the differential effect of red and green on the position of the arm. Taken as an isolated phenomenon, it seems at first inexplicable. However, if we consider it together with the accompanying observable facts as expressing different forms of response patterns of the entire organism, then the phenomenon becomes intelligible. Then we see that not only does green have a different effect than red, but also that it causes deviation in the direction toward flexion (adduction), whereas red works in the direction toward extension (abduction; cf. p. 128). We find, furthermore, that green favors performance in general, in contrast to red. The effect of red probably goes more in the direction of an impairment of performance, in the direction of shock reaction. These different effects correspond, of course, to very definite but different total behavioral attitudes, which find their expression very clearly in the subject's reports of the mood corresponding to the various colors.

The close relation of colors to certain total behavioral attitudes is shown by the fact that the behavior patterns, in turn, can influence color perceptions in a characteristic way.[36] I myself could not as yet strictly prove this experimentally on patients because such experiments offer great methodological difficulties. But on the basis of my experiences with patients, I do not doubt that "experience of a specific color," the "specific mood and attitude," the definite state of the organs, and finally the "performances" of the organism – that all these aspects are but artificially separated factors of a unitary process that represents a

212

coming to terms of the organism with a definite happening in the outer world, called light of a definite wavelength.

What holds for vision seems to hold for all senses in so far as we can draw conclusions from the available experimental results (e.g., of Heinz Werner and Karl Zietz). We can, however, say that aside from the difference in the various sense modalities, the various senses manifest essential conformities. Language often expresses these common characteristics very clearly. We use the same words for experiences in various senses. We talk, for instance, of warm and cold, of agreeable and disagreeable, of bright and dark, of sharp and dull with reference to colors, tones, and smells. Investigations, especially those by Erich Moritz von Hornbostel, indicate the far-reaching conformity of the experience of brightness and darkness in the most varied sensory fields.[37] According to Hornbostel, these phenomena must not be regarded simply as analogies, but as one identical aspect of the various phenomena. Most likely, the same is true for other phenomena, as moods, attitude, and bodily processes (posture, tonus, refraction of the lens, and so on).

These facts lead us to the much discussed problem of synesthesia. The proof of common features in the experience via the various senses has given an entirely new aspect to this problem. We don't have to look any longer for such causes as past experiences to account for the relation between the different sensory phenomena, which was erroneously termed synesthesia. Rather, we should look for the basic organismic configuration that, as a total response pattern, accounts for the conformities in question. We should no longer talk of the "transference" of the effect from one sense to another but of the unitary, homologous pattern. This unity of the senses was overlooked by investigators, because they dealt with the artificial derivatives of all sense experiences as they emerged from the objectifying introspection toward isolatedly given stimuli. Through this objectifying attitude, the common ground of the given sense experiences becomes hidden, and the "segregated content of consciousness" prevails in a differentiated way.

The most important result for our problem is that in all senses we must regard very essential features of the sensory processes as homologous if not identical. This means that we have to understand these common characteristics from a unitary organismic process, the total pattern of which varies corresponding to the respective perceptual constellations and situations. Hence definite localization, in a circumscribed sensual field, can no longer be a matter of discussion. From this point of view, the individual sensory processes are merely individual patterns of the whole organism. For example, what we call green is, on the one hand, an event in the outside world and, on the other hand, a certain pattern of the whole organism of which the objectifying psychological experience of the color, green, is only one aspect that is not even absolutely essential and certainly does not represent the basis of the entire process.

But in this way, is the specificity of the individual senses really entirely lost, and does the problem of specific structures become entirely superfluous? I do not think so. We can only state that if specific areas and specific structures or processes are lost, or if they are imperfectly developed, the objectified conscious color experiences are lacking. Just how far the other processes belonging to them are changed in such a case has not as yet been investigated, as, for instance, the tonus of color-blind people during the exposure to chromatic lights in comparison with people of normal color vision. It seems to me hardly doubtful that here, also, the whole response pattern will be influenced.

Thus, regarding the localization of sensory qualities, we reach the same result as for localization in general. A specific performance, and thus also a perception, is a specific pattern of the whole organism. For the normal organization of this specific pattern, in a so-called sensory performance, those structures are certainly of special importance that we designate as sensory organs or cortical sensory fields; and of course without them the specific sense perception does not take place. It is here that the figure process is formed during a sensory performance. Within this frame of interpretation, the assumption of specific "sense energies," as unique qualitative processes, is justified. However, the figure processes tied to the functioning of certain localities gain their specificity only by virtue of the whole process in which they are embedded; specificity only arises in the whole. If we start from the normal state, that is, from a certain whole process to which the conscious content of a color object corresponds, then the "sensory energies" appear as constant. This constancy, however, is but a special instance, although it is one of particular importance for normal life. According to our view, each stimulation always causes a change of the entire condition, and only apparently a locally confined change. The specific local area is possibly only the best route by which the influence from without can enter. The place of influence does not provide any relevant information as to the real effect. Nevertheless, it may be of great practical significance, because from there, the best performance can be obtained.

This result is of great interest to us on account of its agreement with our general views regarding localization, which were obtained on the basis of entirely different material. But beyond that, it receives particular significance in conjunction with the appreciation of sensory performances and their connections to specific organs, a problem that plays such an important role in animal physiology and biology. Just as in the reflex investigations, we must here never forget that in these explorations of sensory performances, we are also dealing with phenomena in isolation, which might owe their specific character to that artificiality. Moreover, only such methods will really carry us further, which consider the single phenomenon in its significance for the whole organism. Only investigations with that emphasis will give us an understanding of the actual meaning of a phenomenon in respect to its functional significance (e.g., of a color) for the organism in question.

The so-called specificity of the vegetative system

There is still another field in which the problem of specificity plays an important part, namely, in the vegetative nervous system. We have already thoroughly discussed the facts in question, when we showed that they are by no means of such a nature as to justify the idea of isolated processes in this system. In analyzing the experiments of von Brücke and Langley (cf. p. 187), we have come to these results: when an isolated part of the organism is stimulated, the effect of the stimulus is to be understood by the functioning of this part only under this condition of isolation. If the isolated vagus center is excited, the effect is determined by the functioning of this center alone. If a nerve is connected only with the periphery, then the effect of its stimulation is determined only by the functioning of the peripheral organ. This, however, must not be understood to mean that single parts show once and for all the same specificity. The many experiments that we have reported above have revealed that stimulation of the same part, but not in a state of isolation, results in different phenomena, varying with the conditions.

The specificity arises in every case from the special total situation in which the part is embedded.[38] For this reason, we cannot agree with

J.M. Schiff, who on the one hand refutes the specific function of the nerves as we do and on the other hand continues to assume a specificity of the tissues for explanation of the facts.[39] Fundamentally, that means the identical theoretical viewpoint, namely, the assumption of a constant specificity of a single structure. Whether such a specificity exists at all, however, is the problem. It is specificity as such that has become problematic. Actually the same poisons can produce very different reactions in the same tissue, depending on many factors and on the respective situations. This is quite similar to the effect of nerve stimulation. A tissue is not an invariable indicator for the effect of a certain poison; in fact its reaction specificity changes according to the whole situation that is determined by the relation of the tissue to the nerve and to the humoral activities. Critical analysis of the facts, in the field of vegetative processes, certainly does not give us cause to talk of a fixed specificity of certain tissues. But only then would this term have any meaning at all. We are again confronted with the task of understanding the specific performance by the respective total situation.

Our view does not deny, by any means, the special significance of specific structures. Their existence is, after all, beyond question. Indeed, the organism consists of qualitatively different structures. From an extreme standpoint one could go as far as to say that no two localities of the organism are structurally equal and the defect of any part always causes a somewhat different functional change. But this does not imply that that quality, which the functioning of any part contributes to the organism's performance, exists by itself outside that whole relation. The defect of certain fields deprives the performances, the processes, and the experiences of certain qualities. But the specificity itself arises within the functional pattern of the whole to which each part, by functioning, contributes a very specific qualitative tonality.

The So-Called Antagonism
Among the "facts" that conflict with our holistic approach, those that underlie the principle of the so-called antagonism seem especially worthy of comment. According to this principle, a performance is regarded as the resultant of opposing forces. It is exemplified in the unitary effect of two antagonistically operating mechanisms, a phenomenon that, in isolating observations, one almost invariably notices. Such a view is advanced for performances that depend on the nervous system, as well

as for processes in general. It is even found as a general theory of life that, in this light, appears as the expression of a struggle between opposing forces.

"Antagonistic innervation" of voluntary muscles
We do not wish to discuss the problem in its broadest scope; but in keeping with our usual procedure, we only want to examine some of the facts. We start from the well-known problem of reciprocal antagonistic innervation of the muscles that, so to speak, is regarded as an innervation of the antagonist counteracting the activity of the agonist. Sherrington found that in the "spinal cat," it is impossible to bring about the reflexlike contraction of the extensor, while the flexor reflex is released.[40] But on the other hand, it is possible to make the extensor rigidity disappear or to weaken it by releasing the flexor reflex. This contrast became even clearer when Sherrington severed the muscle from its insertion. He could directly observe that, while the flexor contracted, the extensor relaxed and became longer. On these and similar findings of Sherrington and other authors, especially Ewald Hering, the theory of the "reciprocal inhibition" was based and received support by the discovery that the conditions were the same for innervation of the agonist and inhibition of the antagonist with regard to stimulability, latent period, and so on.[41] The "reciprocal innervation" was found not only in movements, released by reflexes, but also in central innervation. Verworn proved that it was a central process.[42] Pathology has shown that the proper connection of antagonistic muscles can be disturbed by the lesion of very diverse nervous apparatuses, from the spinal cord up to the cortex, and therefore all these apparatuses probably have something to do with the antagonistic innervation. However, the opposite effect, in the antagonists, is to be observed only if one stimulates the respective muscle in isolation. During innervation, where the muscle is not stimulated in isolation, one observes not the above effect, but diversified phenomena in the antagonist.

Under certain circumstances — for instance, a coordinated movement — a coinnervation takes place. Sherrington already had found that, at least under special circumstances, as in strychnine poisoning, agonist and antagonist are contracted simultaneously.[43] He, however, interpreted this as reflex reversal under the influence of the poison. But, if we consider natural voluntary innervation, we find that reciprocal relaxation is by no means the typical phenomenon, but at best only a special case. According to the old experiments of Guillaume-Benjamin Duchenne and Rieger, antagonists can behave under this condition quite differently. It has been pointed out by von Brücke that the diversity of the antagonistic innervation depends on the varying outside resistance, against which the movement is executed, and also depends on the variety of the intended performances.[44] When the resistance is strong, that is, strong innervation of the agonist is required, then the antagonists are very little or not at all coinnervated. On the other hand, in finer, more precise movements, both muscles are innervated and cooperate. In rapid, forcefully executed movements the antagonist may appear relaxed; in a movement toward a goal or still more in a fixed posture, both are equally strongly innervated. To regard the state of relaxation as "denervation" or as inhibition is really unfounded. It is simply a case of less innervation, which may appear like a relaxation when the muscle was under stronger innervation than now. The observable fact is the low degree of innervation. Everything else is theory, and in our opinion, superfluous theory. Actually the string-galvanometer experiments of Wacholder show that each time the agonist is innervated it is also in a state of some innervation. He found that even in free movement the antagonist carried an action current.

The relation of agonist and antagonist to each other evidently depends on the kind of performance. This shows itself particularly when muscles, which are not at all connected with the member to be used, as, for instance, in cases of amputation, agonist and antagonist behave differently with regard to their innervation, depending on what performance is intended by the individual. Thus, we find that in an arm, amputated according to Ferdinand Sauerbruch, the flexor and extensor of the free muscles of the upper arm are innervated simultaneously when the patient intends to close his fist, which would require a fixation of the elbow joint (by an analogous innervation of flexion and extension).[45]

These facts are noteworthy because they show that the distribution of excitation in the antagonistic muscles is not alone determined by stimuli from the outside world but also by central processes, by the "intention," and by the whole configurational condition of the organism at the time. It is hardly necessary to say that, normally, events of the outside world also exert an influence. Yet they likewise do not act directly on single parts but indirectly by their influence on the total configuration of the organism. It is essential that the ratio of innervation of agonist and antagonist always depends on the configuration of the whole organism.

But do not these facts undermine the principle of antagonism and perhaps even render it superfluous? Is one justified in regarding the cooperation of muscles under certain circumstances only as the lifting of the "reciprocal inhibition," and in regarding the central innervation of both – in the proper ratio – merely as a modification of the "reciprocal inhibition," as some authors actually do? For instance, one author writes: "The reciprocal innervation of antagonistic muscles is by no means a nonsuspensable modus of physiological processes." But why talk at all of suspension? Would it not be easier to understand a "modification," if one would abandon the assumption of such mechanisms as "reciprocal inhibition" and attempt to understand the various facts through the appropriate change in attitude of the whole organism? One could just as well regard the "reciprocal inhibition" as a "suspension" of the reciprocal cooperation. That shows that neither explanation is expedient. I mention this particularly because it is characteristic and shows where one can be led by a generalization of certain facts, which have been found through isolating experiments.

Our holistic interpretation of the so-called antagonism
The facts find their simplest and most unbiased interpretation in the following: in the case of agonistic and antagonistic muscle groups, which are active during one performance, as in flexion of the lower arm, there are never two antagonistic mechanisms active. We are not even dealing with isolated innervations, but only with one. During voluntary innervation, the excitation is so distributed over a certain group of muscles that, depending on the "intention," sometimes into the one, sometimes into the other sector of the muscle group, more innervation flows. When a definite movement is intended, then, corresponding to the required distribution in the different sectors of the muscle group, the differential excitation in the spinal apparatus takes place. This pattern of excitation, in the various sectors, forms the "figure process" that stands out as a definite Gestalt of excitation distribution, against the rest of the organism, which forms the background. In the total configuration, the excitation of the agonist, or of the antagonist, represents a part that can only be artificially isolated. Since the excitation Gestalt

has a temporal course, it would not speak against the existence of a homogeneous whole process if the change of excitation were to appear in the agonist and the antagonist at somewhat different moments. The excitation might arise slightly later in the antagonist than in the agonist. Of course, any change at any part or locus of this figure must modify the whole figure and the excitation that we observe in various individual parts. To the intention of making movements, for example, a fast or a slow movement or one that has to overcome more or less strong resistance, a different total Gestalt must correspond. And these variations of the whole Gestalt process become manifest in the singled-out parts under examination, which discloses such modifications of the process as relaxation or decreased coinnervation of the antagonist and so on.

If one produces a dedifferentiation of the figure by experimental conditions, then only a simpler figure may develop. Such a dedifferentiation can also be caused through disease, for instance, through lesion in the central nervous system. In these cases the periphery attains an abnormally strong influence and can express itself in the various sectors, the antagonist or the agonist, in different ways. This difference, in turn, depends on the locus of the lesion; for example, whether it is a striatal or cerebellar lesion, and so on. This leads to various forms of disturbances of the whole innervation of agonist and antagonist and to their defective cooperation, because one part of this originally unitary apparatus is affected more, or differently, than the other part. This assumption explains the appearance of disturbances of the "antagonistic bond" in these diseases, especially the variations of the disturbance in different localities. To prove this point, more accurate investigations are necessary. Beginnings of an analysis in this direction are evident in the differentiation between various forms of inability to perform rapidly coordinated movements of antagonistic muscles (in lesions of the central ganglia and the cerebellum – so-called adiadokokinesis).[46]

The dedifferentiation of the pattern may go so far that stimulation reaches only the individual muscles. That happens, for example, in the basic experiments that have led to the theory of antagonistic inhibition. In these cases the contraction takes place in one muscle alone, because no stimulation can reach the other one, if, because of the situation, the effect of the stimulus exhausts itself in the one muscle. In this case, the antagonistic muscle does not undergo any excitation; and even if there were some excitation in it, it could not effectuate itself, on account of the total situation determined by the innervation of the agonist. This, for instance, is the case if the antagonist is already so much stretched that it could respond to excitation only by relaxation. When, however, agonist and antagonist are stimulated in the manner that corresponds to a common performance of the two muscles, then a homogeneous innervation will take place. In other words, we have no occasion to assume a reciprocal antagonistic innervation, but, corresponding to the situation, to the required and to the possible performance, we have simply to assume a variation of the excitation in the relevant groups of muscles. The antagonistic effect shows itself only during extreme isolation, the product of which it is, as we are now well justified in saying. It certainly cannot furnish the basis for the understanding of muscle innervations during real performances. On the contrary, it becomes intelligible only as a border case that arises under specific circumstances. Thus it fits into our whole view without contradiction and without necessitating the assumption of new explanatory hypotheses. We deny the justification of positing the principle of antagonistic innervation and of any antagonistic principle in general.

Our critique may be supported by the discussion of another antagonistic process that plays a special part in the theory of the antagonism, namely, the antagonism of the vagus and sympathicus.

"Antagonistic innervation" of vagus and sympathicus
This question has become the center of interest, especially through the work of Hans Eppinger and Hess on vagotonia.[47]

According to these authors, the nervous system operates as regulator of the vegetative functions, in the sense of an antagonistic influence by way of separate nervous apparatuses of the sympathicus and the parasympathicus. The tonus of these two nerves, determined by humoral influences, the adrenaline and a hypothetical autotonin, is antagonistic. Increased excitability of the sympathicus is found with decreased excitability of the vagus, hypersensitivity for adrenaline entails hyposensitivity for pilocarpine, and vice versa. Normally, there is a balance between the state of excitation in the two nerves. In pathological cases, however, there is an abnormal hypersensitivity or tonus of the vagus, or sympathicus. High tonus in one field precludes it in the other. The clinical symptomatology is explained by a shift in favor of the function of the organs innervated by the vagus or the sympathicus.

Clinical as well as experimental experiences have not really verified the views of these authors. If one regards the relation of the two parts of the autonomous nervous system to the various organs, we find in vagotonia that not all organs innervated by the vagus exhibit symptoms of hyperexcitability and that those organs innervated by the sympathicus exhibit symptoms of hypoexcitability. One recognizes rather, in the symptomatology of the various cases, varying behavior of the single sections, namely, in some organs, signs of hyperexcitability of the sympathicus, in others signs of hypoexcitability of that nerve, in still other organs hyperexcitability of the vagus, and so on. Many clinical papers, especially those of Gustav von Bergmann and his school, have suggested that there is not one single case of pure vagotonia or sympathicotonia. They found that, in cases with changed excitability, these changes always concern both nervous apparatuses, sometimes in an antagonistic, and sometimes in a synergistic way. Therefore, Bergmann talks of autonomous lability or vegetative "stigmatization."

The pharmacological experiments point in the same direction. Direct and isolated stimulation of the vagus has, of course, the opposite effect than the stimulation of the sympathicus, for example, on the rate of heartbeat. The reason for the inclination to regard the sympathicus as the agitating factor is that one usually regards the diminishing of a performance as due to inhibition. But for the same reason, one might just as well ascribe the acceleration, by the nervous accelerans, to an inhibition of the slow heartbeat. There is no reason whatsoever to talk of an agitating and inhibiting factor. One arrived at the idea of these factors through observation of the isolated heart, whose rate of beat was regarded as the normal state that is then retarded by stimulation of the vagus or accelerated by stimulation of the sympathicus. What justifies us in regarding the state of the isolated heart as the normal state, since it is normally embedded in the whole organism? The normal state of the heart corresponds to its functioning within the whole organism in the given situation.[48] According to the given situation of the whole organism, we find a definite excitation of both the vagus and the sympathicus. One could only talk of two different performances, if one could single out the one or the other from the whole process. One has in mind such a separation when speaking of the formation of two different chemical substances. But aside from the terminology, what are the facts concerning the antagonism of the two nerves? Since both nerves are only two sectors of the same mechanism, it is to be expected that the effect of the stimulation of the one will decrease, when the other nerve undergoes abnormally strong excitation. When the "agonist" is stimulated in isolation, the "antagonist" will respond to the stimulus differently than before. This is then mistaken for hypoexcitability of the other nerve, whereas it represents, or at any event could represent, only hypoexcitability in this particular situation. In fact, it seems that this ratio of the excitability between vagus and sympathicus does, by no means, exist under all circumstances.

In a case of vagotonia, the hypoexcitability of the vagus does not continually prevail. Otherwise the patient would always have disturbances. But this is, as K. Ziegler in particular has justly pointed out, as little the case in such a patient, as in a patient with sympathicotonia.[49] The fact that such phenomena can be experimentally demonstrated does not prove anything regarding excitability of these two nerves in tasks in which the whole organism is involved. If symptoms of hyperexcitability of the vagus are found among others, this could be an expression of the disease, which facilitates abnormal reactions, because of the pathological isolation of certain fields. As we have seen, to maintain health means to avoid abnormal reactions, in spite of defect, by changing the milieu or by finding a new adequate milieu. When the vagotonic patient is in such a new adequate milieu, he has no disturbance; but if inadequate demands are made on him, then he suffers. This is especially the case in experimental stimulation. The antithetic excitability, which in a case of vagotonia can be experimentally shown, is an expression of the isolation as it is characteristic for disease. We cannot regard that as a normal state. Pharmacological investigations in normal persons have not proved that the excitation in one nerve is accompanied by hypoexcitability in the other; rather, the opposite seems to be the case.

Reid Hunt found that stimulation of the vagus, after repeated stimulation of the accelerans, retards the pulse more than before.[50] Ernst Billigheimer has proved, in many experiments, that an excitation of the vagus can be found in combination with an increased responsiveness of the sympathicus.[51] He has shown furthermore that, as long as calcium is given to the patient, an increased responsiveness of the sympathicus nerve endings can exist, regarding the pulse as well as blood pressure, and that, after a pilocarpine injection, a higher adrenaline-blood-sugar curve is found than after adrenaline alone. H. Langecker and Wilhelm Wiechowski found in the heart of the frog an increased sympathetic responsiveness when the vagus was in a state of increased excitation and vice versa.[52] Billigheimer was able to confirm the same phenomenon in new experiments.[53] When he produced, for example, a sympathicus-tachycardia through adrenaline and administered calcium at the height of the pulse acceleration (calcium, in regard to the pulse, stimulates the vagus), he obtained quite an enormous drop in the pulse rate, far below the initial level – a clear indication of a hyperexcitable vagus. Similarly, Frank and Isaak found, after simultaneous injection of pilocarpine and adrenaline, not a reduction of glycosuria but a rise of it and a definite increase in blood sugar. In other words, in the case of increased vagus excitation, they found also an increased responsiveness of the sympathicus. On the other hand, the sympathicus seemed less excitable when the excitability of the vagus was reduced. Thus, according to Walter Börnstein's experiments, which Billigheimer mentions, the increase in blood sugar is less in atropinization ("inhibition" of the vagus) than if atropine has not just been administered beforehand.

According to these facts, we would have here exactly the same state of affairs as in the precisely executed movements of voluntary muscles. One who concedes that the antagonism cannot be grounded on differences in the degree of excitability could still think of qualitative differences of the excitation processes. Actually some authors have done so. But this is not justified, as we saw above (cf. p. 217). Langley long ago took a stand against this view. Factually, it has been demonstrated that each of the two nerves can mediate the two specific effects under certain circumstances.

Organismic behavior under "opposed" simultaneous stimuli
Thus, here again we are brought to the result: Antagonistic effects are only found in isolating observation (also in isolation through disease), that is, in reactions under "inadequate" conditions. If we start from antagonistic effects, we must assume inhibition and regulation. Actually, as long as no pathology exists, one finds, in the natural situation, only unitary, total performances that are not caused through isolated excitation of single apparatuses, but are formed through differential configuration of the excitation course, in the various sectors of the whole.

The discussion of the phenomenon of the so-called antagonistic innervation leads us to a more general problem: How does the organism behave when it is exposed simultaneously to stimuli, one of which would lead to the opposite reaction as compared with the other?

We want to discuss this problem by using observations on the influence of stimulation of one side of the body on the position of a limb. Patients with one-sided cerebellar disturbance are especially suited for such experiments, as we have already discussed. Stimuli, which are applied to the diseased side of the body of these patients, are followed by a tilting of the body toward the side of the stimulus. For example, we expose the left eye to light, or the left ear to sound, or we move the position of the head or of the left leg toward the left. Then the spontaneous deviation of the left arm (in a case of left-sided cerebellar disease) increases: if the stimuli are acting in the same direction, then we observe an increase of the deviation, that is, an increase of the process in action.

In another experiment, one may apply, in a cerebellar patient, a cutaneous stimulus to the left side of the body, which results in an increased outward deviation of the raised left arm, and at the same time one applies to the right side a cutaneous stimulus or stimulation of the right labyrinth, or a visual stimulation of the right eye – stimuli that would ordinarily produce a deviation toward the right. Then we can observe various reactions on the left arm: (1) The left arm does not deviate differently than it did before; or, at least, (2) the deviation is stopped; or (3) we obtain a staggering, in the form of an alternating horizontal wobbling to the right and left, as in a "nystagmus."

Which one of the three reactions sets in depends on the relationship of intensity of the left and right stimulus, which, we must remember, can be codetermined by a great many processes in the rest of the organism. The first reaction sets in when one, say the left stimulus, exerts a much stronger effect than the right; the second reaction sets in when the opposite is true; the third reaction, when the difference is not very large. The last case merits our particular consideration. Here both stimuli become effective, without the formation of one resultant effect, but with the appearance of oppositely directed events in temporal sequence. In such a case, we must consider that frequently the reaction that corresponds to the stronger stimulus is more extensive and slower than the other; whereas the latter reaction, which corresponds to the weaker stimulus, is less extensive and faster. This is quite similar to the slower and faster components of nystagmus. That is not a curiosity of this particular case, but, rather, is a general law, which could be verified by many instances. One additional illustration: if one flexes the hand of a cerebellar patient, pointing downward, the large toe of the same side goes in the analogous position. If one now turns the fingers of the same hand upward, while the hand itself remains in the original downward position, then we obtain, in the large toe, a nystagmus-like movement upward and downward. One can see clearly that the alternation of the fast and the slow component of this movement is determined by the respective position of the hand and the finger. The faster component corresponds to the stronger effect of the hand muscles, the slower to that of the weaker finger muscles. If the hand is turned upward and the fingers downward, then the faster phase of the movement of the large toe is upward, and the slower and more intense movement, downward. Again, we see that one single stimulus, the position of the hand and the fingers, can produce an alternating movement. We discussed this fact previously, when we attempted to explain the alternating movements in the legs in case of a transection of the spinal cord, and recognized it as the results of the isolation of certain parts (cf. pp. 126–28). The facts just mentioned are to be understood in the same way. The only difference is that the opposite movement is not caused by processes in the moving part itself, but by processes in the sector that issues the stimuli.

The rhythmic excitation course, basic to the
"coming to terms" of organism and world
Some facts suggest that this alternating form of reaction has a certain significance also in normal performances, as, for example, in voluntary innervation. As is well known, we have, in such a situation, not a single twitch, but a tetanus that shows numerous diphasic currents when recorded on the string galvanometer. (Hans Piper, Rudolf Dittler, Siegfried Garten, and others.) This example is instructive, because it proves that a specific methodology is required in order to determine the type of an excitation process. It points to the fact that, if a certain investigation does not reveal an intermittent character of the process, this is not indicative that such a character is absent, but only that we still lack the correct method to demonstrate it. In the attempt to determine the character of a process, one must first consider that the intermittent

character of the excitation process can become obscured, that in a fast sequence of the same stimuli, the new stimulus may act before the recurrent change of the first process begins or has fully developed. Thus the intermittent character does not appear, or may become so inconspicuous that it escapes even minute investigation. Similar to a quick sequence of the same stimulus, the influence of the whole system may produce an effect on the local processes. In any event, the alternation is the less, the more a performance has reference to the whole, and vice versa. Therefore, we find alternation most commonly in reflexes and in isolated processes, and notice that it decreases when we provide conditions for a more holistic relationship. But even in the best-centered performances, alternation is apparently not entirely absent. It seems that, up to a certain degree, it belongs to the normal life process.

The organism never lives in a completely adequate milieu but must continuously assert itself against inadequate stimuli, that is, against such stimuli that evoke isolated effects. Therefore reactions scarcely ever occur that correspond to a perfectly adequate configuration of the organism and the surroundings. This would be equivalent to an equilibrium state between the organism and the world. In fact, a certain disequilibrium almost invariably exists, for which the organism compensates through the opposite phase. This process usually passes through gradually decreasing amplitudes of opposite phases, through decreasing amplitudes of the curve, until the curve reaches a more or less horizontal line. It is easy to see that voluntary innervation evinces this alternation least. Among the motor processes it is the voluntary ones that are initially best adapted to the surroundings, because from their inception they embrace, in the reaction, possibly all opposing phases, and take place in a very definite milieu, in contrast to the more automatic reactions which are much more determined by an accidental and isolated event in the surroundings.[54]

This phaselike course is nothing but the expression of slight catastrophic reactions, which are inevitable in the process of coming to terms with the world. It is the expression of the equalization process, it is the way of new adjustments and of finding a new adequate milieu. Where this phaselike course goes beyond a definite or normal limit it signifies defective behavior of the organism, danger for its performance capacity and for its existence. Then we have serious catastrophic reactions which are subjectively experienced as shock or as anxiety. Thus we see that the phenomenon of anxiety occupies an important place in the whole process of coming to terms of the organism with the world.

CHAPTER SEVEN

Certain Essential Characteristics of the Organism in the Light of the Holistic Approach

On the Phenomenon of Anxiety

Fear and anxiety. Anxiety has no "object."
The basis of fear is threat of the onset of anxiety

As manifold as states of anxiety may be with regard to intensity and kind, they all have one common denominator: the experience of danger, of peril for one's self. To be sure, this characterization is not sufficient, first of all, because it only describes the subjective experience, which is merely a part of the entire phenomenon. Usually, one believes that this exhausts the facts, that the essential aspect of anxiety is given in the subjective experience. However, if we observe someone in a state of anxiety we can disclose characteristic bodily changes as well, certain expressive movements of the face and the body, and certain states of physiological processes, motor phenomena, changes of pulse rate, vasomotor phenomena, and so on. And we certainly have no reason to exclude these changes from an investigation of the phenomenon of activity. We are even uncertain whether it will not be precisely these changes that will expedite our understanding of the phenomenon.

If we first confine ourselves to the inner experience, we shall find that it is not sufficient to characterize the latter simply as an experience of being endangered. The question arises: Of what type is the danger; and particularly, how does anxiety differ from similar states in which certainly a danger is also experienced? And how especially does anxiety differ from fear? Anxiety does not arise every time one's self is endangered. Pain may endanger us but not necessarily bring anxiety with it. Pain is not even necessarily accompanied always by a negative affective state or tone. It may, in fact, be found along with a certain feeling of pleasure. Anxiety, on the other hand, is always negatively accentuated. Thus, it must be a special kind of danger, for the self, under which anxiety sets in. One might think that anxiety arises when we are confronted with an object that is dangerous in that it threatens a complete overpowering, in other words, that anxiety has something to do with the quality of the object.

But here another question arises: Does the person, in a state of anxiety, become at all conscious of the object? On the contrary, it seems as if, in proportion to the increase of anxiety, objects and contents disappear more and more. Especially in cases of very severe anxiety, as in the onset of psychoses, the patients cannot say what they are afraid of; it is just this condition that is so extremely disconcerting for them. One may ask, Does not anxiety consist intrinsically of that inability to know whence the danger threatens? Is it not essential for anxiety that any reference to an object in the real world is lacking? If this be true, it strikes us as rather misleading to classify the emotional state of anxiety among those emotions that bear such a reference to some object and to regard it, for example, only as the highest degree of fear, as is frequently done. Actually, it may be true that a state of fear, if increasing in degree, may ultimately turn into a state of anxiety. But does this justify us in regarding the state of anxiety as qualitatively equal to the former state of fear, in regarding it simply as a state of increased fear? Could it not be possible that we have here a qualitative change that occurs when the intensity of the underlying cause is increased? And, finally, the assumption that we are dealing with qualitative differences is supported by the fact that two different words, such as "fear" and "anxiety," are used. In German this difference is reflected in such expressions as, "Ich fuerchte etwas; ich aengstige mich." (Henceforth, our use of the word "fear" will correspond to the German *Furcht*, and "anxiety" to *Angst*.)

In the state of fear, we have an object in front of us that we can "meet," that we can attempt to remove, or from which we can flee. We are conscious of ourselves as well as of the object, we can deliberate how we shall behave toward it, and we can look at the cause of the fear that actually lies spatially before us. On the other hand, anxiety attacks us from the rear, so to speak. The only thing we can do is to attempt to flee from it without knowing where to go, because we experience it as coming from no particular place. This flight is sometimes successful, though merely by chance, but it usually fails: anxiety remains with us. Fear differs from anxiety by its character of defense reaction and by its pattern of bodily expression. In fear, there is an appropriate defense reaction, a bodily expression of tension and of extreme attention to a certain part of the environment. In anxiety, on the other hand, we find meaningless frenzy, with rigid or distorted expression, accompanied by withdrawal from the world, a shut-off affectivity, in the light of which the world appears irrelevant, and any reference to the world, any useful perception and action, is suspended. In fear, reassurance is possible by explaining that the environmental situation is actually not threatening or that the possibility exists to overcome the danger. In anxiety, such an assurance is of no avail.

Thus, all investigators who have dealt with the problem of anxiety have sought to distinguish it from fear. I am only mentioning the interpretations of Freud, William Stern, and Géza Révész.[1] The philosophers, especially those whose interest was centered around the phenomenon of anxiety – I mention only Pascal, Kierkegaard, and Heidegger – have been very careful to distinguish between anxiety and fear. With regard to our coming discussion, we may emphasize that Kierkegaard as well as Heidegger considers fear as fear of something, while anxiety in their opinion deals with "nothingness"; their descriptions strongly suggest that anxiety is a state that is without reference to any object. Before we continue our differentiation between these two states, we shall consider somewhat more closely the phenomena that confront us in anxiety.[2]

We have characterized the conditions of brain-injured patients, when faced with solvable and unsolvable tasks, as states of ordered behavior and catastrophic reaction. The states of catastrophic reaction show all characteristics of anxiety. We have attempted to understand the origin of these reactions as the expression of shock, because of inadequate utilization of stimuli, caused by the change of structure in the patient. Observation discloses that, in the state of anxiety, the patient is not really conscious of the impossibility of solving the task and of the danger threatening from it. This can be seen by the fact that the patient does not realize the danger of an object that is the extraneous occasion for the appearance of the anxiety – he is not even capable of this. Because of his specific disturbance, he cannot establish a relation with the object, to wit, he cannot grasp it in such a way that he could appreciate its danger. Apprehending an object presupposes ordered functional evaluation of the stimulus. The fact that the catastrophic condition involves the impossibility of ordered reactions precludes a subject "having" an object in the outer world.

Thus, we find that patients' anxiety has no corresponding content and is lacking in object. The patient experiences, as we might say, not fear of something but simply anxiety. He experiences the utter impossibility of establishing any reference to the world without knowing the cause of that experience. He experiences a breaking down or dissolution of the world and a shattering of his own self. Just as little as he can render to himself a conscious account of an object, just as little can he become conscious of his self. To be conscious of one's self is only a correlate to being conscious of objects. The patient experiences the dissolution of the existence of his personality as anxiety. This shock, in terms of subjective experience, is what we call anxiety. Yet it is not quite correct to say the patient "has" a feeling of anxiety; it is more correct to say the patient "is" or personifies anxiety. In other words, anxiety appears when it has become impossible for an organism to cope in any way with tasks that are commensurate to its real nature. This is the endangering situation.

The above statement, however, must be amended. It is only true as far as we consider the inner experience. But the organism that is seized by the catastrophic shock is, of course, in the state of coping with a definite, objective reality; the organism is faced with some "object." The state of anxiety becomes intelligible only if we consider the objective confrontation of the organism with a definite environment. Only then can we comprehend the basic phenomenon of anxiety: the occurrence of disordered stimulus evaluation as it is conditioned through the conflict of the organism with a certain environment not adequate for it. This objectively endangers the organism in the actualization of its nature. Thus, we may talk of "contentless" anxiety only if we regard the experience alone. To be sure, it is usually in this sense that one talks of anxiety. But this is not quite correct and is due to a false emphasis on subjective experience in the characterization of so-called psychic phenomena. One usually regards bodily phenomena — the physiological processes of the body as well as the pattern of expression — only as the sequelae of the mental condition or, at best, as concomitant phenomena. As we shall explain later, such a point of view contradicts our concept of the relation between body and mind. Mental as well as physical phenomena are, for us, only different aspects of a unitary life process. Thus, what is usually described as anxiety is only that side of the process that presents itself from the psychological aspect.

What, now, is the relation of anxiety to fear? We have already mentioned that, in fear, one always experiences an object that one fears. But what is the characteristic of this object of fear? Is it something inherent to the object proper, at all times? Of course not. We may at one time have an indifferent or positive attitude toward an object and at another time the same object may awaken greatest fear. In other words, what results in fear must be something found only in a specific relation between organism and object. (We leave undecided whether we are, in that case, still psychologically justified in talking about the identical object. "Objectively" it certainly remains the same object.) What is it then that leads to fear? Nothing but the experience of the possibility of the onset of anxiety. What we fear is the impending anxiety. Thus it becomes clear that anxiety cannot be made intelligible from the phenomenon of fear but that only the opposite procedure is logical. The person in fear knows anxiety from past experience and present imagination (anticipation). The person in anxiety, however, cannot know fear, because in the state of anxiety he is incapable of any recollection. The person in fear infers, from certain indications, that an object is apt to bring him into a situation of anxiety.

By the fact that the person in fear is not yet in a state of anxiety but only envisions it, that he only fears that it may befall him, he is not yet so irritated and disturbed in his judgment of the outer world as the person in anxiety. On the contrary – driven by the tendency to get rid of the fear – he attempts to establish special contact with the outer world. He tries to recognize it as clearly as possible and to react to it in an appropriate manner in order to free himself, either by attack or flight, from the impending anxiety situation. Fear is conditioned by, and directed against, very definite contents of the environment. These have to be recognized and removed. Fear sharpens the senses. Whereas anxiety paralyzes the senses and renders them unusable, fear drives them to action. We can escape anxiety only by avoiding situations that might eventuate in anxiety.

Anxiety in infants and animals. The "uncanny."
"Instinct fear" and "experience fear" as the results of critical inadequacy of the organism to stimuli

Our interpretation of anxiety has certain bearings on the problem of anxiety in the infant and in animals. That the infant, even the newborn infant, undergoes anxiety is beyond doubt. His expressive movements indicate this, and most observers agree on this fact. A difference of opinion prevails only regarding the explanation of its origin; and here most authors designate this emotional condition of the infant as fear. Those who explain anxiety by past experience, as the awareness of an impending, previously experienced danger, meet with difficulties in explaining anxiety phenomena in such an early phase of development, in which the child as yet could not have possibly had the requisite experiences. One thus has been forced to assume a hereditary anxiety. In other words, one had to take recourse to experiences not of the individual himself but of his ancestors. Some authors like Stanley Hall go back even as far as to the animal ancestors of human beings. In any event, fear of certain objects is supposed to be hereditary.

Stern has criticized and refuted this hypothesis.[3] He has pointed out in particular that such states of fear, which are always cited as proof for such a view, are by no means established facts. He shows, for example, that the children who were systematically observed by him were afraid neither of the dark, nor of animals, nor of a thunderstorm. If anxiety of certain objects could be observed, then there was reason to assume that the fear of the child is based on actual individual experience. Also Preyer's child showed, for example, no fear of the dark. Yet Stern, too, admits that there are situations in which the child is supposed to be afraid of certain objects, or certain peculiarities of an object, without such fear being explainable by past experience. The child has a feeling of "uncanniness." Stern calls this fear "instinct fear" as compared with experience fear and in doing so quotes observations by Karl Groos, in addition to his own. According to Groos, the fear of the "uncanny" has a pronounced instinctive basis. Through the fear of the uncanny, the child is, so to speak, supposed to choose between what is helpful and what is harmful.

But is it true that the unfamiliar is harmful and that the familiar is helpful? And how would it be possible that the child could have new experiences, or could make new experiences, if it were true that fear keeps the child from the unfamiliar? This view cannot be correct.

But there are still other facts that speak against the recourse to unfamiliarity. For instance, one can hardly say that the child tends to reject the unfamiliar. The opposite seems to be nearer the truth. The situations in which, according to Stern, fear arises in the child are by no means simply characterized by their unfamiliarity. The fear is aroused, as Stern himself points out, by certain formal peculiarities of the objects: the suddenness of their appearance, or the particularly great intensity, or the rapid approach of an object, or the unexpected appearance of familiar happenings in a new context, and others. If it were only the fact of "unfamiliarity," which under these circumstances results in fear, one could justly ask why the child does not accustom itself to such situations. Actually, these formal peculiarities retain their fear-arousing character even in and during the life of the adult.

Therefore, we must seek some inherent factor in those formal qualities which bring about fear. This factor must be sought in the one fact that all these situations have in common, that is, that they all make an adequate stimulus evaluation difficult if not impossible. This is especially the case in the child, because of his incomplete maturity. Not being able to react adequately – that is the shock to the total organism. And to the latter corresponds the subjective experience of the uncanny.

This experience of being at all able or unable to react is primal to the conscious experience of any object. It is a primal experience that something does or does not "fit" into the total situation. This experience precedes the awareness of any object – in the same way as we perceive "likeness" or "contrast" without previous partitive apprehension of constituents – or in the same way as an infant grasps facial expressions before it reacts adequately to other visual elements. The experience of "not fitting" that is identical with the condition of being "unable to cope with" – this is what produces the character of the uncanny and becomes the cause of anxiety in the child.

This view renders superfluous all those fantastic attempts to explain the supposedly inherited fear of the child – for instance, the fear of certain animals that is supposed to spring from the fact that the ancestors had to be on guard against them (as theorized by Hall). This assumption, among others, rests on the quite unacceptable postulate that the now-living infant experiences these animals as the same objects as did the adult ancestors. But all these speculations are unnecessary.

When we observe anxiety in the infant we must carefully avoid interpreting the situation by viewing the objects as they appear to us. Rather, we must start out from the perspective of a coming to terms of the infant's nature with its given environment. Then we shall see that anxiety arises when it is impossible for the infant to cope, in an adequate way, with the environment.

For an explanation of anxiety in childhood it suffices to assume that the organism reacts to inadequate situations with anxiety, and did so in the days of his ancestors, as well as today. The "fear" of Preyer's child of the roaring sea and of water in general can therefore certainly be explained without first wondering, as Hall did, whether this fear is inherited from primeval days when the animal phyla changed from purely aquatic to terrestrial existence. That we are not simply dealing with fear of very definite and constant objects is already shown by the fact that this fear does, by no means, occur always in connection with definite objects but practically only when object and child meet in a very specific way. Thus, the child is not afraid of every body of water, or of the same animal in every situation, or of every loud noise, and so on.

The same objections that can be raised against the hypothesis of inherited fear in the infant are equally valid as arguments against an equivalent explanation of fear manifestations of newly born or young animals before they have had any experience with the object of their fear.

Practically all observers agree that animals do have experiences of anxiety. The explanation of this fact offers no difficulty for our view. If the animal is placed in a milieu in which it is not able to react in an ordered way, we see that anxiety arises, just as in a patient with a brain lesion. Such situations occur, for example, if an animal is brought from its natural environment into captivity or is brought from a familiar keeper to an unfamiliar one who does not yet know the animal's peculiarity and may make demands on it that it cannot meet.

It is very doubtful whether the evidence adduced for the assumption of inherited fear in animals is valid, and such authors as Groos, Karl Bühler, and Stern have presented weighty criticisms. Moreover, one would have to scrutinize very carefully whether the "hereditary" enemy is recognized and feared on the basis of an innate memory of the enemy or whether the inadequate reaction and, with it, the anxiety are not occasioned by certain peculiarities in the encounter between the alleged "hereditary" enemy and the young animal. It should not be hard to settle this question experimentally.

Whether the animal may have fear at all, and how the object that it may fear is perceived by the animal, is completely unknown. In any event, it may be assumed that the phenomenon of anxiety is, in animals, much more frequent than fear, since the latter requires the potentiality of experiencing an independent world of objects in contrast to the organism. Animals hardly have that. It might, however, be possible that certain peculiarities of the situation remind them of former states of anxiety and that fear may thus be aroused in them.

Although it may appear justified to designate the described emotional states in brain lesions as anxiety, one might perhaps hesitate to admit a congruency with anxiety conditions in normal persons. One might especially doubt the correctness of the formal characterization of these states as being the expression of the impossibility to solve tasks that otherwise would be adequate to the normal organism. When somebody is unable to cope with a task, anxiety, in the usual sense of this word, does not always arise. For that, a certain peculiarity of the situation is necessary. In cases of brain lesion, the situation is a special one, inasmuch as the performance capacity is so much impaired in general, that all essential life activities become reduced. For patients, that incapacity to perform means some threat to their existence. In a normal person, this will certainly not always be the case. He will cope with a difficult situation in some fashion without becoming actually endangered in his existence. Therefore in normal individuals real anxiety occurs only on much more serious occasions. Yet, however true it may be that difficult situations do not involve severe anxiety, the concomitant mental state is nevertheless structurally of the same type. The only reason why they do not impress us as anxiety is because they are less relevant to the total personality and its existence. This becomes clearly evident through the fact that a failure, which by itself is irrelevant, may bring anxiety into distinct prominence if it occurs in a situation in which it becomes significant for the very existence of the person concerned, for example, anxiety during any examination.

The significance of anxiety for conquest of the world and for self-realization
It is a matter of fact that the normal person, in his conquest of the world, undergoes, over and again, such states of shock. If in spite of this, he does not always experience anxiety, this is because his nature enables him to bring forth creatively situations that ensure his existence. Thus, the disproportion between his capacity and the demands of the

environment, which may lead to catastrophic failure, is averted to a certain degree in average life. As long as this secure state is not essentially shaken and the existence is not endangered, the shocks are not experienced as anxiety. Even the brain-injured patient is not permanently in a state of anxiety, and we have seen how a transformation and shrinkage of his world spares him from such a condition.

The child behaves, in some respects, similar to the brain-injured patient. It is very frequently confronted with tasks with which it cannot cope and which menace its existence. Thus, anxiety certainly plays a great role in the life of the child. However, it is diminished through safeguards that the adult arranges and that save the child from shocks that otherwise would be too extreme. Furthermore, the anxiety in children is reduced through a peculiarity we must consider more carefully, as it also plays a certain part in the adult's overcoming of anxiety. This peculiarity is the extraordinarily strong and general tendency to action and the urge to solve given tasks, which belongs to the nature and essence of the child. Thus, the pleasurable surprise when the conquest of a piece of the world has succeeded replaces the experience of shock. This drive is so strong that the child not only fails to draw back from the impending anxiety situation but possibly goes out of his way to seek them: "Little John went out to learn the creeps." Not to be afraid of dangers that could lead to anxiety – this represents in itself a successful way of coping with anxiety and, with that, represents the essential difference between a normal child and a brain-injured adult. Especially through this tendency to action does the child manifest itself as an early stage of the normal adult, in contrast to the patient.

As the child grows into the world of the adult, its behavior becomes more even and "ordered." The more it becomes fitted to its environment, the more its "wondering" decreases, but it never disappears completely. The adult is always affected anew by surprise and anxiety, as he is always faced with new outer and inner situations. Just as in the brain-injured person, the normal adult has the urge to diminish his anxiety even though to a much lesser degree. As an expression of this urge, we find in the adult the tendency toward order, norms, continuity, and homogeneity, in principle similar to patients. But apart from this, the normal individual is determined by his urge (already inherent in the child) for new experiences, for the conquest of the world, and for an expansion of his sphere of activity in a practical and spiritual sense. His behavior oscillates between these two tendencies and is influenced sometimes more by the one, sometimes more by the other. The outcome of the two tendencies is the cultural reactions.

But in no way could one claim that this "ordered" world, which culture represents, is the product of anxiety, the result of the desire to avoid anxiety, as Freud conceives culture as sublimation of the repressed drives. This would mean a complete misapprehension of the creative trend of human nature and at the same time would leave completely unintelligible why the world was formed in these specific patterns, and why just these forms should be suited to procure security for man. This becomes intelligible only if one regards them as expressions of the creative power of man and of the tendency to effectuate a realization of his nature. Only when the world is adequate to man's nature do we find what we call security.

This tendency toward actualization is primal; but it can effect itself only in conflicting with, and in struggling against, the opposing forces of the environment. This never happens without shock and anxiety. Thus we are probably not overstating the facts if we maintain that these shocks are essential to human nature, even to all organic life, and if we believe that life must, by necessity, take its course via uncertainty and shock. Even though the tendency to reduce uncertainty, to standardize the environment, may have its correspondence in certain formal peculiarities in science, art, and religion, one cannot emphasize too often that it is impossible to regard the contents of cultural products as the expression of uncertainty and anxiety.

Where anxiety, as the mainspring for the activity of an organism, comes into the foreground, we always find that something is upset in the nature of that organism. Or, in other words, an organism is normal and healthy, in which the tendency toward self-actualization is acting from within, and overcomes the disturbance arising from the clash with the world, not out of anxiety but out of the joy of conquest. How often this most perfect form of actualization is a fact, and whether it exists at all, we leave open to question. In any event, even life in its most perfect manifestation must pass through the disturbances that emerge from the adjustment to the environment. The creative person who ventures into many situations that expose him to shocks will find himself even more often in anxiety situations than the average person. Individuals differ as to how much anxiety they can bear. For a patient with brain injury, the amount is very low, for a child it is greater, and for the creative individual it is greatest.

The capacity of bearing anxiety is the manifestation of genuine courage, in which ultimately one is not concerned with the things in the world but with the threatening of existence. Courage, in its final analysis, is nothing but an affirmative answer to the shocks of existence, which must be borne for the actualization of one's own nature. This form of overcoming anxiety requires the ability to view a single experience within a larger context, that is, to assume the "attitude toward the possible," to have freedom of decision regarding different alternatives. Thus, it is a characteristic peculiarity of man. Therefore, brain-injured persons, whose change we characterized as a loss of the attitude toward the possible, as an impairment of freedom, are completely helpless when facing an anxiety situation. They are entirely surrendered to the anxiety situation, as long as they are not safeguarded against it through an enormous limitation of their world that reduces their human existence to the simplest forms.

The manner in which individual creatures in general, and human individuals in particular, cope with anxiety provides insight into their nature. We have discussed this phenomenon thoroughly because it seems to us particularly important for the knowledge of the essentials of the nature of living organisms. Thus, it pertains not only to anthropology but also to biology in the widest sense.

The So-Called Unconscious and Consciousness

It remains for us to deal with a special problem that is in the center of discussion of recent psychology, particularly subsequent to the fundamental inquiries of Freud. It is the problem of the nature of the so-called unconscious and the consciousness. A discussion of this question seems appropriate if for no other reason than that, in biology, views are also advanced that attempt to carry certain behavior acts of animals back to an "unconscious," in the psychoanalytic sense.

Psychoanalysis and biology

Sándor Ferenczi has demanded, for the investigation of biological phenomena, the application of the psychoanalytic method as a new principle of research.[4] In attempting to demonstrate the procedure of this new "bioanalytic" science by its approach to sexual phenomena, he believed himself capable of making genetic processes quite generally intelligible.

According to Franz Alexander, psychological laws have as much "biological validity," or "biological meaning," as biological laws have psychological validity. There exists a complete reciprocity.[5] Thus, Alexander attempts to compare the arousal of psychological states such as the various stages of Buddhist contemplation, with the "chronological sequence of a regular psychoanalysis." He endeavors to demonstrate that this is a form of regression that leads to the awareness of one's own embryonic development. "The prophetic knowledge of eternal rebirths, of the memory of all forms of existence, and of all geological periods, which Buddha gained after passing over the four Ihana-steps, is nothing but the principle that ontogeny repeats phylogeny. The only difference is that Buddha found it in a completely different way."

Rudolf Brun has attempted to discuss a number of animal observations on the basis of Freud's drive theory and reaches the conclusion that the metaphysical points of view propounded by Freud in his psychology of neuroses are confirmed by biology all along the line.[6] He maintains especially that the dynamic and economic principles introduced by Freud in drive psychology are laws of general biological validity and of pertinence to the drive conflict wherever and in whatever form it is observed. But he goes even further. His analysis of experimentally produced drive conflicts or drive inhibitions in animals (even in organisms that are as far removed from our own physical and psychological organization as the insects), and the analysis of phenomena that can be observed when two incompatible reflexes collide, yields the following surprising result: even the specific economic drive fate (*Triebschicksal*) that inhibited or repressed drives undergo – according to Freud – can be completely proved in the realm of biology (with the one exception of conversion).

Brun must be given credit for having uncovered very important parallels between biological phenomena, arising under certain conditions, and the behavior of the neurotic. The investigations of the Russian analyst A.R. Luria lie in the same direction.[7] He draws the parallel between certain important findings that Pavlov and his pupils have made in their study of the conditioned reflex and its disturbances and the processes that psychoanalysis has discovered. His comparisons are unusually interesting and his conclusions careful. He says, for example, "The eczema, as a peculiar reaction of a dog to a difficult task, is in principle not different from the flight from difficult life problems into a neurotic symptom."[8] One could assume that the author has a biological explanation in mind when he says, "The problem of psychogenesis finds a physiological foundation," and when he calls repression a special case of the parabiotic inhibition of Wedenski.[9] Actually, however, the efforts of Luria also tend in the opposite direction. He discusses the behavior of a dog, in which a flood in the laboratory extinguished all conditioned reflexes. After the reflexes were again acquired, it was possible to make them disappear for a long time by pouring merely a small quantity of water through the door of the laboratory. In discussing these observations Luria attributes the effect to the affectivity and considers this a confirmation of the psychoanalytic claim that a great many apparently organic symptoms are grounded in an emotional basis. This reaction of the dog to water suggests to him "interesting considerations in the sense of bio-analysis" as inaugurated by Ferenczi. Thus it does not become quite clear whether Luria tends more to explain facts discovered by psychoanalysis on biological grounds or vice versa. Also Vladimir Bekhterev has pointed out similarities between biologically and psychoanalytically disclosed phenomena.[10] But he attempts to explain the latter by the former, in the belief that they will find, through reflexology, an illumination that they were lacking before.

Let us sum up this brief sketch of the main lines along which our problem of the relation between psychoanalysis and biology has been treated thus far: we are faced with two more or less seriously opposing standpoints of which Ferenczi and Bekhterev, respectively, can be regarded as the most extreme representatives. Ferenczi attempts to explain biological phenomena through the medium of psychoanalytic thought, while Bekhterev tries to comprehend psychoanalytic phenomena through the medium of biological notions. Our stand on this problem, in pursuance of our general line of thought, will become evident from a further discussion of the unconscious.

We cannot attempt here a detailed discussion of psychoanalysis. We only want to scrutinize its methodological approach from our point of view. We are not concerned with the problem as to which factors have been determinative for the development of the symptoms of a patient in a given case or whether a person can be cured by the psychoanalytic method. We are only interested in determining whether the mechanisms assumed by psychoanalysis are suited and necessary for the understanding of human or animal behavior. Hence we have to take up the problem of the unconscious. Of course, we cannot in any way treat this problem exhaustively, which already has been so much discussed.

The "unconscious." The three behavioral aspects
Beginning with the term "unconscious," we first have to stress that it expresses something negative, something opposed to "conscious." Furthermore, it creates the impression that the same phenomenon can, at one time, have the character of consciousness and, at another time, not. The psychoanalytic postulate actually assumes that the same phenomenon, such as an idea, an act of will, a feeling, a habit, and so on, can be conscious at one time and unconscious at another. Conscious images are said to become repressed in the realm of the unconscious, for example. We shall attempt to describe, in positive statements, those phenomena that have induced scientists to assume such a structure of the unconscious as it is conceived by psychoanalysis. From that we shall see to what extent it is expedient and necessary to use the term unconscious or what can be meant by this term.

What one calls unconscious depends on what one understands by consciousness. Very often one has understood by consciousness the sum of all those contents that are contained in a special realm, in something like a receptacle. But there is no such realm, no such receptacle. We can only speak of conscious behavior as being of such a kind that we are "consciously experiencing something," or, as we will call it, "having something consciously." We shall try to describe how a person who "has something consciously" appears to us and how his inner experiences are. In so doing we discover a person who has a clearcut awareness of a given situation, of his activity, of its purpose and its effect. The world is experienced by such a person as apart from him, and the self is experienced by him as an object akin to other objects.

This is the case in that behavior that we called abstract behavior. With this "having something consciously" or "having consciousness of something," however, the total state of the person in question is not sufficiently characterized.

Another aspect of this phenomenon is certain "inner experiences," usually described as feelings, sets, or attitudes. We may, for instance, have the experience of liking or disliking something, of being under tension or relaxed, of something agreeable or disagreeable, of harmony or disharmony, and so on. Whereas we found that the first aspect of the total behavior could be described as "having an experience," we find that this aspect is better characterized as "being in a certain state." And whereas we find that the first part of the total state of behavior could be described as "having something consciously," the latter may be better described as "the feeling of being in a certain state." In German, there are words which express very well these different types of experience: *bewusst haben*, the first; *erleben*, the second. *Bewusst haben* corresponds to having something consciously, and *erleben* corresponds to inner experience of a certain state. In terms of the relation between organism and environment, the first means "experiencing a distinction between one's self and the world," the second means "to be in the world as part of it," as a cog in a wheel. In the so-called concrete behavior, the second type of experience is in the foreground.

This inner state can never become conscious in the objectifying sense. It can only be experienced as a subjective feeling or setting. If we try factually to describe it, we have to transform it into an object like other objects whereby its primal character of attitude, feeling, and so on, is lost and distorted into a "thing." The mere fact that one can reflect on this subjective state in the same way as one can describe objects led to the belief that it could be made or become conscious. However, that is impossible. Though it goes with, and belongs to, the behavioral aspect of "having something consciously," it never can become conscious as such in the above-indicated sense of this term.

Finally, in the total behavior of a person who "has something consciously," or does something consciously, we have to distinguish a third type of phenomenon. All abstract as well as concrete performances require processes in the body that belong to the respective configuration, for example, automatisms that support and facilitate the voluntary performance. These especially guarantee a definite setting brought on by voluntary activity. As an instance of this we might cite expressive bodily patterns, postures, tones, and so on, which are the physical counterpart of the attitudes and feelings. These processes occur in us without any form of conscious experience. They can be recognized only indirectly, for example, by way of visual perception, as we perceive objects of the outer world. They can never become directly conscious. Neither do we have immediate experiences of those processes, nor are we experiencing them. These processes just occur.

*The configurational relation of the three behavioral aspects: performances
(conscious behavior), attitudes (inner states), and processes (somatic events)*
We shall call these three aspects, which we can differentiate in the
behavior of a person: performances (i.e., the voluntary, consciously
experienced activities); attitudes (i.e., the texture of the affectivity, the
feelings, attitudes, moods, settings, and so on, experienced as inner
states of ourselves); and processes (i.e., the bodily processes or events
that can be experienced only indirectly). These three behavioral aspects,
which can be observed in the human being, are reflected usually in the
ideas "mind," "soul," and "body." We have no objection against such
usage, as long as one realizes that these terms do not describe three distinct spheres of existence of the organism, but that they are merely
abstractions, each of which represents an artificially isolated aspect of
the total behavior of an organism. They may sometimes appear as separate entities, because one or the other aspect of the total behavior is,
at any given time, in the foreground, as figure, while the others form
the background. Which aspect of the unitary behavior shall become the
figure depends on the situation and the kind of adjustment demanded
from the organism as a whole.

Thus, for example, in focusing and comparing definite objects, in
thinking or in voluntary actions, the "conscious" aspect of the total
behavior is in the foreground. When we give ourselves over to an attitude, to a feeling, then that aspect is in the foreground as the predominant factor. In situations in which we behave in neither one of these
ways, the "processes" might dominate the behavior of the organism,
to wit, that aspect always emerges into the foreground that is important for the coming to terms of the organism with the world, under
given conditions. But the other aspects of the characterized unity are
always in action too – as background. This finds its expression in the
fact that one or the other functions normally only if the rest forms an
adequate background.

If we study a person who "has something consciously," we find that
this "conscious awareness of something" is accompanied by a specific
pattern in the sphere of feeling, the sphere of inner experience, as well
as by a specific pattern of the bodily processes. The normal course of
thinking depends on the normal course in the other aspects too. Thinking can take place only while being in a certain attitude, in a certain
setting, and in a certain bodily state. Disturbances in the normal state

of the attitudes or processes derange the conscious actions, thinking, will power, and so on. In the same way, attitudes and even the bodily processes can be deranged by any disturbance in the voluntary conscious actions. Finally, disturbances of attitudes bear consequences for the processes and vice versa. A normal action of the organism demands a normal configuration of the activity of the organism as a whole, a configuration in which we can discriminate, only abstractly, the three aspects mentioned. We have seen that to each situation and to every performance belongs a specific configuration of the organism that varies in such a way that at one time one aspect, at another time another, is in the foreground.

Under certain conditions, all these aspects appear relatively isolated. The conscious aspect is relatively isolated, if we analyze consciously our own behavior while everything else is kept relatively constant in order to avoid disturbance. This is probably only possible for man and presumably represents the most difficult form of human behavior: what is usually called "conscious."

But we can also assume a second behavior, by giving ourselves over to the "inner experiences." In that case, we do not have an objective world; we are living in direct relation to the world, are only feeling, and so forth. This state is "experienced" but not "conscious," in the above sense. Finally, we can center ourselves on the bodily processes, which, however, requires a still greater abstraction from the whole. We can inspect our body in relative isolation, as a physical object, or leave it alone to adjust itself to the environment.

The problem of "aftereffect." No "invasion of the unconscious." Aftereffects of each behavioral aspect are only actualized in the original aspect
Each activity of the organism leaves an "aftereffect," which modifies the later reactions, their course, and their intensities. The aftereffect is especially strengthened when the organism is "touched" again by the same stimulus situation. Yet, remembering, recalling, and so on, are bound to more specific conditions. Not all that we once experienced affects the later reactions or can be remembered in the same way. Remembrance somewhat presupposes a similarity between the situation in which the organism was at the time of the experience, the conditions when remembrance shall take place, and so on. To put it more precisely: An event can be remembered only in that modality in which it

246

appeared first. Remembrance is normally bound to the figure. The background has only an aftereffect in conjunction with the figure to which it belongs. Thus, the three aspects can later affect the behavior only in the same way as they did in original appearance. If a phenomenon were conscious in the characterized sense, it can be effective later only in a conscious way. If an inner experience were figure at the earlier time, it later can have effect only as attitude or feeling, namely, as a setting, influencing other settings. A conscious phenomenon can never work directly on the attitudes, for example. Thus, a phenomenon that was not experienced in the conscious form can never later become directly conscious, and conversely.

However, because the normal course of any performance is tied to the figure-ground formation, changes in background can influence the figure, and with that, changes in the background can affect subsequent performances. There is no direct transition from one event to the other, nor does a direct effect of one on the other exist. All effects are rightly evaluated only if one treats these three abstractively distinguishable behavior-aspects as intertwined into the unity of the whole, which alone has real existence. Only by way of the whole – by this detour, so to speak – can they influence, arouse, or disturb each other. We will see that these indirect influences play a great role in the so-called unconscious phenomena. Usually, behavior presents itself as a state in which one of the three described components alternately stands out more or less dominating, as the figure. Within a certain activity, what is figure at a given moment undergoes manifold changes.

Yet all activity, be it reflection, thinking, feeling, or doing, always begins with a conscious attitude, in the sense of being aware of something, knowing about a situation, the task. Later on, this knowledge simply needs to furnish the general frame, "the background" in which the other, above-described behavioral aspects take their course, without being steadily accompanied by consciousness. The latter has set, so to speak, the frame for the duration of the course of an action. Every "attitude," every physiological process must be initiated by conscious behavior. In other words, conscious direction is necessary for them. But the opposite does not hold. It is true there may be situations in which the normal course of consciousness is aroused by certain bodily processes and emotional experiences. But these processes, in turn, require conscious behavior as their starting point. Consciousness is indispensable not only for initiating an action but also in the case in which a process has been interrupted or blocked, which may be due to failure of the organism or to the influence of external stimuli, with which the organism can deal only in a conscious way. How important consciousness is, becomes particularly evident in cases in which the intervention of consciousness is not possible, as in cases of brain injury. Then, not only is the ability to start wanting, but also any really spontaneous activity, as well as the possibility of spontaneous resumption after a disturbance.

Forgetting and so-called repression in childhood
Processes of the second and third kind may, under certain conditions, attain a high degree of independence. This can be due either to defective integration, in damage of centering, which always means primarily an impairment of the conscious aspect, or can be due to an abnormally strong external stimulation of some parts of the organism. Such functional isolation from the whole may damage the function of the whole organism. This happens in childhood, where normal integration and proper centering has not yet been reached, and in disease. Especially as long as the development is not complete, the single processes are not integrated into that whole that is adequate to the nature of the organism and the human environment. We have good reasons to pay attention to the events when that condition prevails.

The child is immature at birth; its first reactions are certainly not conscious in the defined way. He does not have an objective world but merely one of very "diffused objectiveness." His behavior is essentially characterized by processes in the bodily sphere and by such inner experiences as feelings, attitudes, and so on. In the case of the child, these are relatively lacking in precision, because the possible adjustments are still relatively simple. The whole behavior is embedded in a sphere corresponding more to feelings and attitudes than to conscious objectifying experience. Yet whatever phenomena are found in the child, they are certainly very intense, if for no other reason than because everything takes place in relatively isolated parts, because of the prevailing imperfect centering of the whole or imperfect integration. Isolated processes such as the necessity for satisfaction of hunger and thirst are natural behavior at that time. They lead to equalization appropriate to the present structural organization and are therefore the major determinants in stimulus reactions. The behavior of the child presents the same formal characteristics as reactions in relatively isolated parts. We find abnormally intense reactions, reactions of abnormal duration, greater bonds to external stimuli, a more primitive type of behavior, and reactions in alternating phases.

The child is faced with a world, which at first cannot be, is not recognized by it "as such," and with which it cannot come to terms in an adequate way. Since the stimuli originating from this world do not yet fit the organism of the child, they demand reactions corresponding to a more mature and more integrated organism than the child actually is. Therefore, the organism of the child is not able to accomplish the required actions in an adequate, ordered way. When the child is forced by the outer world to react to such exorbitant demands, then the reactions are imperfect. They are experienced as unpleasant by the child and are very often followed by catastrophic situations that the child meets with defense reactions. We encounter here all these phenomena and sequelae of which we have learned in dealing with the behavior of brain-injured patients. Thus we find catastrophic reactions in the course of the early educational efforts.

At first, the resistance of the child is so weak that behavior can be built up on the basis of conditioned reflexes, as we explained before. Later, a struggle originates between the tendencies of the infant, corresponding to the capacities of its immature condition, and the demands of the outer world. The child begins to fight against the inadequate demands and against the prohibitions of such activities that are appropriate to its maturation level; it struggles against the so-called forbidden. This fight must not be precisely "conscious" for the child; but often the child has definite inner experiences of that kind. It develops certain feeling tones, settings, and attitudes.

While the child is growing up, it becomes more and more able to react to the demands in an adequate way. Thus it gains new adaptations and attitudes, especially when consciousness develops that enables it, if necessary, also to undergo something disagreeable, because it appears appropriate and useful for some other reason or intelligible purpose. The child learns to bear disagreeable things for the sake of actualizing its personality as a multiform entirety.

Thus, the normal development of the child proceeds by way of adaptation through maturation, by "repressing" attitudes and urges that are in opposition to the development of the whole personality. As long as the new performances are not consolidated, reactions of the earlier type can easily occur. Then the prohibited reactions, so to speak, overpower the organism. They may replace the demanded reaction, or at least influence its course. This process may give the impression of invasion from the unconscious. It is a characteristic of the unconscious, from the psychoanalytic view, that this impression is hypostasized into an actual invasion of the unconscious.

The fact of the removal of former reactions is usually described as repression. However, if one thinks of it only in terms of "shoving away," or "splitting off" certain reactions, attitudes, images, ideas, and so on, the denotation "repression" is not correct. The gradual elimination of inappropriate attitudes, feelings, and – in later time – of the conscious ideas is rather a receding into the background than actual repression. Whenever active repression is the case, the repressed processes are factually still effective, and we know how little such an active prohibition is bound to succeed. The elimination really takes place as the maturing organism readapts itself to the environment and gains a new pattern of which the phenomenon to be repressed actually is no longer a part. This process leaves no further room for the former trends and makes them obsolete.

Continual formation of new patterns render ineffective former attitudes
Thus, we find not continual repression but continual formation of new patterns. The factor, which actuates the so-called repressing, is formed neither through prohibitions from without, nor by a censor, nor by an ego, nor by a superego. Rather, through maturation, new patterns of the organism are formed, conforming to the human species in general and to the cultural pattern of that particular milieu in which the child grows up. Of course, one can call this development "ego formation," and of course, the prohibitions, just like other processes in the environment, are codetermining factors in this formation. Yet, the effects of former reactions have not been "forgotten" through repression. Rather, they cannot be remembered because they are no longer part of the attitudes of later life and therefore cannot become effective. We shall see that they can be revived or recalled if the individual is brought into a situation similar to that under which they originated – that is, psychosis or in the psychotherapeutic situation.

For the normal development of the child, it is very important that the counteracting forces should not be so strong that the child is unable to adapt himself gradually to the demands and prohibitions by means of new attitudes that arise from maturation and training. If such overpowering is the case and the child is forced to react to impositions inadequate to the state of his maturation, then catastrophic situations set in; and in turn attempts to avoid anxiety and fear – by substitute reactions and by an escape through nonconscious procedure – also ensue. The child thereby tends to resort to those attitudes of which it is capable, because by these it feels itself protected against the endangering demands. This nonconscious holding on or resorting to certain attitudes cannot only hinder the further adequate development of the child but can also have the consequence that certain attitudes adopted in early stages may persist during its whole life. They can gain the character of habits, if the outer demands and prohibitions, in early stages, have been so incisive that the child cannot develop in a way to overcome them at a later time. These habits can thus persist and can determine the behavior of the child and the adult in an abnormal way; in an abnormal way, because the individual cannot become aware of their meaning, and hence is not able to overcome them – and he cannot become aware of their meaning because he cannot become conscious of their origin. They never were conscious but represented attitudes in a certain situation of infancy that usually cannot be recalled voluntarily in the adult. True, in adult life conscious repression also plays a role, but not in early childhood, or only to a minor degree. At that time, the conscious behavior is so little developed that it can scarcely perform this difficult action. Here, the so-called repression takes place mostly involuntarily, without consciousness.

Because the centering of the organism is not firmly enough established in childhood, phenomena that are in the background can quite easily force themselves into the foreground. But even if they do not enter the figure, they may produce disorder in the normal activity of the organism, with its concomitant phenomena of uncertainty and dread.

The so-called unconscious in neurosis
In the normal adult organism, however, we find in principle such a degree of centering that the stimuli are utilized according to their present significance for the entire organism. Dispositions to former (but

now eliminated) stimulus utilization are no longer or so little effective that no disturbance of the normal, situationally adapted behavior occurs. Of course, this ideal case is not always realized. Even in the normal person, centering and integration may suffer, at least temporarily, as during fatigue or in sleep. Or abnormally intense stimuli may force certain responses so much into the foreground that normal reactions, adequate to the changing situations, no longer take place. Under these conditions, stimulus utilizations may occur that have the characteristics of isolation. Then contents may appear that do not correspond to the present but belong to a former situation in which imperfectly centered reactivity was appropriate to the maturation level of the organism. Then we again have the so-called invasion of the unconscious.

Among the normal phenomena of that kind, particular interest has been focused on the so-called lapses, for the enlightening analysis of which we are so greatly indebted to Freud. It is well known that Freud regarded the lapses as the sequelae of the invasion of unconscious drive effects, which are supposed to originate from repressed ideas. In our opinion, we do not need to assume repression of ideas, for example, but can understand the lapses as aftereffects of particularly intense stimulus utilizations. They need not have been conscious; yet under definite conditions they disturb the course of the performance, which the moment requires, in such a way that the proper excitation Gestalt cannot develop in the normal manner but rather in a more or less distorted way. If the required performance is a conscious act, it will seem as if unconscious processes were invading consciousness. Actually, only disfigurements of the required total excitation Gestalt take place, and these disfigurements naturally find expression in the conscious aspect of that process. What appears just as remembrance, in a situation to which it belongs as an adequate aftereffect, will, in a situation in which it does not belong, be regarded as the invasion of an inadequate and therefore an "alien" event that disturbs the present activity.

Such "invasions" are the more frequent, the more imperfect or defective is the centering of an organism. Therefore they are most characteristic for disease. All the peculiarities Freud enumerates as characteristic for the unconscious correspond completely to the changes that normal behavior undergoes through isolation by disease.

For example, a patient of mine complained that, under certain conditions, namely, as soon as he accidentally sees a naked part of the body of a woman, he is forced to sexual exhibitionism that is very distressing to him. He could not understand why he felt compelled to do such. The patient was not of a very sexual type; on the contrary, he was reserved but had a normal sex life. Only under the above circumstances did he feel an abnormal sex urge, which was disagreeable to him and differed from his usual sex urge, which he liked. The man in general was somewhat nervous and unbalanced but intellectually normal. The treatment disclosed that at an age of 4 or 5, he and his friends, boys and girls, used to play a game they called "milking cows." Both girls and boys undressed, and the girls had to pull on the penis of the boys. He remembered the pleasure they derived from the play. He does not remember whether this game was forbidden; he is inclined to believe that it was not. They discarded that game later. It seems that not an intentional repression took place but that they forgot the game on account of other things. The patient remembered, in the therapeutic conversation, without any resistance. He had forgotten the event because it did not belong to his later life actions. Now, as an adult, in a situation in which he accidentally saw the uncovered legs of a woman, he felt the urge to expose himself exhibitionalistically. He did not know why he was doing that. After some conversation, which induced him to tell all that he remembered of his youth, he recognized the correspondence of his compulsive act with the event in his youth and became able to overcome the compulsion. The connection between the symptom and a special event in his childhood was a compulsive reaction to a certain stimulus. But how can we explain this habit, which looks very much like a conditioned response? Do we have to say that an infantile sex drive produced the play, and subsequently the habit, the connection between the aspect of a naked part of a female leg and the exposure; that this urge was "repressed," and that it came out later in a state of disturbance of the patient in which the "censor" was weakened?

From what we heard from the patient, the whole event was not intentionally repressed in the so-called realm of the unconscious. It was forgotten, and it came out in a situation in which the stimulus was similar to that in situations of childhood and in which the general condition of the man was suitable for the arising of isolated phenomena. Such an isolated phenomenon was this reaction.

Now a very important question: Was the first action – the play – a sexual play? Many people would not doubt that it was. I doubt it. It could have been a harmless play, a sort of imitation of an observed event, that gave pleasure but had nothing to do with the sex sphere in the sense of an adult person, and it might have been so, because nobody had forbidden the play and had drawn the child's attention to the sex problem.

But the emotionally impressive experience in childhood had a strong aftereffect and could become effective if the situation were suitable for this emergence of an old attitude. Now, in the experience of the adult man, it really became connected with sex. But that actually does not mean that it has to be traced back to sex experiences in childhood. The attitude, the habit in the adult, is connected with sex; the same habit in youth could have been connected with a totally different and specific experience. The attitude that comes into the foreground can be the same, and the content can be totally different.

In the psychotherapeutic situation such attitudes are brought into the foreground and then the contents, which the patient utters, are considered as arising from the repressed unconscious. As a matter of fact, they can belong to the present situation, to the adult state that is their origin. But we shall discuss this problem when we have considered another kind of so-called repression.

Certainly, there are events in youth, in which the "forgetting" of something does not run as smoothly as in the mentioned case but in which things are "repressed" because they are forbidden. In such cases, it is not so easy to reproduce the early happenings. We observe what the analyst calls "resistance." And the further explanation reveals that these repressed happenings were connected with dread.

Ambivalence and neurosis
What was the cause of this dread? We defined dread as anxiety corresponding to a condition in which the organism is in a state of danger. We have defined danger as being threatened with impairment in self-actualization. The child entered this situation of danger, because, thanks to its imperfect centering, its tendencies, corresponding to its drive for self-actualization, were in conflict with the demands of the outer world – with the "forbidden." This conflict finds its expression in anxiety. The child escapes such anxiety through building up habits that allow it to avoid these situations. Those tendencies might have strong aftereffects in the background, if they were very important for the self-actualization of the child, but they cannot be made conscious, nor

can they be experienced as attitudes, feelings, and so on, because their emergence into the foreground would bring anxiety with it. However, they may disturb the life of the child, especially because they produce an "ambivalent" state. And they tend to produce that condition the more the child, because of his immaturity or his lack of centering, is exposed to antagonistic, ambivalent reactions. (See chapter 4. *Ambivalence* is used here in the psychoanalytic sense.)

This ambivalent setting, possibly produced by a particular situation in childhood, may, if not overcome by later centering, subsequently find its expression in the whole activity of the individual, namely, in an ambivalent behavior in all the various situations of life, and may thus represent the basic symptom of the neurotic person. That such a state is very easily suited to produce anxiety is clear. We find in the behavior of patients, because of defective centering, for example, pronounced ambivalence similar to that in childhood, for which imperfect centering and the resulting ambivalence are characteristic. Now, if one permits the patient to yield to these phenomena, by offering him protection from catastrophic reactions, as during the therapeutic situation (cf. p. 250), then the patient gives various expressions to these ambivalent processes within himself. Of course, he can express this ambivalence also in words. Here it appears as if the ideas, which correspond to these words, had previously lived unconsciously in the patient. Actually, they represent only the present form of expression by which the patient manifests his ambivalent condition.

That we are not dealing with ideas that have been repressed in childhood, and now emerge from the unconscious, can be seen by the fact that they are frequently of such content that the patient, as a child, could certainly not have had them. It does not conflict with this statement that the expressed ideas can be partly determined by factors that owe their origin to childhood events. Because of the defective centering in the patient at present, such reaction contents, which originated in childhood, will emerge now because they fit into the new situation; they will be remembered and brought into the foreground. Thereby one gains the impression that the patient has "regressed" into a state of childhood. However, this is not a regression to childhood but only the same form of reaction as in childhood. It is now caused in a totally different way, namely, through pathology, that is, reaction in isolated parts. The adult can never really regress to an infantile level.

We find situations in childhood in which the ambivalent attitude is especially directed toward the parents. Of course, it is difficult to say how this ambivalent situation, the so-called Oedipus situation, is experienced by the child. One thing is sure, namely, that ideas, thoughts, definite motives, the "being conscious" of certain ethical norms and of reasons for certain prohibitions – all take a form in the child which is essentially different from those in the adult. Even the "objects" with which the child is dealing are entirely different from those of the adult. The "father," "mother," "child," "ethical norm," "incest," and so on are all contents that can arise in that form only in adults. They are produced only through the highly differentiated form of reaction of the adult and his conscious position in, and philosophy of, life. There is hardly a doubt that, in the child, all these "objects" correspond to an entirely different content than in the adult. Notwithstanding the fact that the child also experiences more than merely feelings and tensions in such situations, the contents, of course, belong to its developmental makeup in that state.[11]

According to the primitive form of reactions in the child, the objectified aspects play a small part, and those aspects prevail that we have described as feelings, emotions, and urges, for example, the simultaneous experience of pleasant and unpleasant feeling tones. It is certain that, at that period, dispositions for ambivalence take form, particularly in connection with impressive experiences, for example, the prohibition of a behavior that is of a strong positive feeling tone. It is no less probable that in later life all sorts of conflict situations that facilitate the tendency to ambivalent behavior also bring to the fore these impressive contents of childhood. To this extent Freud is certainly right, if he ascribes to the so-called Oedipus situation of childhood, and to the mastering of the Oedipus situation, such a special role in the later occurrence of ambivalent behavior. However, he exaggerates by ascribing to this situation such a completely unique preference as compared with the other ambivalent experiences of childhood. Moreover, he thereby commits the error of bringing ambivalence in such close relation to sexuality, because he interprets the "Oedipus situation" from the sexual contents of the adult.

The ambivalent behavior of a neurotic person, who can behave at ease in the psychotherapeutic situation, consists, like that of a normal person, of a great variety of ideas, thoughts, and feelings that are of conflicting values. Among them we also find, of course, conflicts of sexual contents, and among these, in turn, those that have the specific coloration of the ambivalent parent relationship. Their appearance is certainly favored by the strong disposition that may have formed in the so-called Oedipus situation of that person. This may be the reason why this "complex" appears so often in the free associations of the neurotic. But this does, in no way, indicate that the "Oedipus complex" is the determining factor for the ambivalence and is subconsciously supporting it. The "Oedipus complex" is the result of interpretation of the analyst, if he makes a present sexual ambivalence, or more specifically the parental conflict, the central point of reference, and regards the ambivalence that appears in other contents of free associations or in other behavior of the patient, as depending on the ambivalence in that special sphere. Rather, he should regard ambivalence in the sex sphere merely as an expression of the same basic process, namely, as the expression of general ambivalence produced by lack of centering in the sick organism.

In principle, we find here the same methodological mistake that we have previously pointed out; that is, that one fails at the outset to take all symptoms as equivalent and fails to seek for a way of understanding all symptoms. Instead, one phenomenon, which is preferred by chance or by a theoretical predilection, is regarded as the primary phenomenon on which the others are supposed to be depending. When psychoanalysis apparently finds a confirmation of its original assumptions through new observations, we must remember that we were able to state the same about the reflex theory, namely, that on the basis of reflexology, no criticism of the reflex theory is possible, because the principle itself always supplies auxiliary hypotheses to repair the shortcomings.

The apparent confirmation of the basic psychoanalytic theory by further experience leads to the same fallacy, because the new experiences are always obtained in the same way. In psychoanalysis, there is, in addition, a special factor that helps to discover an increasing number of apparent confirmations for the basic theory. Because the analytic doctrine is so widely known, through the spreading of analytic literature, we cannot be surprised that we find, in the free associations, so many confirmations of the analytic thesis.

In summary, there are, in childhood, preferred reaction patterns.

To these belongs the so-called Oedipus situation, namely, the ambivalent attitude of the child toward the object "father-mother." However, this attitude need not have been "repressed." It simply could have receded into the background. In the course of development, new behavior patterns render the existing ambivalent attitude, with its definite contents, ineffective, because the old attitude does not fit the new patterns. This is the same as in memory phenomena in general; something that we have learned arises only when a situation exists to which it belongs. A foreign language, for example, may be immediately remembered in an environment where this language is naturally spoken. In another environment, however, where this language does not fit, to which it stands in a certain contrast, the language does not emerge of its own accord – one must consciously produce it. Of course, the childhood attitudes have not disappeared. They are preserved as dispositions in the background, some of which may even be particularly strong. But they are not relevant, they are not effective, because they do not belong to the milieu of an older person and because ambivalent attitudes in general become less prominent with increasing maturation.

What appears as the unconscious is nothing but the entering of a former reaction pattern of the organism into a present response, when the situation is suitable. It is nothing but a specific form of memory. The emerging of the so-called unconscious is nothing but the result of strong aftereffects of certain patterns, which have not been sufficiently integrated into the properly centered behavior of the whole organism. Without factually belonging to the situation, they effectuate themselves like other stimuli, either on account of their own intensity or because of labile centering of the organism, in the same way as particularly strong, external stimuli. If these abnormally strong aftereffects of certain reaction patterns cannot effectuate themselves, then, at the very least, they may disturb the normal behavior, just as other strong stimuli. They alter the stimulus utilization so that the latter occurs in abnormal fashion. Then anxiety arises as the expression of a continually impending danger of catastrophic reaction. And here we may encounter substitute formations as means to avoid catastrophes. These formations have the same characteristics as those we have met above in the organic patients.

The pleasure principle. The death instinct: Erroneous hypostatizations
of tension and release under isolation. The role of consciousness
Life in the so-called unconscious appears, in Freud's conception, as
dominated by drives, dominated in such a way that it becomes the life
problem to obtain relief from the tension the drives create. This release,
according to Freud, represents the goal of all drives, especially of the
sex drive. The goal of the sex drive is the "becoming free" of the tension of sex − that is the essence of the pleasure principle. The fact that
release is considered the decisive factor shows clearly that release, as
Freud conceives it, has the character of a phenomenon taking place in
an isolated part of the system. As we have emphasized before, equalization and adequate reaction does not mean entering a state of rest
but rather attaining an "adequate mean" of excitation, of tension. The
more, however, a reaction takes place in an isolated part, the more the
only possible reaction is the coming to a state of rest − a removal of
tension. The isolated part of the system has a limited environment. If
we assume that this isolation from the world becomes stronger and
stronger, then hardly any environmental stimuli are left to be registered
by the system, and the system remains in the state of unchanged equilibrium, once it has reached it, the system is released from all tension.
It might, of course, be again thrown out of balance from outside but
will again return to its state of release. To understand release, we need
assume neither drives nor unconscious. This view of Freud, that life is
dominated by a drive, the nature of which is to lead to release, must
necessarily carry us to the further view that Freud, with his characteristic consistency, has finally advanced, namely, that the ultimate goal
is the complete release, or death − the disintegration into the inorganic. When Freud realized that his concept of a libidinal drive does
not cover all aspects of human behavior, he introduced the death instinct. Death becomes the goal of life. Thus life, in its intrinsic character, indeed becomes completely unintelligible. The subject matter
of biology disappears, because life has been argued away through a false
theoretical postulate.

Freud's views become intelligible only if one realizes that they have
been directly transferred from phenomena in sick people to the normal,
from the phenomena in abnormal reactions that formally correspond
to those that we have characterized as reflexes or as parts. From this
erroneous method originates the conflict between "mind" and "drives"

and that peculiar form of "unconscious" that appears during analysis. Obviously it becomes impossible to understand human nature adequately on this basis, and therefore Freud fails to do justice to the positive aspects of life. He fails to recognize that the basic phenomenon of life is an incessant process of coming to terms with the environment; he only sees escape and craving for release. He only knows the lust of release, not the pleasure of tension. Thus, for instance, he does not do justice even to the biological value of sex, to its positive significance for the actualization of the nature of the human being, to the real significance of what he calls the unconscious. This in turn obstructs his appraisal of consciousness phenomena. Consciousness for him becomes something negative, a kind of supervisor whose task it is to see that the other part, which he calls the unconscious, does not break through in an unauthorized manner. In that way, it ultimately remains obscure why consciousness does not tolerate entrance of definite contents. Why should there not be, throughout, gratification of one's lust? Why is man not content with behaving by satisfying his lust? Why does the so-called sublimation lead to culture? No assumption of sublimation of the sex drives can explain this, no matter how significant sublimation may be for special characteristics in the formation of culture. Adequate understanding of the phenomenon "culture" can be attained only through proper evaluation of what we call consciousness and the proper recognition of the specific peculiarities that the human being acquires through the potentiality to have conscious experience. Only then is consciousness recognized in its specific significance for the highest form of coming to terms with the world (as indeed only man seems to exhibit); only then is consciousness freed from a degradation to a sort of useful or harmful epiphenomenon.

At this point, a comparison between the normal and the brain-diseased individual again offers insight into the structure of man and into the special position that consciousness imparts to man within the whole of living nature. No matter how many performances the patients are capable of accomplishing, actually they lack every creative power, any ability to alter their creative activity, corresponding to changing conditions.

It is exactly this factual material that impresses us with the enormous significance of consciousness. This insight compels us to refute that romantic doctrine that has spread, especially under the leadership of Ludwig Klages, who attempts to discredit the mind by contrasting it with the impelling "vital" forces. Klages may be right in so far as he fights against the "overgrowth" of the intellect. But he overlooks completely the fact that the "vital" forces, in the form characteristic for human organization, cannot even become manifest, save in reference to consciousness – the very consciousness Klages tries to root out. Indeed, what remains after the impairment of consciousness is no longer equivalent to the nature of man at all.

Certainly all creative activity originates from the living impulse of the organism to cope productively with the environment. But consciousness is prerequisite in order that productivity may find its manifestation. This is the outstanding characteristic of human creativeness compared with animal behavior. No matter how impotent the direct effect of the mind upon the world may be regarded, it is only through the mind that man reveals his nature. The problem of how the phenomenon of directions in human actions arises has been our particular concern, and we may say that it has been a problem to many generations of philosophers and biologists. To us, it seems that we cannot approach this question without a sufficient appreciation of consciousness. It is ultimately consciousness that determines direction. Only if we keep this in mind are we prepared to deal adequately with the phenomenon of speech, ethical conduct, art, culture, and freedom to act. And only then are we able to understand that these are exclusively attributes of the human being and are absent in animals.

The Organismic Unity of "Body" and "Mind"
Our viewpoint regarding the partitive process leads us to a very definite conception of the psycho-physical problem. In the past, the so-called psycho-physical problem was discussed essentially between philosophers and psychologists, often in a very speculative and not very fruitful manner. During the last decades, the discussion has been carried into the midst of medical practice, especially through the influence of the contributions of psychotherapists.

The psycho-physical problem. No independent realm of "body"
or "mind." No supremacy of "body" or "mind"
We shall base our discussion on practical experience, because this approach seems best suited to bring out the "facts" and thus the material

useful for the theoretical evaluation. The physician must often make a decision whether he should, in a certain condition, use psychological or somatic treatment or both. His decision will be determined by his opinion as to the relation between bodily and psychological processes and the possibility of influencing bodily phenomena by psychological treatment, and vice versa.

The psychotherapist, on his experience, decides in favor of the primacy of the psyche in the genesis and treatment, not only of mental, but also of a great many somatic, pathological phenomena. Some neurotic symptoms that defy any somatic treatment, or even such bodily phenomena as an asthma attack with all its characteristic changes in the lungs, the blood picture, and so on, can be made to disappear by psychological treatment. Or a high and dangerous hypertonia may be reduced to normalcy when the underlying psychological conflict is resolved; the improvement may not merely be temporary but will last until new mental conflicts appear. Anyone who has seen such cases would no longer want to do without psychotherapy as a tool in medicine. For him, the psychological aspect in somatic processes will gain a very particular significance. Thus, it was possible that, to some people, the somatic phenomena appeared almost entirely as an expression of the psychological events and derived significance only as a symbol for those. However, even if the bodily phenomena practically lose their autonomy and if one places them entirely under the influence of the psyche, one cannot nullify the essential difference between the two aspects.

The same holds true for those who emphasize the primacy of the bodily phenomena. They, too, certainly do not deny the significance of the psychological process for normal and pathological somatic events. Sometimes, of course, the basic tendency took in the direction of tracing mental diseases back to bodily changes and of treating the mental in a physical way. True, good physicians always knew enough about the relevance of the "mind" for even bodily diseases, not to neglect it. They had a sufficient appraisal of the great practical implication of psychic phenomena to attribute to the mental aspect a special domain besides the somatic. They were also convinced of their mutual influence. The position that the mind was simply a meaningless epiphenomenon was only possible for the pure theoretician. Physicians, however, in their practice were probably always more or less guided, without explicitly accounting for it, by a theory of interaction.

The opponents agree in recognizing two independent realms: that of the body and that of the mind, and the possibility of interaction. For both, the mind and the body are separate modes of existence. More or less independence and influence are attributed either to the one or to the other, depending on the respective bias. The concordance, in some fundamental presuppositions of these two views otherwise so much opposed to each other, points ultimately to a basic, common denominator. This is the consequence of the same way of thinking, that is, of the atomistic approach.

An unbiased inspection of the pertinent facts, however, reveals the same holistic reference that we have discovered in the description of stimulus reactions. Only, in this case we find, as a component of the reactions besides the somatic ones, "psychological" processes, in the form of "conscious" experiences, or experiences as moods, attitudes, and so on, and such phenomena that are described as "nonconscious" processes.

The relation between somatic and mental processes is exactly the same as that between somatic processes themselves, the latter of which we have discussed above. The results of the body-mind investigations are concerned with the following: influence of psychological on somatic processes (influence of imagination, hypnosis, etc.) and influence of somatic on psychological processes, which latter is such a well-known fact that it is hardly necessary to mention it. We know of definite, alternating, and of opposing effects, no matter whether one starts from the somatic or the psychological process. We know, furthermore, that the effect of a "stimulus" can be understood only by reference to the whole, and so on.

From these observations, we can reach the same conclusion as before. Neither of the two realms can be regarded a priori as dominating and determining the other, leaving to it, at best, a modifying influence. The mind must no more be regarded as the sole expression and the real nature of living organisms than the body. If one makes that mistake, the term "mind" loses its special meaning completely, while at the same time one can also no longer do justice to the "somatic." The "somatic" then would, so to speak, appear only as emanation of the "psyche" and is actually regarded by many as a sort of product of crystallization of mind. How this should be brought about remains completely obscure. There one forgets primarily that what one calls mind is only an abstraction from the real actualization of life in the organism and not something that is given isolatedly. What this has to do with the living organism has to be disclosed, just as must be done for the bodily phenomena. Certainly it is not contained in the organism as part of it. At best, the mind might reflect only one aspect of the organism. One cannot even see the reason why this point of departure should offer the best basis for the comprehension of life.

By proceeding on this basis, one certainly meets the same danger as by attempting to understand life from the somatic point of view. Furthermore, little would be gained if one were simply to supplement the results gained by psychological observation with those gained by somatic observation. Once one has posited the two as different modes of existence, it is impossible to revise this fallacy by any correction. All the difficulties that "pure" psychology encounters over and over again and that it tried to meet in vain by a variety of hypotheses sprang from the fact that it either entirely overlooked the relation between the mind and the living organism or did not regard it correctly.

The "psychological" and the "physical" are indifferent to the real processes. The "functional" significance for the whole is alone relevant
A univocal description of living processes requires that the terms psychological and physical be used at the outset, in a sense indifferent to the real processes, as auxiliary tools of description. Although we are forced to employ these descriptive terms, in other words, to speak of physical and psychological phenomena, we must always bear in mind that, in doing so, we are dealing with data that have to be evaluated in the light of their functional significance for the whole.

On the basis of such a consideration, it becomes intelligible that we meet with the same laws for the "psychological" aspects as for the "physical" and that experiments that attempt to isolate certain aspects (e.g., the so-called processes of consciousness) will produce the same kind of modifications from the "norm" as isolation through pathology.

In the light of our approach, the problem of the interaction between mind and body appears in entirely different aspect. Neither does the mind act on the body, nor the body on the mind, no matter how much this may seem to be the case in superficial observation. We are always dealing with the activity of the whole organism, the effects of which we refer at one time to something called mind, at another time to something called body. In noting an activity, we describe the behavior of the whole organism either through the index of the so-called mind or through the index of the body.

In order to prevent misunderstandings let us state that we deny neither the "psychical" nor the "physical" in their uniqueness, we merely demand that the psychological and the physical should be treated as phenomena that have to be evaluated as to their significance for the holistic reality of the organism, in the situation in which we observe it.

The Constants. Preferred and Ordered Behavior

The analysis of a variety of phenomena has strongly impelled us to the holistic view of the organism. Yet it has not furnished a decisive stand regarding a substantiated knowledge of the structure of the organism. It has principally shown us only which ones of the observable phenomena are unsuited as a departure for our goal. True, we have disclosed some essential traits of the functional organization of the organism, for example, the importance of visual discrimination (in the analysis of calcarine-lesion), the significance of definite patterns of gait (through analysis of the movements of animals after amputation of limbs), the specific significance of the abstract behavior, the difference in significance of flexor and extensor movements, and so on. But these are all more or less incidental results. We still cannot give an account of why we regard precisely these phenomena as essential traits of the organism. We need guidelines that permit us to make systematic determinations. We need a criterion that enables us to select from the multitude of observations those facts that are suited for the determination of the real nature of an organism.

The criterion as to whether a single phenomenon is such a characteristic of the organism is, we believe, given in the fact that it is an intrinsic factor in the maintenance of the relative constancy of the organism. In contrast to the diversified and even contradictory character of the partitive data, the organism proper presents itself as a structural formation that, in spite of all the fluctuations of its behavioral pattern in the varying situations and in spite of the unfolding and decline in the course of the individual's life, retains a relative constancy. If this were not the case, it would never be possible to identify a given organism as such. It would not even be possible to talk about a definite organism at all. We shall attempt to use this criterion of the maintenance of constancy as our guiding principle in selecting the facts that should serve as a basis for our conception of the organism. What are the processes that are apt to maintain the constancy of the organism?

The "preferred" behavior

We can consider an organism at one time, in the usual analytic way, as composed of parts, members, organs, and, at another time, in its natural behavior; then we find, in the latter case, that by no means all kinds of behavior, which on the grounds of the first consideration would be conceived as being possible, are actually realized. Instead we find that only a definite, selective range of modes of behavior exists. These modes we shall classify as "preferred behavior."[12]

To illustrate this phenomenon, we have ample choice in the various fields of animal and human behavior. We know, for example, that animals, when dropped, always fall in a very definite position. In order to explain this, one has posited certain postural reflexes. If we bring parts of their bodies into an abnormal position – for instance, if we turn the head toward one side – we find a compensation for this abnormal position, in the assuming of a new, definite position. Or, if this is prevented, the posture of the rest of the body changes until a definite total position is again achieved. Thus, the animal has the capacity, within a certain degree, of adapting itself to environmental situations through very specific positions of the body. This takes place also in the case of being dropped. In spite of diversified environmental situations, it is always able to return to its balanced position, which we call the "preferred position."

In "decerebrated animal," the number of positions that are thus possible is considerably less and can be exactly determined experimentally. For instance, a definite position of the head corresponds to a very specific position of the trunk and the limbs. Thus, we find here relatively simple conditions for the explanation of the origin and preference of certain positions, in the reflexively fixed connections of the limbs, as in the squat position of the rabbit, and so on.

Thus, it may seem as if simple, reflexively fixed connections would ensure the preferred positions. The facts determined by the investigations of Magnus, his pupils, and many others regarding the "postural reflexes" have contributed a great deal to support the theory of the reflex structure of the performances of the organism. But the results have mostly been obtained from decerebrated animals, and the circumstances are by no means so simple in the intact animal and in man. The variety of possible "normal" positions, corresponding to the same outside stimulus situation, is much greater. Thus one can observe, provided that the visual performances are not interfered with, various other preferred positions. This is usually explained simply by the appearance of additional stimuli, by a modification of the original reflex through additional reflexes. The theory of differential shunting is supposed to satisfy these new phenomena by the assumption of more complicated reflex mechanisms. We have previously pointed to the difficulties of this theory, which arise when an almost unlimited number of variations appear, which in turn compel one to take recourse to an almost unlimited number of shunting mechanisms. Before attempting another explanation, we want to report on a number of facts that will illustrate the existence of preferred behavior in man and that will give us the possibility of a more accurate check.

First, we must emphasize that one finds in nondecerebrated animals, especially in the higher ones, and particularly in man, a far greater number of actually realized positions and postures than presumed in the reflex theory. Even in the same stimulus situation, opposite postures occur. Thus, to a definite position of one limb, by no means always corresponds the same preferred position of the rest of the body. To a turning of the head toward the right belongs a turning of the body and the extremities toward the right. But there is still another preferred position that is directly opposite to the first one. For example, it happens not infrequently that in paying attention to something on our right, we must turn our eyes and head in this direction and at the same time grasp something located at the left, with the left arm. In such a case, where head movement toward one side and arm movement toward the other belong together, an entirely different relation between head and arm position is "preferred" than in the first instance.

Such an "ambiguity" of relations becomes particularly obvious in the following cases: occasionally we find in a patient that a passively induced head position has a close bond to a certain arm position, and this bond is so strong that it cannot be overcome passively. However, this connection can be immediately loosened if the patient attempts to perform a task that requires another, reverse connection. The new task causes the new connection promptly to appear (cf. p. 124). How

267

is it possible that we obtain an opposite coupling in which the "reflex connection" was so extraordinarily strong? We must assume that entirely different factors are decisive to bring about this apparent "deviation" from the established connection.

As we have mentioned, the number of possible positions becomes much larger in the higher animals, and especially in human beings; the relation to the stimulus is no longer so unambiguous. Still it remains noteworthy that the number of possible positions and other behaviors is by no means indefinite. They are not numerous enough to correspond to the quantitative variability of the environmental situation. Human beings do not always exhibit the capacity to respond adaptively to every change of outer-world demands, to any change of the stimuli imping-ing on a part of the body. The human organism much rather prefers def-inite reactions to others and contents itself with a definite, not very large number, of such reactions, even if the environmental changes vary to a much greater degree. If a person has the task of pointing to a cer-tain place that lies more or less sideward, he executes the pointing movement of the arm by no means always in the same manner, at least as long as he is not influenced in any way. If the object at which he is required to point is slightly sideways, he points, without moving the rest of the body, only with the extended arm, in such a way that the angle between arm and the frontal plane of the body is obtuse, about 130° to 140°. If the object at which he should point is in a more for-ward position, then the arm is no longer moved alone, but the trunk, too, is moved somewhat toward the left, the pointing arm still form-ing approximately the same angle with the frontal plane of the body as before. If the object that is to be pointed out lies more outside, say, to the extreme right side, then the body turns so far to the right that, when the subject points, the angle between the frontal plane and the arm is again essentially the same as before. Of course we can also behave differently: we can point forward, while our body remains fixed. But this is not the natural way, since it requires a special imposition, pos-sibly because the situation demands that the body must not or cannot be moved.

Thus, the organism seems to have the tendency to prefer a definite relation in the positions of arm and trunk, instead of conforming with the varying environmental demands, although this could very well be done by altering the preferred arm-trunk position. The problem is:

Which ways, which situations, which positions are preferred, and why?

If one requests a person, while standing, to describe a circle, he will usually describe a circle of medium size in a frontal parallel plane with the extended index finger of the right arm, while the arm is half flexed in the elbow. Larger circles, circles in another plane, or possibly executed with the extended arm, seem unnatural and uncomfortable to such persons who naively would proceed in the above manner. But when their trunk is bent forward, then it is natural for them to describe the circle in a horizontal plane. One might think that the horizontal circle simply results from executing the arm movement in the same relation to the upper part of the body and is only due to the changed bodily posture. But if this were true, we would find, in this bent-over position, only a circle in the oblique plane. Yet actually the circle is in the horizontal plane. In this position, apparently, the circle in the horizontal plane corresponds to the preferred situation. Accurate analysis shows that the way of describing this circle is univocally determined by the total situation of the subject. By total situation, we also mean to include the factor of the subject's attitude toward the task. Therefore, the circle is not made by all subjects in the same way, but in a specific situation, by each one in a specific way that he prefers quite naively to all other alternatives.

Through this simple experiment, one can easily differentiate several types of individuals. In one type, the objectifying attitude prevails. This type prefers to describe a small circle in an almost-frontal parallel plane. Another type is more motor, has a prevailing motor attitude, and describes a large circle with the extended arm by excessive movement in the shoulder joint. Actually he does not describe a circle at all but leads his arm around in a circle for which an excessive excursion is the most natural. These variations in the execution of the circle manifest differences between men and women, between persons of different character, vocations, and so on. But always — and this is the essential point — we find, together with the preferred way a task is executed, the experience of greatest "comfort," "naturalness," and the greatest accuracy of performance, in spite of the fact that, from the pure motor point of view, we have highly diversified coordinations between the individual parts of the body. If one forces a subject to proceed by using such coordinations that do not come naturally to him, then the procedure is immediately experienced as uncomfortable and the result is not as good. Apparently, the preferred behavior is determined by the total attitude of the performing person.

If we ask somebody to stretch out his arm we find, as long as we give no special instruction, that hand and fingers are slightly flexed, that the thumb is a little lower than the rest of the fingers, that the fingers are somewhat spread, especially the little finger, and that the palm of the hand is turned downward, directed somewhat toward the midline of the body. Any other position of the hand in this situation is distinctly felt as uncomfortable, and we try to avoid it as far as possible or to bring the hand back into the more comfortable position. If we are asked to extend the arm forward, with the palm directed upward or outside, we feel the distinct inclination to turn the hand back into the aforementioned position, and a continuous volitional effort is required to prevent this.

If someone who is accustomed to hold his head somewhat obliquely is forced to hold it straight, this is not only a special effort for him, but after a certain time the head will return to the usual, "normal" position, unless he prevents this by continuously paying attention to the position of his head. If, in going to sleep, one assumes a variety of positions, one will very soon regain a definite natural position in order to fall asleep. So many hindrances to falling asleep are simply due to the fact that one is prevented by some circumstances from assuming this natural position. If we trace the causes for assuming these positions, we find a great variety of bodily and psychological factors. But they are almost always fixed for a given individual.

This preference for a definite behavior, relatively independent of the outer situation, is found especially in perceptions. When angles between 30° and 150° are optically presented, not all steps of the differential threshold are experienced as equal. What we do recognize primarily are "acute," "obtuse," and "right" angles.[13] These are the preferred impressions, around which all others are grouped. Each of the preferred impressions has its range. An angle of 93°, for example, appears as a "poor" right angle, deviating somehow from the preferred impression and not as a characteristic impression of individual uniqueness. In the tachistoscopic experiment, it is the circle that is easiest to recognize; polygonal figures are perceived as circles.[14]

Also tactually the circle is preferred. If three places of the skin, arranged as a triangle, are touched successively, it results in the impression of a circle.[15] Similar preferences in the field of vision are the impression of the square, certain curves, symmetry against asymmetry, and the vertical against a somewhat obliquely inclined line. Emil von Skramlik has shown that a number of illusions in the cutaneous sense are caused by the fact that our perceptions depend on normal posture and that, in abnormal, unaccustomed placement of the stimulus area, the perceptions are transfigured in the direction of the experience during the normal position.[16] If two stimuli touch simultaneously the volar side of the end section and of the second section of a finger, the former one, which touches the tip, seems to lie higher. Skramlik explains this and similar illusions on the basis that the normal position of the hand is the grasping position, in which the fingertips are really higher. Börnstein and I were able to show, in entirely different investigations, that this grasping position is actually a preferred position.[17] Thus the "illusion" is caused by the tendency to a specific preferred situation. Instead of talking of an illusion, one could also talk of transfiguration or assimilation to a specific preferred situation. Corresponding phenomena exist in the field of tones. The fourth and the fifth are preferred. Small deviations leave the perception relatively unaffected, but larger deviations are experienced as an impurity of the fifth, as a bad fifth, and so on, without one always being able to say in which direction the experience deviates. Finally, in the field of colors, we have, in proportion to the great variety of colors (according to their wavelengths), only a very limited number of qualitatively different color experiences (e.g., in the research of Sander).

In patients, corresponding phenomena can be observed even much better than in normal persons, especially in patients with disturbances of the funtioning of the cerebellum or the frontal lobe. This manifests itself so that patients, while executing an uncomfortable movement in a task performance, invariably lapse into the more comfortable movement, unless they are intensely concentrating on the demanded movement. Usually it suffices to have the performances carried out with closed eyes to bring about this phenomenon. We find then that, even against their will and most of the time without their knowledge, the comfortable position sets in.[18]

Thus, for a patient with disturbance of the left frontal lobe, the preferred position of the head is a slight tilting toward the right (new natural position). If one brings the head passively into a straight position, or over to the left, or even further to the right, then one finds that the head returns, without knowledge of the patient, into this new natural position in which it ultimately will remain. The same happens if the patient brings his head intentionally into such an "abnormal" position and pays no further attention to it.[19]

In the above-mentioned task of pointing to a place, it becomes clear that the patients prefer a certain plane of action even more strongly than normal persons. This is especially the case because the spatial domain, in which the execution takes place, is in itself much more limited than in a normal person.

Often in the field of vision, the assimilation of an oblique line to a vertical one is particularly instructive. The presented line may deviate considerably from the objective vertical and still be experienced as a vertical. It becomes especially apparent when a patient sees this line as a vertical irrespective of whether it deviates to the right or to the left. This was the case in one of Weizsäcker's patients.[20] I have observed similar phenomena. If I showed one of my patients a stick, one foot long, from a distance of two yards, at first in a vertical position and then in a 10° inclination toward the left or the right, she did not notice the difference, but saw always only a vertical rod. Similarly, a stick was always seen horizontally, even if deviating 10° from this position.[21] Only in deviations above 10° did the patient see that the stick was oblique. When the stick was turned from the vertical into the oblique position, she did not see the movement until the stick reached and continued beyond the region where the oblique position of the stick could be experienced.

The characteristics of preferred behavior and its explanation
In summarizing these facts we find the following:

1. The organism realizes only a certain number of definite performances. It by no means realizes all those that were to be expected from the material obtained through isolating experiments on parts of the organism.

2. The organism has the tendency toward very decidedly preferred ways of behavior, be it in perception, motility, posture, and so on.

3. In situations in which the task requires a behavior in approximation to the preferred behavior, we find assimilation to the preferred behavior.

4. The preferred situation is subjectively characterized by the feeling of comfort, agreeableness, security, and correctness.

5. In nonpreferred behavior, we have subjectively the feeling of "not fitting," "disagreeable," "unsatisfied," "difficult," and "of more deliberate execution."

How is this preference of certain decided ways of behavior to be explained? Among the available attempts of explanation, the following types may be differentiated:

1. There is an attempt to explain these phenomena through certain conditions of the pertinent field in which the preferred behavior takes place. Thus, for example, one tries to explain the preference of the visual vertical by its retinal projection on the vertical meridian of the retina. This, of course, barely fits the facts in normal cases. If we turn the head or assume a horizontal position, the objective vertical remains for us vertical, although it is now projected on an entirely different retinal meridian. In order to explain this on the basis of the above assumption, special auxiliary hypotheses would be required. Actually, the objective vertical coincides with the vertical meridian of the retina only in one special situation, namely, during the upright position of the body, a special position of the head and the eyes. This is certainly a very characteristic and preferred posture for human beings but one that is actually only rarely realized in life. It would be extremely strange if all visual impressions of direction were referred to a position that, in itself, is so rare. But especially pathology has shown impressively that, experiencing a vertical can certainly not be determined once and for all by the excitation of a specific retinal meridian. We know of patients with a one-sided tonus disturbance who have the impression of obliqueness while the head is in the vertical position and the objective vertical is projected on the vertical meridian of the retina; and a line that is somewhat oblique produces the impression of being straight. But still more characteristic is the fact that the identical stimulus, the retinal image on the same meridian, may at one time cause the impression of verticality, at another time of greater or lesser obliqueness, all depending on what other stimuli influence the body. We refer to this in order to demonstrate that the peripheral process, the retinal stimulus, cannot alone be the decisive factor.

One other example is preferred behavior in motor processes; when one tries to explain the fact that the optimal performance of pointing occurs approximately always in the same plane, one has appealed to the mechanical arrangement of the moved limbs. One refers, for instance, to the way in which the arms are fixed in the shoulder joint. Others, who reject this assumption, like K. Flick and Karl Hansen, have taken recourse to the state of tension of the muscles by which the plane of motion is fixed.[22] The preference of a certain plane, outside of the sagittal plane, is caused, according to them, by the fact that "pointing positions in abduction positions take place under increased stretching or tension of the abductors, and vice versa. The more to the side the starting position is, the more the countereffect of the tensed muscle group has to come into action. Thus a variably great error in pointing, in the positive or negative sense, is brought about."[23] In other words, the preference for this plane is referred to the state of equilibrium between the two muscle groups during the movement.

As far as the state of equilibrium of the muscle groups is concerned, this explanation probably does correspond to the actual state of affairs. Still, it is not really an explanation, because the question arises: Why does a state of equilibrium exist just in this plane? One could answer this question only by again referring back to the mechanical arrangement (which, however, the authors refuse), unless one would refer to entirely different factors as determining the balance of tension. The latter is actually necessitated. We know that the state of tension in a certain muscle changes according to the position of the other parts of the body, according to the condition of the whole organism. Thus, if, in the plane in question we find, during the experiment, a state of equilibrium between the abductors and adductors, this can only be so, because it corresponds to the total situation. We shall see that this is actually the case, when we discuss how the preferred plane of the pointing can be modified by the condition that prevails in some parts of the body or in the entire remaining organism. The state of local tension in the above-mentioned plane shows a state of equilibrium, because a preferred situation prevails and not the opposite. This leaves us with the task of explaining why, in this situation, this specific plane is the preferred one in the pointing performance. We see then that, here as well, the facts necessitate an explanation that cannot confine itself by taking only the conditions in the periphery into account. The central processes, the whole of the organism, must be considered in order to arrive at an explanation. How this must be conceived, we shall discuss later.

2. There is a second group of attempted explanations that take an essentially different direction. They trace the preferred behavior to a more formal principle that is propounded in two forms:

First, one believes that the determining factor for the preference of certain patterns is to be found in their simplicity and in a particular "innerness" (Ipsen). This problem was discussed particularly in an attempt to explain how the so-called good Gestalten in perception are brought about. "The preference for turning the head to the source of sound can be understood as caused by the tendency to obtain as simple an auditory experience as possible" (Koffka). But what is simple? That certainly cannot be determined on the basis of the content of the process or of the experience. The determination will depend on whether one departs from isolable "part contents" or from the whole. By the fact that something is "a figure," a Gestalt, it apparently becomes simple for us. This probably also holds true with regard to physiological processes. But this is precisely the problem: Why is something a Gestalt? Simplicity and pregnanz, after all, are nothing but essential characteristics of a Gestalt. But what causes a Gestalt? This is what we really wish to know.

Second, similar in principle, only different in direction, is the assumption that the organism has the tendency to behave according to the principle of least energy expenditure. According to this view, the preferred behavior corresponds to the least possible expenditure of energy, a view that was already developed by Ernst Mach and then by Köhler, A. Gatti, and, in great detail, by Richard Hamburger.[24] As much as we subscribe to this view in general, nevertheless the question arises again: Why is the situation in which the preferred behavior appears the one of least energy expenditure? We agree with Matthaei when he says that the principle of "minimum energy" descriptively does not seem to indicate more than the "tendency to simplicity."[25] After all, the minimum energy consumption is not a proven fact but only a theoretical hypothesis. But even if it were a universally proven fact, it would still require explanation. This is really our problem, which can be formulated as: For what reasons are the "preferred" ways of behavior preferred? Why do we do the best, the most comfortable, and the most correct pointing, in a definite realm? Why are the vertical and the square preferred visual Gestalten, and so on?

To answer the question, we first have to scrutinize the whole situation in which the preferred behavior occurs. Usually, one has made the mistake of not taking the total situation into consideration, because one has not appreciated its relevance for our problem.

3. Numerous observations in this respect, have shown that actually all changes in the rest of the organism do modify the preferred behavior in a certain field. They may make it less preferred; and they may make a less preferred behavior a more preferred one. This is illustrated by the following facts:

(A) *Influence of peripheral changes on preferred behavior*
a) Influence of sensory stimuli on motor performances. We were able to determine in numerous experiments that the plane for pointing can be displaced by a variety of stimuli (tactual, visual, auditory, etc.) and always toward the place of onset of the stimulus.[26]

b) Influence of motor processes and positions of the individual members on motor performances. As stated in detail elsewhere, the plane of correct pointing can be changed, in a regular manner, by changes of the positions of the other arm, the head, the eyes, and the legs. These facts in general can also be easily proved in normal people.

c) Influence of processes of which the person is not conscious. Particularly important is the fact that peripheral changes, which do not become conscious, are of equal influence on the manner of pointing as on the locality of the preferred plane during pointing.[27] One may determine, in a cerebellar patient, the preferred plane during a sagittal movement of the arm of the unaffected side, say, the left. This can be done by having the patient indicate in what position the movement is most comfortable or by determining where the pointing, in a pointing experiment, is most correct. Then one asks him to raise the arm of the other, the diseased side, in which condition the arm begins to deviate, because of the existing abduction tendency.

Now one sees that, depending on the position that the unconsciously deviating arm has just reached, the plane varies and is always moved toward the right in correspondence with the degree of the deviation. One could assume that the preferred position of the left arm is displaced toward the right during the deviation of the right arm, because the attention of the patient is shifted toward the right on account of the processes in the right arm. However, two things speak against this assumption. One is the proof that the deviation does not become conscious. The following experiment corroborates this: if one asks the patient to close his eyes and point with one hand to the center of the other hand, which has been voluntarily raised, he points at first almost correctly. If the arm now deviates, the patient still points approximately to the old place, even after the arm has already reached an entirely different position, and is astonished if he does not find the hand. The old place to which he points is somewhat shifted by the deviation, but in any event is far distant from the real place.

Another proof for the nonconscious deviation is the following: in the beginning, and even after the deviation has attained a certain degree, the preferred position still remains approximately the same. The displacement sets in only after the deviation has increased in accordance with the latent period, which is characteristic for tonus processes. If it were a question of attention, then we should find the displacement especially in the beginning, when the patient raises the arm. But at this time, no influence can be observed. Thus, we can assume that the displacement of the plane is determined by the deviation that takes place nonconsciously. The fact that the influence reveals itself only after a certain extent of deviation, corresponding to the latent period for tonus processes, speaks especially in favor of the physiological character of the influence.

d) Just as peripheral stimuli have an influence on the preferred behavior in motor performances, so in the same way we find that motor and sensory processes influence the preferred behavior in performances of perception. For example, the subjective vertical can be changed through sensory stimuli (labyrinth stimuli, cutaneous stimuli, etc.), as well as through changes in the position of limbs.

The preferred situation in one part may be modified through a combination of various sensory and motor (conscious and nonconscious) processes in other parts – as can be demonstrated in a variety of different experiments. The influence always appears to be lawfully dependent on any changing factor. This influence can be directly determined quantitatively, insofar as sensory and motor processes are at all comparable.

e) Furthermore, the significance of the time factor is quite noteworthy. Small changes that, in themselves, have little or no effect become effective if they last long enough, almost as effective as stronger stimuli in shorter duration.[28] We have had repeated occasion to state that red color changes a performance by impoverishing it; objects presented in red color seem less clear than those in green color. This fact is exaggerated by an inadequate, "bad" position of the head, for example, if the head is held straight, while slight obliqueness is the preferred position in an individual patient. When one presented to such a patient a red piece of paper next to a green one of equal size, the red color "diffused" over the green, the red paper seemed larger and the green one smaller.[29] Therefore the patient was not capable of reading Jakob Stilling's well-known pseudoisochromatic tables, which can be read only if one discriminates clearly between the green and the red dots. However, when the head was brought into an oblique, that is, into the preferred position, then the disturbance was reduced and disappeared almost completely during a short exposure of the object, and the patient was then able to read Jakob Stilling's tables. But the disturbance immediately reappeared as soon as the red color was presented a little longer. In other words, increasing the stimulus duration had the same effect as an impairment of the performance by introducing a change in the motor or sensory field. This and similar observations point again to the great importance of the time factor for the ordered course of an excitation (cf. pp. 140ff.) and so also for the realization of the preferred behavior.

(B) *Influences of centrally located changes on preferred behavior*
What we have said about the influence of peripheral changes, of course, is true only with reservations. According to our view, all these are indeed changes of the whole organism. One can talk of peripheral influences only insofar as the place of origin of the stimulus, which produces the change, is peripherally located. But we find the same influence when the place of origin is centrally located, when the changes are aroused from within, when we find a changed attitude of the examined individual. This becomes most evident in the differential effect of positions, which superficially are apparently identical, but which, however, in connection with a different attitude, actually have a different meaning for the individual.

Such a situation can be easily created by asking the subject at one time simply to turn the eyes sideways, without gazing at anything (possibly with closed eyes, in which event the experiment succeeds more readily) and, at another time, by asking the subject to focus sideways on something, for example, to read something. In these two cases, we have almost the same change of the eye position, but the change is of an essentially different significance. In the first instance, we have a pure, meaningless eye movement; in the second instance, a purposeful "looking at" in order to see something. The two attitudes influence the preferred plane for the pointing in an entirely different manner. In the pointing task, the pure eye movement causes a shift of the plane in the opposite direction to that of the eye movement, whereas the "looking at" movement causes a shift in the same direction as that of the eye movement. We find corresponding influences on auditory and kinesthetic localization arising from the differential significance of the eye movements (because of the different attitudes). What we want to emphasize here is not simply the fact that the difference in the total attitude of the individual, that is, a psychological factor, exercises a different influence on the position of the preferred plane and that it can change the state of peripheral tensions. Rather, we are interested here in emphasizing especially that the influence depends in a lawful way on the momentary total attitude of the individual. This means that subjective experiences have the same effect as objective changes of the body. In accordance with our view of what is mental and what is physical, we are not astonished over the above findings (cf. p. 261), we are not surprised that the influence of inner experience can be modified by peripheral physiological factors, which are not even consciously experienced. Inner experience is only one factor among others. It has been found that any bodily or psychological change of the organism influences the preferred behavior. We might be justified in talking of "any" change, although in the course of our numerous examinations not every possible incident could be covered.

Thus, preferred behavior, realized in one field, depends on the condition of the whole organism in a given situation.

This finds its expression also in the fact that any adequate behavior, any adequate performance, can be disturbed, if one induces a nonpreferred behavior in another part; and an imperfect performance in one field can be improved by influencing other fields. Let us assume that, because of a change in tonus, a patient has an abnormal pull to one side; then the body attempts to adapt itself to it. If it succeeds it is, of course, an abnormal situation in comparison with the normal position; but the organism is freed of a number of disturbances. The patient, for instance, may keep his body or head tilted toward one side. In this

279

situation he is normal as a whole, he walks properly, does not fall, his subjective vertical corresponds to the objective situation, and so on. But if one compels him to keep his head objectively straight, then all disturbances again set in. Through the slight slanting position of the head, the course of the excitation in the whole organism has actually become ordered. This is not only in general a sign that there is no such thing as an isolated process but also that each apparently isolated event means a change in the whole organism and, specifically, that preferred behavior in one field always means preferred behavior of the whole organism.

So far, we have discussed facts of, and general laws for, the occurrence of preferred behavior. Its intimate relation to the whole may suggest the question whether this tendency represents an essential factor in the organization of the organism. The preferred situation is subjectively characterized by the experience of feelings of comfort, agreeableness, security, and correctness. It is exactly this criterion that we employ to determine the situation in which preferred behavior occurs. We ask the subject to move the arm in the various sagittal planes up and down until the movement seems most comfortable and agreeable. To this experience, the second characteristic of preferred behavior, the objective characteristic, corresponds. It is the performance that is best, does most justice to the task, and is most adequate. The plane attained in this manner is the one in which the subject can perform the most correct pointing movement and in which the threshold is the lowest. We probably will not go wrong if we bring the feeling of agreeableness, ease, and correctness into relation with the same state of affairs that is expressed by the objective findings, namely, in preferred behavior, the organism is coming to terms with a given environmental situation in a way that is most adequate and corresponds best to its nature. Thus, we may continue to say that the tendency toward preferred behavior is an expression of the fact that the organism seeks again and again a situation in which it can perform adequately. How is the most adequate situation characterized as compared with the others?

Any performance signifies the reaction of the organism to a definite environmental situation. It signifies the change of the previous state. In our specific case it signifies a change of the motor situation corresponding to the previous state of the sensory apparatus. Performance under definite stimulation at first depends on the preceding, the starting situation. But we saw that this determination is not sufficient, that we have to include the tendency toward equalization by virtue of which that situation is brought about, in which the best performances can be produced. Thus the tendency toward the preferred situation corresponds to the equalization process; it is the latter that always brings the organism anew into the situation in which it is capable of the best and most adequate performance. In other words, this tendency is a means to maintain the order of the organism in spite of the influences of interfering stimuli.

The fact that definite kinds of performances occur in the situational preferred behavior becomes instrumental for determining what the essential attributes (constants) of the organism are.

Ordered behavior and preferred behavior
We were hoping to obtain material for an adequate conception of the organism by determining the preferred ways of behavior. But could it not be possible that the relative constants of the performances in these preferred situations (in which we find preferred behavior) are caused by the fact that the observations were made under a certain isolation and constant conditions similar to those in the reflexes? This could be the case even without the experimenter always being aware of it. It could be caused by accidental circumstances that even in the laboratory situation, could escape the observer. Cannon and his pupils have shown that animals can continue to live after the destruction of the entire vegetative system, that is, they show a constant, normal behavior, for example, with respect to intake and assimilation of food, temperature, pulse, and so on. But could it not be possible that this behavior of the animals was conditioned by the fact that the environment of the laboratory protected them from the demands of their "naturally adequate" environment and that this was the reason the destruction of such an important system did not cause catastrophic reactions in them? If they were forced to live in their normal milieu, their reactions would certainly rapidly become inconstant and they would perish. The constants that are achieved in the laboratory are reached at the expense of performances very essential for the organism. The constant determined in this manner is certainly not the one that corresponds to the natural conditions. Yet it is just the latter that can alone serve as a basis for an adequate concept of the organism's constants.

Preferred behavior, as ordered behavior, pertains to the whole organism
We must seek a criterion that will make more certain that we are actually dealing with the attributes of the organism in "natural" life situations. Such a criterion may be offered by our finding that preferred behavior in one field is possible only if it belongs as well to the whole organism. Only then is ordered behavior actually realized. If we want to decide, during the investigation of one field, whether a phenomenon that appeared to be a preferred behavior is an "essential" and genuine one, we must at the same time pay attention to the rest of the organism. We are dealing with genuine attributes or constants if we find, by examining as many fields as possible, order and "adequate performance" in the rest of the organism, rather than rigidity and uniformity, as in the reflexes. This is the criterion of ultimate validity that available methodology can offer (cf. p. 305). In this way we apprehend certain characteristics of the organism with which we are dealing, certain norms and constants of its nature. Here we are approaching the frontiers of the science of living entities.

The performances of the organism correspond to these constants. It would be better not to speak here of functions. The term "function" may be better reserved for the formal structure of the activity, while "performance" means the concrete action in which the organism actualizes itself. Goethe spoke in this connection of "Dasein in Tätigkeit" ("Being in actuality").

Thus we obtain a number of constants as characteristics of the nature of an organism — constants in the ways of behavior, constants regarding the sensory and motor threshold, "intellectual" characteristics, constants of "affectivity," "psychic" or "mental" and "physical" constants, constants in the field of temperature, respiration, pulse, and blood pressure, constants in the sense of a certain proportion of calcium and potassium, and of certain types of reaction toward poisons (allergies), blood types, and so on. In the living organism, we continually observe a tendency to approach these relative constants or "average mean"; or in better terms, we are only in position to speak of one and the same organism, if, in spite of temporary changes, these constants become manifest. The more constants we can ascertain, the more the at first rather formal concept of the nature of an organism gradually becomes filled with those contents that we usually call "facts," in the real sense of forming a natural science.

Two types of constants — as to species and to the individual
From among these constants, we must differentiate two groups: constants as the expression of the essential nature of the species and the individual constants corresponding to the organism under consideration. On the basis of the constants of the species, the life of the normal and especially of the defective individual cannot be sufficiently comprehended, notwithstanding certain congruencies between the individuals of the same species. For that objective, an acquaintance with the nature of the individual, that is, with the individual's normal constants, is prerequisite.

One constant, particularly characteristic for the individuality, has to be especially emphasized: the constant in the temporal course of processes. The important role that a specific temporal sequence of processes plays in the ordered activity of the normal organism can be seen, for example, in that we can regard the pathological phenomena in the neuropsychological field, as predominantly an expression of a change in the temporal sequence. Not only the analysis of the symptoms shows this, but also the investigation with time-measuring methods, for example, chronaxie and electro-encephalogram.[30] Every human being has a rhythm of his own, which manifests itself in the various performances but of course in various ways, yet in the same performance always in the same way. A performance is only normal when an individual can accomplish it in the rhythm that is his adequate rhythm for this performance. Just as for physiological processes, like heart beating and respiration, this is valid for the physico-chemical processes. The time constant indicates a particular characteristic of the personality.

It is possible to supplement our knowledge of the constants by regarding a long time sector of the life of an organism. This "anamnesis" enables us to bring out more clearly the adequate constants. A closer analysis of that life course, the factors of which make for ordered and disordered behavior, can furnish a distinction and possible relation observable among the adequate, the genuine constants, and the more casual reaction patterns. The problems of acquired reactions of so-called conditioning, of "maladjustment," and so on, and the specific trends of the personality, operating in all these modifications by experience, can thereby be elucidated.

CHAPTER EIGHT

On Gestalt Psychology and the Theory
of the Physical Gestalten

Our basic view agrees in many respects with Gestalt psychology. However, the conception I am trying to develop is not simply such a "psychological physiology" based on a Gestalt view, as scholars like Matthaei
are striving after.[1] On the contrary, such an attempt to apply views and
laws of one field of research to another seems very problematic to me,
as long as it has not been proven that the two fields are of the same
nature (cf. pp. 35ff.). Such an attempt seems to me to be particularly
questionable in the present instance because, in my opinion, psychology could well be regarded as a special field of biological knowledge,
but not conversely. In an attempt to obtain biological knowledge we
must start from the facts that obtrude on us and must try to understand
them. In doing so, many things that we have learned from Gestalt psychology will be useful to us.

Yet my guiding principle has been a different one, inasmuch as the
"whole," the "Gestalt," has always meant to me the whole organism
and not the phenomena in one field, or merely the "introspective experiences," which in Gestalt psychology play quite an important part.
From here, also, certain differences arise between the views advanced
by Gestalt psychologists and those advanced by me.

These differences concern, to begin with, the appearance and the
nature of preferred events, of "good Gestalten." According to Gestalt
psychology we are dealing with a self-organization of the "excitation"
field occasioned by a stimulus, with a "segregation" that is determined
by the events in the field and that takes place according to certain laws
of organization. Thus, for example, the factors "similarity" and "nearness" lead to a distinct patterning in a unit, as compared with other
constellations. Simple and regular figures, as well as closed wholes,

seem to form more easily and more usually than irregular forms, and so on. "The process of self-distribution" has a decided "preference" to correspond to definite field requirements.[2] According to Gestalt psychology, how does this preference originate? The answer seems to be twofold.

First, Gestalt psychology is primarily and mainly based on phenomenally given experiences and seeks to determine the Gestalten that appear in those and the laws which govern them. Wertheimer writes, "The given is itself 'gestaltet' in various degrees: what is given are more or less well 'gestaltet,' more or less definite wholes or whole-processes, frequently with very concrete whole-attributes which are following laws of inner determination, characteristic whole tendencies, and with parts conditioned by the whole." Second, Gestalt psychology points to certain objective factors of Gestalt formation, such as Wertheimer originally formulated with his terms: factor of nearness, homogeneity, simplicity, symmetry, closure, and so on.

What we are striving for is to grasp not merely the actual "giveness" of Gestalt phenomena but their corresponding objective stimulational factors. What will turn out to be a Gestalt for an organism depends predominantly on the organism's structure. To be sure, the structure of the world is not indifferent to it. It appears that the biological facts may be suited to teach us what it means when world is experienced as Gestalt and when not, and from where the above-mentioned "preference" comes.

Preferred Behavior and Gestalt

Good Gestalt as a definite form of coming to terms of
the organism with the world
The "preferred situations," to which the good Gestalten belong, show characteristics that indicate not only a reference to the organism in general but also a very definite kind of activity of the organism. The preferred situation is characterized by the fact that, in it, the performances are executed in the promptest, most correct manner, and with the best possible self-assurance. In the preferred situation, the sensory thresholds are the most constant and the lowest. The movements that are demanded by the situation take place in the most adequate and most definite way, and distribution of "attention" occurs that guarantees the

best apprehension of the world in accordance with the situation. From all this it follows that preferred behavior, good Gestalt, or whatever one chooses to call it, represents a very definite form of coming to terms of the organism with the world, that form in which the organism actualizes itself, according to its nature, in the best way.

With this view in mind, we can do more than simply state that good Gestalten are directly given experiences. Rather, they become intelligible as to their causation. Tendency toward preferred behavior means self-organization of the system, in the sense that the tension equalizes itself toward the "adequate mean" that alone makes possible such phenomena as the constancy of the thresholds, of the performances, constancy, and stability of the world (cf. p. 102).

Thus, the recognition of the essential nature of an organism is prerequisite for proper evaluation of what is a good Gestalt. It seems that the variety of possibilities, which the world in its entirety offers, are of such a sort that the greatest variety of creatures can find adequacy. If this were not the case it would not be possible that so many different creatures exist. On the other hand, it certainly is probable – even though it requires closer investigation – that, corresponding to the inherent properties of the world, only a limited number of Gestalt possibilities (potentialities of patterning) really exist, that is, that only creatures of definite organization can "be." Since, for many creatures, certain characteristics of the "good Gestalt" are qualitatively the same, it is to a certain extent possible to deduce the Gestalten from the structural organization of nature.

Thus, investigation of the Gestalten does not merely teach us something about the functional patternings of the organism but teaches us also about essential features of nature. As long as our point of departure is provided by the material of phenomenally given experience, the Gestalt can just be described as "given." As long as we base our findings on observations that are emphasizing this sort of "relief phenomena," then the thus-established laws of Gestalt perception will correspond to this type of approach. The latter represents an observational method, during a certain perceptual isolation, on the part of the subject. Thus, the perceptual Gestalten, by which the theory was originally and preferably guided, show a number of characteristics that indicate a great conformity with the typical peculiarities of somatic reactions in isolation. The discussion of these peculiarities should be suited to provide further insight into the causes of many a "preference" for certain segregations.

The first peculiarity that we point out is the ambiguity in the reaction to an objectively constant stimulus constellation. This ambiguity has been verified on a variety of material, acoustical, optical perception, and so on. It always has been emphasized that this ambiguity is, so to speak, dependent on the Gestalt process itself. Thus, the alternation of figure and ground, in the previously mentioned figure of Rubin, depends only seemingly on the choice of the observer. Köhler writes: "One definitely sees those features together which, in the intended Gestalt, belong essentially together, one makes, for a while, a strong though vain effort – but nothing happens. Yet suddenly, unexpectedly, when one perhaps already doubts that it will ever succeed, the new formation suddenly is there. And, conversely, one focuses one of the possible alternatives, and tries to retain it with all the effort of 'collective attention.' Suddenly one is surprised by the fact that another pattern has come out in spite of one's intention to retain the first. The new alternative might be quite unfamiliar, and now attention, so to speak, lags behind."[3]

This is certainly true for this experiment but does not indicate that this emergence of reversal of figure and ground is a characteristic of "normal," "natural" Gestalt processes. It could be possible that this alternation is the consequence of the special situation in which the Gestalten appear in this case, that it results from the special nervous excitation pattern prevailing. We are familiar with this alternation of figure and ground from our discussion regarding the so-called reflex reversal and have learned to understand it, in that instance, as the result of stimulus reaction in "isolation." Possibly the same condition may frequently apply to the situation in which visual Gestalten appear in laboratory experiments.

We have seen, furthermore, that in spite of all alternating phases, there exists a constancy in the reflex phenomenon at a given moment, determined through the maintenance of constancy in the rest of the organism. We have also seen that the reflexes vary when changes in the rest of the organism take place. Consequently, the respective behavior proved to be related to a very definite configuration of excitation within the whole organism, and one part thereby being strongly isolated.

Actually, we can alter the perceptual Gestalten experienced in one sensory field by varying the excitation state in the rest of the organism. So, for example, the objective vertical corresponds no longer to the normally preferred configuration if one, simultaneously with the visual presentation, stimulates the subject's labyrinth or applies ice to the surface of the neck. Then a line, somewhat tilted to the opposite side of the stimulation, is experienced as vertical. The good Gestalt in one field can be converted into a bad one through all sorts of sensory, motor, and other changes in the organism, and vice versa.

The Gestalten, which are given in perception through one sensory organ, are Gestalten that belong to a very definite condition of the organism, namely, to an isolated stimulus utilization in one part, while the rest of the organism is artificially kept relatively constant. Thus, it is intelligible that one can regard them as the expression of self-organization of the nervous processes but only, as such, in a part of the system. The more one part is isolated from the whole, the more its function is determined alone by the configurational excitation in that part, during the isolation (cf. pp. 117ff.); namely, as long as events within the rest of the organism are prevented from interfering, in other words, as long as these other processes are kept constant. This constancy is one of the conditions necessary for the "self-organization in a part," a fact that one must not forget in the description of any given Gestalt phenomenon.

Stability and reality
Besides this ambiguity, Köhler emphasizes the stability of certain phenomena. "The perceptual things in our visual field," according to him, "are, as a rule, very stable wholes."[4] He points out that certain "field parts" segregate themselves as forms experienced as, and adequate to, the real. But as long as it is possible that other field parts might just as well immediately stand out as the Gestalt, one must ask why it is precisely these which segregate themselves? Köhler also tries to explain this stability by the self-organization in the field, by the dynamic properties of the field itself. We have met this stability twice before: first, in the conditioned reflex, that is, in the strongest isolation of stimulus and the afflicted part of the organism, and, second, in the ordered, normal coming to terms of the organism with the world.[5] With regard to our present problem, the first type of stability is certainly not to be considered here, but only the second one. However, the second type

is a phenomenon of stability in reference to the whole organism.

This fact would mean that stability and "real" form (adequacy) are not to be explained by self-organization in a part of the system but by an adequate reaction of the whole organism. One may put it in other words: Stability and "real" form are to be explained by self-organization of a field, in this case, of that field that is the whole organism in a given situation. Stability would then be the expression of the fact that something is experienced by us as real. Reality means that something features in the adequate stimulus reaction of the whole organism, that such a form of reaction prevails that makes ordered behavior possible and, with it, the realization of the essential nature of the organism. In other words, a thing is not real because of its stability; rather it is stable because of its "reality." Within the realm of Gestalt theory, Hornbostel has apparently come closest to such a conception.[6]

If we investigate pure sense perceptions, as, for example, the visual phenomena of Gestalten in the laboratory, then we find on the one hand stability similar to that of the conditioned reflexes and on the other hand instability as in alternating phases of the reflex reversal. The visual phenomena, under such laboratory conditions, appear to us as relatively unreal. Yet if we regard a figure on paper as a drawing of an object, then it becomes a little more real, and at the same time a little more stable. "Inversed" figures – such as von Hornbostel's – show a greater character of reality, not only on account of the experience of three dimensions but also because the individual mental set already necessitates a far-going participation of the whole organism. As von Hornbostel has shown, definite mental sets of the observers belong to the respectively experienced figures. And that means a definite coming to terms of the whole organism with the world. However, since even in this case the relation to the whole of the organism is somewhat artificial, these object formations appear strangely real and unreal at the same time, uncanny in their realness, in their simultaneous stability and instability. The more one succeeds in maintaining one attitude, the more real and stable do these object formations become. The parallelism between reality and stability on the one side, and unreality and instability on the other side, becomes particularly evident in such experiences in which it is possible to alternate between an attitude of reality and unreality, as is the case in the above-mentioned figure of Rubin.

Köhler thinks that unstable events appear when the forms are dissolved "by accidental, unfavorable structure of the environmental field, or by purposeful camouflage."[7] This is certainly true, but to define the structure of the environmental field as accidentally unfavorable seems too indefinite. This unfavorable structure can be better defined. It is isolatedness. The favorable condition in which perceptual things appear stable is the one in which the organism as a whole fits itself into its environment, that is, the one in which the world appears real. It is not enough to say that constancy and stability cannot be understood from the retinal image alone and that they arise in the organism. Rather, it is necessary to try to understand stability and lability as definite forms of an organism's coming to terms with the world.

All this goes to show that reality arises when a single event is embedded within the functional organization that corresponds to an organismically ordered reaction.

Any alternation and thus any equivocality is always the expression of the fact that the whole organism has not yet reached the preferred situation. At the same time we have to bear in mind what we have pointed out before, namely, that a certain degree of instability is always present, because of the imperfect state of centering. This, however, is not an instability that is, so to speak, imposed from without, but is an instability that corresponds to the unfixed pattern of the determining inner factors. The better centered and integrated a personality is, the more definite and stable are these "Gestalten."

Having suggested that the Gestalten disclosed by the descriptive and experimental approach are phenomena in relative "isolation," the doubt arises, in their case, as well as in that of the reflexes, whether the experiences thus gained can teach us anything directly regarding the behavior of the organism. There is no doubt that the laws found by Gestalt psychologists, frequently approach reality very closely. The reason for this achievement may be that Gestalt psychology was particularly apt for discovering phenomena that have the character of "constants." In fact, the Gestalt psychologists, by their experimental research, have made relevant contributions to the understanding of "constants" in terms of the nature of the organism. Nevertheless, it is easily seen that these results have been achieved more through the ingenuity of the experimenters than through a systematically grounded conception of the organismic whole. Such a foundation is rather necessary because only on such a basis can "deviations" such as the above-mentioned instability, become intelligible, and because only then can one systematically elaborate which of the stated phenomena have to be regarded as "constants" and which not.

Thus, in the light of our general view, the tendency toward the good Gestalt finds its explanation as an organismic phenomenon. The explanation lies in the tendency toward preferred behavior, which is the essential prerequisite for the existence of a definite organism. It is a special expression of the general tendency to realize optimal performances with a minimum expenditure of energy as measured in terms of the whole. The operation of this tendency includes the so-called "prägnanz," the closure phenomenon, and many other characteristics of Gestalt. In fact, they are only intelligible from this tendency.

Only through analysis of the interactional totality of the outer and inner field do the reasons become clear just why a certain pattern, a certain action appears as a "good Gestalt." On this basis, also, the effects of such external and internal conditions as the constellation of the stimuli, personal factors as mental set, age, memory, type, and so on, become intelligible, all of which are factors determining the forming of good Gestalten.[8]

Simplicity and minimal expenditure of energy in good Gestalten
Moreover, the meaning of "simplicity" as well as that of "minimal expenditure of energy," in the case of "good Gestalt," becomes comprehensible. One need merely realize that the best Gestalt means the best for a coming to terms of organism and world, of adjustment in a definite situation, that is to say, during a definite task. The task must be accomplished if a state of balance and Gestalt are to arise at all. Thus simplicity can be defined only on the basis of the demands of the individual task. Therefore, Matthaei argues – but not quite justifiably – that if economy were to be regarded as the fundamental goal, then the phenomena of equalization and leveling should be far more frequent than those of segregation.[9] According to Matthaei, the relief phenomena should be regarded as very high energy gradients. It is certainly not simply a question of equalization and of "minimal energy expenditure" per se but of minimal energy expenditure for performance of a definite task.

It segregation is required for a performance in a situation, then the simplest possible process producing the tension necessary to the segregation is the one that demands the minimum energy expenditure. If we take the respective task into consideration, then the good Gestalt is a simpler kind of performance of the task in question than the performance of the bad Gestalt. The latter is more difficult because it would imply realization and maintenance of "inadequacy." Thus, for example, it requires more energy and it is more difficult to maintain a nonpreferred position of the hand than a preferred position.

We saw that without reference to the whole organism we simply cannot make any statement regarding the characteristics of "Gestalt," not even whether it is simple. With my concept of the tendency to "good Gestalt," as a tendency to the preferred and most suitable behavior of the whole organism in specific situations, I am, therefore, referring to the Gestalt theorem, because a far-reaching agreement exists in our basic philosophy. This conformity, however, should not cause us to obscure divergencies with respect to further research of such important problems as the above, especially when we have to deal with the ultimate and indeed primary questions of the methodological approach to the organism.

In this connection, we should not fail to mention that many a hypothesis and suggestion in Koffka's *Principles of Gestalt Psychology* and Wertheimer's publications, such as *Denken der Naturvoelker*, tend toward a conception of the principle of "prägnanz" in the more functional and more holistic sense of "fitting together" of the organism and the environment, similar to my own endeavor.[10]

The Theory of Physical Gestalten

We considered it necessary above (cf. p. 261) to reject any parallelism between bodily and mental events and maintained that any such relation is conceivable only indirectly by reference to the whole of the organism. Nevertheless, there is a possibility that the phenomena in the two fields were in such a congruency that, from this, we could obtain insight into the nature of the organism. The atomistic approach to mental processes gained probability because it was confirmed in the prevailing theory of physical events. When the Gestalt character of mental events was demonstrated it seemed at first as if a gap had opened that could not be bridged. It seemed impossible to compare mental phenomena, even as to structure, with physical phenomena, conceived to be atomistic. The same held true for the mental as for biological phenomena.

Wertheimer, in connection with his study on seen movement, has attempted to develop a theory of the processes in the brain matter in correspondence with the Gestalt theory of mental events.[11] In doing so he deviated from the then-current view by opposing the idea of brain processes as a connection between isolated single excitations and by introducing the notion of a holistic excitation process. His further innovation was to claim a dynamic nature of the excitation process that corresponds to the mental phenomena. Also Georg Hirth and I have already described a brain event as always taking its course as a whole and have stressed that the brain correlates of certain mental patterns must be regarded as systemlike, structured, functional wholes of a dynamic character.

But all these conceptions really represented only analogous images derived from the model of the mental events. There was no proof that the brain processes actually had such a structure or that there were any physical systems at all, in which processes would take place in the assumed way. The physico-chemical investigations of the brain up to that time could not give us any information with regard to this question.

In this state of affairs, it was of fundamental importance when Köhler attempted, in his book concerning the physical Gestalten, to demonstrate the holistic character of physical processes.[13] This offered the possibility of paralleling the holistic mental structure with a similar one in physical systems. Köhler, for example, states that the distribution of electricity on the surface of a conductor has a Gestalt character, in the sense of the "Ehrenfels criteria." The charge distribution can neither be composed from the charges in the individual parts, nor can it be broken down piece by piece. Any change of charge at any place changes the distribution as a whole. The physical Gestalt, according to Köhler, is just as little the sum of its parts as the melody is the sum of its notes. Physical Gestalten are transposable just like mental Gestalten, that is, they are independent of the size of the charge of a conductor, as well as of the size of the conductor itself. They merely depend on the form of the conductor, the topography.

It was Driesch who first called attention to the difficulties of comparison that lie in the factor of topography. In doing so, he pointed to the difference in nature between the physical Gestalt and the organism: the topography of the physical Gestalten that is fundamental for them and depends on the external conditions. For the topography of the organism, on the other hand, such a dependency cannot be shown. One could say that the topography of a physical system depends on the "limiting conditions," that the structure of the topography is not given with the material. We easily overlook this difference, because the constancy of the topography is preserved by the experiments as limiting conditions of a particular kind or is at least protected against the influences of the environment. The topography of the organism on the other hand is relatively autonomous, a given fact. Within certain limits, the organism can remain intact by virtue of its own nature in spite of great differences in environment; it selects autonomously, so to speak, the milieu that is adequate to it within the world. In any event, the processes within the organism are not exclusively determined by the environmental variations. And what is more, no matter how much they are codetermined by the environment, they would be utterly unintelligible, if considered from the environment alone (cf. pp. 84ff.).

The process of regulation, which Köhler tried to verify in physical systems, differs in the same sense. According to Köhler, it is possible – no matter what the initial situation – that physical systems, similar to organisms, modify themselves according to the direction of lowering potential when the tension is changed; "provided that the conditions, set by the system, permit the reaching of a state of equilibrium," they will again reach the initial situation. It has been pointed out that this phenomenon is not generally valid but only when certain arrangements are made, like the suspension of a pendulum that is prior to the return to a certain state of equilibrium.[14] Aside from that, it is not important for the organism to return to a state of equilibrium, but it is important for it to return to a very definite state. This return, however, is only possible by procuring a special arrangement, that is, a special topography that, for a certain range of initial states, always enforces the same ultimate state of equilibrium of the organismic processes.[15]

The problem of topography in Gestalt theory
In reply to such questions, Köhler has again discussed the processes in physical systems, especially the problem of topography. He says: "In physical processes two sorts of factors determine events at every moment. In the first class belong the actual forces of the process itself, they represent the dynamical side of it. In the second class we have

those properties of the system, which may be regarded as constant conditions of its events."[16]

One of these conditions is the topography, representing the spatial arrangement, for example, the arrangement of a wire in the form of a net. Between the various physical systems there are "enormous differences in the relative influence which the limiting topographical conditions and the inner dynamic forces exert upon the course of events." In some, the conditions set by the topography are dominant, while in others they are relatively irrelevant. "The most extreme case will consist in a system where preestablished topographical arrangements exclude all processes except only one." In such a system, to be sure, the movement is still determined dynamically, "whereas the direction is strictly enforced by topographical arrangement. These are the mechanic arrangements and contrivances which we set up. To such arrangements correspond the prevailing conceptions regarding the structure of the nervous system, the nature of nervous processes and the assumption of inherited and acquired apparatuses, connections and mechanisms."[17] But Köhler rightly claims that mechanistic models do not fit that idea of events in the nervous system, which the phenomenal facts compel us to develop.

There are, however, other kinds of physical systems that are suited to serve as such models, namely, those in which topography does not play an essential part. Köhler says that there are systems "in which the course of events is not at all completely determined by topographical arrangement. Let us regard a particle of water which moves within a constant stream through a narrow tube. For what reason, besides inertia, does it move? Because pressure on one side is greater than on the other. Movement takes place only in one direction because the wall of the tube precludes all other possible effect. Thus the particle according to the mechanistic principle moves along in a rigidly given line. Now let us assume that the tube disappears and that the drop and (with it the entire stream of water in the tube) becomes part of a larger body of water. Probably the particle will also move in the new environment. But now it is exposed to the influence of forces on all sides and its movement will fall in the direction of whatever will be the resultant. Apparently this movement is no less determined than was the movement in the tube; but now there are no special local arrangements which fix one single direction as the only possible one. Thus in the new situation also the path of locomotion of the particle becomes dynamic, i.e.

it is determined at each instant by the resultant of forces at its respective place. From this it follows that usually the locomotion will take on a quite different path, depending on which total situation of the whole system prevails at a given moment which we consider. But also the movement of the particle itself partakes in bringing about the dynamic situation which it encounters in the various points of its course. This is a simple example which could be replaced by an unlimited number of others."[18]

Köhler does not overlook the fact that this larger body of water also has a boundary and thus a topography that codetermines the distribution of forces acting on the particle. But he is inclined to regard them as irrelevant, as not "essential" in comparison to the inner dynamic effects. The drop of water moves because movement, in accordance with the pressure gradient, has the tendency to equilibrate this gradient. This is certainly true. But is it not true only because the body of water is artificially isolated from the world? Does the spatial distribution in the second case really result from the effect of the forces that are present and effective within the stream? I dare not decide whether, in this case, the topography is not codetermining, even though it is more removed, or whether the event can follow simply the internal conditions (inner dynamics) only because it is protected from external influences by such a removed topography. I also would not venture to decide which of the factors in this case are essential and which are not.

If it is true that in a physical system, without the influence of topography, dynamic behavior leads by itself to a certain distribution and order comparable to organismic processes, then this question arises regarding the organism: Could this self-distribution not be caused by the fact that, although the process in a part is not directly determined through the processes in the rest of the organism, it is still indirectly guaranteed in its course, by being embedded in a certain excitation pattern of the rest of the organism? In other words, in this case the process may only take place undisturbed in a circumscribed field, because the rest of the organism is kept constant.

If this be true, then it could be explained why, also in the example of Köhler, the processes in a sector seem so independent of the condition in the rest of the organism. Inasmuch as it is this constancy in the rest of the whole system, which alone could guarantee the ordered behavior in the sector, one might designate the condition in the rest of the organism as topography. Instead of a topography within the sector itself, which governs the processes in it, we would have to deal with a topography constituted by the condition of the surrounding field, that is, the rest of the organism. This, by the way, is not a totally sufficient guarantee for maintenance of real order. Such a topography can in no way bar several alternatives of order ("instability") from arising, that is, cannot secure one and the same constant order, as it is characteristic for the behavior of the organism and necessary for its life.

If the rest of the organism is not constant, then instability of behavior can occur in parts that clearly indicate their dependence on further parts of the system, and, ultimately, on the whole. We have met numerous examples of this sort. Köhler does not overlook this relationship and talks, in this sense, of events covering the total field. This means that they bring about a mutual equilibration of tensions. But does this actually correspond to the performances of the organism? We have already shown that this is not the case; rather, that "equilibration" means the return to a definite state of tension, which corresponds to the respective situation and which in its particular pattern can be understood only by considering the "essential nature" of the organism.[19] This nature, in its specific qualitative structure and in its respective state, represents, so to speak, the topography that codetermines the course of behavior.

This is certainly not a fixed and rigid topography, as the customary view presupposes, as, for example, in the concept of a specific anatomical structure of the nervous system. It is rather a topography that is itself of a dynamic character, which changes according to the various situations that the self-actualization of the organism makes necessary. The individual configurations that this organismic topography takes on are held together by the continuity of the organism's pattern of self-actualization. Or better, these individual topographic phases are nothing other than the factors of the organismic being itself, which the investigator delineates. Thus we arrive at the same result to which analysis of the physiological processes, and that of the vegetative system, have brought us. The simple regulation of a disturbance of the equilibrium, through equilibration of the tension, could at best lead to an equilibration that is bound to the changing milieu; could at best lead to release of tension. Behavior could alternate between disturbance and rest, but could never result in performances that require the return to an adequate state of tension, relatively independent of the milieu, but dependent upon the whole (cf. pp. 95, 103ff.).

All events in the organism, even though they may take place in parts, are holistic. The more they take place in isolated parts, the more mechanistic they become, and the more they become like "physical Gestalten" in Köhler's sense. The reason for this is that they occur in parts that are relatively isolated from the whole and that are embedded in a relatively stable and constant topography (the rest of the organism). The regulation in such parts corresponds to that in physical systems. The "topography" in the isolated parts is a structure that has been artificially segregated from the whole topography of the entire organism and thus has become relatively fixed. It is a structure that, in this form, in the normal activity of the organism, does not exist at all, or only in exceptional cases. In the normal activity of the organism, every part has a topography that changes according to the functional situation of the whole organism.

Through our explanation, the characteristic difference between the performances, under change and constancy, becomes intelligible; whereas, in Köhler's view, it remains unaccounted for. Köhler really cannot do justice to this difference between the processes because he starts from two similar ones, which differ only in that they occur at one time in a part of the system, and at another time in the whole field, that is, cover smaller or larger fields. We, however, believe we can do justice to these facts because we regard every process as one within the entire organismic field, and because we try to explain the difference between performances as two essentially different formations of the whole field. One formation is the so-called isolated activity in one sector during artificially maintained constancy in the rest of the system, and the other formation is the activity of the entire organismic field. The aspect of those processes that unitarily cover the whole of the organismic field is matched by the observations of the characteristic orderliness in the performances within the organism, when operating as a whole. The other aspect is matched by those laws that we found pertinent to patterns of responses and processes, during isolation.

Here we are always confronted with a relative inconsistency and lack of orderliness in the performance. This lack of homogeneity is caused by an imperfect formation of the topography in that particular case, as compared with that of the whole organism under normal conditions.

It is a topography that structurally does not suffice to give to the process a specifically consistent orderliness, so that this process is delivered over to its own inner dynamics – namely, in so far as its structural parts are but imperfectly determined by the whole organismic field. It is one of the consequences thereof, that an alternation of opposite phases becomes possible. This is exemplified by the reflexes and other introspective experiences, when artificial segregation and relief formation is the case, as in Rubin's ambiguous figures, or the Gestalt configuration within single sense organs. What Köhler calls the self-organization of the field is an expression of behavior in defective topography – defective in relationship to the topography that represents the whole organism.

Summary of the two holistic notions
Let us summarize certain characteristic differences as they have arisen in the two holistic views discussed.

1. The notion of "physical Gestalt" refers to states of dynamic equilibrium. In our organismic concept we have developed the idea of equalization toward a level, adequate to the organism's functional self-actualization. Only this equalization concept makes intelligible the fact that a certain state of tension can represent a state of equilibrium.

2. The individual "field forces" including vectors, for example, cannot be defined merely in terms of the "field" itself. As Köhler also emphasizes, these forces can only become understandable by their embeddedness in the whole. But this whole cannot be taken simply as another, more complicated field. One has to realize that it varies constantly according to the varying situations. Reducing the entire situation to "field forces" would therefore imply the necessity of introducing new variables again and again.[20] And since the functional significance of these variables depends on the respective "task," in reference to the potentialities of self-actualization, we are referred back to the organism as chief determiner of the "field forces." (In this dispute we have not even touched on the problem of the "biographical factors," which, in addition, would reveal the methodological difficulty of the concept of field forces, regarding the control of variables.) However valuable the practicability of these terms for descriptive purposes of definitely circumscribed situations may be – if hypostasized to a real interplay of forces, or "vectors" – they will inevitably lead to the above-mentioned predicament.

3. The functional significance of "field forces," "valences," even of preferred Gestalten, and constants cannot be determined in a physicalistic-causal sense of objectivity. Determination is only possible from the specific organization of the organism that can be inferred only from its forms of coming to terms with "stimuli."

4. From this interrelatedness of functional significance and specific organization in structure, it follows that the constants, "good Gestalten," and so on, are not necessarily identical in the various species, nor even in different human individuals. Wherever similarities are found, they point to similarities of structural organization. This statement does not in any way advocate an interpretation as to mere "arbitrariness" and "meaninglessness" within the relation of organismic beings and their respective milieus. Our emphasis on the specific organization as basic for functional significance merely shifts the aspect of nonarbitrary, nonmechanical patterns, from laws of the physical field to the above-mentioned interrelatedness.[21]

5. With the principle of isomorphism, one tries to establish a direct parallelism, or correspondence, between physical Gestalt processes and the mental configurations. Viewed from our organismic conception, this is inadequate. Every part event, be it physical, be it mental, refers to the whole. And only by way of the whole is it related to the other event, be it physical or mental. The whole of the organism therefore supports all partitive phenomena of either aspect, which are nothing but different expressions of that unitary "meaningfulness."

6. The claim of isomorphic and invariably "nonarbitrary" Gestalt patterns does not leave sufficient room for a positive determination and explanation of a phenomenon that is, in particular, an attribute of the human being. We have called it "abstract behavior," embodying in this notion the ability of voluntary shifting, of reasoning discursively, oriented on self-chosen frames of reference, of free decision for action, of isolating parts from a whole, of disjoining given wholes, as well as of establishing connections, for example, in learning.

One cannot evaluate the phenomena under isolation as being exclusively negative and contrary to nature. How far they may reach into lower organized beings we are unable to tell. However, human behavior will never become understandable in its specific complexity if one does not realize that the very organization of the human being consists in the potentiality to behave partitively as well as holistically. The phenomena of active self-limitation and of culture – differentiated as it is into manifold aspects of life and nature – demand that capacity of shifting, of "compartmental" activities, the ability to represent to oneself different contents as separated and belonging simultaneously to the same frame of reference.[22] Without that, and without the "attitude toward the Possible," abstract behavior could not exist – a trait without which human culture is inconceivable.

7. The comments presented in points 1–4 do not offer insurmountable discrepancies between the Gestalt theory and my own theory. In my concept of the configurational process in the organism, the figure, in the sense of Gestalt, already represents a partitive phenomenon. If the scope of holistic events were enlarged to include the entire organism, then the Gestalt principle would become sufficiently broad to fit all the facts that may not have, as yet, been covered.

The Problem of Parts and Whole

But by what right do we ascribe to the organism properties entirely different from those which we ascribe to its parts? After all, are these events in the parts less alive? The first question concerns the basic problem of our entire discussion. After reading my arguments, one could object: "Why do we stop at the organism as a delimited whole? Is not the organism also only a part, namely, a part of a greater entirety?" One certainly would have to answer this in the affirmative. Furthermore, one cannot be allowed to overlook the consequences of this relation by arguing, for example, that the determinants of the superindividual whole should be regarded to be of such different dimensions that one could consider them relatively insignificant in comparison to the individual determinants. This argument is untenable. Regarding the effect of any superordinated whole, no general statement can be made. However, one should not simply gloss over the problem involved here; we are too aware of the relativity of our knowledge to commit this fault. All our knowledge is incomplete in a qualitative rather than quantitative sense. In our cognitive procedure we halt with the individual as a preliminary whole, simply because we here arrive factually at a relatively satisfactory result, or at least, at a much better result than if we started in the customary manner from the parts (cf. pp. 69ff.).

But what about the question of the "being alive" of the parts? This is certainly a difficult and very serious question. One could assert that the parts are alive and also that they are not alive. They are alive only insofar as they are supported externally or from the whole. For example, animals with certain "essential" defects will die unless man "supports" the still-possible "part performance" by providing particularly favorable milieu conditions. In man, however, part processes can be supported by man himself. The organism bears the relatively isolated part; we "bear," as one says, a defect (cf. pp. 325ff.). When the defect can no longer be borne by the remaining, relatively unimpaired organism, then the defective organism lacks the power of self-regulation. It loses its autonomy, its state of being alive, it is nearer death, is no longer the organism with which we were dealing before, is no longer just a defective organism (i.e., one that bears its defect) but is another organization, is somewhat a negation, a privation, in other words, is "sick."

Further facts seem to offer another difficulty. The part seems, by no means, to be necessarily always such an isolated formation. One of the main objections against the mechanistic view of life processes is supported by the fact of self-regulation by which the organism, in spite of its defect, is supposed to become restored. There are experiments that show us the miracle of fertile eggs of sea urchins that, when cut in half at a certain stage of development (after one mitosis), can develop into two whole sea urchins. These and similar experiments have led to a refutation of the mechanistic view and to a revival of vitalism.

Do these facts not contradict our assumption that contained a sort of degradation of the isolated parts from full vitality to an inferior vitality? Of course, we have to take the experiments into account. However, we have to put their interpretation to the test. Here we can be guided by our experiences regarding the events that take place when one calcarine area is destroyed. We have previously compared them with the events in the regeneration of a part of an egg of a sea urchin to a whole one. We have seen that in calcarine destruction, in spite of the destruction of one half of the central visual apparatus, a restoration of the subjectively most important visual performances is achieved. We did emphasize, in this phenomenon, that a defect for the whole organism still remained, which is not so relevant to it and which can be "borne." We have conceived it as a general and fundamental fact in all recoveries with a remaining defect. In this sense we have really denied any actual regeneration.

But what about the facts in the above-mentioned and similar experiments? The experiments are not, throughout, of the same kind. First, the success has only been obtained in early phases of the development; only then was a new whole formation reached. C. Lloyd Morgan, to be sure, has shown that one can produce whole formations at a later age also, as, for example, when one shakes mechanically the frog egg that had been divided in half.

If one takes these experiments together, we can conclude that whole formations occur only at an age in which the differentiation is, so to speak, still very much in the initial stages, so that a division is really a quantitative division of material that is equal throughout the structure and of the same functional potentiality. One probably is justified in assuming that the shaking destroys differentiations of the structure that possibly had already formed, and, so to speak, structurally rejuvenates the ova. From a certain stage on, if one does not shake the ova one does not obtain whole formations but only half formations, or the ova may perish altogether. This fact shows that as soon as differentiated structures are at all existent, no regulation or regeneration occurs.

But in another respect the facts remain at least unclear. Several questions arise that one cannot answer strictly, because one probably has not paid sufficient attention to them. Do the regenerated ova have the same life span, which is certainly one of the essential traits of an organism, or do they have an untimely death? Are special milieu conditions requisite for their preservation? Finally, we must point out one more factor, which, to be sure, is very frequently not noticed: the new regenerated formations are not as large as the normal ones. If the size of an organism were only determined by feeding, this difference would be of no interest. But this is certainly not the case. Size is also one of the essential characteristics. If the size were much smaller than the size of an organism that developed from a normal ovum, this would be a property that certainly requires careful observation, at least with regard to the total behavior of the organism. At this point, we are confronted with a number of questions. Yet I do not believe that we have reason to change our views on the basis of the facts supplied by the regeneration experiments. At any rate our discussion is suited to call for new experimental arrangements that take into consideration all the problems stated.

CHAPTER NINE

The Nature of Biological Knowledge

All disputes of antiquity and modern times, up to the most recent time, are caused by the division of that which in its nature God has produced as one whole.

             – Goethe, *Analyse und Synthese*

Characterization of the Nature of Biological Knowledge

It is hardly to be questioned that by determining the organism's constants we have come much closer to the essential characteristics of an organism than we would have by any resort to the phenomena that have been revealed through reflex investigations. Yet our knowledge is still far from complete. We never know whether we have considered a large enough number of constants. The constants themselves are still somewhat equivocal because they also are obtained by an isolating procedure. After all, the method of determining constants depends on a formal criterion: the ordered condition in other parts of the organism, whenever genuine preferred behavior occurs in one field. Thus we find, for example, when a definite blood pressure represents the preferred state of the respective organism, that perceptions, motility, and so on, are functioning orderly. However, we cannot determine from this constant what the actual contents of vision or the contents in other fields are. We may even get as far as determining the absolute and relative threshold of perception by this method. However, we are not equipped to define contents and qualities as readily as the governing principle that makes for the occurrence of all these contents or qualities within the general frame of the preferred behavior. We must not forget that the criterion of preferred behavior, that is, the constants, is a more or less preliminary one and that it cannot furnish us an indication of the actual cause for the direction of the organismic course of events in actual living.

We deny, however, the possibility of gaining biological knowledge on the sole basis of the phenomena that can be determined by the analytic methods (cf. p. 308). In saying this we by no means underrate the significance of these phenomena. But we do not accept them simply as undistorted manifestations of the nature of the organism. They must first prove their "significance" for the organism. These observations are the material with which we have to deal, but the value the separate phenomenon has for our understanding of the behavior of an organism depends on our conception of the latter. Thereby phenomena lose the apparent character of self-evident facts. Thus what biology in general believes to be the basis of its body of knowledge, the "facts," becomes the most problematic. For this reason, in the history of science, many facts have proved to be meaningless for the progress of our knowledge. This skepticism towards so-called facts is a basic requirement for fruitful work in all branches of natural science. Only this skepticism eliminates existing bias by preparing the ground for posing the fundamental question: Which phenomena are biologically relevant, and which are not; which phenomena are biological "facts," and which are not? The criterion of that relevancy can be offered only by a conception of the organism in its qualitative organization and holistic functioning.

This conception is not a mere synthesis of the separate phenomena. It is true that the latter point to the organization in question, but we cannot obtain such a picture of the organism directly from them. Neither can it be obtained by means of the simple inductive method. It is not a question of generalizing or of applying to other circumstances the results of previous observations and thus of enlarging our knowledge progressively by induction. This factor certainly plays a large part in concrete scientific work. But it does not furnish us with knowledge, nor does it make a scientific description of biological phenomena possible. Yet neither is the process of biological knowledge a deductive procedure. We do not adhere, in any way, to the a priori method of preconceived categories applied to the nature of life, to the differences between animals and man, and so on.

After all, what is the character of the picture of the organism we are seeking? It is not by a mere addition of brick to brick that we try to construct this building, but it is rather the actual Gestalt of the intrinsic architecture of this building that we try to discover, a Gestalt from which the phenomena, which were formerly equivocal, would now become intelligible as belonging to a unitary, ordered, relatively constant formation of a specific structure. We are seeking a whole in which one can differentiate, among the observed phenomena, between the "members" that really belong to it and the less relevant, contingent connections of arbitrary parts. We do not look for a ground in reality that constitutes Being but for an idea, a reason in knowledge, by virtue of which all particulars can be tested for their agreement with the principle – an idea on the basis of which all particulars become intelligible, if we consider the conditions of their origin. We can arrive at this picture only by a form of creative activity.

Biological knowledge is continued creative activity, by which the idea of the organism comes increasingly within reach of our experience. It is a sort of ideation equivalent to Goethe's "*Schau*," a procedure that springs continuously from empirical facts and never fails to be grounded in and substantiated by them.

To advance such a type of cognitive procedure may at first give the impression that we are headed for, and leading into, metaphysical or even mystical fields. This criticism can be readily refuted by pointing to such a trivial biological phenomenon as the acquisition of any performance by learning, like bicycling, for example. We execute inappropriate movements of our body, such as are determined by partitive aspects and are only partially relevant for correct bicycling, until suddenly we are able to maintain our balance and to move on in the correct way. All these initial exercises have only an indirect connection with the actually achieved performance. Of course, they are not aimless but are merely incorrect movements that in themselves never lead directly to correct movements. Nevertheless, they are necessary because, by continuous modification of the movements, the correct performance will be reached. However, the correct movements appear suddenly when a state of adequacy between the procedure of the organism and the environmental conditions is attained. This adequacy is experienced by us. The procedure in this situation also includes the insight into the correct procedure in bicycling. We continue trying to bring about this procedure until it becomes the unique performance that we set going when we want to ride a bicycle.

The attainment of biological knowledge we are seeking is essentially akin to this phenomenon – to the capacity of the organism to become adequate to its environmental conditions. This is a fundamental biological process by virtue of which the actualization of organisms is made possible. Whenever we speak of the nature, of the idea, picture, or conception of the organism, we have in mind these essentials for the realization of adequacy between the organism and its environment. And these are the principles of composition of that picture that biology has to grasp. In so doing, the cognitive process of the biologist is subject to practically the same difficulties of procedure as the organism in learning; he has to find the adequacy between concept and reality.

In practice, the difficulties that this method may seem to entail are not as great as they appear in theoretical reflections. In practice, we usually venture to pass over from the plane of partitive facts to this other form of cognition. We can be less concerned about doing so the more we have become conscious of the theoretical justification and its consequences. In practice, we usually proceed in such a way that, from the facts gained by analysis, we sketch a picture of the whole organism, which in turn instigates further questions and investigations, so long as we encounter discrepancies between this picture and factual experience. On the basis of new inquiries, the picture of the whole is again modified, and the process of discovering new discrepancies and new inquiries follows, and so on. By such an empirical procedure, in a dialectic manner, a progressively more adequate knowledge of the nature of the organism is acquired, and an increasingly correct evaluation of the observed facts, as to whether they are essential to the organism, is obtained.

"Analytic" and "synthetic" approach

The difference between our holistic approach and that based on the reflexes is frequently understood as a difference between analytic and synthetic method. But this is an error. Scientific research is always founded on analysis and, on the other hand, will never proceed without a certain synthesis. If one understands by synthesis the preliminary summary of the analytically gathered facts, nothing can be said against it. There is probably no scholar who does not, in this way, continuously give account to himself of separate data. Such a procedure can be very useful for further research, particularly because it reveals the mistakes of the prevailing views – the breaches in their theoretical bulwark. But it furnishes us with as little insight into the true nature of things as does the analytic procedure. Actually, we must hold against the synthetic approach the fact that it does not confine itself to a preliminary synthesis but claims itself able to form a coherent and adequate picture of reality. In this way – that is, through a false evaluation – the analytically found facts are treated as part facts of the "true nature" that one investigates, and are regarded as the constituents out of which the structure of that reality is built. We know what these facts are, and therefore a synthesis of such piecemeal material is no more true to reality than the material itself.

The arguments by the "analysts" against the "synthesists" hold equally against the analysts themselves. When, for instance, Weizsäcker demands, instead of the "ambition of the synthesis" (for which the holistic consideration is being reproached), "the surrender to that which *is*," he misunderstands the character of the analytically gained facts, as well as the analytical character of true holistic approach. My reproach against an investigator who fundamentally has the holistic outlook might seem strange. My criticism arises on this point because I believe that a holistic approach must be completely univocal, if it is not going to be a discredit to the entire point of view. One cannot regard mechanism and mind as opposites and at the same time subscribe to both of them. If one does this, everything becomes ambiguous. If we want to attain to a final clarity concerning the reflex, the most urgent requirement is univocality in the definition of the concept. If one talks of the reflex as an "unnatural, but not unreal event" and by "real" means "not a theoretical hypothesis," the point of view is one with which, according to my previous statements, I certainly agree.[1] After all, the reflex is a phenomenon in the organism. It is unnatural insofar as it is not one of the "natural" reactions, one of the "performances." If we wanted to use the reflexes for construing organismic order, we would have to ask: How can we, keeping the artificiality of the conditions in mind, utilize the experiences from the reflex investigation for the understanding of the performances? Yet it would hardly be possible to answer this question, because it presupposes that we already know what the natural conditions are. In turn, this assumption implies that we already know the natural performances of the organism, whereas actually we want to gain information regarding them, through the reflex investigation. Investigations under artificial conditions can never lead to knowledge of natural performances. Thus it is impossible to regard the reflexes as unnatural processes and to assume at the same time that one can obtain from them an insight into the "natural" performances of the organism.

The fact that the reflex is a process in the organism does not mean that it belongs to the real nature of the organism. Reality, in this sense, means that a process belongs to the true "nature" of the organism. In this light, "unnatural" and "unreal" are the same. Thus, considering that the reflex is an unnatural process, the question cannot be: What can we learn from it for the performances of the organism? The question must rather be restated as: What does the reflex mean, viewed from the performances of the whole organism? There is a fundamental difference between these two questions. The first assumes that an advance in knowledge is possible by going from the reflex to the performance. The second presupposes the knowledge of the performances of the organism as necessary in order to understand the reflex as one of the "real" but not natural performances of the organism. Thus, our question challenges the assumption that the reflex possesses a character of "reality" for the organism. It charges any attempt to understand the performances as being composed of reflexes, with not "surrendering to that which is," with intellectual preoccupation and with having leanings toward a false synthetic approach. By saying this, we do not intend to deny that reflexological investigations have disclosed many facts of importance for the recognition of the "real." But in so doing they have never offered an explanation that justifies us to proceed directly from the reflexes to the performances.

The concept of adequacy and reality

Just as the concept of reality proved to become equivocal, so also the concept of adequacy meets with the same fate. Whenever, in the normal life situation and in the natural environment of an organism, a stimulus evokes a movement corresponding to the natural organization of that being, one speaks of adequacy. In assuming that this occurs also in the reflexes, one talks of adequate stimuli in those cases as well. But this is in reality impossible. As long as "adequate" is meant to indicate that stimulus and movement correspond to the nature of the organism, then the meaning of the word is unequivocal. But such a definition does not fit the reflexes that, to say the least, represent unnatural reactions. The constant relationship between a definite stimulus and a definite movement, which is characteristic for the reflexes, has really nothing to do with adequacy per se. Actually the term "adequate" becomes useful for the definition of a reflex movement only if the concept of "naturalness" is introduced into the definition. Thus for Weizsäcker "an adequate reflex movement" is one "which as a typical, biologically intelligible movement follows a typical stimulus, resembling natural conditions!" It should be noted that this definition of a reflex does not take into consideration the only real characteristic of a reflex, namely, the constant relation between stimulus and movement. Instead, a new factor is introduced – that of "natural condition." This is similar to the above discussion of what is "real," which was so equivocal that it invalidated the entire definition. Why should this adequate movement still be called reflex movement? Actually, all reflexes have been determined up to now, under the most unnatural conditions possible. Weizsäcker, quoted above, also used the term "unnatural." We must clearly differentiate between reflex reactions, characterized by a constant relation between stimulus and movement and for which the reflex laws have been established, and adequate performances, which cannot be understood on the basis of reflex constancy. During these adequate performances, rather natural conditions must prevail, and they can be "understood biologically" on the basis of the organism. The question then should be restated as: Can reflex movements provide us with anything for understanding adequate performances, or vice versa? This is a question of fact aiming at "that which '*is*.' "

The use of the term "adequacy," in connection with the greater naturalness of a situation, suggested itself when it was discovered that the usual reflex definition was not sufficient in cases where the same stimulus leads to different performances. The reflex appeared to be modifiable when one investigated variations under different situational conditions; and that modification was designated as adequate, which corresponded to the natural condition. Finding that a circumscribed reflex reaction can be changed through added stimulus conditions is in itself no argument against the reflex theory and does not invalidate it. This leads, as the literature shows, only to the hypostatization of more complicated reflexes. Whether we shall ever reach an understanding of the performances in this way and be able to determine adequate reactions – that is the question. I do not believe so, and, moreover, I think Weizsäcker does not believe it either. Otherwise, how could he speak of unnatural conditions in the reflexes? He could have spoken only of imperfect conditions in some reflexes.

Criticism of the reflex concept must be radical and fundamental, or else it misses the mark, or even creates confusion, by the entailing equivocality. It is radical if it disregards all theoretical speculation and confines itself to "that which is," that is to say, if it tries to determine what sort of process the reflex represents from the point of view of the organism. Then the reflex may prove to be a fundamentally inadequate reaction, arising under unnatural conditions, not as the expression of a natural response of the organism but as an expression of an injury, or, at best, as a reaction in a border situation (cf. p. 139).

The principle of exactness

The main reason one would like to retain the reflexes, at least in some form, is the assumption that they alone permit exact determinations. But this exactness holds only for fictitious life processes, transformed by actively intervening forces. Thus, Weizsäcker wants to confine reflex investigation to physiology, which, according to his views, is alone exact as compared to biology, which has a different methodological foundation and which he regards as inexact. Certainly one may make such a distinction, but it leads to the question of how to distinguish physiology from the inorganic sciences and of what such a physiology contributes regarding the understanding of the organism.

We do not want to discuss, at this point, the problem of accuracy. We only wish to ask what good is accuracy if the results are unsuited for comprehension of the living organism? Organic nature cannot be understood with the tools of mathematical, natural science (cf. pp. 314–15). Thus, the approximation that the biologist can attain is not one in the mathematical sense but is one in the sense of approaching a prototype, "*Urbild*," of the organism. We must take this into account, or forgo the concept of adequacy, because it means nothing but adequacy in regard to the "essence" of the organism, as we recognize it in the "prototype." Nothing seems to be so precarious as to want the latter and at the same time cling to the concept of exactness of mathematical natural science. Such an attempt would imply the desire to understand adequacy on the basis of the reflex concept and at the same time to include the natural condition as an auxiliary concept. This, by logical necessity, reintroduces just that problem of the organismic prototype, which one wanted to avoid. One has to be aware of the consequences of this circular reasoning before scrutinizing the doctrine of the reflexes. Either one forgoes any reference to an organismic prototype, and thereby avoids any reference to adequacy, and makes only piecemeal statements of "what is," or one subscribes to the organismic reference, and thereby faces all phenomena as "they really are and what they mean."[2]

The Epistemological Relationship Between
Biological and Natural Science[3]

The symbolic character of knowledge in general

From the customary point of view in natural science, objection will possibly be found to our conception of biological knowledge, especially with regard to two contentions: first, the postulate of the prototype character of the organism, and second, the incompleteness and imperfection in the determination of that prototype. Regarding our first claim, our procedure does not deviate essentially from that which competent scholars have regarded as the essence of knowledge in natural science. "In the same measure," says Heinrich Hertz, "in which the skepticism toward a naive copy theory of knowledge has grown, it has become more and more the task of natural science to create images or symbols which were suited to gain a coherent understanding of the empirical facts." The mathematico-physical scientist was the first one to realize clearly the symbolic character of his basic tools, as Ernst Cassirer explains. Hertz considers the urgent and most important task of natural science to be that of enabling us to predict future experiences.[4] However, the method that natural science uses for deducing the future from the past consists in making " 'fictitious images or symbols' of the outer objects, of such a sort that the images, in the logical order of ideas, will always be suitable to represent those objects in their physically necessary order. Once we have succeeded in deducing from previously collected data images of the required consistency, then we can develop from them in a short time, as from models, the consequences which will appear in the outer world after a longer time or as the sequelae of our own interference.... The images, of which we speak, are not concepts of things; they coincide with things in one essential point which lies in the fulfillment of the stated postulate; but for their purpose, it is not necessary that they coincide with the objects in any further way. Indeed, we do not know, and have no way of learning, whether our images of things coincide with things in any other regard than only in this one fundamental relationship."[5] According to Cassirer, by this pronouncement the concept of symbol "becomes, so to speak, the central point and focus of our entire epistemology in physics."[6] This is the dividing line between mere empiricism and physical theory, as Pierre Duhem especially has expressed it.[7] There is no direct transition from collecting and ordering of facts, as empiricism does it, to physical knowledge. Cassirer believes it is a matter of a μετάβασις εἰς ἄλλο γένος, a transition to a new perspective. "Instead of the concrete data, we use symbolic images, which are supposed to correspond to data on the basis of theoretical postulates which the observer considers as true and valid.... The significance of these concepts is not manifest in the immediate perception, but can be determined and secured only by an extremely complex process of intellectual interpretation."[8] This conceptual interpretation represents the character of physical theory.

The type of biological knowledge, which we here advance, agrees in its fundamental tendency with the above-characterized epistemological approach. We think one should not content oneself with a mere ordering of empirical findings, and we deny a direct transition from these findings to the objective of knowledge in biology: the comprehension of the prototype of the organism. In biological, like physical, knowledge, it is necessary that "creative power of imagination" become effective. However, in my opinion there remains a difference between the two kinds of knowledge. The symbols that biology requires for the coherent representation of the empirical facts are of a kind other than those in physics. The physical symbols are characterized by the fact that diverse systems of symbols can coexist and are in practical use at the same time. I am thinking here, for example, of the fact that the wave theory and the corpuscular conception in the light-quantum theory are both valid at the same time.

Such a multiplicity of theories is not theoretically tolerable for the physicist and does not necessarily obstruct his practical dealings. Yet such a procedure would not satisfy the requirements of biological research. As previously pointed out, we consider the assumption of different principles of explanation for the processes in the organism as untenable. This conclusion is connected with the fact that, in the field of biology, knowledge and action are very intimately related (cf. p. 339) and that we need a basis for knowledge and for action that will always do justice to the whole organism, because in this field every action concerns the whole. If the reference to the whole is insufficient, the action may possibly be correct for a part, artificially isolated. But it will distort the functioning of the whole. Therefore we cannot be satisfied with symbols that correspond only to part processes. And therefore we have to reject, for example, the scheme that serves as the basis of reflexology. Our knowledge must come closer to the "real" than is requisite for a science of inorganic nature. We need symbols that are not as essentially alien to the observed phenomena, as is permissible for the symbols of physical science; the latter in extreme cases can confine and content itself with a system of fictitious "signs" (mere models). Certainly biological knowledge also remains a set of symbols; and we are also dealing with "substitutes" but not with representation by simple arbitrary "signs." We need a more complete image of an individual concrete character that as much as possible must match the particulars from which we build it up. After all, we do not regard the particular data as mere appearance but as something that pertains to the reality of the whole organism, although it is insufficient for the direct cognition of that. Biological understanding, furthermore, can never be satisfied with finding laws of relation between completely undetermined, theoretically assumed elements. The symbols, the theoretical representations in biology, must, in principle, include quality and individuality in all their determinations. Biological descriptions must exhibit definite qualitative organization. The symbol must have the character of a "Gestalt."

Thus it is possible that, in spite of agreement in the basic procedure, natural science may see itself in opposition to the method of cognition here propounded. This contrast has often become apparent and has led to opposing tendencies within biology and even to heated controversies between the scientists. One faction advocated the exclusive use of the analytic method, the other the exclusive use of the holistic point of view. A classic example for this contrast is found in the well-known controversy between Georges Cuvier and Geoffroy Saint-Hilaire, which Goethe has so vividly described and used as an opportunity to characterize the two points of view.[9] He speaks of two different modes of thinking, represented in these two scientists. One clings to a dissective attitude, and the other makes the idea the guiding principle. One corresponds to an analytic discursive, the other to an organismic principle. These two modes of thinking are distributed "in such a way that they are hardly found together in one individual, and so also not in science; and where they co-exist separately they cannot be reconciled with each other."[10] It seems to us, however, that a competent natural scientist, especially a biologist, must possess the faculty of combining both points of view, although he may at times not admit it. In other words, he must at one time use the dissective approach, at another, the holistic. Sufficient understanding can only be gained when these two forms of cognition influence and supplement each other continuously. Was this not true of Goethe himself?

The incompleteness of biological knowledge and the
acausality in cognition of natural science
It is clear that, when based on the procedure that we have chosen, our knowledge in the field of biology can never be final, and that we must content ourselves with an increasing approximation to the truth. But this approximation must not be understood in the sense of the approximate value of a mathematical series that increases in correctness, the more decimal points we are able to determine, and where we can be satisfied with a limited number of decimals. It may be that biological knowledge frequently has a similar character. But in principle it is of an entirely different kind.

Biological knowledge is not advanced by simply adding more and more individual facts. In the process of biological understanding, it is not true that facts that gradually become included in the "whole" as parts can be evaluated simply quantitatively, so that our knowledge becomes the more firm, the more parts we are able to determine. On the contrary, each single fact has always a qualitative significance. This single, new fact may perhaps revolutionize the entire conception on the basis of former findings and demand an entirely new idea, in the light of which the old facts may have to be evaluated in a radically different way. Completeness and definiteness of cognition is only possible by recurring to certain explicit or inexplicit metaphysical presuppositions that we reject.

However, if one considers biology only as the knowledge of the phenomena, which have been determined by the analytic method, then one must either renounce the understanding that comprehends the organism as a whole, and in so doing really renounce cognition in biology in general, or one must resort to metaphysical and speculative doctrines in order to comprehend an organism. We refuse to adopt any such procedure, although it has, in recent years, been advanced not infrequently. In such cases the factor of irrationality usually creeps in quite unintentionally and is often obscured by a pseudoscientific terminology. In the last analysis, even such concepts as "inhibition," "higher centers," and so on, are based on such a procedure. We reject such a procedure, not only because it goes along with determinations that are not empirically verifiable and are often merely negative, but also because it invites all sorts of speculations and fictitious explanations.

Needless to say, our approach takes a fundamentally different course. Although it aims to gain knowledge of the organism's nature by a method deviating from that of the analytic-synthetic procedure, and although it considers it the very task of biology to gain a true vision of the various organisms in their specificity, nevertheless it springs from the conviction that this method is as accurate as the so-called exactness of natural science. It belongs to the nature of such an epistemological viewpoint that cognition be relatively incomplete and ultimately undefined. The student must remain permanently aware of that insufficiency and be prepared to shift as soon as newly arising facts may demand it. We shall see later on how important this active character is for biological knowledge. At present, we are concerned more with the factor of "acausality" that, for our view, is part of biological cognition. In this respect, it does not basically conflict with natural science. On the contrary, it is remarkably close to views taken by eminent natural scientists on the grounds of more recent investigations concerning the structure of the atoms and the quantum theory in particular. According to these views, processes on the "microscopic level" are governed by probability laws, not by strictly causal principles.

Recently some scientists have formed conceptual models of the atomic structure that are quite akin to those prototypes that we have postulated for biology. They are similar, especially in the respect that they are not equivalent to strictly causal relations and exhibit a somewhat individualized character. Any prediction of a physical nature faces a certain amount of acausal free play, according to Pascual Jordan.[11] "All changes in the state of an atom," says Nils Bohr, "must be described in accordance with the indivisibility of the energy quanta as individual processes; whereby the atom passes from one so-called stationary state into another."[12] At another place, he says, "Quantum physics makes one recognize 'fundamental discontinuities of processes.' Light emission and absorption is connected with discontinuous transitions between stationary states." This represents a further analogy: we differentiate also in biology between processes having continuity and order, those that are comprehensible, and those having discontinuity and disorder, those that are incomprehensible ("catastrophic situations").

Especially Bohr and, after him, Jordan have pointed out the parallelism between physical and organic processes, the former basing his statements particularly on the fact that the determining processes in the organism are of microscopic (submicroscopic) nature.[13] According to Bohr, the reaction of the organism can be divided, from the physical point of view, into two spheres. First, the sphere of macroscopic causality in which all reactions occur according to causal, mechanical, and chemical laws. Second, the sphere of the directing activity, down to processes of atomic order that, although not causally determined in their course, set going the macroscopic events. The behavior of the organism, in a specific instance, always lacks causality, according to Bohr. Just as one relates the lack of causality in atomic processes to the change produced in the processes themselves through the very fact that they are being observed, so does Bohr consider the acausal processes in the organism even more difficult to observe than the atomic processes. The acausal processes are located in the inner sphere of the organism, which he regards as the seat of that unity of reaction potentialities that constitute an organism.

The far-reaching analogy of this view of the organism with ours is obvious. This view as well admits, by reference to a causally, not completely comprehensible nature, that determination is only possible by probability. Here this determination by probability takes on, however, a specific qualitative characteristic through the relatively constant individual structure of the organism. In this connection, it is interesting that Bohr also points to the striking stability of the organism as a characteristic difference between inorganic and organic processes, a property that has assumed fundamental significance for our entire conception.

One might believe that if in inorganic nature acausal phenomena need be assumed only in the microscopic processes, then the same

318

would hold true for the organism. One might believe that here, as well as in inorganic nature, mechanism and causality reign on the macroscopic level. Since our observations are essentially concerned with macroscopic phenomena, our knowledge would not be affected by the lack of causality. Whether organic processes are macroscopic or microscopic, we do not want to decide here. As mentioned above, Bohr believes that the latter is the case. But let us assume that we are dealing essentially with macroscopic phenomena. Would that mean that we are dealing with strict causality in our findings? All physico-chemical investigations and all physico-chemical interferences with the organism, where we would most expect definite causal relationship, actually never yield results of absolute constancy but only averages or probability values. The results are always influenced by a causally "intangible" personal factor. We may understand digestion in the stomach as a physico-chemical process to such an extent that we can influence it systematically in its individual aspects through specific physico-chemical intervention, that we can remove disturbances, and so on. Still we must not forget that these rules of influence are strictly valid only for investigation outside the organism in a test tube or in situations in which we segregate the stomach artificially from its connection with the organism. We must, further, not forget that under natural conditions we have constant results in a certain number of cases, and there also, only approximately constant ones. Still we are not able to state from where the deviations come, and especially what other effects we produce at the same time that are possibly unfavorable for the whole organism.

The state of affairs is quite similar in all other physico-chemical applications to the organism. This is particularly true as to the quantitative conditions of such experiments (cf. p. 75). Through all these incongruities, we need not be deterred in medical treatments, simply because, in practice, we can be satisfied with a reasonable percentage of equal effects, especially regarding extent and quantity, and because, rightly, we are interested in producing at first the effect on a specific place. This is of practical importance in localized diseases. It is suitable to circumscribed processes and also corresponds to those border situations to which we conceded a sort of effect in the sense of the reflexes.

But all this does not represent phenomena during adequate functioning of the organism. It would hardly be possible to prove that causal relations prevail in those processes that belong adequately to the nature of the organism. Whenever a phenomenon seems to be causally explicable, then it occurs, as in the fixed reflexes, only under conditions of isolation, by which the rest of the organism does not disturb these processes. The disclosure that the course of a process in such a situation is causally determined does not, however, justify the assumption that the course within the whole organism takes place in a similar manner.

Entelechy and "reason in knowledge"
But is it necessary to conceive this acausal process, which we have just discussed, as the expression of peculiar forces, real, but different from the usually assumed mechanical causal linkages, for example, of entelechies? The entelechy theory is found today not only in natural philosophy, which is concerned with the organisms, but also in the speculations regarding the structure of the organic world in general.

If one goes so far as to differentiate, in inorganic events, between processes that are to be understood as mechanistic and others that are to be understood as nonmechanistic, then one may also understand matter as the manifestation of the entelechy. Especially, the views of Herman Weyl could lend support to such an approach. According to his so-called *Agenstheorie* the physical field is not closed but is only the substratum in which the effects of the transspatial "material" agent manifest themselves.[14] The forces, the effective units that determine material events, the events in spatial matter, are all of transspatial nature; "experience very clearly indicates another form of causality than the one fitting the frame of the field theory; namely, that if the field is left to itself, it remains in a homogeneous state of quiescence and becomes excited only through something else, the 'spirit of unrest.'... Matter is the agent which excites the field...although the material particle is hidden in a spatial environment, from which its field effects originate, it actually exists beyond space and time."[15] Thus, it becomes necessary to assume higher units of action (quanta) in order to understand the processes in the realm of matter. Thus Kurt Riezler, too, arrives at the conclusion: "As long as the theory of the physical world does not yield an order which is closed in itself, but rather admits gaps in the determination which cannot be filled by physically comprehensible factors, so long do we have neither reason nor right to deny the existence of other forms of structure, like wholeness.... We must assume," Riezler says, "that the latter or analogous structural forms may prevail wherever physics meets gaps in causal determination, and must realize that its instruments are failing it."[16] In consequence, one could assume that nature represents a stratified hierarchy of various entelechies to which certain ways of manifestation like matter, organic life, and so on, would correspond.

I do not feel competent to decide as to whether such a point of view is necessary for understanding of inorganic nature or not. But is such a view necessary for understanding organic events? I believe not. Within the framework of scientific method, we can and must confine ourselves to such assumptions as are requisite for making the facts intelligible. This requirement is met by the holistic reference, which deals with the "essential nature." The latter we attempt to recognize in its structure by way of the dialectic procedure of cognition indicated above.

We are not afraid of the term "entelechy" in so far as it is a metaphysical conception but primarily because it is much too general and undefined. For example, Driesch decrees that, regarding entelechy, one must not imagine anything further than that it is a regulating principle that cannot be characterized any more precisely. We are afraid of the term because it has too much the character of a correction, necessitated by errors made elsewhere, as is actually the case. The cause of these errors rests in the conception of the organism as a mechanism. Our analysis has shown that, with the exception of border situations in which the organism is endangered (cf. p. 139), there are no such part processes in the organism that can be understood mechanistically, but that every life process has a specific holistic pattern. Since it was on no occasion necessary to assume mechanistic processes in order to understand life, we do not need to speculate on "entelechy."

In the first place, what we call the essence of nature is not to be understood as having metaphysical existence, but only as a basis for cognition – "a reason in knowledge." It is of an exclusively positive character, the determination of which becomes more precise as science advances. It has never a negative function. This "essence of nature" cannot be dissected mechanistically into parts, but it is a structurally articulated organization. True, we can dismember it, so that we construe "parts"; but this is only the case when we actually take it apart, that is, split it into its physico-chemical elements. In every physiological dissection – and this is true also for many experiments carried out with the knife – we create a mixture of these "part elements" and real "whole members." It is our task to discriminate, in this mass of phenomena, the true "members" from the artificial "parts," and further, to investigate the former as to their functional membership character in the organism and what significance they have for it.

Whole and "members"

The last point requires more precise elaboration. The question may be raised whether there is any sense at all in speaking of the existence of members, in view of the organismic whole. Are not such members merely the result of the isolating procedure? At any rate, one must not regard the relation between members thus determined, that is, the "essential constants," and the organism, as a relation between lower "action units" and the higher unit of the organism. Neither can one see in them the manifestation of "lower entelechies" as compared to the "higher entelechy" of the organism, or as part and subwholes as compared to the "whole" of the organism. Likewise, of course, we cannot follow any hypothesis claiming such subdivision of the whole into subwholes and antagonism between them.

We reject also that special form of conflict that Emil Oldekop introduces with his concept of "polarity relations."[17] This author thinks that the assumption of the customary vitalistic dualism, which consists in the antagonism of two completely disparate substances, has recently become untenable through the proof of the existence of both mechanical and nonmechanical events in both inorganic and in organic nature. He wants to replace this dualism by the "polarity relationship of the whole to its members," with the "polar tension between the 'tendency towards unification' of the superordinated action unit and the tendency towards self-preservation of the members" – an antagonism that, according to the author, is found throughout all of nature. This dualism can in no way be resolved, because it is "the expression of the basic primal fact, that the 'form' of the whole is a unity which cannot be derived from the multiplicity of its members, and vice versa, the multiplicity of the members cannot be deduced from the unity of the form."

In such a consideration one forgets, however, that even the members themselves are artificially separated parts of the organism, which stand out only under the isolating view. One overlooks that the organism is, of course, articulate (differentiated into members) but does not consist of members: the members that we distinguish neither compose the organism, nor are they antagonistic to it, because the organism is nothing but the members themselves. There is neither a struggle of the members among each other in the organism, nor a struggle of the whole with the members. Whenever any such phenomenon appears it is either due to an illusion or to an isolating consideration, as in the so-called antagonism, or it is the expression of an improper centering that reaches far into the "normal course of events." Performances are not the product of compensation of mutual tensions between members of the organism. Only deterioration or imperfect adaptation of the organism makes members stand out abnormally. Then we find tensions that, however, do not really exist between members themselves or between the whole and its members, but between the organism and the environment.

The assumption of a tension between members suggests itself only when one overlooks the "functional" character of a member and reifies it. It is only too easy to err in this direction, if one talks of lower and higher entelechies. Therefore, we had best avoid such notions, especially since we really cannot deduce anything from them and they in no way further us in our knowledge.

So-called purposiveness
Just as we had to reject vitalism and the idea of entelechy, so too do we reject the teleological approach. To be opposed to strictly causal reference need not imply leanings to teleology. At most, the concept of the so-called inner purposiveness in the sense of Kant, could be taken into consideration. Driesch has emphasized that teleology, in the realm of life, demands really only one principle, namely, that of wholeness. The problem is to determine conceptually the factor of constancy that the organism displays, notwithstanding all the modification it undergoes during its life course. Following Driesch, Emil Ungerer says: "If an individual object of nature preserves itself, during Becoming, in the form of a whole, and if, during Becoming, certain processes appear, which condition the preservation of this wholeness, we may describe these processes as 'purposive' in a mere descriptive sense."[18] In inorganic nature, he means, there are no "purposes" but only one purpose, namely, the preservation of the wholeness of a thing during Becoming. "All other purposes are meaningless for causal quest. In teleological consideration of a process in the organism, it does not matter whether it can be subordinated to a purpose, but rather whether it contributes to preserva-

tion of the wholeness of this organism (or of a higher wholeness, in case one exists)." I agree with Ungerer so far as to reduce the term "teleological" to this mere descriptive use and, furthermore, with his demand that the term "purposive" would be best avoided altogther. Accordingly, we have not used it in our presentation. Following the example of Karl Ernst von Baer, one could rather speak of an "end." According to him "purpose" is an intended task, whereas "end" is a given direction of activity, an intrinsically predetermined effect. The idea of an intended task is superfluous for an understanding of the organism, but that of a definite end (the actualization of its essence) may be very fruitful for our understanding of the organism. Yet the idea of "end" must also be taken only as a guiding notion for the procedure of knowledge rather than in a metaphysical sense, as it appears in von Baer. In this sense, one can describe the concept of wholeness, as a category, as the category that substantiates and encompasses the subject matter of biology.

CHAPTER TEN

On Norm, Health, and Disease.

On Anomaly, Heredity, and Breeding

An organism that actualizes its esssential peculiarities, or – what really means the same thing – meets its adequate milieu and the tasks arising from it, is "normal." Since this realization occurs in a specific milieu in an ordered behavioral way, one may denote ordered behavior under this condition as normal behavior.

On the Determination of Normality

Health and disease

A great many different attempts have been made to determine normality. According to an idealistic view, one regards a person as normal, or more or less abnormal, in the degree to which he corresponds to a certain philosophically founded ideal. Thus Hildebrand would want the concept of the norm to be formed according to such an ideal type, as that of a hero. Any such idealistic norm concept is but of little use, because it will always differ according to the respective philosophy of life. Furthermore, it always carries an extrinsic character, because its frame of reference is not oriented on any reality but, rather, would have to justify itself in reality. Even if the idealistic norm concept would do justice to the "constants" of the species, by forming the ideal according to these constants, it may nevertheless fail with respect to the individual.

What we need is not only a generally valid concept of the norm, which should avoid the "subjective," but a concept on the basis of which the concrete facts can really be comprehended. On the basis of such views, a statistical concept of the norm seems almost more useful. The latter certainly may be very valuable for specific practical purposes that require statements regarding the average. But it cannot be used to determine whether a given individual is to be regarded as normal or abnormal. The statistical norm concept cannot do justice to the individual. Yet, according to our previous discussion, we can only be satisfied with a concept of norm that is suited for this purpose.

Before we can elaborate on this in detail, we first want to discuss more closely another concept, to which it is in many respects related – the concept of health and that of its opposite, disease. In that way, we hope to obtain material that will enable us to make a decision regarding the norm concept. Furthermore, such a discussion seems expedient for our principal problem, because the concepts of health and disease by no means concern only the physician but the entire field of biology.

It may be stated as certain that any disease is an abnormality but not that every abnormality is a disease. No matter how we may define normality there are certainly many digressions from the norm that do not mean being sick.

But what is being sick? Many will agree with Ehrenfried Albrecht that a general definition of such concepts as normal, healthy, and sick is not possible and that these concepts are determined by traditional convention, thus naturally being afflicted with the problems of these conventions.[1] According to Karl Jaspers, disease is a concept of value that depends more on the prevailing conception of the respective cultural sphere than on the judgment of the physician.[2] The decision whether a phenomenon is pathological has, according to him, really no factual significance. The thoughtful psychopathologist, for example, would really place no emphasis on such a general judgment as "disease." I should not like to take issue with this argument as long as it remains purely academic. However, it seems questionable to me whether fact-minded science could get along without the concept of disease, which after all expresses a fact, although it may be difficult to formulate the fact precisely. Others, as for example Mainzer, say that disease is "not at all a category of the science of life, but only a medical or pre-medical concept."

In our discussion, we shall disregard those who seek to determine disease extraneously – as something that, so to speak, befalls the patient. We shall deal only with those who regard disease as a change of the organism. Thus we really are more concerned with the problem of being sick than with that of disease. (Still, for the sake of simplicity, we shall in general use the term disease for the phenomenon that we mean.)

326

Disease not determinable as to contents, nor as
deviation from a superindividual norm

Various studies usually seek to determine disease as a deviation, as to contents, from the condition of the organism during the state of health, or as a deviation from a norm that is to be determined as to contents. The ambiguity of the concept of disease shows itself then as the consequence of the ambiguity of the concept of norm. From an "average norm" or an "idealistic norm" (cf. p. 325), it is certainly, in general, impossible to derive a definition of disease as to contents. Strictly as to contents, there is, on this basis, no far-reaching fundamental difference between the healthy and the diseased organism. But it is questionable whether one is justified in saying, as Mainzer does, that there is "no difference regarding healthy and diseased life." In our opinion, normal life has something to do with ordered behavior. In this event, it would be possible that, although there might be no difference between healthy and diseased life, with regard to contents, there still could be a difference with regard to form. Possibly all attempts to determine disease up to now were doomed to failure, because one was looking for determinations as to contents. These cannot be found on the basis of a superindividual "norm." The possible failure in determining disease by this procedure leads then to the assumption that disease is no category of the science of life. Such a result should have made one suspicious of the original premise. How is it thinkable that disease and health should not be biological concepts! If we disregard, for a moment, the complicated conditions in man, this statement is certainly not valid for animals, where disease so frequently decides whether the individual organism is "to be or not to be." Just think what detrimental part disease plays in the life of the undomesticated animal, that is, the animal that does not benefit by the protection through humanity! If the science of life is supposed to be incapable of comprehending the phenomena of disease, one must doubt seriously the appropriateness of, and the truth in, the intrinsic categories of a science so construed.

But let us put aside, for the time being, this problem of definition and see how the patients themselves and the physician go about distinguishing health and disease. I believe they proceed at first by not focusing on the contents. True, the physician as well as the patient can become suspicious as to health, when recognizing deviations from the usual behavior with regard to content, as for example, abnormal fatigue, palpitation of the heart, nausea, headache, swollen feet, and so on. But neither for the physician nor for the patient are these manifestations of diseases in themselves but, at best, signs that a disease may exist. The experience of being sick does not necessarily contain any definite kind of change as to contents. And the physician, when he decides whether he is dealing with a case of disease, is, for the most part, guided by criteria entirely different from the proof of a change as to contents. At least, the good physician will proceed in this way as long as his ingenuous apprehension of health and disease is not biased by the knowledge of innumerable scientific details.

Definition of disease presupposes a conception of the individual nature
Now what is the basis for passing the judgment "He is sick"? It is the observation of a peculiarly changed, of a "disordered" behavior, the observation of that type of reaction that belongs to the catastrophic. The objectively verifiable changes of particulars, in pulse, temperature, and so on, are to the physician practically only a confirmation of the correctness of his assumption. And likewise the patient himself experiences disease primarily as a basic change of his attitude toward the environment, as uncertainty and anxiety – the subjective manifestations of catastrophic condition.

This characterization shows that being sick is experienced neither by the physician nor by the patient as a change regarding contents but rather as a disturbance in the course of the life processes. Therefore not every deviation from the norm, as to contents, appears as disease. It actually becomes a disease only when, as L. Friedmann states correctly, it carries with it impairment of and danger for the whole organism. Using a provisional and more general description, which may later require a more specific determination, we may say that a condition can be designated as a disease when it endangers "existence." Thus, being sick appears as a disturbance of function, whereby the changes as to contents may merely occasion the feeling of illness. Regarded in themselves, the changes do not need to be disease. Pathological phenomena are the expression of the fact that the normal relationships between organism and environment have been changed through a change of the organism and that thereby many things that had been adequate for the normal organism are no longer adequate for the modified organism.

Disease is shock and danger for existence. Thus a definition of disease requires a conception of the individual nature as a starting point. Disease appears when an organism is changed in such a way that, though in its proper, "normal" milieu, it suffers catastrophic reaction. This manifests itself not only in specific disturbances of performance, corresponding to the locus of the defect, but in quite general disturbances because, as we have seen, disordered behavior in any field coincides always with more or less disordered behavior of the whole organism.

With this definition of disease as a disturbance of the course of the processes, we are, in general, in agreement with a number of authors. Thus, for example, we can agree with Otto Lubarsch, who characterizes disease as the disturbance of the vital equilibrium, or with Hugo Ribbert, who calls it the result of insufficient or completely lacking adaptation to harmful influences, or with Viktor Schilling, to whom disease is a disturbance of the ordered biological course in the organism, which disturbance can no longer be removed through the usual degree of regulation.[3] Our view is particularly close to that of Ludwig Aschoff and that of A. Grothe.[4] Aschoff defines disease as any disturbance in the course of biological processes "by which the organism is endangered in its biological existence." Regarding this definition, it would seem to us that the characterization of existence as biological, in the usual sense of the word, is too narrow. However, I cannot agree with the objection of Friedmann that this definition is too narrow because the clinician unquestionably knows pathological conditions that do not endanger existence. This objection would be valid only if one were always to think of death when thinking of danger, for existence. But the objection does not hold if one considers that danger means always endangering the actualization of the "performance potentialities" essential to the individual organism. This danger can manifest itself in objective disturbances as well as in subjective experiences. But it can also exist objectively without the person becoming subjectively conscious of it.

Disease as "defective responsiveness"
Our view probably comes nearest to Grothe's. We agree completely with him that disease can be determined only by means of a norm that permits taking the entire concrete individuality into consideration, a norm that takes the individual himself as the measure; in other words, as an individual, personal norm. According to Grothe, the individual

is the measure of his own normality. Health is defined by the fact "that the manifestation of life of an individual fits completely his biological requirements which emerge from the encounter of his physiological 'performance potentiality' with his external life situation." This "fitting" is described as responsiveness. Disease is "defective responsiveness resulting objectively in impairment of the capacity and duration of performance, and subjectively, in suffering." Any attempt to determine health and disease on this basis makes prerequisite, of course, the determination of the "nature" of the individual person in question. On the basis of our previous presentations, we see in this point no difficulty for Grothe's view. But another difficulty arises.

If regaining health consisted of bringing about a sufficient removal of the deviations from the individual's norm that had been caused by the disease, then health could be regained only by a complete restitution of the former normal state (*restitutio ad integrum*). This, however, would limit incisively the concept of health, as compared with the customary usage of the term. After all, there are undoubtedly people who do not consider themselves sick, although a defect may remain. Grothe escapes this difficulty, but only apparently, by assuming that the patient is capable of compensating, through morphological and functional adaptation, for the deviation from his individual norm with respect to performance capacity and duration. The patient becomes well in spite of residual defect, because he replaces the lost performances by others. This idea is based on the presupposition that deficiency in function of one part, can be compensated by increased function of other parts. Thus the total performance may remain essentially unchanged. But this presupposition is very dubious. It was possible to conceive it only as long as one considered the performances of an organism as composed of partitive performances and as long as one assumed, so to speak, a special agent for the regulation of the whole by the aid of which a lost performance could be replaced by another. But if one regards every single performance as depending on the whole, as a special expression of the whole, then it is really no longer possible to assume a substitution per se. Indeed, substitution seems to take place only under a superficial examination. We gain this impression when, in spite of a defect, the organism continues to perform somewhat adequately, so that the individual no longer appears as being essentially disturbed.

The restoration of health

Careful analysis shows that the former way of performing and the former way of coming to terms with the former milieu is never reached by the patient. We consider it very important to make this point completely clear. The reader may be surprised that we reject the assumption of any compensation for lost performances (in spite of the fact that we have defended such a far-reaching relative independence of performances from their normal substratum, and in spite of the fact that we regard any performance as one of the whole organism).

First of all, observation itself makes this conclusion compelling. But to object to the idea of compensation does not contradict our view of the relation of performance to the substratum. As much as we are convinced of the relative independence of the individual performance from a definite localized substratum, we are equally certain that normal performances are limited to the strict integrity of the organism throughout, in terms of its normal structural organization. In a formation that is qualitatively and structurally as highly differentiated as the organism, there is no such thing as compensation. If lost performances return, this is either possible through restitution of the damage or through the execution of performances that are similar only in their effect. But then we will always find a simultaneous loss of other performances or a shrinkage of milieu. To regain health, while the defect remains, is possible only under certain limitations. Since the main criterion for regaining health is the restitution of order, any other remaining change may at first be left unnoticed, as long as it does not impair at all or impairs to only a slight degree ordered behavior. We shall see later, that this order depends, however, on a minimum of essential performances.

Health is not restored, as Grothe assumes, through compensation or substitution for disturbances as to contents. Rather it is restored if such a relation between preserved and disturbed performances is reached, which makes (in spite of residual defects) "responsiveness" possible anew. This relationship is independent of an injury of a definite substratum. If certain changes do not indicate danger, then they do not make for disease but are only deviations that remain irrelevant as long as the individual is able to meet the psychological and physical demands of his personal milieu in spite of these changes – in other words, is not menaced in his "existence."

This may be the case, to mention a few examples of Grothe, when the heart is too small, or in physiological albuminuria, abnormal vaso-motility, and so on. Individuals with such changes appear healthy because they are adapted to a very specific personal milieu. That the adaptation to a personal milieu is a basic requirement for their health shows itself in the fact that they take sick as soon as this adaptation is not present, for example, as soon as "normal," average demands are made on them. In a similar manner, even a normal individual may take sick when demands far beyond his average potentialities are made on him.

It is not a valid objection against such a definition of disease that, on its basis, for example, a patient with an ulcer of the stomach or a malignant tumor may be designated as healthy, namely, as long as no disturbances of his responsiveness have become obvious. First, the assumption that there are no disturbances can be traced, to a certain extent, to an insufficiency of observation on the part of the patient as well as of the physician. Second, such an objection is unjustified from our point of view because it is altogether too short-sighted in considering, as it does, the organism only in its present situation and in not considering that single phenomena can be evaluated properly, only if one regards them as a part of the total life of the individual, particularly also with regard to his future. We may designate a person with such stigmata as being healthy only if we do not expect any disturbance of responsiveness in the future. If that is the case – and to decide this is really the basic requirement of a medical diagnosis – we should certainly designate the patient under consideration as being sick.

Thus, being well means to be capable of ordered behavior that may prevail in spite of the impossibility of certain performances that were formerly possible. But the new state of health is not the same as the old one. This observation marks the main difference between our view and that of Grothe. Just as a definite condition as to contents belongs to the former state of normality, so also a definite condition as to contents belongs to the new normality; but of course the contents of both conditions differ. This conclusion, which follows as a matter of course from our concept of the organism, which is also determined as to contents, becomes of the greatest importance for the physician's attitude toward those who have regained their health. From any superindividual norm, disease cannot be determined as to contents, while from the individual norm this can be done very well. If the individual has lost

332

essential contents, he becomes sick. To become well again, in spite of defects, always involves a certain loss in the essential nature of the organism. This coincides with the reappearance of order. A new individual norm corresponds to this rehabilitation.

How very important the regaining of order is for recuperation can be seen from the fact that the organism seems primarily to have the tendency to preserve, or gain, such capacities that make this possible. The organism first of all appears set on gaining constants anew. We may find in recovery (with residual defect) changes in various fields as compared with the former nature of the organism; but the behavior shows that the character of the performances is again "constant." We find constants in the bodily as well as in the mental field. For instance, as compared with the former behavior, we find a change in a pulse rate, blood pressure, sugar content of the blood, in thresholds, mental performances, and so on, but this modification is one of newly formed constants in the respective fields. These new constants guarantee the new order. We can understand the behavior of the recuperated organism only if we consider this fact. We must not attempt to interfere with these new constants because we would thus create new disorders. We have learned that fever is not always to be combated but that an increase in temperature may be understood as one of those constants that are necessary to bring about the recovery. We have learned to treat quite similarly certain forms of increased blood pressure or certain psychological changes. There are many such alterations of constants that today we still attempt to remove for their alleged harmfulness, whereas it would be better not to interfere with them.

Deeper insight into the nature of neuroses, as well as brain lesions, has shown us that deviations from the norm are not always signs of disease. On the contrary some of them belong to the processes in the patient that protect him from certain dangers naturally involved in the change to new normality. We have learned to regard certain deviations as a necessity for well-being. They belong to the type of milieu change (cf. p. 56) that permits a relatively ordered behavior and thus protects the organism from demands with which it cannot cope.

Summary of our concept of disease and health

1. Well-being consists of an individual norm of ordered functioning, expressed in definite constants, responsiveness, and in decidedly

preferred ways of behavior (essential nature, individual adequacy, individual average mean of equalization processes, and so on).

2. Disease is a disordered functioning, that is, defective responsiveness, of the individual organism as compared with the norm of this individual as a whole. This disorder is disease insofar as it endangers self-actualization.

3. The change in content does not constitute the disease but is an indicator of the existing functional derangement of the whole.

4. Recovery is a newly achieved state of ordered functioning, that is, responsiveness, hinging on a specifically formed relation between preserved and impaired performances. This new relation operates in the direction of a new individual norm, of new constancy and adequacy (contents).

5. Every recovery with residual defect entails some loss in "essential nature." There is no real substitution.

In its tendency to maintain optimal performance and to attain new ordered functioning, the diseased organism either adapts itself to a less relevant defect by yielding to it, or adjusts itself to a stronger defect by reorganizing the impaired performance at the expense of others (shift). In either case, the new order necessitates a shrinkage or diminution of performance potentialities (essential nature) and of milieu.

The two types of adaptation to a defect
It seems that the adaptation to an irreparable defect takes essentially opposite directions. Either the organism adapts itself to the defect, or, so to speak, yields to it, or resigns itself to that somewhat defective but still passable performance that can still be realized, and resigns itself to certain changes of the milieu that correspond to the defective performances; or the organism faces the defect, readjusts itself in such a way that the defect, in its consequences, is kept in check. We have already mentioned these two kinds of behavior in our discussion of the sequelae of calcarine lesion. There we saw that the onset of each of these two types of behavior is related to the degree of the disturbance. The same can be verified in many different fields.

We want to demonstrate this, here, with a particularly instructive example. In patients with one-sided cerebellar lesion, we often find a "tonus pull" toward the diseased side. All stimuli that are applied to this side are met with abnormal intensity, with abnormal "turning to the stimulus." This leads to deviation in walking, to a predisposition to falling, to past pointing, and so on, all toward the diseased side. Usually the patients display simultaneously an abnormality of posture in the form of a tilting of the body, especially of the head. As long as the patient remains in this abnormal posture he feels relatively at ease, has less subjective disturbances of equilibrium, less vertigo, and so on. His objective performances, such as walking, pointing, and so forth, are better. Deviations may diappear completely. However, the subjective, as well as the objective, disturbances immediately reappear as soon as the patient reassumes the old, normal position of the body. Apparently the abnormality of posture has become the prerequisite for better performances; it has become the new preferred situation. Thus, we consider the abnormalities of posture as compensation processes, similarly as Pötzl considered them. Apparently, compensation is brought about in some cases by tilting toward the diseased side, in others toward the healthy side.

How can this behavior be explained? Like any other kind of defect, a cerebellar defect results in two kinds of symptoms: First, symptoms that consist of disturbances of certain performances and second, those that consist of a general disorder of total behavior which is determined by catastrophic phenomena, corresponding to the inadequacy of reactions. Through the posture anomaly, not only are the specific performances improved but also the catastrophic reactions are diminished. A new order exists that can be reached in two ways. One way is for the organism to yield to the tonus pull. Through tilting of the body toward the side of the pull, a position is reached in which equal stimuli produce an equal effect on both sides.[5]

But this change is of value to the organism only if this oblique position does not in itself become a disturbance, for instance, if it becomes impossible in this position to maintain the whole body in balance. Therefore the tilting toward the diseased side appears only in patients with a relatively minor impairment. Only in such cases is the old way of procedure preserved. We have here the same conditions as in hemiamblyopia. The other way is to be observed if the impairment is so strong that the patient would immediately fall over if he were to tilt toward the side of the disturbance. Then we find a posture anomaly toward the opposite side, that is, the healthy side. The abnormal, strong tonus pull in stimulation of the diseased side is balanced in such a way that, because of the posture anomaly – meaning, in this case, abnormal effort – the common environmental stimulation of the healthy side now also becomes effective with abnormal strength. In this way a state of equilibrium is again obtained, in this case through a change of the type of behavior, through new adjustment, as in complete destruction of the calcarine in hemianopsia. This kind of adaptation is more active, more voluntary. Gradually, however, it becomes so much a matter of course that the patient is then hardly conscious of the abnormal posture. He only knows that thereby he feels better, for example.

The two kinds of adaptation are not equally relevant for the organism as a whole. The first involves more security, is more automatic, and is usually accompanied by an improvement not as great as the other. The second involves less security, requires more volitional behavior, and therefore leads more readily to fluctuations; yet the performance in the special field may be more improved. Since, as we have seen, the main point is to achieve ordered behavior, we find, as long as the performance in the special field is at all sufficient, that the first, more secure kind of adaptation, sets in. The second type appears only when the first no longer serves the purpose, that is, if it cannot attain a sufficiently fair performance in the special field, or as we have already said, if an unbearable impairment of the whole organism should occur.

In these two different kinds of adaptation, we are dealing with general rules of which one must be mindful. Only then do apparently contradictory symptoms in an injury of the same character become intelligible. This holds equally for phenomena in diseased human beings as for those in experiments with animals.

If we analyze the various kinds of adjustment and particularly the significance of the milieu demand for the development of adaptation, the basic law that dominates the life of the organism becomes especially clear. It is of paramount importance for the organism to attain a condition that is adequate to its "nature," in this case to its modified nature. On the basis of our view, this can be well understood, because only then are performances possible. Thus, it can happen that adaptation to a defect does not operate so much in the direction of regaining former performances but rather in the direction of achieving ordered behavior. Of the performances that in themselves are still possible, those are actualized that can be utilized within the framework of the new ordered behavior, or at least do not disturb it. Ordered behavior is aimed at, even at the expense of certain performances that in themselves would still be possible if the milieu were a different one.

The tendency toward preservation as expression of decadence of life
In this pathological condition, the tendency to preserve the present state may become the means of survival. If the biologist rests his theory on observations of such conditions, then a drive toward self-preservation may appear as an essential trait of the organism, whereas, actually, the tendency toward self-preservation is a phenomenon of disease, of "decadence of life."

The necessity of obtaining a new, suitable milieu depends on two factors, as does life in general. It depends, first of all, on the "nature of the organism" itself, as much as on the world. Here, however, we are particularly interested in the second factor, the significance of the "world." The changed organism must find, in the "world," a new "milieu."

In our discussion of the processes in calcarine lesion we have pointed out that the readjustment occasioned by a defect is always accompanied by a limitation of the performances, or a shrinkage of the milieu. We find the same phenomenon in all recoveries with a remaining defect. It is self-understood that animals, after amputation of limbs (cf. p. 188), cannot cope with all the demands that they "normally" could meet. One easily overlooks these limitations, because one pays attention, first of all, to the restoration of particularly important performances. For example, one pays attention to the restoration of locomotion in animals after amputation of the leg, or of the function in a certain muscle after transplantation in human beings, and so on. We know that, after transplantation, the restored energy is seldom greater than one third of the energy of the control muscle and that the transplanted muscles suffer abnormal fatigue in the originally "normal" performances. One is easily deceived in experiments with animals and assumes a far-reaching adaptability because one overlooks that the animals do not live in their natural situation. It is human care that saves them from certain tasks so that the resulting limitation does not become apparent. So, for example, in the experiments of Cannon, the animals were not exposed to the "normal" fluctuations in temperature, the normal struggle for food, the normal necessity to escape from enemies, the normal danger of bleeding to death, because laboratory conditions were favorable in these respects.[6] Yet these animals were unquestionably defective in many respects. They were actually much less protected against the influence of cold and warmth, they could not maintain a constant body temperature independent of the outer-world temperature, and similar phenomena.

Readjustment is only possible if, simultaneously, provision is made for the required restriction of milieu, in such a way that no stimuli, which might occasion catastrophic reactions, can affect the organism. We have seen earlier how patients with brain injury gradually gain this new milieu and what form it takes. But they can obtain the new milieu only if fellow men make it possible by providing an environment adequate to the new condition. To produce such a state is the goal of medical practice in general. Insofar as medical therapy does not eradicate the damage, it consists only in rearranging the milieu. To avoid misunderstandings, I should like to point out that the term "rearranging the milieu" is to be understood in the broadest sense. Thus, it includes the necessity of taking certain drugs continually, to keep within a certain mode of living, of avoiding situations or indulgences in the somatic or psychological realm, of renouncing or of entering certain human relationships, and so on. We shall see, in the discussion of acting in the biological sphere, what extraordinary difficulties are encountered.

Before dwelling on further consequences of our view, we have to comment on the individualistic character that our description of health seems to bear. Adequacy, in the sense of "responsiveness," manifests itself in the greatest performance capacity of the respective individual. While our description completely abstains from stating the contents of the performances, it is, on the other hand, independent of any a priori conception of man, permitting a stress on either the individualistic or collectivistic aspect of his nature. Our determination makes no decision, in this respect, and is of course not "individualistic" in the sense of being egocentric. Our problem is not the person as an individual, but individuality. It is quite possible that the social attitude, the character of concrete group membership, belongs essentially to man. If this is true, then that atttitude belongs to the individual norm of humans, and health will be maintained only when this essential trait, among the others, finds realization. I personally adopt this point. If, however, such an attitude did not belong to the norm, then the claim for social behavior would be totally inadequate and would, therefore, be incompatible with ordered behavior, and so also with health. No matter what the decision on this question may be, the concept of norm, which we have advanced here, can be employed.

Since ordered behavior has such an extraordinary significance for the injured organism, the restriction of the milieu under certain conditions might become so great that the restriction itself may in turn become a cause of catastrophic reactions. This may be the case if the limitation incapacitates the organism for executing other "essential" performances. For example, when certain mental activities that seem indispensable to the patient have been made impossible through some bodily incapacitation, then life, in such limited form, becomes inadequate to him. Then, not infrequently, by what might be termed a protective measure of nature, the patient is spared a catastrophe by losing the awareness of his change (cf. pp. 49ff.). For instance, this loss of awareness of change appears in cortical injury or in very serious bodily diseases like tuberculosis, carcinoma of the uterus, and so on. In the most serious cases, the patient loses consciousness altogether.

But there are border situations in which a severe bodily impairment already exists, but consciousness of the condition has not yet disappeared. In such situations, intense psychological conflict may arise. Then we find the tendency toward self-destruction as the ultimate possibility of adaptation, although fatal for the individual. And therewith, suicide occurs as an expression of the most serious catastrophic shock, caused by the realization of the impossibility of existence. This conflict situation becomes very important for the deliberations of any medical treatment. Such treatment will always have to be guided by the consideration as to whether the shrinkage of the milieu, which every treatment entails, does not limit, for the individual, the possibilities of self-actualization beyond the point of what is bearable. Thus it will sometimes be necessary to tolerate a certain disturbance, a "symptom," as more bearable than the curtailment of more essential performances resulting from greater limitation of the milieu. On the other hand, one will have to make the demands as high as possible, because only then does real responsiveness occur. Demands that are too low can also prove to be an obstacle for bringing about the optimal order of performances.[7]

Biological Knowledge and Action
Here we are facing one of the most difficult tasks. We have to decide which course should be taken. Obviously, it is not sufficient to base this

decision on the changes as such, which the patient manifests. Rather it is imperative to consider the entire premorbid personality of the patient and his transformation by irreparable changes.

The imperfection of all biological knowledge, its incompleteness in principle, appears in all its severity, when it becomes the basis of our actions. We cannot avoid this difficulty by saying that the conception that we gain of the organism is no more than a symbol and that it becomes the foundation for our actions as a fiction, in the sense of an "as if" philosophy (e.g., Hans Vaihinger).

Some physicians have conceived medical practice as being determined by such fictions. But that cannot be so. Oriented by fictions, one can never arrive at definite action. Our cognition is truly no fiction. Though cognition is, of course, limited by the extant state of knowledge and therefore subject to change, it is still real. There is no other reality for the person in action. For medical practice, the body of knowledge, at a given time, is actually the reality.

While, on the one hand, the situation impels us to act, on the other hand, action itself becomes a source of knowledge for us. After all, all certainty arises from verification that knowledge finds in action, or from its correction through action. Thus medical, and probably all biological, cognition is very closely tied up with actions; yet not in the sense of a pragmatism determined by extraneous norms, but as action dictated by reality, which in turn can be grasped only through knowledge. The relation between this type of action and knowledge is not meant to be an extraneous one between two independent factors, like the usual connection between theory and practical application in medical science. Rather, knowledge and action are interrelated in a dialectically determined manner. Knowledge without action is no knowledge, and action without knowledge is no action. Both mutually originate in each other, in the test of their fruitfulness, as well as in their adequacy to reality, and their aptitude to maintain nature, rather than to disturb or to distort it. In the physician, to speak concretely, knowledge and action arise together in their suitability to help preserve, as far as possible, the living human being in its specific nature.

This "cognition action" demands free decision because of the ever-existing incompleteness of biological knowledge. Here, the holistic conception manifests its quite unique significance for medicine, in the relationship between physician and patient. If regaining health means loss of essence, this implies greater dependence on the environment, stronger bonds to environmental events; a decline from multiform, living behavior to a more limited, compulsive, mechanical behavior; a disintegration from a personally patterned, uniquely directed, behavioral organization to reactions governed more by the law of causality. In short, it means limitation of freedom. This, however, implies that medical decision always requires an encroachment on the freedom of the other person.

Thus the whole problem complex of the concept of freedom enters into medical practice. The difficulties are aggravated, since in any treatment the free decision of the patient himself must not be disregarded. Thus, the patient frequently has the choice whether he wants to accept – corresponding to the change caused by the disease – a limitation of the milieu and the resulting limitation of freedom, or less limitation and more suffering instead. If the patient bears more suffering, he will gain in possibilities of performing since therapeutic measures may be apt to reduce suffering but at the same time diminish the performances. He must choose between a greater lack of freedom and greater suffering. It is quite obvious that this is not a superficial alternative but that this decision touches metaphysical depths. Thus, quite often, it is in disease than an individual reveals his true nature.

Does it not surpass the competence of the physician, in such a situation, to give counsel or, what is more, guidance? At any event, he will be able to do so, only if he is completely under the conviction that the physician-patient relationship is not a situation depending alone on the knowledge of the law of causality but that it is a coming to terms of two persons, in which the one wants to help the other to gain a pattern that corresponds, as much as possible, to his nature. This emphasis on the personal relationship between physician and patient marks off, impressively, the contrast between the modern medical point of view and the mere natural-science mentality of the physicians at the turn of the century. Although it may often seem as if the physician were interfering only with the bodily or mental event, he must always keep in mind that any effective interference, no matter how apparently superficial, must affect the patient's essential nature. He must remember that any interference, since it springs from freedom, affects the freedom of another person. From the holistic approach, this statement is self-evident.

Thus, action leads us not only to deeper understanding in general, insofar as we check on our ideas regarding part processes by the effects that our actions have but also to a deeper understanding of the nature of the specific organism in question. The impossibility of grasping the phenomenon of disease in a way other than by introducing the factor of freedom leads us to the recognition of an important attribute of man, namely, recognition of his potentiality for freedom, his necessity to realize his nature by free decision.

However, this difficulty in action, because of the responsibility for the specific nature of a patient, exists in a similar manner in dealings with any living being whatsoever. And since we are so far from a real knowledge of the essential nature of animals, we should not interfere with their mode of living without remaining conscious of this problem.

Our discussion has led us to a subject that seems far removed from the usual biological topics. With the concepts of freedom and responsibility we enter into the spiritual sphere and seem to remove ourselves from natural science. To be sure, this is not the first reference of this kind that we have made during our attempt to understand human behavior. After all, freedom is merely the expression of that kind of behavior that the analysis of brain-injured patients has led us to regard as an essential attribute of human nature. We shall encounter these spiritual problems in the following discussion of the concept of anomaly.

On Anomaly and Species

The assumption that a qualitative change as to content is part of recuperation with residual defect opens the way for a discussion of the relation between disease and anomaly. Anomaly always represents a deviation as to content from a norm in some way defined. Also, in dealing with the problem of anomaly, we want to discuss primarily the conditions in man. Of course, there certainly are anomalies in animals. But in the first place, they are usually much more difficult to describe because we are much less trained to identify them. This difficulty begins even when we are faced with members of "races" with which we are less familiar. And in the second place, it is almost impossible to determine, in animals, the nature of a species so clearly that a deviation from it could be characterized with any degree of certainty. This difficulty is due to the interference of man, as in breeding, feeding, and so on. The so-called purity of species, which undoubtedly is essentially the product of human breeding, certainly cannot serve as a criterion.

Anomaly differs from disease in two ways. It does not necessarily entail a shock to the individual's being. It requires for its understanding, besides closer reference to the individual proper, reference to a larger social unit. Certainly, individuality in general is to be viewed only within the larger frame of social relations; and its "responsiveness" is, at the same time, determined by this relation. We have seen that recuperation, in spite of defect, requires the cooperation of fellow men or, in more general terms, it must be embedded in the community of fellow man.

But the converse can also be true: lack of responsiveness can arise from a disturbance of the relation to the wider social field. This plays an important part, for example, in the origin of many mental diseases. For anomaly, the relation to the social field is still more primary. Anomaly can be understood only in reference to a "superindividual" norm.[8] But as long as this norm is determined, so to speak, only negatively in comparison with the individual norm and as long as this "superindividual" concept is filled with inherently alien contents, just so long will we remain in the sphere of those atomistic approaches that we have rejected. Furthermore, in this instance it is expedient to aim at the prototype of this more comprehensive "entity." Oriented about this prototype, "anomaly" can become intelligible as a phenomenon that appears under certain circumstances that can be definitely revealed. In our attempt to arrive at such a comprehensive prototype, we are confronted with difficulties still greater than in the determination of the individual whole. One may, according to Uexküll, define the species as that number of different individuals that, when crossed, can still produce offspring, capable of living and propagating.[9] Here we find, as in the individual norm, that the potentiality "to be" is the basis for the determination of the prototype. It cannot be overlooked that the concept of potentiality – "to be" – is somewhat undefined. Particularly with reference to man, it requires that his entire complicated psychophysical nature be taken into consideration.

Regarding the superordinated whole, concepts like "tribe," "family," "species," "race," "nation," "state," and "humanity" are yet to be defined. The problem arises as to whether they are genuine forms of Being that facilitate the understanding of the individual Being – the object with which we are ultimately concerned. Of course, we cannot take

343

up the difficult problems that are here involved. However, an understanding of anomaly, its effect on the individual, and its handling by society can be obtained only through a clarification of these concepts.

Anomaly has to be considered in two respects: on one hand, from the point of view of the wider "entity" to which the anomalous individual belongs by "nature"; on the other hand, from the point of view of the more specific community in which he lives. This means, in this case: on the one hand, "mankind," on the other hand, the specific communities, such as "nation," "race," and so on.

The first classification, definition of anomaly as deviation from human nature in general, will be simpler than the second, the character of which is very problematic. Certain phenomena will immediately be regarded as not human, as deviation from the "human." There is hardly any disagreement that certain peculiarities are characteristic traits of every human being. Here a naive prescientific knowledge of human nature comes to light. It only seemingly conflicts with this idea when we find, in certain human "races," customs and observances that appear "inhuman" to the civilized and when various races indulge in such mutual criticisms. It is exactly by means of such examples that one can demonstrate that such criticism often does not correspond to the facts, for example, that the experiences and motives in group behavior may be entirely different from those that were assumed or, in general terms, demonstrate that these "findings" were errors that have sprung from an isolating approach.

If, for example, we single out one feature from its natural context in the life pattern of a "primitive" people and subject it to a measuring principle intrinsically foreign to it, then we must arrive at the same false generalization as in reflex theory. In order to describe correctly and understand the structure of an individual phenomenon, we have to refer to the total pattern to which it belongs. With this frame of reference in mind, a great many "inhuman" phenomena have turned out to be very human! This discovery signifies that caution is imperative. Here we are still in the first steps of empirical research, although especially the last decades of anthropological research have brought many advances. We must get over the habit of judging "other" people by our own standards, and we should attempt to understand these phenomena more from their pertinent nature; and then many peculiarities that at first appear as differences between ourselves and the "others" will turn out to be

344

nothing but modifications of essential aspects of human nature that occur under certain circumstances – as the expression of a special development of human traits.[10]

For example, it is easy to show that, in so-called primitive man, various traits have experienced a development different from that in so-called civilized man. But we will have to beware of inferring, from these differences in development, "lower" or "higher" organizations and races. We shall discuss below what meaning, if any, these words may have. To the extent that further experience will teach us that individuals of completely different extraction may develop almost alike, if reared in the same environment, the more such conclusions as to lower and higher races will be ruled out. Then the phenomenon of a difference in skin color will certainly no longer be reason for construing differences of value.

The decision whether, and to what degree, if any, such differences may exist can be approached only by a true cognition of the essential nature of the respective groups. We are here not only at the very beginning of our knowledge but are also faced with a jungle of confusion that is artificially preserved through all kinds of prejudices, which in part are certainly the outgrowth of, and maintained by, moral deficiencies. In part, however, they owe their origin to the errors of the isolating procedure. A proper, holistically oriented view certainly would disclose many an error in this field. I should not fail to emphasize here that many authors, in the present controversy on racial issues, abuse concepts such as "essential nature" and "holistic reference."

The prototype of the organism and the "essential nature" at which we are aiming in our analysis has nothing to do with evaluations, indoctrinated by some ideology that is nothing else than the expression of a political creed and bias. All theorems hitherto advanced to suggest the inferiority or superiority of a particular group or entity are based on a misconception and abuse of what is factually holistic. Instead of carefully investigating what really belongs to the essential nature of a group – apart from historico-economic pattern – they introduce unscientific axioms, for instance, the myth of blood, and others. All notions of that kind are totally unjustified when spuriously linked to the methodology and results of modern empirical research or to posited whole-part relations.

Such confusions regarding the judgment of the "nature" of a race, or even the decision as to whether such a thing as race exists at all, make a correct judgment of anomaly particularly difficult. This judgment would require scientific fundaments that we do not as yet possess. Usually it is oriented around accidental findings in the concrete environment. The latter are evaluated according to the average somatic and mental peculiarities and, in addition, to the prevailing prejudices. Therefore, it is possible that the same anomalies may find quite different evaluation as times change. In the evaluation of an anomaly, the question of the disturbance by it stands much in the foreground. On this point, our consideration coincides again with the procedure for deciding what disease is. In the latter case, the frame of reference is the "Being" of the individual, whereas in anomalies, it is the Being of a larger entity, the existence of which might be threatened with catastrophic shocks by disturbances through the anomalous individual – now or in the future.

If the anomaly is such that the individual in question continuously meets, in the milieu in which he lives, tasks that he cannot solve, then, in turn, anomaly becomes dangerous for him. He is forced to withdraw – to limit his milieu – or he will perish from the continual catastrophic reactions to which he is exposed. At any rate, he will not be able to "actualize" himself essentially. As far as actualization is possible he will very probably represent a danger factor to the community, although this might frequently only supposedly be the case. Then the community will reach the conclusion that it has the right to rid itself of this individual. Every race theorist who, on the assumption of "superior" and "inferior" races, wants to exclude the members of the "inferior" race as perniciously anomalous acts in this irresponsible way. Any such procedure, in order to be biologically justified, would have to employ methodologically the holistic reference in two ways, first in deciding on the possibility of lesser or greater value of a race and second in estimating the potential danger of the anomalous for the community: that danger may be represented more through his hereditary mass than through his personal existence. All this exemplifies the error that arises from assuming as absolute the phenomena obtained through isolating procedure.

Heredity and Breeding
In the atomistic interpretation of hereditary processes, the attempt to explain the origin of an individual through the sum of separate heredi-

tary factors, we have, in the usual procedure, a complete analogy with the procedure of reflexology. Certainly nobody will fail to admire Gregor Mendel's experiments and to appreciate the knowledge that we have gained through them regarding heredity and partitive characteristics — especially if one adds the more recent experiments that have shown the possibility of singling out, in subtle ways, circumscribed features in experiments on heredity.

But just as there is no way from the reflexes to an understanding of the organism as a whole, so also is there no direct way from partitive characteristics, which genetics singles out through analysis, to an understanding of the genesis of an individual! If we think that there is such a direct connection, we make the mistake of regarding certain peculiarities as characteristic for the individual. On the contrary, special peculiarities gain their significance by their being considered within their functional "belongingness" to the whole of an individual. As H.F. Jordan has emphasized, it is not true that we are dealing with the inheritance of independent elements, but rather with total characteristics. According to him, the effect of the gene can be understood only from its relation to the whole.

But even in the results of the atomistic type of genetic experiments, essential, total characteristics of the respective organisms become manifest. The mere fact that dominant and recessive factors exist at all indicates that some factors are more related to the essential nature than are others. Recessive characteristics are probably due to the fact that the crossing of a creature with another having other dominant traits causes mixtures that do not possess the same hereditary potency. In competition with the dominant factors the recessive ones cannot make themselves effective, or only with difficulties, and therefore appear only when there is a crossing with an animal that has an affinity for this particular trait.

Probably the dominant hereditary factors are traits that are related to what we have called the "constants." But these constitute the individual only in the respective concatenation as given through the greater or lesser effectiveness of recessive factors. The knowledge of the factors and their hereditary value in the experimental procedure offers us but very preliminary information regarding the genesis of the individual. One usually overlooks this fact because the exact genetic experiments are made on animals, or even plants, where it is not only difficult or almost impossible to grasp such a thing as individuality, but also where our view is so biased by our interest in artificially selected elements that the experimenter therefore sees practically only these.

The decision as to which is a dominant and which a recessive characteristic presupposes real knowledge of the nature of the individual to which they belong. Thus one must not be surprised that the evaluation of the actual phenomena becomes increasingly difficult and that new superordinated factors have continually had to be introduced in order to be able to retain the original genetic atomistic concept.

A few quotations from recent papers may show that our critical remarks are in accord with the more recent views of well-known geneticists.[11] "One must never forget that the individual gene acts only in interplay with the other constitutional elements of the geno-type and with the life-situation."[12] "All pheno-typical details are determined by the configurational type to which they belong.... It is probably no exaggeration to say that each gene, in the germ-plasm, influences several or possibly many parts of the body, in other words that the entire germ-plasm is active in the development of every part of the body" (in the view of Morgan). "In the drosophila, a great many factors, at least fifty, participate in the formation of an eye color.... Careful observation has disclosed that each individual gene does not influence only one characteristic, but many, probably the entire body."[13] Heinrich Poll writes: "The atomistic character of the genetic conception strongly demands compensation in form of a holistic view such as a theory of differentiation or 'Melistik.' The 'unio mystica' of the units does not take place on the basis of a secondary union of primally preexisting particles ('Meronten'). This idea assumes a primary disjointedness of members ('Melonten'), the independence of which can be made perceptible only secondarily."[14] These words of Poll indicate the holistic tenor of modern genetics. Because I am lacking sufficient experience of my own in this field, I do not dare to decide whether, from such a view, the gene is recognized as a "part" gained through a definite method, in a way similar to that we have shown for the reflexes.

One of the main errors of geneticists, namely, to apply to human beings the laws deduced from breeding experiments in plants or lower animals, owes its origin particularly to this failure to recognize the atomistic character of the isolating method. Genetics has practically nowhere proved to be so fatal as in this simplified method of "transfer." To begin with, geneticists overlooked the fact that the breeding experiments took place under quite unnatural conditions. They were concerned with planned inbreeding, with the bringing about of "pure lines," and with the selection of attributes that were not chosen with respect to whether they were relevant to the essential nature. Thus one was able, in the last analysis, to breed creatures with properties arbitrarily singled out.

The experiments that genetics really has carried out were not experiments in heredity, in the sense of an experimental observation of the natural genesis, but experiments of the drill type (cf. pp. 380ff.) with all their characteristic positive and negative aspects. As long as breeding is not concerned with the knowledge of the essential nature of creatures and the way of their heredity but rather with the breeding of specific traits useful for man, just so long are the experiments useful – as useful as the overpowering of nature through technology. They have provided a certain insight into the essence of nature, but only insofar as they have disclosed how far such application of force to nature is bearable, which in turn reveals certain characteristics of creatures. Finally they have provided us with some information regarding the aids necessary to make existence in this "border state" possible.

If it were the task of human genetics and eugenics to breed human beings with definite traits, irrespective of man's essential nature, then one could possibly concede that results of plant experimentation would be applicable to human beings. To be sure, such experiments in human beings would hardly yield the expected success. The human species could probably not really live in the border situation in which the pertinent experiments have to place them. The capacity limits of existence might be overstepped at the same time and so many catastrophic reactions result that the properties that the "breeding" intended could not be achieved. Breeding could only result if it turned on and aimed at traits essential to the human subject. But then it would have to be altogether different.

In all such experiments, one overlooks the fact that one of the essential traits for the human being is individuality and freedom, and that these can be curbed only up to a certain point without endangering the capacity of its existence. The reality of intellect, of self-determination, which even in its most primitive form represents essential human characteristics, dooms to failure any breeding experiment of the usual type.

However, if the regulation of hereditary conditions aims not at specific characteristics but aspires to meliorate the human race by eliminating the unfit individuals, such endeavor presupposes a thorough knowledge of the significance of individual peculiarities for human natures. And who would venture any decision in this respect at the present state of research! Even in the field of study where, relatively, we know the most concerning the harmful effects of pathological changes on the progeny, if we consider the matter without bias we realize that nothing definite has as yet been ascertained. The reason is that we can neither determine nor predict when and where abnormality becomes harmful or, perhaps, extremely valuable for the individual and the community as well.

For example, let us consider only the discussion on sterilization of manic-depressives, the disposition to which disease is undoubtedly hereditary to a high degree. Who would care to doubt the capability – if not superiority – of many an individual with greater or less manic-depressive predispositions. If one considers oneself justified in interfering with human self-determination, even as far as the progeny is concerned, one may do that only at one's own risk. But we should not attempt to take recourse to "inherent" nature for the justification of such a procedure, in regard to the foundations of which we do not yet possess, and can scarcely ever hope to possess, knowledge.

Having said all that, it must appear unusually difficult to gain the correct attitude for our dealings with anomalies in the sense of a deviation from an average or, even more so, from an ideal type. The situation is somewhat different if we regard anomaly from the point of view of the individual norm. One will have to find the milieu best suited for the anomalous. Society will have to do this from the twofold point of view, namely, to protect itself from the dangers of anomaly and at the same time to enable the anomalous individual to exist. In the ultimate analysis, there is no essential difference between the two points of view. After all, it becomes necessary for society to protect itself only so long as the anomalous individual does not live in the proper milieu. If he lives in a proper milieu, he is not dangerous, because he is in an ordered state. This result seems important to us, because it offers us the criterion for the only correct way of biological action. True, one can extinguish what one considers anomalous. But then the question arises whether, in so doing, one acts in accordance with the "essence of Being," whether one does justice to freedom – that trait that our discussion of the phenomenon of disease and of anomaly has proved to be the very characteristic of human nature.

CHAPTER ELEVEN

On Life and Mind.

The Problem of Organismic Hierarchy

> Man is neither angel nor animal, and it is unfortunate that he
> who tries to make of him an angel, makes of him an animal.
>
> – Pascal

The So-Called Antagonism Between Life and Mind

If what is usually designated as mind really belongs to human nature,
then we cannot avoid this problem of mind. According to our basic
stand, we do not concede the existence of anything "apart from" or
"additional to" but always regard the organism as a whole in which segregation of any sort is artificial and in which every phenomenon is a
manifestation of the whole.

The idea of an antagonism between "nature" and "mind" is ages old,
and one has tried in various ways to overcome this bifurcation. It is usually considered as an antagonism between consciousness, thinking,
"act," on the one side, and life and immediate Being on the other side.
In recent times, this view finds its most rugged expression in the philosophy of Klages which gives definite preference to life, and in which
mind appears as the opponent of life, as a power that is hostile to life.
To Max Scheler, mind also appears in opposition to life, although under
an entirely different evaluation, directly opposite to the one of Klages.[1]
For Scheler, no transition from mind to life exists. "The new principle
which makes man man, is outside of anything that we call life in the
widest sense of the word." It is a principle opposed to anything called
life. It does not mean an enhancement of natural life energies, but their
inhibition, a turning away from all that life is driving toward. Man, as a
"spiritual" being, is no longer tied to his drives and his immediate
milieu; he is milieu autonomous, and as we should like to call it, "world

open." For the human being alone has "world." To him, as well as to the animal, "the world is given originally, as centers of resistance – and reaction. While the animal submerges 'ecstatically' in them, the human alone is the creature which can elevate these experiences to objects." It is characteristic for him that he is able to say "no" to the vital sphere; he is an "ascetic of life."

From the metaphysical point of view, it is this that determines man's peculiarity and superiority as compared with all other manifestations of life. Yet, for Scheler, it is a matter of course that the mind is neither the product of asceticism, nor that it originates from the repression of drives through sublimation – as Freud holds. Rather, that "negative" activity proper, of "saying no" to reality, constitutes, so to speak, "the source of energy, and with that, man's potentiality to manifest himself." Mind in itself is powerless. It is only able to direct and guide by presenting ideas to the drive impulses. "The goal and end of all finite Being and Becoming is the mutual penetration of the originally powerless mind, and the originally demonic urge, an urge blind towards all spiritual ideas and values."

Objections in this direction are apt to arise against this profound philosophy. What one understands by mind will always depend on what one understands by life and nature. It seems to us that in general the conception of mind is (and for Scheler also) determined by an incorrect notion of the phenomenon of life, because one has torn it, "isolated" it, from the whole to which it belongs. In this way life has become imbued with characteristics not really attributable to it, a mere artifact of isolating description. If one takes life in the sense of a "blind urge," it is already dubious whether, from that basis, animality can be satisfactorily understood; certainly it cannot if one regards "drive" as determined only by extraneous stimuli and satisfaction as the simple release of tensions.

All our arguments against the possibility of a mere drive theory of behavior are to be recalled at this point. Even animal behavior indicates holistic patterning and individuation, neither of which can find their realization through mere drive release. Here great caution in evaluation of the data is imperative. The observations usually originate from such situations, which by themselves occasion a special behavior and which in turn might then easily appear as the result of drive release. If, subsequently, a deviation is observed, a new drive (or variable) is only too readily at hand to solve the puzzle. The drive theory, through the simplicity of its explanations, that is, through the deceiving simplicity that the term itself involves, impedes the exploration of animal life, which still lies in complete darkness. Certainly we have no reason to assume that for the animal there exists a world in the objectified sense (cf. p. 210). But this still does not make the animal a creature that is simply passively bound in a frame of certain drives, driven only by environmental stimuli. It appears this way only in isolating considerations.

As we have seen, animal behavior cannot be understood as a summation of single processes. It points, rather, to an individual organization, on which basis alone it becomes intelligible as the expression of the tendency to actualize itself according to the circumstances. In this general characteristic of animal nature, I find myself in agreement with Alverdes, Frederik Buytendijk, and others. Likewise for the animal, the environment is not given as absolute but arises in the animal's being and acting. Further, the so-called drives are manifestations of the animal in definite situations that only indicate its nature; they are not attributes by which the animal could be directly understood. We must not only reject a characterization of the animal as a creature determined by drives and the environment, but also that of man as a sum of drive systems and mind, where the mind would inhibit life. This view also reflects the misconceptions of the isolating approach, the tendency to elevate the phenomena obtained by this method to absolute and real entities. As to the isolating approach, phenomena that allow for a classification into two opposing realms can be produced very readily. Or, to state it more carefully, if one desires to understand human nature, one must try to understand these phenomena as the manifestations of one unitary being, as phenomena revealed through the isolating manner and changed in a specific way through that isolation.

In the conception of man, this dualism suggests itself because only in the rare moments of his adequate actualization, only in a state of full "centering" does that holistic entirety manifest itself, in which entirety there is no conflict between "drives" and "mind." Because of a lack in perfect centering, which is part of the imperfection of human nature, usually such contrariety, corresponding to isolation, becomes phenomenally obvious. Nevertheless, it would be a mistake to regard these phenomena as flowing from two separate realms, because that would exclude any adequate apprehension of behavior. Once a philosophy has divorced "vital sphere" and "mind," they can never become reunited thereafter. No matter how such union may be defined, it never corresponds to the real and original entirety. Here the same is true as in all instances in which a contrast between body and soul, between reflex and performance, between perception and action, has been established. But the reverse is quite possible: proceeding from that holistic entirety, one can understand the particulars as partitive regulations or limitations of the whole.

The so-called vital sphere and the life process as a whole
What Scheler calls the "vital sphere," if it is presumed to be synonymous with animal behavior, does not exist in human beings. Such an assumption would do an injustice to the animals as well as to human beings. What appears to us to be animal-like is usually a behavior in which the human species has lost, to a large degree, the specifically human characteristic, that is, a behavior that represents a reduction of human nature, be it through illness, poisoning, or abnormal outside stimuli. However, what really remains has only a very superficial resemblance to animal behavior. It lacks the holistic reference to the essential nature of ordered behavior, which characterizes the normal life of animals. It is disordered, distorted, and mechanical. The attempt has often been made to compare the performances of patients to those of animals, even to go so far as to explain the phenomena as the emergence of animal characteristics. Nothing could be further from the truth.[2] Thus the presupposed characteristics of the "vital sphere," in Scheler, do not stand the test. Scheler's phenomenological analyses of human nature and its discord, and of the antagonistic forces that manifest themselves in it, are certainly enlightening. But as Cassirer argues, "by shifting in his interpretation from an assumed antagonism as to functional contrast, to an assumed antagonism as to substance, Scheler obstructs true understanding. It becomes unintelligible how two so antagonistic potencies can be active in one being, without a further regulating principle."[3] We again face the theorem of antagonism, which we have to reject here as before. Moreover, Scheler's theory leads to a conflict in itself, as he does not ascribe to mind real existence (as to life) but regards it as a pure "act." This raises the particular difficulty of how it is at all possible that the powerless mind could influence "brute" life. Cassirer says: "If one wants to solve this riddle, one has to

go back to a common metaphysical world substrate, which connects what is, and always will be plainly heterogeneous for us, and nevertheless unites it into one whole. By assuming this of course, the Gordian knot would not be untied, but cut in two." This necessity of introducing additionally a common, basic world substrate as a means to establish order is similar to the way of thinking that has necessitated the auxiliary assumption of regulative centers.

Cassirer puts the question, How is it to be understood that life, if it is only a blind urge, can follow the model that the idea places before it? How, on the other hand, could the mind accomplish this arrest, this peculiar damming of the life forces and drives, if it were originally simply powerless?[4] According to Cassirer, this difficulty evidently can be solved only if, recognizing the antagonism between mind and life, one understands the mind not merely as a static factor (Stillsteher) but recognizes its actively as being of the same kind as that of life, differing only in direction: the mind is thereby conceived as taking charge of the indirect forming of images, and life as taking charge of the immediate operating and performing. Then the difference is not that life is only operative and the mind only formative and inoperative but rather that, in comparison with the direct operation of the vital sphere, the operation of the mind is indirect. "Then the tension between the ego and the environment is not to be conceived of as immediately discharging; the spark, so to speak, no longer jumps directly from one to the other. Rather the mediation occurs in a way that, instead of going through the medium of processes and reactions, leads through the medium of creative forming. Only at the end of this long and difficult detour of inner creative activity does reality again enter man's horizon."[5] This asceticism that Scheler has described as characteristic for the mind "is not the turning away from life as such, but an inner transformation and reversal which life in itself undergoes. In this reversal, in this turning from 'life' to the 'idea,' we do not find the antagonism between a static principle and one of motion, nor an inactive principle of rest, as against 'the restless flow of Becoming.' The manifold worlds of imagery which man places between himself and reality (i.e. the intermediate sphere of symbolic forms) have not the purpose to remove and repel reality but to gain through distance the proper perspective, in order to raise reality to visibility as compared to the mere palpability which immediate proximity imposes."[6]

If one regards life and mind not as two transcendentally separated entities but rather accepts them as merely functionally contrasting operations, then it is no longer necessary "to regard the mind as a principle which is foreign or hostile to all life, but it can be understood as a turn and reversal of life itself – a transformation which life undergoes in itself to the degree in which it passes from the sphere of mere organismic patterning and performing into the sphere of symbolic forming – of ideational forming.... The drama proper does not take place between life and mind but in the center of the realm of the mind, in its very focus.... Therefore, the mind is not only – as Scheler has defined it – the ascetic of life, not only the potentiality of 'saying no' to all vital spheres, but mind is the principle which is capable of negating itself."

We can well subscribe to this interpretation, inasmuch as it describes mind and life as two manifestations that, by virtue of their cooperative action, their mutual negation and reconciliation are peculiar to the nature of man. Yet the presentation of Cassirer seems to us open to misunderstandings on account of the still-remaining ambiguity of the terms "life" and "mind." In the last analysis, both terms are unsuited to describe that dimension in which the tension takes place, the tension that manifests itself in the two contrasting phenomena of "mind" and "life" – of "intellect" and "urge." The possible ambiguity becomes immediately obvious if one compares, for example, the following sentences of Cassirer. On the one hand he says that asceticism is an "inner transformation and reversal which life undergoes in itself...the mind must be understood as a turn and reversal of life itself."[7] On the other hand he says: "Is not life after all something else and something more than blind urge?"[8]

If these two versions are to be reconciled and if we interpret Cassirer correctly, then the latter sentence voices his basic concept more unequivocally, inasmuch as life and mind now appear merely as two different aspects of one and the same being within this being proper, which in itself issues the energy of "forming" and "acting." Only in this case the antagonism would not be one between two contradictory potencies of nature, an antagonism for which one could not predict how it would ever resolve itself.[9] Only then would it become clear that the antagonism between mind and life corresponds to a struggle within that unitary entity that we describe as "essential nature."

Clear, unambiguous terms seem necessary to us at this point, not because of a superficial pedantry but because only then does it become possible to avoid certain factual ambiguities that would easily creep into the reader's interpretation through loose usage of the terms "mind" and "life." Otherwise, life as it appears in the human being, and as it appears in animals, would be easily confounded. Cassirer himself is inclined to make this mistake when, for example, he follows the opinion that also "relatively very complicated instinct-performances of animals seem to be nothing but chain reflexes," and when he talks of "vital sphere" as if it were something similar in man and animal, as if it were exactly that which characterizes life. But life in animal nature is something different from life in human nature. This difference can become a true problem only if one does not obscure it by using the same terms in treating man and animal. That which is superordinated, and to which mind and life belong, we are inclined to call organism, entity of a specific kind, or at times simply life, though not in the usual sense of the word.

One cannot talk of a negation of the vital sphere through the mind, because neither the vital nor the mind are separate potencies. The tension under which the human being lives, which suggests the idea of two antagonistic forces within him, is based on the fundamental characteristic of human nature: the potentiality to focus on the "possible," to arrest, so to speak, the world in its course, to picture it, and to shape the coming to terms with the world by virtue of this ability. This does not only equip the human subject with what is called "mind," but it also renders him susceptible to the risk involved in the adjustment to the world and drives him toward negation or conquest. To say no is fundamentally the expression of becoming conscious of the tension that arises in the coming to terms of the human organism with the world. The coming to terms in turn passes through catastrophic reactions and is experienced as conflict and resolution within man. The catastrophic reactions in general do not simply negate the "other" but represent only a transition for the purpose of coming to terms of the organism and the other, during which adjustment, performance alone develops.

Likewise the negation of the world by the mind represents only a transition toward ordered existence, in which the tensions are balanced and performance emerges. The mind does not deny the senses (the "vital") but gives form to the phenomena that appear through the senses; thereby it helps to achieve that adaptation by which nature and mind, artificially separated through isolating analysis, preserve the unity in which human nature alone actualizes itself. It is a complete misapprehension of the essence of the mind, if one regards as its task only the negation of what the vital sphere furnishes. The negation is only the transition to a higher, or real level of existence, in which "mind" and "life" operate in unison, and in this sense the negation is ultimately taken back. The negation is similar to the catastrophic reaction that is conditioned through the separation between the self and the "other." This contrast creates the tension that as a transition leads to the real existence in an always-positive sense. As long as the human being only negates within himself that which we call nature, he is not himself, but at best only in a struggle, insufficiently centered and unproductive.

The human being's surrender to nature is never an act purely confined to the vital sphere. Only through artificial isolation do we find something that we can call purely vital. And if at all, it is only possible in the human subject; only his ability to isolate parts artificially, and thus to surrender these parts of himself to adjustment with the environment, creates the so-called vital sphere that has similarities with what we have called drill.

It is only reason that enables a creature to be "more bestial than any beast." No such sphere exists in animals. In the human species it becomes most obvious through defective integration, as in disease. Then we see that the drive becomes outstanding. But we may also see simultaneously, or in a change of conditions at different times, that the world narrows down to such an extent that neither the mental nor the "vital" find a place. Impairment of the conceptual function (representational, or "propositional," as Head called it) also takes from the human being the possibility of giving himself over to the senses. Such patients, for instance, require a very special outside aid in order even to initiate sexual intercourse.[10] In general, an exaggerated strong drive is out of the question in such cases. On the contrary, only when the immision of the sexual organ has taken place through purely extraneous manipulation can the sexual act be set going.

In the sense of reason in knowledge, we attribute equal importance to "mind" and "vital sphere" as essential traits. But we certainly do not deny that the tension in the human being is of a specific quality; it does not consist, as in animals, only in the momentary feeling of danger and anxiety but becomes conscious and takes on factual, objectified form.

360

Thus this tension makes an entirely different attitude possible, which manifests itself in the phenomenon of fear and of the freedom to cope with it, that is to say, to realize oneself in spite of danger, and to shape the world. All shaping of the world, everything we call culture, becomes intelligible only from this concerted effort of "mind" and "vital sphere," or better of the unitary whole of human nature that is shaped in this particular mold.

Our view of the mind within the total of human nature has, so we trust proved that the problem of mind is justified in the frame of biology, and also that it has to be included, because only in this way has it been possible to differentiate between man and animal.

Biology and ontology
To be sure, one could doubt whether this topic could still be called biology. Perhaps some people would think it better to talk of ontology, since all experience evidently becomes intelligible for us only by referring it back to a sphere that one customarily does not call the sphere of life. Still we should like to retain the term "biology." When we speak here of life, of nature, of organism, we use terms which certainly can easily be misunderstood because they are so burdened with all kinds of often-discussed definitions. But there is certainly no doubt as to how we want them to be understood here: all creatures have a specific nature, and all represent wholes having the character of an individuality. Therefore we can obtain insight in all living forms by one methodological principle – the holistic. This is, to a certain extent, an anticipation, but we believe it is justified through the direct observation of nature.

In man, mind (consciousness, intellect) is as much part of this individual whole as the attitude (feelings and so on) and the somatic (bodily processes). We call the whole the living being, because only in this way are we able to include the relation between consciousness, the feelings, and the somatic. As long as nature manifests itself in the form of the living body, the mind, if it is part of it, has something to do with the body as it has with all other behavioral aspects. This standpoint has the advantage that one is able to regard every phenomenon within empirical reach, the reflexes as well as the mind, primarily as data. This standpoint does not commit one to any theory that may lead in the wrong direction. Nor does it prevent one from asking: What is the place of this or that phenomenon in the whole? What does it mean for the whole?

Only from such a view is it possible to consider man and animal on a unitary basis. We need no longer fear that, from the height to which the analysis of the mind of man has led us, a descent to "biological being" is not possible. It is this holistic approach, comprising all aspects, which is our concern. We are not interested in developing general postulates for an anthropology, no matter how important this task may appear to us. But the holistic approach, with man as the starting point, should furnish us with the basis for gaining an understanding of life phenomena. We can refute the objection that scientific dealing with human nature leads in principle beyond the sphere of life and that the general postulates for knowledge of man differ from those of the rest of living beings.

I hope that I may not be misunderstood. By assuming a common basis of knowledge, we do not intend to claim that the difference between man and animal is merely one of degree. The common factor rests first in the similarity of the total organization, in the similarity as to holistic structure. Along with this similarity another similarity as to particulars can be found in isolating techniques. But this similarity would not necessarily signify equality. It could, at the most, refer to a unitary, basic plan that manifests itself in similar details in man and animal. The details themselves could then have different meanings in each instance, since all phenomena gained by the isolating method achieve significance only by virtue of their relation to their respective whole.

The line of demarcation between two species seems to us indeed insurmountable, and thus also the line of distinction between human beings and animals. One thing we know: the human being cannot be regarded as a creature in which something was only added to the animal. Johann Gottfried von Herder already has recognized this clearly. He says: "One has taken the human intellect as a separate force in the soul which man obtained as a special addition in preference to all animals. This is, of course, philosophical nonsense, no matter how great the philosophers may be who say so. All individualized powers of man and animal are nothing but metaphysical abstractions. They are abstracted because our weak intellect could not grasp them all at once. They are treated in separate chapters, not because they operate compartmentally in nature, but because a textbook presents them best in this way.... Yet every-

where, the whole, undivided life is at work." Every segregated peculiarity is lawfully connected with every other. And Herder concludes, "If
man had drives of the animal kind, he would not have what we call reason.... If man had the sense of animals, he would not have reason."

We must continually bear in mind such considerations whenever
we compare single items of various creatures and whenever we attempt
to establish a hierarchy of living beings, unless we want to commit grave
errors by false analogies.

The Hierarchic Structure of Life

> In the human mind, just as in the universe, there is no top or
> bottom. All parts have an equal claim upon a common center
> which manifests its hidden existence in the harmonious
> relationship of the parts to it.
>
> — Goethe, *Rezension zu Stidenroth*,
> "Psychologie," Ges. naturwissensch. Schriften

The problem of adequate criteria

The analysis of the changes in cases of brain lesion has, in the beginning of our presentation, suggested that the organism is stratified as to
higher and simpler performance levels and that this may hold for all life
in general. We meet this problem in various discussions, in the discussion of the scale from the inorganic to the organic, from plants to animals, and in the animal phyla itself, from the lower to the higher orders,
up to the human species. We meet it in the discussion of the hierarchy
of performances within a single organism and finally in the discussion
of the scale from lower to higher human individuals or human races.

As far back as Plato we find the attempt to bring the three powers
of the soul, which he considered hierarchically stratified, in relation
to the arrangement of the body as to head, chest, and abdomen. Cuvier
talks of a hierarchy in which the central nervous system, as the center
of the animal functions, occupies the highest level, the heart and the
circulatory organs are centers for the vegetative system next below, and
the lowest are the digestive organs that as the sources of matter and
energy take care of the preservation of life.

A hierarchy is usually assumed within the individual organ systems
themselves. For example, in the nervous system the brain is regarded

as the "higher" organ as distinct from the peripheral, the "lower" organs. In the circulatory system, the heart is regarded as the center as compared to the peripheral blood vessels. But we must be very cautious with these and similar hierarchic differentiations, because the division between higher and lower sections within one system is very much subject to the bias of prevailing views. With changes of the latter, the type of distinction itself may undergo great changes.

Today, for instance, the heart has lost much of its predominance as compared to the capillaries. For the nervous system, the situation is similar. During the last decades, parts of the "old brain" have gained more and more significance as compared to the former central position of the cortex, and some would even regard the medulla oblongata as a center for consciousness. It is a problem to what extent the cortex or even the entire nervous system occupies a key position in mental phenomena and whether it must not at least share it with the ductless glands.

With the increasing impossibility of considering the morphologically segregatable organs as isolated apparatuses, an entirely different view comes more and more into the foreground. It became increasingly doubtful whether the differentiation, according to organs, does not owe its origin simply to the fact that some characteristics are more striking and whether these characteristics have really anything to do with the assumed differentiation.

This new conception by logical necessity does not draw the line of demarcation between the morphological and structural boundaries but rather establishes partitions, which cut across the organ systems within the entire body, thereby creating new functional members. The new principle of articulation tries to do greater justice to the idea of a functional organization of the whole organism.

In this connection, new significance may accrue to old notions, which distinguished organismic life as to such basic functions as reproduction (nutrition, growth, propagation), irritability (reaction to stimuli), and sensitivity (conscious sensation) – a tripartition that Schelling conceived as fundamental for the organization of the realm of nature. The new functional idea suggests also Cuvier's analysis, which established a hierarchy of the various organ systems, wherein the system that carried the greater weight for the unitary and complete character of the whole would rank the highest.

We have emphasized before that the rehabilitation after damage

points to an articulated organization according to functional significance. We thought we were justified in assuming that the behavior,
which is impaired or lost through cortical lesion, represents a behavior
particularly significant and essential for human existence. We differentiated between an objectifying and an immediate, concrete, behavioral attitude and spoke of a disintegration to a lower level in those
patients who have lost the objectifying attitude. We have attempted to
characterize the two kinds of behavior, mainly as to their manifestations
in psychological material, such as perception, action, and other functions. We might describe them also in terms of the "expression Gestalt"
or in terms of various somatic processes. Thus, for example, a different energy expenditure is found in the objectifying, voluntary behavior than in the immediate concrete behavior. We know that fatigue, in
a voluntary performance, is stronger than in an involuntary performance.
Of the bodily phenomena, which are expressions of these two types of
behavior, we want to emphasize one in particular: it is the difference
between the significance of the flexor or adduction movements and the
extensor or abduction movements (cf. pp. 127, 343).

The differential functional significance of flexor and extensor movements
Let us summarize in short what we already know: in weak stimulation
one finds, according to Sherrington, a preference of the ipsilateral extensor reflex, whereas only after stronger stimulation the flexor reflex
appears. In cerebellar impairment, we observe a tendency toward extensor and abduction movements (Dusser de Barenne). Decerebrate rigidity, which manifests itself in extensor and abduction posture, can be
"inhibited" through stimulation of larger sectors of the cerebellum.
Transection of the midbrain causes, in the animal, a rigidity of the
extensor and abduction muscles (standing reflex, Sherrington). When
the pyramidal tract in the midbrain is stimulated, we obtain a preference
for the flexor movements (Graham Brown). In chronaxie investigations,
the flexors normally show a lower chronaxie than the extensors, which
is reversed in the foot muscles when the pyramidal tract is injured.
When the cortex is stimulated, flexor reaction occurs more readily
than extensor reaction. Repeated stimulation or preceding stimulation
of the same area of the cortex produces a reversal of effect, which is
more pronounced from flexor to extensor than vice versa.[11] In cerebral injury in particular, the flexors are affected as in hemiplegia of

the leg in the adult or in hemiplegia of the arm in early childhood.

If we sum up these facts, we find everywhere a closer relation of the flexor movements to the cerebral cortex (and to the cerebellar cortex, which apparently represents only an appendix of the former) and of the extensor movements to the deeper lying apparatuses.[12] Thus, weak stimulation of the spinal animal is followed only by extensor movements, and stimulation of the cerebral cortex only by flexor movements. From this we may conclude:

1. Flexor and extensor movements differ in their significance for the organism.

2. The relation to the whole (for which the cerebrum is certainly of great importance) is more intimate in the flexor movements than in the extensor movements.

If we follow other aspects of the organism's behavior, especially that of man, from this functional point of view, we obtain further interesting material. When attention is distracted, we find, in the more "involuntary," more automatic movements, a preference for extensor and abduction movements (e.g., in the involuntary movements during distraction of attention, described by Riese and myself). We know the same for the movements when one stretches to relax. Yawning, also, is usually accompanied by involuntary outward movements of the arms.

In contrast to this, the flexor and adduction movements play a considerable role in voluntary performances. In executing accurate performances, we prefer flexor and adduction movements, while extensor and abduction movements come into the foreground when the performance requires more strength than precision. In abduction, the movements are, of course, voluntarily initiated also. Later on, however, they are continued more independently of us and run "involuntarily." Therefore they cannot be so easily arrested or be carried out so precisely. We throw a ball with extension and abduction movements when it is more a question of strength and distance; however, when greater accuracy is required – for example, when we want to hit a definite goal with a ball – we throw with flexor movements. In the first instance the arm is stretched, in the second, more flexed. This difference becomes particularly clear in writing. Those parts of the letters in which accurate execution is important, like the arcs, slings, and little hooks, are to a great extent executed with flexor and adduction movements, while the straight lines, especially at a letter's end, in which precision is not as important as speed, are executed with extensor and abduction movements.

We may say that the flexor and adduction movements belong more to the voluntary, the extensor and abduction movements more to the involuntary, performances. The former are more holistically determined and of higher functional significance for the intrinsic nature; the latter are of less intimate relation to the whole, are of less functional significance. They rank lower in the functional hierarchy inasmuch as they require the initiation of the voluntary activity and belong to performances that do not originate as much from the center of the personality. The flexor movements have a closer reference to the self, the extensor movements, more reference to the external world.

This also finds expression, for example, in the different influence of color stimulation on flexor and extensor movements. We have already mentioned that green facilitates the performance capacity of the organism and makes the execution of performances more adequate to its nature. In comparison with red, green favors more the flexor movements, allows the organism to be more "itself," and lets it act more "spontaneously," while red causes a stronger attention (distraction) from the outside.[13]

Thus, the difference of the flexor and adduction movements on the one hand, and the extensor and abduction movements on the other hand, becomes a manifestation of different attitudes of the organism to the world. The flexor movements emphasize more the self in contrast to the world, the influence of the ego factor in the apprehension of the world, and, with that, render possible the emancipative distance between ego and world. This finds its specific expression in the convergence of the eyes, the bending of the head and its turning toward the object (usually located slightly below and before us), in fixating it, that is, in the voluntary "grasping" of the world. In contrast to this attitude, a certain surrendering to the world corresponds to the extensor and abduction movements, a more passive mode of being "in" the world, a state of the ego submerged in the world. To this belongs a relaxing convergence of the eyes, backward tilting of the head, and abduction of the arms. The difference can best be illustrated if we contrast the total behavior, the bodily and mental attitude of a person who is concentrating intensely on an object, with that of a person who dances and, touching the ground with nothing more than the tip of his toe, surrenders himself completely to the outer world.

Any impairment of the organism, but especially one of the cerebrum or the cerebellum, is always more disturbing to the voluntary, the flexor, performances. At the same time, it affects the capacity of the ego to emancipate itself from the world, surrendering the organism more to the world and making it more an automaton.

With this in mind, we may be in the position to earmark certain basic differences between human and animal nature. The difference between flexor and extensor movements is much less pronounced in animal than in man. Yet even in the animal the extensor movements are in closer relation to the automatic function than the flexor movements. Thus we find in the so-called dead faint of animals the tendency toward abduction and extension. In some animals, like the turtle, the mere removal from natural support releases, reflexively, the tendency to that posture.[14] Osvaldo Polimanti's proof that this reflex appears independently of the position of the animal but is closely related to inspiration (biologically the most important function) points to the primitive character of this reaction. Human inspiration is also facilitated by extension and abduction of the extremities. Thus, in human beings, this tendency to abduction is still related to inspiration, although the two performances are no longer so rigidly connected that they could not be separated. However, during forced inspiration, during dyspnoea, the abduction and extension movements again become automatically more apparent.

In animals, we find neither such a strongly expressed differentiation in the use of flexor and extensor performances, nor do we find that a defect of the cerebrum has, in their case, such a different effect on the two kinds of movements. Correspondingly, the animal seems to us, also in other respects, to be far more bound to the outer world; it lacks freedom and the possibility to set itself off from the world.

Thus, we can see, in the differentiation between flexor and extensor performances, the expression of two basic ways of behavior, which might well be used for establishing a hierarchy. With this criterion, we could distinguish between a higher and a lower level.

This assumption of the differential significance of the flexor and extensor performances is not intended to mean a particular specificity of the extensor movements. We are not at all concerned to differentiate between flexor and extensor movements, nor flexor and extensor muscles, but only between flexor and extensor performances. Under different circumstances, the muscles with which these are performed, may vary. In spite of that, the characteristics of flexor or abduction performances remain the same. They do not in the least depend on the activity of single muscle groups of the body but on the whole. They are an expression of different attitudes of the whole. Not every flexor movement can simply be regarded as a flexor performance in the above sense.

An illustration of this is the grasping reflex, which is certainly a very primitive phenomenon but manifests itself in a flexor movement. In this instance, the flexor movement has an entirely different significance. In stimulation of the palm, the simplest reaction is the turning-to movement. How little this movement has in common with a real performance can be seen by the fact that if, in patients, the extensor side of the hand is stimulated, we may obtain an extension movement as another turning-to reaction. This movement certainly cannot be taken as an attempt of coming to terms with the environment, in the sense of an object-directed performance, of doing something with the object. After all, this movement is totally unsuited to accomplish this. Still another factor shows clearly that, in these cases, we are actually dealing with the opposite of a real performance. As a matter of fact, we are dealing with a state of being surrendered to the world. Thus, we find that patients who cannot let go of an object, once in the condition of the grasping reflex, hold on the firmer, the stronger the stimulus becomes. This is even true if the stimulus becomes painful, in which case it certainly would be part of a meaningful adjustment to the environment to let go of the object. Thus, not every flexor movement is a flexor performance, and what we have said above holds only for the latter. In normal life, to be sure, flexor movement and flexor performance almost always actually coincide, as long as they are not movements in certain artificial "drilled" performances.

No criteria of hierarchy according to organs or organ systems
Such distinctions, as that of the differential significance of the flexor and extensor performances, bring us closer to the hierarchical organization of the organism. From this approach, it becomes apparent that the organization is not one according to organs or organ systems in the usual sense of these words. One member or "part" may be concerned with all the various phenomena that we can determine through isolat-

ing procedure. Because of the fact that a specific way of behavior is prerequisite for specific contents and specific performances, certain contents may drop out if the respective behavior type is absent. This may lead one to the false assumption that disintegration proceeds according to contents and performance fields, or organs and organ systems, and that, in turn, may lead one to assume a structural organization of hierarchical integration according to performance fields, organs, and organ systems. We reject any such conception.

The problem of "centering and richness"
We want to explain, by an example, how little such a view is suited for an understanding of the phenomena. It has been assumed that the nervous system should be regarded as higher than the sexual system. If one observes, however, how disease proceeds with distintegration, one cannot say that it reduces the nervous system and leaves the sexual system intact, although to superficial observation the sexual system may have even assumed greater importance. Actually, however, it turns out that the performances that are in close relation to the sexual system are also changed. And they are changed in the same manner as the mental and intellectual performances. The attitude toward the erotic sphere has been modified in the same way as the total attitude toward the world. Just as the latter becomes more stimulus bound, less independent and less ego determined, so also does the former become more passive, less discriminating, and more disconnected from the ego. If the words were not so easily misunderstood, the difference could be best expressed by such terms as a degradation from erotics (love sentiment), which embraces not only "physical" but also "mental" and "spiritual" contents, to bare sexuality that lacks the more spiritual and the more subtle bodily qualities.

The erotic sphere in itself does not represent a lower level, but it will represent a lower level only when it has become isolated, has become plain sexuality. That this cannot possibly be regarded as loss of "inhibition," which presumably the higher nervous system normally exerts on the "lower" sexual system, can be seen by the fact that all other performance systems are changed in similar fashion. Moreover, even the function of the nervous system and mental life may become, in turn, changed through a primary impairment of the bodily organ systems and particularly of the sexual system. It should be stressed that

370

here too the isolating approach brings mutual influences of presumably discrete factors deceptively into the foreground. As soon as one has undertaken an artificial separation into organ systems, one is, as in the division of performances into reflexes, for example, bound to find the phenomenon of mutuality of effect. This rule is effective in mental and intellectual processes as well. Individuals may indulge not only in excesses of the senses but also of the soul and intellect, when the latter become autonomous and detached from the world. Then the excesses of soul and intellect show formally the same characteristics as the sensual sphere, if isolated from the total personality.

We must not discriminate between the sexual and the nervous-psychological systems as two parts of the organism having different valence. Rather, the various higher and lower behavior types cut across these systems that, taken as such, are products of isolation. But neither must we regard these two behavior types as strictly separate, and as higher and lower levels existing side by side. Actually, we find the two ways of behavior as separated and therefore distorted only under certain isolating influences, as in defective integration and centering of the organism. Normally, the two exist in a total configuration in which one or the other comes only temporarily into the foreground. When one of the systems thus becomes "figure," the other is somehow always present at the same time.

Depending on the various patterns of centering, we can distinguish between three principle forms of human behavior, which we recognize in the prototypes: the thinker, the poet, and the man of action. In the thinker, the conscious, objectifying behavior is particularly in the foreground. But it becomes dangerous if he neglects the "nonconscious," the "experienced" (cf. pp. 240ff.) mode of living activity, because then his work becomes an excessive indulgence in thinking, suspended *in vacuo*. In the poet, the "nonconscious" attitudes, feelings, moods, and so on, prevail. For him it is disastrous if he does not pay tribute to "objective" reality and to verification in action. Then his work becomes exuberance and redundance of sentiments estranged from reality. The man of action, finally, is in danger of losing himself completely in the milieu situation unless he comprehends, at the same time, the world in its objective aspects and does not lose sight of its entirety, which likewise has to be experienced and "lived through." Otherwise he becomes a destructive machine. If one or the other aspect usurps the foreground in a way detrimental to the total individual, then we have to deal with deficiency as a result of defective centering of the adequate configuration.

Thus the vigor and cohesion of centering reveals itself as a measure for the level of organization of life. The highest form of centering manifests itself in a number of formal attributes that ultimately represent one and the same thing but that are, as a rule, named differently: freedom, meaningfulness, action springing from the whole personality, productivity, capacity to meaningful actions, capacity to adequate shifting in attitude, capacity to absorb milieu expansions or modifications, and so on. To this indicator of "level," we might add a second factor: capacity to absorb richness of content (of world material). We have already seen that the second factor is also conditioned by the factor of centering, and that when centering is impaired, the capacity to absorb richness of content is impaired also. However, it figures as a special factor, as the expression of the qualitative organization of the organism. We rank an individual the higher, the greater his power is of cohesive centering in encompassing "world," that is, the milieu corresponding to human nature.

In this sense, we can speak of the two above-mentioned types of behavior as being higher or lower and can talk of a hierarchy. The low level of existence in the sick, as compared to the normal level, can be characterized first by shrinkage of world, privation of "personality" through limitation of degrees of freedom, and second through defectiveness of centering. The first manifests itself through a narrowing of the world, with regard to quantity and quality. The second manifests itself in a lower grade of integration and firmness of subjective experience, reduced "openness" toward the world, reduced versatility in attitudes, and a lowering in the direction from actively "conscious" behavior to a more passive way of "living." The impairment of centering finally manifests itself in defective coherence of the environment for the respective person and a stronger bond to a specific milieu.

Centering and richness of the apprehended world as
criteria for the level of organization
The two characteristics for determining the rank in the hierarchy, centering and richness of the apprehended world, must also be regarded as nothing but two sides of one whole, because neither one is effective

and thus really present without the other. However, they can furnish us with a guiding line for the differentiation of levels within the field of all life phenomena. The "formal" guiding line, of more or less cohesive centering, is easier to use than that with regard to richness of contents. Observation easily shows us that, by his nature, the human being is the most centered creature of all. His centering is less easily disturbed, he is less bound to a specific milieu and is less affected by its change.[15] This is so not because the milieu does not affect him (as in the reflexes, which are detached from the whole) but rather in spite of the effects of the milieu. Among living beings, the plants seem to us to be the least centered, representing the lowest level of individualization.

It may be much more difficult to form a scale according to the different degrees of richness. In this instance, the diversity of the nature and milieu of the various species – as judged by their performances – does not at all permit a simple, quantitative ranking. After all, there is "world," which is apprehended by some animals but not by human beings, who occupy the "highest" rank. There are so many variations regarding the patterning of individual apparatuses, as of the senses, the motor mechanisms, and so on, that a comparison is impossible, as long as we do not have a scaling basis that comprises all Being. All attempts to arrange the individual animal classes in a scale based on the development of specific organ systems have brought, at best, only a superficial ordering that is quite inexpedient for the comprehension of the stratification of living nature in general. In this connection, it is easier to make many negative comments on the present attempts than to provide starting points for a positive, meaningful rank order.

For all comparisons between man and animal, one must observe the principle that any singularity cannot be compared as long as it has not been recognized in its significance for the organism to which it belongs. Comparative anatomy has often made grave mistakes in this respect, by drawing comparisons on the basis of very superficial analogies. Also, where tissues of similar structure are compared, for instance, the tissue of the cortex, one must be extremely careful in inferring from the extension and structure of the cortex to the respective level of an animal in the hierarchy. After all, we know much too little regarding the specific significance of a certain structure for the entire organization, and we know nothing as to whether we can compare specific performances or capacities, such as intelligence, in the individual creatures.

373

The insurmountable difficulty, which is involved in any attempt to classify animals according to individual organs, should make us wonder whether we are actually on a passable road. In any event, a determination of the nature of the individual creatures, or species, is at least a prerequisite for any such attempt.

Phylogeny and ontogeny
On the basis of our presentation, we obtain a new view of the problem of phylogenetic and ontogenetic development. The question of evolution is usually seen as a development from the lower to the higher creatures. An actual genetic emergence of the latter from the former is assumed. All the objections that we have just considered stand in the way of such an attempt. In principle, also, it remains implausible how the "more perfect" should arise from the "less perfect." The opposite would be rather more intelligible. The fundamental thought that mature observation impressed on us and that we adopted as an orienting principle, is that the less perfect becomes intelligible as a variation and aberration of the "perfect," but not the opposite.

Besides, I cannot see in what way our knowledge can be advanced, if we trace one phenomenon to another, if we assume an evolution of phenomena. Usually, such an assumption has only hindered further research. The difference of species can probably be best understood as different degrees of approximation to a prototype, similarly as the differences between individuals are degrees of approximation to a prototype of the "species." In this case, I would also like to postulate that every phenomenon must be understood on its own grounds, just as we have demanded for the reflexes.[16] If this were not possible, then it would be better to acknowledge that one is unable to explain a phenomenon than to lead research into a misinterpretation of facts.

The situation seems to be somewhat different regarding the ontogenetic development. Here we truly have phenomena that are observable and belong to one and the same organism. Here one can also make various statements regarding the emergence or transition of one stage from another. But here as well, one should attempt to understand each stage from the respective present condition. In doing so, one must certainly not overlook that the effect of the former stage continues into the next, just as we find the effect of former generations in the phenomenon of so-called heredity.

374

We must content ourselves with these few words regarding the problem of evolution, which is certainly obscured by a mass of prejudices.

If we summarize all the difficulties encountered in the attempt to establish hierarchic scales, we find that they all go back to the difficulties that the problem of the individual nature of an organism sets before us. In addition to that, such an attempt requires determination of the relative position of each creature within the realm of living beings, and this presupposes the knowledge of that realm in its entirety. In other words, each single phenomenon (individual, species, etc.) refers us back to the next-higher whole. Only with a known reference to the superordinated whole would it be possible to properly evaluate how that being, to which the observed phenomenon belongs, exists in reality. In attempting to bring order into the animal phyla, we have to realize clearly that here also, in starting from the individual, we are referred to the whole and may be led to a view of the whole. However, synthetic procedure is not the way to ascend from the particular to the whole. A few gifted individuals may be inspired to envision the Gestalt of that prototype, which we, who are only capable of an isolating approach, meet in the confusing multitude of phenomena. We can at best attempt to gather the material from which, some day in the future, a conception of this prototype may arise. Again we are restrained to modesty.

One general remark: Every creature is, so to speak, simultaneously perfect and imperfect. Regarded in isolation each creature is, within itself, perfect, well organized, and alive. With regard to the entirety, however, it is imperfect to various degrees: the individual creature, as compared with the entirety of nature, shows the same sort of being that an isolated process in the organism reveals in comparison with the whole of the organism, imperfection and rigidity, existence only in being within the whole, only by support of the whole, like a reflex. Therefore, it is doomed to die as soon as this support ceases. Therefore, it is by its very nature transitory and on the road to death.

CHAPTER TWELVE

Knowledge and Action

Biology and Action

In our approach to nature, we usually distinguish between two attitudes, one of cognitive apprehension and one of acting. But this characterization is not exhaustive or sufficiently adequate. It would be better to speak of an attitude of immediate experience and one of analytic (anatomizing) reflection; these two attitudes correspond to two different kinds of knowledge and of action. As long as we behave in the first manner we do not differentiate sharply between living and inanimate nature.

Nature confronts us, so to speak, as a still undismembered unity; and by no means is this mode of apprehension only that of nonerudite, unsophisticated, or primitive man. It may even be present in the Weltanschauung of the scholar, along with his scientific, analytical approach. Moreover, it frequently determines and pervades his ultimate conception of nature. The eminent physicist, also, though resting entirely on the empiricism of the anatomizing method in natural science, may exceed, in his ultimate ideas of nature, the bounds of this empiricism. These ideas of nature are frequently implicit or explicit categories or concepts and are required for dealing with the holistic character of life. Then one has to concede that the results gained by the analytic method represent only one "part aspect" of the whole world — just as if they were cut out from the world's totality.[1] The epistemologically conscious biologist arrives at a similar conclusion. From the living world surrounding us, those phenomena, which everywhere can be grasped by the physico-chemical method, shape themselves to a special partitive aspect.

By virtue of this isolating, dismembering procedure one can readily abstract and single out from living phenomena those on the physico-chemical "plane." But the attempt to reintegrate the elements thus abstracted, to reorganize these split-off segments into the reality of living nature, is doomed to fail. This vain attempt, however, is made again and again, overlooking the fact that it is possible to understand the part on the basis of the whole but that it is not possible to comprehend the whole on the basis of the parts.

The theoretical natural scientist – for example, the theoretical physicist – usually cannot arrive at a direct action from the attitude of immediate experience. His action is usually confined to elaboration of that part of the world that becomes prominent through the anatomizing procedure. His work can take two directions: he either tries to make the experiences obtained by the analytic method increasingly useful for knowledge, or his activity is directed against the forces of nature in order to master them for the benefit of man. Usually the theoretical physicist leaves this kind of action to the technologist who applies physics, chemistry, and so on.

Before discussing the character of applied sciences, we return once more to the behavior of the biologist. From our point of view, it is evident that, no matter how much he employs the analytic method for obtaining real knowledge, real insight into the depths of nature, the departure from the "immediately given" will always dominate. Also from this perspective, a "part" of nature shapes itself that can be comprehended only through analysis and the significance of which, for the understanding of organic life, is a continual problem to the biologist. Thus the biologist's procedure does not differ essentially from that of the theoretical physicist. Only his kind of "centering" data, his organization of facts within the body of knowledge, are different. Whereas the eye of the physicist is especially directed to that part of the world that can be apprehended by the isolating method, the view of the biologist is more directed to the other aspect.

However, to this different centering, a different way of action corresponds. The physicist can leave acting in the world to the technologist; the biologist cannot do this, particularly insofar as he may be a physician. He is forced to interfere actively with nature, unless he confines himself to being a purely natural scientist, which has often been the case in recent medicine. We have previously seen that his knowledge, by its very procedure, calls for action because action as such is one of the sources of his knowledge.

But there is still another reason for his acting in person: The subjects with whom he is dealing require his interference, especially if human beings are concerned. Yet human beings oppose any interference in the form of plain violence and would ultimately perish from it. They demand that the physician help them to regain the possibility for existence. The biologist who deals with animals is likewise forced toward practical activity by the keeping of, taking care of, and breeding of animals. To be sure, his attitude is usually somewhat different from that of the biologist who deals with man. All animal care ultimately refers back, somehow, to usefulness of the animal for man, although it may become detached from this pragmatism, as is the case of hobbies or animal care in zoos.

With the category of usefulness, however, this type of action approaches the characteristics of technology. The procedure in animal care, however, is somewhat restricted by the fact that if it neglects to do sufficient justice to the animal nature it jeopardizes the existence of the animal (cf. p. 281). Granted that in the treatment of man, sociological, political, or other purposes of extrinsic character may be imposed on him, still, under this influence, the nature of the person to be treated is the center of interest. Only from this situation, therefore, can we appreciate clearly the character of acting in its reference to biological knowledge and its strict contrast to acting in the technological application of natural science.

Action in Technology and Education

Every technology means violence to nature; and even where it utilizes or exploits natural energies by direct manipulation, it is able to serve its purpose only in opposition to nature. Moreover, the aim of technology is not to render the natural energies available and instrumental, but rather to protect its products against their encroachments. Around its products, it builds protective walls against nature, within which nature does not function, but rather the knowledge that results from analytic procedure, culminating in the form of machines. Only in that way are machines, for example, able to last.

The biologist will act in this manner only when he is not concerned with living creatures as such, as, for instance, in breeding for human purposes, or if his lack of knowledge still obscures his adequate understanding of the nature of a living creature and its appropriate environment. Since biological knowledge, in most cases, lacks completeness, we are frequently forced to do so. But this predicament is manifested only in the imperfection of our actions and not in our goal. Since our actions are guided by the desire to contribute in a meaningful way to the preservation of living beings, our goal can be none other than to provide for a creature an adequate environment that allows for the most complete realization of its nature.

This manifests itself in the purest form in the task of the physician and the educator. We have commented already on the activity of the physician; the activity of the educator takes on a complexion not much different. But here we approach more closely the limits of human perfection as they are given in the imperfect knowledge of pedagogic means and ends and moreover are grounded in the imperfect adaptation of man to the world in which he has to live. Many of the pedagogic measures spring from the necessity of standardizing the individual to the norms of the respective civilization and culture, a necessity that must be borne. It is not sufficient to encourage and help the child in the practice and development of his innate potentialities – which is the ideal of any biologically founded pedagogy concerned with the development of the individual according to its nature. Yet the demands of civilization compel the educator to utilize, to a certain extent, mere drill.

Practice and drill
Regarding the performance of the organism, there is a fundamental difference between practice and drill, a difference only too often overlooked.[2] Both aim at the best performances possible, but practice aims more to attain the optimal performances attuned to the nature of the organism, whose development, to the highest perfection possible in a given environment, is the objective. For this purpose, a knowledge of the organism's essential nature is necessary, and the task consists in bringing forth the greatest adequacy between organism and environment. Thus all practice implies those inner experiences, which we have described as characteristic of preferred behavior, no matter which performances are involved. With that goes the experience of an actualized personality. From this alone springs true insight and the acquisition of fruitful knowledge – all of which is fundamentally different from drill and rote learning.

In drill, the acquisition of a certain performance is at first unrelated

to the nature of the performing being. It is achieved by bringing a somehow isolated part of the organism into a relation with a certain part of
the environment and establishing such a firm tie between the two that
the external event (stimulus) is followed by the performance (response)
with the greatest promptness. The prototype of the drill is the conditioned reflex. Such a reaction bond depends, in principle, on a safe-
guarding from all possible interferences. This safeguard is furnished by
the prevailing isolation while the performance in question is in demand.

In the animal, this safeguard is accomplished by preventing, through
force, all performances that are essential to the animal, except the one
reaction in question. Gradually, on account of the special arrangement,
the animal comes into a condition in which this isolation of certain
events takes place almost passively without any resistance on its part.
The animal has been gradually deprived of its individuality. Usually, drill
remains a continual discomfort for the animal and is tolerated because
of anxiety (punishment) or its counterpart (reward). Drill is the more
successful, the more the trainer manages to press the adequate performances into the service of the drilled actions; in other words, the more
he can bring drill into relation with the natural potentialities of the
respective organism. Then it becomes best fixed and rooted and may
even become somewhat agreeable to the animal. In this respect, bad
and good drill differ, inasmuch as the latter always contains a great deal
of practice.

In human learning, drill also plays a particular part. But that it is not
the adequate method of learning can be appreciated immediately from
the fact that the learning of any inadequate performance is extremely
laborious and tedious. In any event, the "acquisition" of adequate performances succeeds much better. From this follows the expediency of
a special method of learning. The learning must be inspired by the
aspect of adequacy for the respective individual with regard to the selection of the material as well as to the method of learning. But this procedure, oriented on adequacy, is usually not sufficient. Corresponding
to the imperfect adequacy of the environment to their nature, human
beings more or less have to take recourse to drill. However, drill – if it
is not to be doomed to failure – must become substantially related to
the personality of the learner. And thereby, one human attribute offers
a supporting basis: the human being is probably the only creature that
possesses the potentiality of partitive isolation within the organism and,

at will, of exposing parts to stimuli. In this way, these parts become attuned to stimulus settings in such a way that, under the same environmental conditions and under the volitionally produced identical isolation, the same performance sets in. To a certain extent, we need such "inadequate" performances in order to cope with the world. Yet they are not so completely inadequate, as long as they are acquired with insight into the inescapable demands of the world and as long as one is determined to deal with these necessities even in an "inadequate" way. From this it follows that human learning does not always represent adequate practice, insofar as it consists in drill. Furthermore, drill is only effective through insight into, and realization of, its necessity, on the part of the learner. It is only fruitful as voluntary, deliberate "self-drill." In this respect, human learning by drill does not involve a complete aberration from the basic trait of "biological acting," which ultimately arises only when it is necessary to help a being to actualize itself.

CHAPTER THIRTEEN

Concluding Remarks

We have come to the end. At times our presentation may have seemed too critical, too negative. I have certainly made generous use of that marvelous peculiarity of human nature, namely, the capacity to say no. But I hope that the reader will have realized that in so doing I have always been interested only in clearing the path for the positive, for what is really constructive, although at the present time this may be so sparse that it constrains us to be modest. I am deeply convinced that life never manifests itself in negative terms; therefore any personal and objective criticism, in the form of simple negation, is repugnant to me on account of its sterility. My aversion to any personal controversy goes so far that I have expressed it by omitting, as much as possible, the names of those against whose work I was compelled to raise objection. After all, only the subject matter counts. And criticism is important only when a false viewpoint appears with ponderous arguments and blocks the path for further progress. That this attitude does not involve sterility may be seen by the fact that it has offered me inspiration for manifold research for many years, and also from the fact that criticism has directly resulted in many new problems – as our presentation shows.

The viewpoint that we have advanced does not readily enable one to master a problem. Rather, it compels one, in every individual problem, to see its foundation, to approach it as closely as possible. And because the foundation can be seen vaguely, though not touched, this viewpoint keeps us always open-minded and prepares us for revising our concepts on the ground of new findings; it does not deceive us as to the provisional nature of every result; and it instigates further research. This viewpoint, furthermore, never really permits one simply to set aside or neglect problems that have not as yet been clarified, because it considers nothing to be a priori inessential. After all, one can never be certain that some such apparently inessential point will not shed the light required to illuminate the darkness of the depths.

We have already emphasized that to be aware of incompleteness does not hinder human action, and, moreover, that it is this very incompleteness that imbues such action with the responsibility characteristic of human nature. Thus, our scientific procedure is apparently commensurate with the character of the human being in general, manifesting itself mainly in three phenomena: in the potentiality of complete devotion to Being, in the potentiality to keep modestly at a distance from it, and in the potentiality to act with free decision in placing the personality at stake.

I believe one will feel that this book is not the outcome of a mere academic attitude, although it does defend a specific theory with a certain fanaticism. Rather, I have been prompted to write it because my concrete research work continually forced me to give an account of what I was actually doing. Therefore, the book turned out to be principally a methodological discussion. It does not attempt to provide a presentation of the living world but to discuss the means by which we may arrive at its comprehension. Yet the material that it contains is not intended merely for exemplification, nor merely to indicate the extent of the grounds on which my conception is founded – all this would not justify the quantity of material that, at times, may somewhat overwhelm the reader. The material is essentially supposed to demonstrate over and over again that method as well as theory must originate from nothing but the most concrete evidence.

It seemed particularly necessary to me to demonstrate this, since the discussion led us ultimately into realms that are far removed from usual biological considerations. I hope that the reader will realize that this digression into philosophical problems is not determined by the casual, personal inclination of the author but that the material itself imposes the obligation on us, if we desire to find our way through it. I also hope our presentation will have shown that our attitude throughout reflects what we have emphasized in the Introduction, namely, the intention to approach the material with as unbiased an attitude as possible, to be guided by the material itself, and to employ that method which the factual material dictates to us. If this intention has necessitated considerations that one customarily calls philosophical, one will,

I hope, realize, by the way in which these considerations have grown out of the material, that they actually belong to it. I hope, furthermore, that it will be realized how irrelevant and little pertinent to reality such lines of demarcation are, which one usually couches in the contra-distinctive terms of "empirical research" and "philosophical (meta-physical) reasoning."

It is not our objective to ascend from the empiric realm to that of ideas, from the finite to the infinite. Such an approach is already biased; it already presupposes a very definite, theoretical point of view. Un-biased research shows that no empirical data can ever become really intelligible unless grasped from an ideational frame of reference and unless viewed from a conceptual plane. It even shows that these defini-tional distinctions themselves – "philosophical" and "empirical" – are of nothing but a provisional nature. Any research that disregards this fact is caught in a labyrinthine jungle, no matter how entrancing it may appear in giving the illusion of great variety. Thus from empirical expe-rience, there arose for us the methodological, the crucial problem: How does Gestalt emerge from this chaos? We had to call into ques-tion the evaluation of many findings, but not simply to put them aside. We have never been satisfied unless we comprehended, at least in prin-ciple, these findings in their specific form, endeavoring always to deter-mine their significance for and within the realm of living nature. Under our examination, many a finding has certainly lost the character of facts which it formerly seemed to possess. We frequently had to deprive such findings of a claim upon definite validity and significance in a given branch of science. Thus, we have denied any adequacy to the scientific principle of mere random dissection of nature, and made the scrutiny of the factual character of every phenomenon the center of our inquiry into nature. To be sure, we know only too well that research cannot always take a direct path to the facts, that frequently false trials are req-uisite to reach a goal, that the shortest way is not always the most fea-sible, and that it may be more correct to take a detour than to attempt in vain to overcome insurmountable obstacles which lie along the short-est road. Nevertheless, the principle of trial and error, in that form in which it is frequently met, should never have attained such prominence in science.

The facts for which we are searching are those that enable us to describe the nature of the organism unequivocally, to "understand" it.

385

In our attempts to determine the organism's intrinsic character, we always started from the concrete, individual phenomenon, and thus tried to gain sight of its real nature.

To this approach, the nature of the "partitive" disclosed itself, and proved itself determinable only by reference to the whole to which it belongs structurally and qualitatively. The "partitive" revealed itself as an "unnatural" state of the organism under isolation of certain often very arbitrarily selected parts. Thus the "partitive" proved itself unsuited to derive the whole from it. All individual parts pointed beyond themselves to the whole, to a base differing from the parts themselves, to a center to which they owe their functional reality and by which they achieve their place (i.e., order of the parts). As to the nature of this base, mere empirical observation can never furnish a definite determination. For empirical research, it is sufficient to characterize this base as the reason for knowledge, as a heuristic principle that renders possible the comprehension of all these partitive phenomena in their reference to the organism – thereby makes them reconcilable with each other. One may say furthermore: This "reason for knowledge" is not a concept in the abstract sense, but has the character of a concrete entity. It has the character of a prototype, and as such, contains more than the "parts," which after all are only its manifestations. It is a prototype that reveals itself in an increasingly pronounced and differentiated way whenever the situation makes it possible or demands it. Here we have found parallels to what Goethe has brought into concrete visualization with his notion of the "Urpflanze" as the prototypic principle of differentiation into manifold forms of plants.

Only if and only to the extent to which we succeed in bringing the "prototype" in sight, can we attempt to approach such problems as the relationship of organisms to each other, their belonging to kinds and species, their level in a hierarchy of life, and so on.

To be sure, the material for the knowledge of this prototype (pp. 312ff.) can only be obtained by the isolating method of empirical investigation. It is our task to discriminate from among the great number of phenomena those "constants" or norms through which we may come closer to the nature of the organism. This is the way from the artificially produced "part processes" to those phenomena "in which, through many variations, their real, common base is revealed," though only to a man who, with the proper power of mind, is capable of grasping "the engendering point from whence wisdom spontaneously springs as an offering to us."[1] Then the prototype arises before us in a receptive-creative act, though always only in incompleteness. From this point of view, the organism appears to us as a "Being" of relatively constant and qualitatively specific nature. Analysis reveals that certain general laws govern the existence of the organism. Only by the fact that every change, conditioned by environmental stimuli, is equalized in adequate time toward an adequate mean, does the organism retain its main, formal characteristic, that is, its relative constancy, which guarantees its existence as well as its identifiability. Therefore, we called this "principle of equalization" a basic biological law.

Quite in general, we may say that the organism is a Being enduring in time, or if we may say so, in eternal time; for it does not commence with procreation, certainly not with birth, and does not end with death. What we mean by the terms "birth" and "death" are merely certain landmarks like others, for example, like puberty and menopause. Their real nature is yet to be determined. But they belong essentially to the existence within the course of time prehensible to us, to the "life" of the organism from impregnation down to death. And therefore these features must be regarded as instrumental for our conceptions of the prototype, just as any other apprehensible state during the life course. Many an event in the life course becomes intelligible only from the anamnesis – from the so-called hereditary factors; many another event in turn becomes intelligible from the subsequent biography – from death.

The fact that the organism represents, so to speak, a historical being makes it imperative to consider the time factor in dealing with any detail. All performances must be determined not only according to quality and spatial conditions but also according to their temporal index. A performance is normal or "adequate," if it shows an adequate temporal structure (see pp. 104, 275). If, in a statically minded approach, we arrest for a moment *in abstracto* the development in the course of time, then the organism may possibly appear perfectly embedded in a world that it fits like a statue in its mold. But we may also strike another moment in which a grave discrepancy exists between the organism and the world. In the first instance, our impression of the organism seems to correspond completely to the prototype – it is from such static impressions that the prototype forms itself for us. In the second instance, a strange organism appears before us, showing at best only a distorted semblance of the prototype. On this basis, we would never be able to obtain a prototype. These two moments represent, on the one hand, Being-in-order, in adequate stimulus evaluation, and on the other hand, Being-in-disorder, in inadequate stimulus evaluation, in "catastrophe." If the organism is "to be," it always has to pass again from moments of catastrophe to states of ordered behavior. Catastrophic shocks, that is, traumas of existence, arise when the organism clashes with the world in the productive coming to terms with it. They really signify as much a concussion of the world as of the organism itself. They represent a disequilibrium that must be overcome, if the organism is not to lose its existence. This balancing process occurs through mutual adjustment of the organism and the world and is realized because the organism is able to find its "milieu" in the world.

If it is true that these catastrophes are the expression of a clash of the individuality of the organism with the "otherness" of the world, then the organism must proceed from catastrophe to catastrophe. But this is not its intrinsic Being, rather only the transition to its true realization. The clash, so to speak, provides only a shake-up from which the repatterning, that is, the real pattern, the real performance, the revelation of the organism and the world, emerges. Indeed there is no performance without a new region of the world becoming manifest.

In these moments of performance, we find the organism in an ordered state and specific Gestalt, on the basis of which we form our conception of the organism. Such are the situations of preferred behavior, toward which the organism, changed and shaken by the outer world, repeatedly strives. Such are the phenomena from which we derive the constants of the organism; such are the moments of its real existence, when the organism is its real self, as compared with states of deterioration and enslavement to the world that must always be overcome to make performances possible. From this point of view, "being in order and existence," "meaning and being," are the same; and "being" signifies nothing other than a self-realization that keeps in step with the conquest of the world, that is, inclusion and transformation.[2] This leads on the one hand to what, in terms of the individual, is experience, on the other hand, to what in terms of the world is organization and patterning. Thus organism and world realize themselves simultaneously and grow from the sphere of potentiality into that of actuality.

Life has always a positive character; it never manifests itself in negative terms. All attempts at an explanation that necessitates the assumption of negative factors, for example, such concepts as inhibition, antagonism, struggle between opposing lower and higher forces, and, finally, such concepts as "negation" of the "vital forces" through the mind, are unproductive. Wherever negative factors seem to operate, this is either due to false theoretical presuppositions that demand an amendment through the introduction of such negative factors, or it is due to the erroneous hypostatization of processes as absolute, which actually belong to performances, occurring in antagonistic phases insofar as they are considered in a state of isolation.

This criticism is as valid for the theory of "antagonistic" movements, as for the so-called antagonism between the mind and the "vital sphere." The phenomena that have occasioned the doctrine of such interpretations are only an expression of the process of coming to terms with the world under continual tension. Although individual phenomena become really intelligible to us only if we regard them positively as pertaining to a unitary, holistic being, still we have had to restrict this view to a certain degree. We have seen that a certain amount of fluctuation in antagonistic phases is evidently part and parcel of the normal process. We had to admit that we can volitionally impede processes in the organism (pp. 186, 301) – that it belongs to human nature to oppose, in some measure, the drive impulse by means of the mind. We even had to admit more: in reality the self-realization of the organism by no means exhibits consistency throughout. Every creature is easily drawn back and forth. In human beings, especially, consistency, perfect centering, and integration are almost the exception. The human subject seems to oscillate between passion and reason, between drives and intellect. One might argue: What right do we have to minimize these more frequently observed phenomena, to subordinate them to the unitary whole that is neither consistently nor completely realized throughout? Why do we not proceed in the opposite manner, starting with the variety of the individual phenomena, with the existence of reflex and inhibition mechanisms with drives and intellect, and attempt to explain life on the basis of these phenomena through their counterplay and interplay? Why do we not take offense at the incompleteness of knowledge in determining the whole? And why do we take offense at the inadequacy of regulating principles that one is compelled to introduce, in order to maintain consistency, if one makes the single phenomenon the starting point?

One may reply to this that the difference between the two views is the following. In the atomistic approach, advancement of knowledge hinges on theory, while in the view we have advocated, it clings to empiric data. To be sure, the former also aims to scrutinize and revise its theoretical views through experience, and it amends the theory on proof of new observations. But these corrections are done rather with hesitation. No matter what field we may consider, we shall always see that an old theory is given up only very reluctantly even if new data challenge it; that one rather takes recourse to all possible amendments and auxiliaries, before the theory is entirely rejected. Usually, experiences that do not fit are at first simply left "outside," and one does not refrain from granting validity to two or more theories at the same time.

Such procedures are impossible for us in principle. Since every new additional experience is never simply one more, standing apart from the others, it forces us rather to reconsider the entire theory, if for no other reason than that an experience becomes a "fact" only if it fits into the whole. In this respect we cannot accept compromise and have to uphold unceasingly the cause of the scientific attitude. Yet ultimately our procedure is rooted in a more profound conviction: this is the conviction that a state of greater perfection can never be understood from that of less perfection and that only the converse is possible. It is very feasible to isolate parts from a whole, but a perfect whole can never be composed by synthesizing it from the less perfect parts. True, the reflex can be understood as a manifestation of the whole, as a special condition during isolation of a part, but the whole can never be comprehended from the reflexes.

When centering is defective, when parts are split off from the whole, it is certainly possible that the outcome is antagonism, for example, a contest in the field of perceptions or drives or something in the nature of a struggle between "mind" and "drives." Then it is even possible that a so-called drive may become so pathologically dominant that it is mistaken for a true, essential characteristic of the normal organism, as in the anthropology of Freud. But from such partitive phenomena, it will never be possible to understand, even approximately, the inner coherence and unity of holistic behavior. From no single phenomenon does a path lead to the whole; yet it can be comprehended as a privation of the whole. The possibility of such privations is no objection to the holistic organization; rather, they express the imperfection in self-realization resulting from a lack in potency of "essential nature." This lack is either innate, through defective genesis – or, as one may say, through a deprivation of the grace of endowments – or it is acquired through disease, or is a sequel of overpowering demands by the environment.

It is well worth noting that we meet this imperfection in disease, and among all creatures, especially in man. The first is easily understood because disease means reduction of centering. The second would indicate that for man, of the creatures, ideal centering is most difficult to achieve; and this in turn points to the specific intricacy of his organization. This finds expression in individuality, the one factor that may be regarded as the ultimate reason no being can ever attain a realization completely corresponding to its nature. Individuality in no way means simply that "I" exist, but that there are, simultaneously with me, "other" creatures; and that fact necessarily implies incomplete realization of every individual, it means impact, catastrophic reactions, antagonism, competition between creatures, and struggle between "mind" and "life" (p. 353). The higher the organization, the more differentiated and the more individual the creature, the greater is the inner imperfection, together with the relative perfection. Therefore, we find in man, along with the most pronounced and developed individuality and the greatest relative perfection, forces adverse to both. This opposition may go so far that the "mind" can "say no" to "life." Evidently such a creature must meet with great obstacles and conflicts in order to realize its nature.

Realization is determined by its structural organization as much as by its capacity to tolerate or overcome catastrophes. Every defect destroys structure; and this is the cause for frequent occurrence of inadequate stimulus reactions, that is, catastrophes, in a milieu that would formerly have been adequate. Such occurrences can be obviated through nothing but performances, which one can achieve only if he finds the adequate milieu. That achievement implies limitation of his world, corresponding to the limitation of the premorbid performance capacities. At this stage, the organism is really and solely striving for "preservation." The manner in which an organism copes with a defect is always characteristic of its individual nature. This reveals itself not only in the quality of the performance – that is, in the scope and differentiation of his world – but equally as much in the strength with which shocks can be resisted without breaking the organism (pp. 240, 303).

At this point the analysis made it indispensable to include the intellectual power, the "mind," as an instrinsic characteristic of human nature. In man alone, the privation of essential performances and limitation of world can be mitigated, because he has the capacity to bear insufficiency, that is, suffering. This capability is the characteristic of human nature and reveals the very highest form of life in the phenomenon of freedom.

In deliberate limitation of our textual scope, we have regarded the organism primarily as individual Being. Here we halt and confine ourselves to an understanding that, of course, is only preliminary. Many phenomena of the organism point beyond the individual. First, any attempt to regard the essential peculiarities of an organism, or of the kingdom of living creatures in its entirety, as forming a hierarchy, is oriented on the presupposition of a prototype of the entirety of living creation. Two criteria seemed to us suitable as guiding principles for determining the "level" of a living creature. One is its degree of perfect centering, and the other is its richness or abundance. However, we were not definite as to the justification of such an attempt, which may already constitute an artificial separation.

Depending on how we regard it, every organism appears to us as relatively perfect or relatively imperfect. It is relatively perfect if considered as an ordered entity commensurate with its individual nature. It is more or less imperfect in comparison with the nature of its class or species, and more so, in comparison with the whole of nature.

The individualization, which always means an emancipation from the superordinated whole, be it species, group, and so forth, involves a necessary contrast between the individual and his fellow men and so brings about that imperfection that manifests itself in the catastrophic form of all coming to terms of the organism with the world. In that fact is given the transitoriness of all living beings bearing a specific individuality. This may well be the only genuine, real imperfection by the very nature of life, the imperfection that is inherent in life as such. It shows itself in the incompleteness of the individual's participation in that reality to which it belongs according to its nature. All the minor catastrophic reactions to which the organism is continually exposed thus appear as inevitable way stations in the process of its actualization, so to speak, as the expression of its inescapable participation in the general imperfections of the living world (pp. 363ff.). This is a different imperfection from that due to defective genesis (changes) caused through extraneous influences that impair the individual in its centering so much that it is no longer capable of realizing its individuality even proximately. In such cases, imperfection becomes "disease," that is, existence in "transition" becomes existence in "decay," and is destined for death. That such a privation in essential nature is at all possible — especially when we meet it in our fellow men, and thus when it comes so close to us — this is the most stirring experience that the biologist can have. However, this perturbing shock is transfigured into admiration for nature and veneration for its benignity. One realizes that, simultaneously with the privation in essence, the awareness of this privation may be lost, and thus the victim is spared the catastrophic shock that such awareness must necessarily carry with it.

Notes

INTRODUCTION

1. Hermann Jacques Jordon, *Allgemeine vergleichende Physiologie* (Berlin: de Gruyter, 1929), p. 338.

2. See Kurt Goldstein, "Die Lokalisation in der Großhirnrinde," *Handbuch der normalen und pathologischen Physiologie* (Berlin: Springer, 1927), vol. 10, pp. 600–842, and "Die pathologischen Tatsachen in ihrer Bedeutung für das Problem der Sprache," *Sitzungsberichte über der XII Kongress für Psychologie* (1931).

3. Johann Wolfgang von Goethe, "Meteore des literarischen Himmels," in *Zur Naturwissenschaft im Allgemeinen (Plagiat)* (Stuttgart: Cottasche Buchhandlung, 1867), vol. 35/36, p. 218.

CHAPTER ONE: METHOD OF DETERMINING SYMPTOMS

1. Kurt Goldstein, "Das Symptom, seine Entstehung und Bedeutung," *Archiv für Psychiatrie und Neurologie* 76 (1925).

2. Kurt Goldstein, "The Problem of the Meaning of Words," *Journal of Psychology* 2 (1936), "The Significance of the Frontal Lobes for Mental Performances," *Journal of Neurology and Psychopathology* 17 (1936), "The Modifications of Behavior," *Psychiatric Quarterly* 10 (1936), and *Über Aphasie* (Zurich: Fuessli, 1927); Kurt Goldstein and E. Katz, "The Psychopathology of Pick's Disease," *Archives of Neurology and Psychiatry* 38 (1937); Kurt Goldstein and J. Marmor, "A Case of Aphasia, with Special Reference to the Problems of Repetition and Word Finding," *Journal of Neurology and Psychiatry* 1.4 (1938); Mary Marjorie Bolles, "The Basis of Pertinence," *Archives of Psychology* 212 (1937); Mary Marjorie Bolles and Kurt Goldstein, "A Study of Impairment of Abstract Behavior in Schizophrenic Patients," *Psychiatric Quarterly* 12 (1938); Eugenia Hanfmann and Jacob Kasanin, "A Method for the Study of Concept Formation," *Journal of Psychology* 3 (1937), and "An Experimental Study on Concept Formation in Schizophrenic Amnesia," *Journal of Psychiatry* 95.1 (1938); Aaron B. Nadel, "A Qualitative Analysis of Behavior Fol-

lowing Cerebral Lesions," *Archives of Psychology* 224 (1938); Adhëmar Gelb, "Psychol. Analysen hirnpatholog., Fälle. IX. Über eine eigenartige Sehstörung ('Dysmorphopsie'), infolge von Gesichtsfeldeinengung," *Psychologische Forschung* 4 (1922), and "Psychol. Analysen hirnpatholog., Fälle X. Über Farbennamenamnesie," *Psychologische Forschung* 6 (1925).

3. Goldstein, "The Problem of the Meaning of Words."

4. Adhémar Gelb and Kurt Goldstein, *Psychologische Analysen hirnpathologischer Fälle* (Leipzig: Barth, 1920); Kurt Goldstein, "Kritisches u. Tatsächliches zu einigen Grundfragen der Psychopathologie," *Schweizer Archiv für Neurologie und Psychiatrie* 34.1 (1934).

5. John Hughlings Jackson, *Selected Writings*, ed. James Taylor (London: Hodder & Stoughton, 1932).

6. Goldstein, *Über Aphasie*; Gelb and Goldstein, *Psychologische Analysen*; Leendert Boumann and Abraham Anton Grünbaum, "Experimentell psychologische Untersuchung zur Aphasie und Paraphasie," *Zeitschrift die Gesamte Neurologie und Psychiatrie* 96 (1925); W. Benari, "Psychol. Analysen hirnpathol. Fälle VIII, Studien zur Untersuchungen der Intelligenz bei einem Fall von Seelenblindheit," *Psychologische Forschung* 2 (1922); Klaus Conrad, "Versuche einer psychologischen Analyse des Parietalsyndroms," *Monatschrift für Psychiatrie und Neurologie* 84 (1932); Henry Head, *Aphasia and Kindred Disorders of Speech* (New York: Macmillan, 1926); Wolfgang Hochheimer, "Psychol. Analysen hirnpathol., Fälle XIII, Analyse eines 'Seelenblinden' von der Sprache aus," *Psychologische Forschung* 16 (1932); F. Lange, "Finger-Agnosie und Agraphie (Eine psychologische Analyse)," *Monatsschrift für Psychiatrie und Neurologie* 76 (1930), and "Analyse eines Falles von Lautagraphie," *Monatsschrift für Psychiatrie und Neurologie* 79 (1931); Eva Rothmann, "Untersuchung eines Falles von umschriebener Hirnschädigung mit Störungen auf verschiedensten Leistungsgebieten," *Schweizer Archiv für Neurologie und Psychiatrie* 33 (1933); H. Scheller and H. Seidemann, "Zur Frage der optisch-räumlichen Agnosie," *Monatsschrift für Psychiatrie und Neurologie* 81 (1932); Friedrich Wilhelm Siekmann, "Psychol. Analysen hirnpath. Fälle. XIV. Psychol. Analyse des Falles Rat," *Psychologische Forschung* 16 (1932); Willem von Woerkom, "Über Störung des Aufgabebewußtseins in einem Falle von Tumor des Frontalhirns," *Monatsschrift für Psychiatrie und Neurologie* 70 (1928), and "Psychopathologische Beobachtungen bei Stirnhirngeschädigten und bei Patienten mit Aphasien," *Monatsschriften für Psychiatrie und Neurologie* 80 (1931); F. Wolpert, "Die Simultanagnosie," *Zeitschrift für die Gesamte Neurologie und Psychiatrie* 93 (1924), and "Über das Wesen der literalen Alexie. Beitrag zur Aphasielehre," *Monatsschrift für Psychiatrie und Neurologie* 75 (1930).

7. Hereafter, we shall speak in this context of a "performance field."

8. Bolles and Goldstein, "A Study of Impairment"; Hanfmann and Kasanin, "A Method," and "An Experimental Study"; Nadel, "A Qualitative Analysis."

9. This term is logically related to the German word *Prägnant* often found in Gestalt literature.

10. Gelb and Goldstein, *Psychologische Analysen*; Goldstein, "Kritischens"; Konrad Zucker, "Über die pathologischen Funktionen bei amnestischer Aphasie," *Monatsschrift für Psychiatrie und Neurologie* 87 (1933), and "An Analysis of Disturbed Function in Aphasia," *Brain* 57 (1934); Max Isserlin, "Die pathologische Physiologie der Sprache," *Ergebnisse der Physiologie* 29 (1929), 33 (1931), and 35 (1932).

11. Rothmann, "Untersuchung eines Falles."

12. Gabriel Anton, "Über die Selbstwahrnehmung," *Archiv für Psychiatrie* 32 (1899).

13. *Ibid.*; Emil Redlich and Guilio Bonvicini, *Über das Fehlen der Wahrnehmung der eigenen Blindheit bei Hirnkrankheiten* (Leipzig: Deuticke, 1908), "Weitere klinische und anatomische Mitteilungen über das Fehlen der Wahrnehmung der eigenen Blindheit bei Hirnkrankheiten," *Deutsche Zeitschrift für Nervenheilkunde* 41 (1911), and "Weitere klinische und anatomische Mitteilungen über das Fehlen der Wahrnehmung der eigenen Blindheit bei Hirnkrankheiten," *Neurologische Zentralblatt* 30 (1911); Fritz Hartmann, *Die Orientierung* (Leipzig: Vogel, 1902).

14. Arnold Pick, "Über das Verständnis des eigenen Defectes bei Aphasischen," *Monatsschrift für Psychiatrie und Neurologie* 43 (1918).

15. Franz Kramer, "Nichtwahrnehumung der Hemiplegie," *Zeitschrift für die Gesamte Neurologie und Psychiatrie* 2 (1915); Karl Bonhoeffer, "Casuistische Beiträge zur Aphasielehre," *Archiv für Psychiatrie* 37.1 (1903).

16. Kurt Goldstein, "Beobachtungen über die Veränderungen des Gesamtverhaltens bei Gehirnschädigung," *Monatsschrift für Psychiatrie und Neurologie* 68 (1928).

17. Walter Cannon, *The Wisdom of the Body* (New York: Norton, 1932).

18. Kurt Goldstein, "Über die gleichartige funktionelle Bedingtheit der Symptome bei organischen und psychischen Krankheiten; im besonderen über den funktionellen Mechanismus der Zwangsvorgänge," *Monatsschrift für Psychiatrie und Neurologie* 57 (1924).

19. Gelb and Goldstein, *Psychologische Analysen;* Wilhelm Fuchs, in Adhëmar Gelb (ed.), *Psychologische Analysen Hirnpathologischer Fälle. Untersuchungen über das Sehen der Hemianopiker* (Leipzig: Barth, 1920), and "Eine Pseudofovea bei Heimanopikern," *Psychologische Forschung* 1 (1922); Kurt Goldstein, "Zur Frage der Restitution nach umschriebenem Hirndefekte," *Schweizer Archiv für Neurologie und Psychiatrie* 13 (1923).

20. Kurt Goldstein, "Über monoculäre Doppelbilder," *Jahrbuch für Psychiatrie und Neurologie* 51, pt. 1/3 (1934).

21. Fuchs, "Psychologische Analysen," and "Eine Pseudofovea."

22. Adhémar Gelb, "Die psychologische Bedeutung pathologischer Störungen der Raumwahrnehmungen," *Kongress für Expermentelle Psychologie, 1925* (Jena: Fischer, 1926).

23. Erich R. Jaensch, "Analyse der Gesichtswahrnehmungen," *Zeitschrift für Psychologie* 4 (1909).

24. Alfred Bielschowsky, "Über monoculare Dyplopie ohne physikalische Grundlage," *Gräfes Archiv für Ophthalmologie* 46 (1898).

25. Kurt Goldstein, "Zur Theorie der Halluzination," *Archiv für Psychiatrie und Neurologie* 44 (1909).

26. Otto Pötzl, *Zur Klinik und Anatomie der reinen Worttaubheit* (Berlin: Karger, 1919), and "Über Störungen der Selbstwahrnehmungen bei linksseitiger Hemiplegie," *Zeitschrift für die Gesamte Neurologie und Psychiatrie* 93 (1924).

27. Henceforth, by "analytic" we mean anatomizing or dissecting.

CHAPTER TWO: THE ORGANISM VIEWED IN THE LIGHT OF RESULTS
OBTAINED THROUGH ATOMISTIC METHOD

1. Paul Hoffmann and F. Kretschmer, *Untersuchungen über die Eigenreflexe* (Berlin: Springer, 1922).

2. Charles Scott Sherrington, *The Integrative Action of the Nervous System* (New Haven, CT: Yale University Press, 1911).

3. Charles Scott Sherrington, "Antagonistic Muscles and Reciprocal Innervation," *Proceedings of the Royal Society of London, Series B: Biological Sciences* 90 (1897-98).

4. E. Sanders, *Ber. Verhandl. d. Sächs. Gesellsch. Wiss.* (1867), ch. 19.

5. F.R. Miller and Charles Scott Sherrington, "Some Observations on the Buccopharyngeal Stage of Reflex Deglutition in the Cat," *Quarterly Journal of Experimental Physiology* 9 (1915).

6. Charles Scott Sherrington, "Reflexes Elicitable in the Cat from Pinna Vibrissae and Jaws," *Journal of Physiology* 51 (1917).

7. Silvestro Baglioni, "Sui reflessi cutanei degli anfibii e sui fattori che li condizionano," *Zeitschrift für allgemeine Physiologie* 14 (1912).

8. B. Luchsinger, *Pflügers Archiv* 27 (1882), p. 190.

9. Viktor von Weizsäcker, "Reflexgesetze," *Handbuch der normalen und pathologischen Phsyiologie* (Berlin: Springer, 1927), vol. 10, pp. 35–102.

10. Jacob von Uexküll, "Ein Wort über die Schlangensterne," *Zentralblatt für der gesamte Physiologie* 23 (1909); Hubert Fairlee Jordan, *Pflügers Archiv* 110 (1905), p. 553.

11. Charles Scott Sherrington and S.C.M. Sowton, "Reversal of the Reflex Effect of an Afferent Nerve by Altering the Character of the Electrical Stimulus Applied," *Proceedings of the Royal Society of London, Series B: Biological Sciences* 83 (1911).

12. J.S. Beritoff, "Reflexumkehr durch Verstärkung oder Verlängerung der peripheren Reizung," *Pflügers Archiv* 201 (1923).

13. Rudolf Magnus, *Körperstellung* (Berlin: Springer, 1924).

14. Frigyes Verzär, "Reflexumkehr (Paradoxe Reflexe) durch Ermüdung und Schock," *Pflügers Archiv* 183 (1920).

15. Christian Kroetz, "Allgemeine Physiologie der autonomen nervösen Korrelationen," *Handbuch der normalen und pathologischen Physiologie* (Berlin: Springer, 1931), vol. 16, pp. 1729–1821; Kurt Goldstein, "Die Neuroregulation," *Ergebnis der innere Medizin und Kinderhlk* 32 (1932), and "Die Neuroregulation," *Verhandlung der Gesellschaft für innere Medizin* (Wiesbaden: Congress, 1931).

16. Goldstein, "Die Neuroregulation," and Kurt Goldstein, "Über induzierte Tonusveränderungen," *Klinische Wochenschrift* 4.7 (1925), "Über die Funktionen der Kleinhirns," *Klinische Wochenschrift* 3.28 (1923), and "Über induzierte Veränderungen des Tonus," *Schweizer Archiv für Neurologie und Psychiatrie* 17, pt. 2 (1926).

17. Magnus, *Körperstellung.*

18. Kurt Goldstein and Walther Riese, "Über induzierte Veränderungen des Tonus," *Klinische Wochenschrift* 2.26 and 2.52 (1923) and 3.5 (1924).

19. In connection with those phenomena, cf. the numerous papers on "induced" tonus by Ernst Wodak and Martin Henry Fischer, my coworkers, and me; Kurt Goldstein and Walther Riese, "Über induzierte Veränderungen"; Ernst Wodak and Martin Henry Fischer, "Zur Analyse des Barany'schen Zeigeversuches," *Monatsschrift für Ohrenheilkunde* 58 (1924), and "Eine neue Vestibularisreaction," *Münchener medizinische Wochenschrift* 69, pt. 93 (1922).

20. Kroetz, "Allgemeine Physiologie."

21. Jakob von Uexküll, *Theoretical Biology* (London: K. Paul, Trench, Trubner, 1926).

22. Albrecht Bethe, "Plastizität und Centrenlehre," *Handbuch der normalen und pathologischen Physiologie* (Berlin: Springer, 1930), vol. 15, p. 1175.

23. *Ibid.,* p. 1179.

24. J. Moritz Schiff, *Gesammelte Beiträge zur Physiologie* (Lausanne: J.B. Baillière, 1896), vol. 3, p. 251.

25. Paul Weiss, "Die Funktionen transplantierter Amphibienextremitäten," *Archiv für Entwicklungsmechanik* 102 (1924), "Neue experimentelle Beweise für das Resonanzprinzip der Nerventätigkeit," *Biologisches Zentralblatt* 50, pt. 6 (1930), "Das Resonanzprinzip der Nerventätigkeit," *Pflügers Archiv* 226 (1931), "Erregunspecificität und Erregunsresonanz," *Ergebnisse der Biologie* (1928).

26. See esp. Samuel Detwiler, *Neuroembryology* (New York: Macmillan, 1936).

27. Uexküll, *Theoretical Biology.*

28. Kurt Goldstein, "Das Kleinhirn," *Handbuch der normalen und pathologischen Physiologie* (Berlin: Springer, 1927), vol. 10, pp. 225–31.

29. Bethe, "Plastizität," p. 1217.

30. *Ibid.*, p. 1215.

31. *Ibid.*, p. 1219.

CHAPTER THREE: THEORETICAL REFLECTIONS ON THE
FUNCTION OF THE NERVOUS SYSTEM

1. Kurt Goldstein, "Zur Theorie der Funktion des Nervensystems," *Archiv für Psychiatrie* 74, pt. 2/4 (1925), and "Das Symptom, seine Enstehung und Bedeutung für unsere Auffassung vom Bau und der Funktion des Nervensystems," *Archiv für Psychiatrie* 76 (1925).

2. Thomas Brown, "Die Großhirnhemisphären," *Handbuch der normalen und pathologischen Physiologie* (Berlin: Springer, 1927), vol. 10, pp. 418–522.

3. Charles Child, *Physiological Foundation of Behavior* (New York: Holt, 1924).

4. August Pütter, *Vergleichende Physiologie* (Jena: Fischer, 1911).

5. Kurt Goldstein, "Über die Halsreflexe des Menschen," *Deutsche Zeitschrift für Nervenheilkunde* 77, pt. 1/6 (1922), "Die Topik der Großhirnrinde in ihrer klinischen Bedeutung," *Deutsche Zeitschrift für Nervenheilkunde* 77 (1922), and "Das Kleinhirn," *Handbuch der normalen und pathologischen Physiologie* (Berlin: Springer, 1927), vol. 10, pp. 222–93.

6. Inez Wilder, "Ein unbeachtetes biologisches Gesetz, sine Bedeutung für Forschung und Praxis," *Wiener Klinische Wochenschrift* 2 (1931).

7. Christian Kroetz, "Allgemeine Physiologie," *Handbuch der normalen und pathologischen Physiologie* (Berlin: Springer, 1931), vol. 16, pp. 1729–1821.

8. Kurt Goldstein, "Kritisches und Tatsächliches zu einigen Grundfragen der Psychopathologie," *Schweizer Archiv für Neurologie und Psychiatrie* 34, pt. 1-2 (1934).

9. Jakob von Uexküll, *Umwelt und Innenwelt der Tiere* (Berlin: Springer, 1921).

10. Constantin von Monakow, *Die Lokalisation im Grosshirn* (Wiesbaden: Bergmann, 1914).

11. J. Stein, "Pathologie der Wahrnehmung," *Handbuch der Geisteskrankheiten* (Berlin: Brumke, 1928).

12. *Ibid.*, p. 381.

13. Conrad Rieger, "Wie geht es in dem Gehirn zu?" *Zeitschrift für die Gesamte Neurologie und Psychiatrie* 94 (1925).

14. Albert Theodor Poffenberger, "Some Unsolved Problems in Human Adjustment," *Science* 87 (1938).

CHAPTER FOUR: MODIFICATION OF FUNCTION DUE TO
IMPAIRMENT OF THE ORGANISM

1. The Babinski phenonmenon describes the dorsal flexion of the big toe when the

sole of the foot is stimulated. For those unfamiliar with anatomy we remark that the so-called dorsal flexion is executed by the extensor of the big toe.

2. John F. Fulton and Allen D. Keller, *The Sign of Babinski* (Springfield, IL: Thomas, 1932).

3. Michael Kroll, D. Markow, and N. Kantor, "Über Muskeltonus und Chronaxie," *Nervenarzt* 5 (1932).

4. Kurt Goldstein, "The Sign of Babinski," *Journal of Nervous and Mental Disease* 93 (1941), p. 288.

5. *Ibid.,* p. 286.

6. *Ibid.,* p. 291.

7. Fulton and Keller, *Sign.*

8. Kroll et al., "Über Muskeltonus."

9. Fulton and Keller, *Sign.*

10. Kroll et al., "Über Muskeltonus."

11. Charles Scott Sherrington, *The Integrative Action of the Nervous System* (London, 1923), and "Reciprocal Innervation and Symmetrical Muscles," *Proceedings of the Royal Society of London, Series B: Biological Sciences* 56 (1913).

12. Thomas Brown, "Die Großhirnhemisphaeren," *Handbuch der normalen und pathologischen Physiologie* (Berlin: Springer, 1927), vol. 10, pp. 418–522, and "Die Reflexfunktionen des ZNS m. bes. Berücksichtigung d. rythm. Tätigkeit beim Säugetier," *Ergebnisse der Physiologie* 1.13 (1913) and 2.15 (1916).

13. Ernst Wodak and Martin Henry Fischer, "Eine neue Vestibularisreaktion," *Münchener medizinische Wochenschrift* 69, pt. 93 (1922).

14. Bela Mittelmann, "Über länger anhaltende (tonische) Beeinflußungen des Kontraktionszustandes der Skeletmuskulatur des Menschen," *Pflügers Archiv* 196 (1922); Kurt Goldstein and Walther Riese, "Über induzierte Veränderungen des Tonus," *Klinische Wochenschrift* 2.26 (1923), and "Über induzierte Tonusveränderungen beim Menschen. VIII. Mitteilung: Über den Einfluß unbewußter Bewegungen resp. Tendenzen zu Bewegungen auf die taktile und optische Raumwahrnehmung," *Klinische Wochenschrift* 4.7 (1925).

15. Goldstein and Riese, "Über induzierte Tonusveränderungen."

16. Edgar Rubin, *Visuell wahrgenommene Figuren* (Kopenhavn: Syldendalsche Bookhandel, 1921).

17. Mary R. Harrower, "Some Factors Determining Figure-Ground Articulation," *British Journal of Psychology* 26 (1936).

18. Thomas Brown, "Die Reflexfunktionen," and "On the Nature of the Fundamental Activity in the Nervous System," *Journal of Physiology* 48 (1914).

19. Compare the summary in Kurt Goldstein, "Das Kleinhirn," *Handbuch der nor-*

malen und pathologischen Physiologie (Berlin: Springer, 1927), vol. 10, pp. 222, 256, and "The Function of the Cerebellum from a Clinical Standpoint," *Journal of Nervous and Mental Disease* 83.1 (1936).

20. Konrad Zucker, "Über die pathologischen Funktionen bei amnestischer Aphasie," *Monatsschrift für Psychiatrie und Neurologie* 87 (1933), and "An Analysis of Disturbed Function in Aphasia," *Brain* 57 (1934).

21. Karl Lashley, *Brain Mechanisms and Intelligence* (Chicago: University of Chicago Press, 1929); Isadore Krechevsky, "Hypothesis in Rats," *Psychological Review* 39 (1932), and "Brain Mechanisms and Variability," *Journal of Comparative Psychology* 23 (1937).

CHAPTER FIVE: THE NATURE OF PARTITIVE PROCESSES

1. Viktor von Weizsäcker, "Reflexgesetze," *Handbuch der normalen und pathologischen Physiologie* (Berlin: Springer, 1927), vol. 10, pp. 35–102.

2. Kurt Goldstein, "Über die Abhängigkeit der Bewegungen von optischen Vorgängen," *Monatsschrift für Psychiatrie und Neurologie* 54 (1923).

3. Paul Hoffmann, *Unters. über die Eigenreflexe menschlicher Muskeln* (Berlin: Springer, 1922).

4. N. Bubnoff and Rudolf Heidenhain, "Über Erregung und Hemmungsvorgänge innerhalb der motorischen Hirncentren," *Pflügers Archiv* 26 (1881).

5. Siegmund Exner "Zur Kenntnis von der Wechselwirkung der Erregung im Zentralnervensystem," *Pflügers Archiv* 28 (1882).

6. Thomas Brown, "Die Großhirnhemisphaeren," *Handbuch der normalen und pathologischen Physiologie* (Berlin: Springer, 1927), vol. 10, pp. 418–524.

7. Albert Leyton and Charles Scott Sherrington, "Observations on the Excitable Cortex of the Chimpanzee, Orangutan, and Gorilla," *Quarterly Journal of Experimental Physiology* 11 (1917).

8. Hermann Jacques Jordan, *Allgemeine vergleichende Physiologie* (Berlin: de Gruyter, 1928); Kurt Koffka, *The Growth of the Mind* (New York: Harcourt, Brace, 1925); Gordon W. Allport, *Personality, A Psychological Interpretation* (New York: Holt, 1937).

9. Apart from Karl Lashley's painstaking analysis, the work of Edward Stuart Russell offers excellent observations on this point: Karl Lashley, "Experimental Analysis of Instinctive Behavior," *Psychological Review* 45.6 (1938); Edward Stuart Russell, *The Behavior of Animals* (London: Arnold, 1934).

10. See this term in similar connection in Trigant Burrow's writings.

11. Koffka, *The Growth of the Mind* (New York: Harcourt, Brace, 1925).

12. L. Gustav and K. Wolf, "Kindespsychologische Experimente mit bedingten Reflexen, *Zeitschrift für Kinderforschung* 46, pt. 4 (1938).

13. Conwy Lloyd Morgan, *Habit and Instinct* (London: Arnold, 1896).

14. Karl Lashley, "Contributions of Freudism to Psychology," *Psychological Review* 31 (1924), and "Cerebral Control versus Reflexology," *Journal of General Psychology* 5 (1931).

15. Allport, *Personality.*

16. *Ibid.*

17. Kurt Goldstein, Carney Landis, William A. Hunt, and F. Clark, "Moro Reflex and Startle Pattern," *Archives of Neurology and Psychiatry* 40 (1938); Kurt Goldstein, "A Further Comparison of the Moro Reflex," *Journal of Psychology* 6 (1938).

18. Henceforth the terms *potentiality* and *capacity* will be used interchangeably.

19. Hans Spemann, "Die Erzeugung tierischer Chimären durch heteroplastische embryonale Transplantation," *Archiv für Erwicklungsmechanik* 43 (1918).

20. Hans Spemann, "Über die ersten Organanlagen des Amphibienembryo," *Archiv für Erwicklungsmechanik* 43 (1918).

21. Jordon, *Physiologie.*

22. *Ibid.,* p. 343.

23. *Ibid.,* p. 345.

24. *Ibid.,* p. 348.

25. *Ibid.,* p. 346.

CHAPTER SIX: ON THE CONCEPTION OF THE ORGANISM AS A WHOLE

1. E. Metzger, "Tonusveränderungen auf optische Reize," *Verhandlungen der Ophthalmologischen Gesellschaft* (Heidelberg, 1925), vol. 45; Kurt Goldstein and Otto Rosenthal, "Zum Problem der Wirkung der Farben auf den Organismus," *Schweizer Archiv für Neurologie und Psychiatrie* 26 (1930).

2. Kurt Goldstein and Walther Riese, "Über induzierte Veränderungen des Tonus bei normalen Menschen," *Klinische Wochschrift* 2.26 (1923).

3. Michael Kroll, D. Markow, and N. Kantor, "Über Muskeltonus und Chronaxie," *Der Nervenarzt* 5 (1932).

4. Kurt Goldstein, "Über den Einfluß motorischer Störungen auf die Psyche," *Zeitschrift für Nervenheilkunde* 84, pt. 4/6 (1924), and "Über induzierte Tonusveränderungen beim Menschen," *Zeitschrift für der gesamte Neurologie und Psychiatrie* 89, pt. 4/5 (1924); Kurt Goldstein and Walter Börnstein, "Über sich in pseudospontanen Bewegungen äußernde Spasmen," *Zeitschrift für Nervenheilkunde* 84, pt. 4/6 (1924).

5. Adolf Freusberg, "Reflexbewegungen beim Hunde," *Pflügers Archiv* 9 (1874).

6. Hans Cohn, "Weitere Beobachtungen über Haltungs- und Bewegungsstörungen," *Zeitschrift für der gesamte Neurologie und Psychiatrie* 125, pt. 2/3 (1930).

7. Herbert Spencer Jennings, "Behavior of the Starfish: *Asterias forreri*," *University of California Publications in Zoology* 4 (1907).

8. Friedrich Alverdes, *Biol. genrl.* 3 (1931).

9. E. Gergens, "Über gekreuzte Reflexe," *Pflügers Archiv* 14 (1877).

10. Silvestro Baglioni, "Sui reflessi cutanei degli anphibii e sui fattori che li condizionano," *Zeitschrift für allgemeine Physiologie* 14 (1912).

11. Rudolf Magnus, *Körperstellung* (Berlin: Springer, 1924).

12. J. Stephan Szymanski, "Untersuchung über eine einfache natürliche Reaktionstätigkeit," *Psychologische Forschung* 2 (1922).

13. Albrecht Bethe and Martin Fischer, "Plastizität und Centrenlehre," *Handbuch der normalen und pathologischen Physiologie* (Berlin: Springer, 1931), vol. 15, pp. 1045, 1175.

14. Otfrid Foerster, "Restitution der Motilität und Sensibilität," *Deutsche Zeitschrift für Nervenheilkunde.*

15. Albrecht Bethe, "Über Nervenheilung und polare Wachstumserscheinungen am Nerven," *Münchener mediziniesche Wochenschrift* 52 (1905).

16. Foerster, "Restitution."

17. John Newport Langley, "Note on the Experimental Junction of the Vagus Nerve in the Cells of the Superior Cervical Ganglion," *Proceedings of the Royal Society of London* 62 (1897).

18. Franz von Brücke, "Allgemeines über Tatsachen und Probleme der Physiol. nervöser Systeme," *Handbuch der normalen und pathologischen Physiologie* (Berlin: Springer, 1929), vol. 9, pp. 25, 645, and "Über die reziproke, reflectorische Erregung der Herznerven bei Reizung des N depressor," *Zeitschrift für Biologie* 67 (1917).

19. Wolfgang von Buddenbrock, *Grundriß der vergleichenden Physiologie* (Berlin: Karger, 1928); Bethe and Fischer, "Plastizität."

20. Kurt Goldstein, "Über die Plastizität und Centrenlehre," *Handbuch der normalen und pathologischen Physiologie* (Berlin: Springer, 1931), vol. 15, pp. 1131–74.

21. Cited in Rupprecht Matthaei, "Über die Funktionsregulierung im Zentralnervensystem bei experimentellen Eingriffen am Organismus," *Deutsche Zeitschrift für Nervenheilkunde* 115 (1930).

22. Kurt Goldstein, "Über Zeigen und Greifen," *Nervenarzt* 4, pt. 8 (1931).

23. Matthaei, "Über die Funktionsregulierung."

24. Albrecht Bethe and E. Woitas, "Studien über die Plastizität des Nervensystems," *Pflügers Archiv* 224 (1930).

25. Kurt Goldstein, "Über die Abhängigkeit der Bewegungen von optischen Vorgängen," *Monatsschrift für Psychiatrie und Neurologie* 54 (1927).

26. Kurt Goldstein, "Lokalisation in der Großhirnrinde," *Handbuch der normalen und pathologischen Physiologie* (Berlin: Springer, 1927), vol. 10, pp. 600–842.

27. François Moutier, *L'Aphasie de Broca* (Paris: Steinheil, 1908).

28. Constantin von Monakow, *Lokalisation im Großhirn und der Abbau der Funktion durch corticale Herde* (Wiesbaden: Bergmann, 1914).

29. See the particularly characteristic material available on the localization of motor aphasia, in *ibid.*

30. *Ibid.*

31. *Ibid.*

32. The comprehensive experimental research on this subject by Heinz Werner, Karl Zietz, and others is related by George Hartmann. Heinz Warner, *Einführung in die Entwicklungspsychologie* (Leipzig: Barth, 1928); Karl Zietz and Heinz Werner, "Über die dynamische Structur der Bewegung," *Zeitschrift für Psychologie* 105 (1928); Karl Zietz, "Gegenseitige Beeinflussung von Farb- und Tonerlegnissen (Studien über experimentell erzeugte Synästhesie)," *Zeitschrift für Psychologie* 121 (1931); George Hartmann, *Gestalt Psychology* (New York: Ronald, 1935).

33. We use the term *objectifying* to signify an attitude in which the subject is directed toward an object in the outer world and disregards his personal reactions to it. This attitude can concern inner experiences (e.g., feeling, emotions) as well.

34. Wassily Kandinsky, *Form und Farbe in der Malerei*; Johann Wolfgang von Goethe, *Zur Farbenlehre* (Stuttgart: Cotta'sche Buchhandlung, 1867), vol. 33/34.

35. Kurt Goldstein and W. Jablonski, "Über den Einfluß des Tonus auf Refraktion und Sehleistungen," *Graefe's Archiv für Ophthalmologie* 130, pt. 4 (1933).

36. *Ibid.*

37. Erich Mortiz von Hornbostel, "Über Geruchshelligkeit," *Pflügers Archiv* 227 (1931), and "Die Einheit der Sinne," *Melos* 4 (1925); trans. in Willis Davis Ellis, *Source Book of Gestalt Psychology* (London: Routledge, Kegan & Paul, 1938).

38. George Ellett Coghill, *Anatomy and the Problem of Behavior* (New York: Macmillan, 1929).

39. J. Moritz Schiff, *Lehrbuch der Physiologie des Muskel- u. Nervensystems* (Lahr, 1858).

40. Charles Scott Sherrington, "Further Experimental Note on the Correlation of Action of Antagonistic Muscles," *Proceedings of the Royal Society of London, Series B: Biological Sciences* 84 (1911); Charles Scott Sherrington and S.C.M. Sowton, "On Reflex Inhibition of the Knee Flexor," *Proceedings of the Royal Society of London, Series B: Biological Sciences* 52 (1911).

41. Heinrich Ewald Hering, "Über die Wirkung zweigelenkiger muskeln auf 3 Gelenke und über die pseudoantagonistische Syringie," *Pflügers Archiv* 65 (1897), and "Beitrag zur experimentellen Analyse coordinierter Bewegungen," *Pflügers Archiv* 70 (1898).

42. Max Verworn, "Ermüdung, Erschöpfung und Erholung der nervösen Zentra des Rückenmarks," *Archiv für Anatomie und Physiologie* (1900).

43. Charles Scott Sherrington, "Notes on the Arrangement of Some Motor Fibres in the Lumbosacral Plexus," *Journal of Physiology* 13 (1892), and "On the Reciprocal Innervation of Antagonistic Muscles," *Proceedings of the Royal Society of London, Series B: Biological Sciences* 76 (1905).

44. Franz Theodor von Brücke, "Über willkürliche und kramphafte Bewegungen," *Sitzungsberichte der Akademie der Wissenschafte Wien* 75/76 (1877).

45. Albrecht Bethe and Hans Kast, "Synergische und reciproke Innervation antagonistischer Mukeln," *Pflügers Archiv* 194 (1922).

46. Kurt Goldstein, "Das Kleinhirn," *Handbuch der normalen und pathologischen Physiologie* (Berlin: Springer, 1927), vol. 10, pp. 222–319.

47. Hans Eppinger and Walter Rudolf Hess, "Die Vagotonie," *Samml. Klin. Abh. (Path. Stoffwechsel)* 9/10 (1910).

48. Regarding the fact that it has a relative constancy, like all performances, cf. below, pp. 265ff.

49. K. Ziegler, "Beobachtungen zur Pathophysiologie des vegetativen Nervensystems," *Deutsche medizinische Wochenschrift* 1 (1931).

50. Reid Hunt, "Direct and Reflex Acceleration of the Mammalian Heart with Some Observations on the Relations of the Inhibitory and Accelerator Nerves," *American Journal of Physiology* 2.5 (1899).

51. Ernst Billigheimer, "Über einen Antagonismus zwischen Pilokarpin und Adrenalin," *Archiv für experimentelle Pathologie* 88, pt. 3/4 (1920), and "Vergleichende Untersuchungen über die Wirkung und Wirkungsweise des Calciums und Digitalis," *Zeitschrift für klinische Medizin* 100, pt. 5 (1924).

52. H. Langecker and Wilhelm Wiechowski, "Zur Pharmakologie des Froschherzens," *Verhandlung der Deutsche pharmacologische Gesellschaft Archiv für experimentelle Pathologie* 96 (1923).

53. Ernst Billigheimer, "Regulationsmechanismus des vegetativen Nervensystems," *Klinische Wochenschrift* 1 (1931).

54. Kurt Goldstein, "Über die Abhängigkeit der Bewegungen von optischen Vorgängen," *Monatsschrift für Psychiatrie und Neurologie* 54 (1923).

CHAPTER SEVEN: CERTAIN ESSENTIAL CHARACTERISTICS OF THE ORGANISM IN THE LIGHT OF THE HOLISTIC APPROACH

1. Sigmund Freud, *Hemmung, Symptom und Angst* (Vienna: Internationaler Psychoanalytischer Verlag, 1926); William Stern, *Psychology of Early Childhood* (New York: Holt, 1930), and *General Psychology from the Personalistic Standpoint* (New York: Macmillan, 1938); Géza Révécz, "Zur Psychology der Fucht- und Angstzustände," *Zeitschrift für angewandte Psychotherapie* 59 (1931).

2. Kurt Goldstein, "Zum Problem der Angst," *Allgemeine aerztl. Zeitschrift für Psychotherapie* 2, pt. 7 (1927).

3. Stern, *Early Childhood*, and *General Psychology*.

4. Sándor Ferenczi, *Versuch einer Genitaltheorie* (Vienna: Internationaler Psychoanalytischer Verlag, 1924).

5. Franz Gabriel Alexander, "Der biologische Sinn psychischer Vorgänge," *Imago* 9 (1923).

6. Rudolf Brun, *Biologische Parallelen zu Freuds Trieblehre* (Vienna: Internationaler Psychoanalytischer Verlag, 1924), p. 29.

7. A.R. Luria, "Die moderne russische Physiologie und die Psychoanalyse," *Internationale Zeitschrift für Psychoanalyse* 12, pt. 1 (1926).

8. *Ibid.*, p. 44.

9. *Ibid.*, p. 49.

10. Vladimīr Bekhterev, *Allgemeine Grundlagen der Reflexologie des Menschen* (Leipzig: Deuticke, 1926).

11. Stern, *General Psychology*; Jean Piaget, "Principal Factors Determining Intellectual Evolution from Childhood to Adult Life," *Harvard Tercentary Publications* (1937).

12. Kurt Goldstein, "Zum Problem der Tendenz zum ausgezeichneten Verhalten," *Deutsche Zeitschrift für Nervenheilkunde* 109 (1929).

13. Max Wertheimer, "Untersuchungen zur Lehre von der Gestalt," *Psychologische Forschung* 1 (1922); trans. in Willis Davis Ellis, *Source Book of Gestalt Psychology* (London: Routledge, Kegan & Paul, 1938).

14. Hans Rupp et al., "Discussion," *Bericht VI Kongr. Exper. Psychol. Göttingen* (Leipzig: Barth, 1914).

15. Vittorio Benussi, "Kinematohaptische Scheinbewegungen," *Bericht VI Kongr. Exper. Psychol. Göttingen* (Leipzig: Barth, 1914).

16. Emil von Skramlik, "Lebensgewohnheiten als Grundlage von Sinnestäuschungen," *Die Naturwissenschaften* 13 (1925).

17. Kurt Goldstein and Walter Börnstein, "Über sich in pseudospontanen Bewegungen äussernde Spasmen und über eigentümliche Stellungen bei striaeren Erkrankungen," *Deutsche Zeitschrift für Nervenheilkunde* 84 (1925).

18. Goldstein, "Zum Problem."

19. *Ibid.*, cf. pictures, no. 12, fig. 21, p. 24.

20. Viktor von Weizsäcker, "Über eine systematische Raumsinnstörung," *Deutsche Zeitschrift für Nervenheilkunde* 84 (1924).

21. This was observed in Weizsäcker's patient; see *ibid.*, p. 267.

22. K. Flick and Karl Hansen, "Über die Einwirkung der Labyrinthreizung," *Deutsche Zeitschrift für Nervenheilkunde* 96 (1927).

23. *Ibid.*, p. 202.

24. Ernst Mach, *Die Analyse der Empfindungen* (Jena: Fischer, 1903); Wolfgang Köhler, "Gestaltprobleme und Anfänge einer Gestalttheorie," *Jahrsberichte für der gasamte Physiologie* 3 (1922); A. Gatti, "Über die Entstehungsweise visueller Complexe," *Intern. Kongr. Psychol. Groningen* 1926 (Groningen: Nordhoff, 1927); Richard Hamburger, *Neue Theorie der Wahrnehmung und des Denkens* (Berlin: G. Stilke, 1927).

25. Rupprecht Matthaei, "Das Gestaltproblem," *Ergebnisse der Physiologie* (1929).

26. Kurt Goldstein, "Zur Methodik des Zeigeversuches," *Der Nervenarzt* 2, pt. 8 (1929).

27. Goldstein, "Zum Problem," and "Zur Methodik."

28. Ralph Lillie, *Protoplasmic Action and Nervous Action* (Chicago: University of Chicago, 1923).

29. Kurt Goldstein and W. Jablonski, "Über den Einfluß des Tonus auf Refraktion und Sehleistungen," *Graefes Archiv für Ophthalmologie* 130 (1933).

30. Lillie, *Protoplasmic Action*; Edgar Douglas Adrian, *The Basis of Sensation* (New York: Norton, 1928), and *The Mechanism of Nervous Action* (Philadelphia: University of Pennsylvania Press, 1932).

CHAPTER EIGHT: ON GESTALT PSYCHOLOGY AND
THE THEORY OF THE PHYSICAL GESTALTEN

1. Rupprecht Matthaei, *Das Gestaltproblem* (Munich: Bergmann, 1929).

2. Wolfgang Köhler, *Psychologische Probleme* (Berlin: Springer, 1933), p. 100.

3. *Ibid.*

4. *Ibid.*, p. 129.

5. As we have seen, instability belongs to the processes in isolated parts disregarding special cases of stability in isolation, like the conditioned reflexes.

6. Erich Moritz von Hornbostel, "Über optische Inversion," *Psychologische Forschung* 1 (1922).

7. Köhler, *Probleme*, p. 127.

8. William Stern, *General Psychology* (New York: Macmillan, 1938).

9. Matthaei, *Gestaltproblem*, p. 54.

10. Kurt Koffka, *Principles of Gestalt Psychology* (New York: Harcourt, Brace, 1935); Max Wertheimer, "Experimentelle Studien über das Sehen von Bewegung," *Zeitschrift für Psychologie* 60 (1911), and "Über das Denkender Naturvolker," in *Drei Abhandlungen zur Gestalttheorie* (Erlangen, 1925). This biological aspect of "fitting together" as an implicit underlying principle of Gestalt theory has been pointed out by Martin Scheerer, *Die Lehre von der Gestalt* (Berlin: de Gruyter, 1931).

11. Wertheimer, "Experimentelle Studien," and "Denkender Naturvolker."

12. Koffka, *Principles*; Georg Hirth, *Die Epigenesis der Merksysteme* (Munich, 1898).

13. Wolfgang Köhler, *Die physischen Gestalten in Ruhe und im stationären Zustand* (Erlangen: Philosophische Akademie, 1924).

14. Ewald Oldekop, *Über das hierarchische Prinzip in der Natur und seine Beziehungen zum Mechanismus-Vitalismus Problem* (Reval: Wassermann, 1930).

15. *Ibid.,* p. 14

16. Wolfgang Köhler, *Gestalt Psychology* (New York: Liveright, 1929), p. 111.

17. *Ibid.,* p. 113.

18. Köhler, *Probleme,* p. 85.

19. Therefore we have preferred to speak of equalization toward an "average" state of excitation, adequate to the nature of the organism (cf. pp. 103ff., 161).

20. Edward Tolman, "The Determiners of Behavior at a Choice Point," *Psychological Review* 45 (1938).

21. Jerry Carter, Jr., "An Experimental Study of Psychological Stimulus Response," *Psychological Record* 2 (1938).

22. William Kilpatrick, ed., *The Educational Frontier* (New York: Appleton-Century, 1933).

CHAPTER NINE: THE NATURE OF BIOLOGICAL KNOWLEDGE

1. Viktor von Weizsäcker, "Reflexgesetze," *Handbuch der normalen und pathologischen Physiologie* (Berlin: Springer, 1927), vol. 10, pp. 35–102.

2. Therefore, in our description of the reflexes, we did not bring into focus the fixed-reflex reaction alone, but brought into focus all its modifications, and that altogether is "what really is."

3. The term *natural science* means here and henceforth physical science.

4. Ernst Cassirer, *Philosophie der symbolischen Formen* (Berlin: Cassirer, 1923, 1928, 1929), vols 1–3; Heinrich Hertz, *Die Prinzipien der Mechanik* (Leipzig, 1894).

5. Hertz, *Prinzipien.*

6. Cassirer, *Philosophie.*

7. Pierre Duhem, *La théorie physique, son object et sa structure* (Paris: Chevalier & Rivière, 1906).

8. Cassirer, *Philosophie.*

9. Johann Wolfgang von Goethe, "Über Mathematik und deren Mißbrauch," in *Zur Naturwissenschaft im Allgemeinem* (Stuttgart: Cottasche Buchhandlung, 1867), vol. 36.

10. *Ibid.*

11. Pascual Jordan, "Die Quantenmechanik und die Grundprobleme der Biologie und Physiologie," *Die Naturwissenschaften* 20 (1932).

12. Niels Bohr, "Die Atomtheorie und die Prinzipien der Naturbeschreibung," *Die Naturwissenschaften* 18 (1930).

13. Jordon, "Die Quantenmechanik"; Bohr, "Die Atomtheorie."

14. Herman Weyl, *Philosophie der Mathematik und Naturwissenschaft* (Munich: Oldenburg, 1927).

15. *Ibid.*

16. Kurt Riezler, "Die Krise der Wirklichkeit," *Die Naturwissenschaften* 16 (1928).

17. Ewald Oldekop, *Über das hierarchische Prinzip in der Natur und seine Beziehung zum Mechanismus-Vitalismus-Problem* (Reval: Wassermann, 1930).

18. Emil Ungerer, *Die Regulationen der Pflanzen* (Berlin: Springer, 1926).

CHAPTER TEN: ON NORM, HEALTH, AND DISEASE

1. Ehrenfried Albrecht, "Grundprobleme der Geschwulstlehre," *Frankfurter Zeitschrift für Pathologie* 1 (1907).

2. Karl Jaspers, *Allgemeine Psychopathologie* (Berlin: Springer, 1923).

3. Otto Lubarsch, *Die Allgemeine Pathologie* (Wiesbaden: Bergmann, 1905); Hugo Ribbert, *Das Wesen der Krankheit* (Bonn: Cohen, 1909); Viktor Schilling, "Über die Erweiterung des Krankheitsbegriffes in der internen Medizin durch die verfeinerten neuen Untersuchungsmethoden," *Verhandlungen der Gesellschaft für innere Medizin* 41 (1929).

4. Ludwig Aschoff, *Vorträge über Pathologie* (Jena: Fischer, 1925); A. Grothe, *Grundlagen ärztlicher Betrachtung* (Berlin: Springer, 1921).

5. It would take us too far afield to explain the reasons in greater detail; cf. Kurt Goldstein, "Das Kleinhirn," *Handbuch der normalen und pathologischen Physiologie* (Berlin: Springer, 1927), vol. 10, pp. 222–317.

6. Christian Kroetz, "Allgemeine Physiologie," *Handbuch der normalen und pathologischen Physiologie* (Berlin: Springer, 1931), vol. 16, pp. 1729–1821.

7. Kurt Goldstein, "Über die Plastizität des Organismus," *Handbuch der normalen und pathologischen Pysiologie* (Berlin: Springer, 1931), vol. 15, pp. 1132–74.

8. Through incorporation of the individual's existence into a more comprehensive whole, Being is never detached from individual nature, and, moreover, the existence of this superordinated whole can manifest itself nowhere but in the individual proper. We want to emphasize this point expressly.

9. Jacob von Uexküll, *Theoretical Biology* (New York: Harcourt, Brace, 1926).

10. Kurt Goldstein, "Die Bedeutung der Psychopathologie der Sprache für die Anthropologie und Ethnologie," *Intern. Kongr. für Anthrop. und Ethnol.* (London, 1934).

11. Compare the discussions in Uexküll, *Theoretical Biology*, regarding species, race, etc., with which we are in far-reaching agreement.

12. Wilhelm Ludwig Johannsen, *Elemente der Exakten Erblichkeitslehre* (Jena: Fischer, 1909).

13. Herbert Spencer Jennings, *Prometheus; or, Biology and the Advancement of Man* (New York: Dutton, 1925), and *The Biological Basis of Human Nature* (New York: Norton, 1930).

14. Heinrich Poll, "Genetik und Melistik als Grundlage des ärztlichen Denkens," in *Einheitsbestrebungen in der Medizin* (Dresden and Leipzig, 1933).

CHAPTER ELEVEN: ON LIFE AND MIND

1. Max Scheler, *Die Stellung der Menschen im Kosmos* (Darmstadt: Reichel, 1929).

2. Kurt Goldstein, "Die Lokalisation in der Großhirnrinde," *Handbuch der normalen und pathologischen Physiologie*, vol. 10 (1927).

3. Ernst Cassirer, "Geist und Leben in der Philosophie der Gegenwart," *Die neue Rundschau* 41, pt. 2.

4. *Ibid.*, p. 244.

5. *Ibid.*, p. 256.

6. *Ibid.*, p. 259.

7. *Ibid.*, pp. 259–60.

8. *Ibid.*, p. 252.

9. *Ibid.*, p. 254.

10. Julius Isaac Steinfeld, "Ein Beitrag zur Analyse der Sexualfunktion," *Zeitschrift für die Gesamte Neurologie und Psychiatrie* 107 (1927).

11. Thomas Brown, "Die Großhirnhemisphären," *Handbuch der normalen und pathologischen Physiologie* 10 (1927).

12. Goldstein, "Die Lokalisation."

13. Kurt Goldstein and Otto Rosenthal, "Zum Problem der Wirkung der Farben auf den Organismus," *Schweizer Archiv für Neurologie und Psychiatrie* 26 (1930).

14. Osvaldo Polimanti, "Über einen Starrkrampfreflex bei den Schildkröten," *Zeitschrift für Biologie* 62 (1914).

15. The fact that there is a greater possibility for inner conflict is no contradiction; on the contrary it seems to belong to his nature. See p. 391.

16. Here I would like to quote a statement from Goethe, regarding "evolution" (from a study on Spinoza): "Even if it seems to us that one thing is brought forth by another, this is not so. Rather one living being occasions the being of another and necessitates its existence in a definite condition. Thus, every being has its original existence within itself, and also therewith the intrinsic rule according to which it is."

Chapter Twelve: Knowledge and Action

1. In this connection, see the quote from Kurt Riezler on p. 320.

2. By drill, I mean every sort of so-called training, without primary insight.

Concluding Remarks

1. Johann Wolfgang von Goethe – cf. "Abhandlung über den Zwischenknochen." Bedeutende Förderung durch ein einziges geistreiches Wort" (1823).

2. William Stern, *General Psychology* (New York: Macmillan, 1938), p. 73, has introduced a similar notion by his term "introception."

Index

This edition designed by Bruce Mau
Type composed by Archetype
Printed and bound Smythe-sewn by Maple-Vail
using Sebago acid-free paper